HRD in the Age
of Globalization

New Perspectives in Organizational Learning, Performance, and Change
JERRY W. GILLEY, SERIES EDITOR

Ethics and HRD
by Tim Hatcher

High Impact Learning
by Robert O. Brinkerhoff and Anne M. Apking

Transforming Work
by Patricia Boverie and Michael Kroth

Philosophy and Practice of Organizational Learning, Performance, and Change
by Jerry W. Gilley, Peter Dean, and Laura Bierema

Assessing the Financial Benefits of Human Resource Development
by Richard A. Swanson

The Manager as Change Agent
by Jerry W. Gilley, Scott A. Quatro, Erik Hoekstra, Doug D. Whittle, and Ann Maycunich

HRD in the Age of Globalization

A Practical Guide to Workplace Learning in the Third Millennium

New Perspectives in Organizational Learning, Performance, and Change

Michael Marquardt
Nancy Berger
Peter Loan

BASIC
BOOKS
A Member of the Perseus Books Group
New York

Books published by Basic Books are available at special discounts for bulk purchases in the United States by corporations, institutions, and other organizations. For more information, please contact the Special Markets Department at the Perseus Books Group, 11 Cambridge Center, Cambridge MA 02142, or call (617) 252-5298, (800) 255-1514, or e-mail special.markets@perseusbooks.com.

Set in 10.5-point Minion by the Perseus Books Group

Library of Congress Cataloging-in-Publication Data

Marquardt, Michael J.
    HRD in the age of globalization : a practical guide to workplace learning in the third millennium /
Michael Marquardt, Nancy Berger, Peter Loan.
        p.   cm.—(New perspectives in organizational learning, performance, and change)
    Includes bibliographical references and index.
    ISBN 0-465-04383-6 (alk. paper)
    1. Personnel management.   2. International business enterprises—Personnel management.
3. International organization—Personnel management.   4. Manpower planning.   5. Intercultural
communication.   6. Organizational learning.   7. Globalization.   I. Berger, Nancy O., 1951–
II. Loan, Peter.   III. Title.   IV. Series.

HF5549.M3195 2004
658.3—dc22
                                                                                    2004006148

Publisher's Note

Organizations are living systems, in a constant state of dynamic evolution. *New Perspectives in Organizational Learning, Performance, and Change* is designed to showcase the most current theory and practice in human resource and organizational development, exploring all aspects of the field—from performance management to adult learning to corporate culture. Integrating cutting-edge research and innovative management practice, this library of titles will serve as an essential resource for human resource professionals, educators, students, and managers in all types of organizations.

The series editorial board includes leading academics and practitioners whose insights are shaping the theory and application of human resource development and organizational design.

Contents

Preface   *xi*

Acknowledgments   *xv*

Part 1 ■ Context of Global HRD

1 ■ Globalization and HRD   3

2 ■ Culture and HRD   16

Part 2 ■ Roles of HRD

3 ■ Design and Development of
Global HRD Programs   43

4 ■ Delivery and Assessment of
Global HRD Programs   59

5 ■ Consulting Across Cultures   70

6 ■ Administration of Global HRD Programs   80

Part 3 ■ Levels of Global HRD

7 ■ Global HRD for Individuals   95

8 ■ Teams and Global HRD   109

9 ■ HRD in Public and Nonprofit
    Global Organizations   123

10 ■ HRD in Global Corporations   135

11 ■ HRD for Development of
     Communities and Nations   158

Part 4 ■ HRD Best Practices and Programs
Around the World

12 ■ Europe   175

13 ■ Middle East and North Africa   189

14 ■ Africa   202

15 ■ China   218

16 ■ Japan   231

17 ■ South Central Asia   246

18 ■ Southeast Asia and Korea   260

19 ■ Central Asia   271

20 ■ Australia and the South Pacific   283

21 ■ Canada   296

22 ■ Latin America and the Caribbean   305

23 ■ United States   317

Part 5 ■ Future of Global HRD

24 ■ Megatrends in Global HRD   335

Helpful Web Sites   *355*

References and Suggested Readings   *357*

Index   *369*

Preface

As the 21st century begins, the challenge of enabling people everywhere on the planet to learn and work effectively across human cultures and international borders has never been more critical to the survival and success of organizations and nations. Change, chaos, and a globalized marketplace are hallmarks of today's workplaces and communities. Better-trained and dedicated people make the world a better place for all of us.

Over the past thirty years the three authors have assisted thousands of individuals in living, studying, and working in some 150 countries around the world. We have worked with hundreds of companies, government agencies, and private voluntary organizations. For the first twenty-five years, two factors were obvious to us:

1. Most organizations did not recognize the need for preparing people to work in other cultures; they assumed that American ways and business practices were the norm and that a manager or sales representative who was successful in Boston would be equally successful in Bangkok or Buenos Aires. Thus little money or effort was spent in global human resource development (HRD).
2. Information about living and working in other countries was fairly limited, most of it available only in Peace Corps manuals or State Department reports. Only with the advent of the Internet and the development of powerful search engines did it become easy to find information about almost any issue or topic in every country.

Today, the chaos of a highly competitive marketplace and a politicized world impel all of us to become better informed and educated, more flexible, and continuously updated. We must be better prepared for the enormous transformations that are taking place in the social, political, economic, educational, and religious institutions around the world. We must remake our organizations, rendering them more responsive to the rapid revolutionary changes occurring at both the global-strategic and the local-tactical levels. We must prepare our societies for the elimination of slow-learning organizations and non-value-adding jobs. We must prepare for emerging bodies of information, expertise, skill, and knowledge that we can barely imagine today. In brief, we must be prepared for almost anything.

Those of us in the global HRD arena must be willing to adopt new and difficult strategies for getting things done. We must be willing to reframe our attitudes and postures, our thinking, and our mindsets. We must become involved in a continual learning process that quickly outstrips and dates the knowledge that we thought was so valuable yesterday.

The world over, public and private organizations face enormous demands and expectations from within and without. Increasingly, leaders in these organizations are turning to human resource professionals for assistance, ideas, and strategic direction. Human resource development is in ascendancy. The art and science of empowering people, organizations, and communities to create maximum productivity, quality, opportunity, and fulfillment has never encountered so many challenges and opportunities.

As organizations struggle to remain viable and competitive globally, strategic planners and human resource professionals need to collaborate more intensely in designing and developing strategies that are at once productive and humane. The most successful organizations and communities in the 21st century will be those that adopt a focused and integrated learning process and incorporate new global strategies and new global skills.

HRD professionals must be able to operate successfully on a global scale as well as in the myriad of unique, sometimes contradictory local cultures. They need to learn from the best of each nation's HRD technologies, ideas, and visions. The aim of this book is to provide the reader with the best HRD ideas and programs in the world so that he or she can learn from them and then adapt and apply them in future actions.

Audience for This Book

This book is written for:

- HRD professionals who are responsible for designing, delivering, and/or administering HRD programs across cultures and borders
- Global consultants, curriculum developers, and executive coaches

- Leaders and managers of global companies or companies seeking to go global
- Students and those who are considering a career in global HRD

Overview of Book

The book is divided into five sections:

1. *Context of Global HRD* (chapters 1–2) examines the economic, political, and social environment in which HRD professionals now operate, as well as the impact of culture on every aspect of the work of HRD.
2. *Roles of HRD* (chapters 3–6) explores the four major roles of the global HRD practitioner: developing workplace learning activities, delivering HRD programs, consulting with global organizations, and administering HRD programs around the world.
3. *Levels of Global HRD* (chapters 7–11) considers the role and responsibility of HRD at the individual, group, and organizational levels as well as the community and national levels.
4. *HRD Best Practices and Programs Around the World* (chapters 12–23) surveys twelve regions of the world in terms of their cultural, political, demographic, educational, linguistic, and sociological dynamics and provides profiles of innovative HRD programs in each region.
5. *Future of Global HRD* (chapter 24) identifies fourteen global megatrends that will have an impact on human resource development around the world and describes how leading-edge organizations and HRD professionals are already incorporating these trends in their strategic planning.

Global HRD is a wonderful profession, one whose importance and relevance is growing in today's world. We hope this book will contribute to shaping the vision, attitudes, and convictions of HRD professionals, managers, leaders, and students—all of whom have the potential to improve the world of work and the work of the world in the 21st century.

Acknowledgments

This book is the product of the authors' combined one hundred years of work in global human resource development and draws on the experiences, insights, and support of family, professional colleagues, clients, students, and friends. Each of us would like to personally acknowledge those who made this book possible and our global work so meaningful.

For Peter: Countless people prepared me for this project, but some stand out. The love and support of my wife, Ceola, and my children, Dena and Willie, have eased me through many transitions—most recently, that from bureaucrat to writer and trainer. Julius Nyerere, Paulo Freire, Carl Bauer, Jane Jacobs, and David Korten shaped my thinking and attitudes about human development. John Hogan, Kathy Rulon, and Brenda Bowman fortified my reverence and respect for truth. Arthur Wille and Vance Ross taught me about courage in difficult times.

For Nancy: My contributions to this book were shaped over three decades by many individuals and organizations in the United States and abroad. Special thanks go to Rotary International, the International Executive Service Corps, and Winrock for their willingness to send me abroad and to my colleagues in Vladivostok, Russia; UNIDO; the ESCEM school in Tours, France; and the Singapore and Malaysian Institutes of Management for valuable lessons in cross-cultural understanding. To all my international friends, colleagues, and students—too numerous to name individually—I extend my sincere appreciation for hours spent sharing ideas and philosophies. Heartfelt thanks also go to my parents, whose decision to send me on a high school trip to Europe launched my lifelong quest to understand other cultures, and to my husband, Ken, for his perseverance during my absences and encouragement to follow my dreams.

For Mike: My journey into the land of global HRD has been guided and blessed by many giants in the field—Len and Zeace Nadler, Angus Reynolds, Tom Jaap, Gordon Lippitt, Don Roberts, David Waugh, Wayne Pace, Gary McLean, Danielle and Thomas Walker, Steve Rhinesmith, Bob Kohls, Pierre Gheysens, and Penti Sydanmaanlakka, among many, many others. I wish to thank my global family—wife, Eveline, from Switzerland; son, Chris, from Peru; daughter Stephanie from El Salvador; and Swiss-American daughters, Catherine and Emily—who have so enthusiastically supported my work in some one hundred countries during the past thirty-five years.

All of us are especially grateful to the folks at Perseus Press who made this book possible—particularly Senior Project Editor Kay Mariea, for her comprehensive and responsive coordination of the writing and publication of this book; and Steven Baker, copy editor extraordinaire, who improved our writing and identified every error.

Finally, we would like to acknowledge the many contributions made by the pioneers in the International Federation of Training and Development Organizations (IFTDO) and International Society for Intercultural Education, Training, and Research (SIETAR) who blazed the early trails of global human resource development.

MICHAEL MARQUARDT
Reston, Virginia

NANCY BERGER
Midlothian, Virginia

PETER LOAN
Hyattsville, Maryland

Part 1

Context of
Global HRD

Globalization and HRD

It is time for people to move beyond an awareness of the urgency of global competition and begin to develop skills for success in the global arena.

Nancy Adler

Introduction

Over the past twenty years, the peoples of our planet have become widely interlinked via worldwide telecommunications, technology, trade, and travel. We have entered the global age. We share many global values and practices, and we work, increasingly, for global organizations. Globalization both symbolizes and creates a convergence of economic and social forces, values and tastes, challenges and opportunities.

Our deepening and intertwining linkages have created a single marketplace, spurring the need for global corporations whose success depends equally on developing their human resources and restructuring their strategies and operations. Human resource development (HRD) will become companies' critical lever for success in the global age. World-class global HRD is the ultimate key to executing the bold visions and strategies needed for global success.

Bartlett and Goshal (1998) note that organizations which operate globally must now compete for the most important resource of all—talent. Continuous learning and the development of intellectual capital have become an organization's most valuable assets. The difference between global success and

3

global failure depends on how well organizations select, train, and manage their employees. In a recent BBC interview, TNT's CEO for Asia remarked that a lack of trained human resources was the only factor preventing TNT from growing even faster.

Global HRD enables organizations to more effectively utilize their human resources in building global success. It enhances leaders' abilities to develop business opportunities, strategically link human resources and organizational goals, improve job satisfaction and retention of global staff, and improve the quality of products and services on a worldwide basis.

However, all too often, HRD efforts and activities are planned and undertaken with insufficient awareness of, or regard for, the unique differences and needs that a global context and multicultural environment demands. Most people who are deployed in overseas assignments are given little or no cultural preparation; too often, companies assume that practices within their own country are the norm and that what works for a manager or sales representative in Chicago will work just as effectively in Beijing or Santiago.

What Is HRD?

Human resource development is a relatively young profession that emerged in the middle of the 20th century and quickly evolved and grew in importance in corporate circles. As a young profession, it is still shaping its identity and developing the best ways to make a better workplace for companies around the world. A December 2003 survey of 1,340 readers of the journal *T+D* reported that the "name or label preferred by people in the profession" was equally divided between *human resource development* and *workplace learning and development*.

Swanson and Holton (2001) define HRD as a "process for developing and unleashing human expertise through organizational development and personnel training and development for the purpose of improving performance" (p. 4). Another popular definition is Chalofsky's (1992): "HRD is the study and practice of increasing the learning capacity of individuals, groups, collectives and organizations through the development and application of leaning-based interventions for the purpose of optimizing human and organizational growth and effectiveness" (p. 179). These two definitions highlight the ongoing debate in the academic and corporate arenas about whether HRD should focus on *learning* or *performance*.

HRD is generally distinguished from HRM (human resource management), in that HRM focuses more on personnel-related issues such as job design, human resource planning, performance management systems, recruitment, selection, staffing, compensation and benefits, employee assistance programs, and union/labor relations. Today, however, the two functions are overlapping more and more as HRD professionals recognize the HRM function's critical importance and impact on every aspect of workplace learning and performance.

McLagan (quoted in Galagan, 2003) notes that the HRD field is metamorphosing from closed rational systems focused on structure to dynamic models inspired by new views of the universe that emphasize process and participation. The role of HRD is to develop human capabilities in the workplace by using all the tools at our disposal, including the best of technology, systems thinking, active learning, organizational learning, economics, learning theories, psychology, sociology, anthropology, and cultural synergies.

The Practice of HRD Around the World

HRD scholars have identified nine specific factors that differentiate the current practice of global HRD from traditional domestic HRD (see Table 1.1):

1. *Learners/trainees:* In global HRD the composition of trainees includes one or more of the following categories:

- Local/host country nationals (e.g., Australians training in Australia)
- Expatriates/parent country nationals (e.g., American employees of the U.S. company who are among the trainees in Australia)
- Third-country nationals (e.g., Japanese who are among the trainees in Australia)

Global HRD trainees in the United States may also include any or all of the above categories. For example, the training director of Toyota in Kentucky trains Americans of various ethnic groups as well as Japanese and Europeans.

2. *Culture:* Simply defined, culture is a way of thinking, acting, and living that is shared by members of a group and that older members pass on to new members. Culture shapes the group's and each member's conscious and subconscious values, assumptions, perceptions, and behavior. It provides the group with systematic guidelines for how they should conduct their thinking, actions, rituals, and business. Since HRD professionals and trainees may come from several different cultures, the cultural dynamic impacts every aspect of global HRD. The concept of culture as well as the levels of culture—corporate, ethnic, national, regional, and global—is treated elsewhere in this chapter as well as in chapters 2–6.

3. *Administration:* The coordination and management of HRD programs on a worldwide basis involves numerous unique administrative issues such as

TABLE 1.1 Factors Impacting Global HRD

1. **Learners/trainees**
2. **Culture**
3. **Administration**
4. **Learning styles**
5. **Physical and financial resources**
6. **Political and economic environment**
7. **Role of trainers**
8. **Language**
9. **In-country HRD partners**

transportation, relocation, cultural orientation, language translation, host government relations, housing, facilities, and support services. Chapter 6, Administration of Global HRD Programs, discusses each of these issues.

4. *Learning styles:* In many cases, trainees possess different learning styles from that of their trainers. One's learning style is based on one's education system at the formal and nonformal levels as well as a variety of cultural influences on learning. For example, some trainees may be accustomed to a philosophical, didactic, deductive, collaborative, rote style of learning, while others have experienced a style that is practical, individualized, inductive, and questioning.

5. *Physical and financial resources:* The resources available to the global HRD practitioner may vary from large, luxurious facilities equipped with the best learning technologies to an outdoor classroom with no flip charts and handouts that are meaningless to illiterate trainees. Equipment may no longer function and may require unavailable or unaffordable parts. Trainees may be seated at executive tables, in child-sized desks, or on the floor. Promised supplies, equipment, and materials and even cotrainers may arrive late or not at all.

6. *Political and economic environment:* The HRD program may take place in a country whose government is democratic or totalitarian, military or civilian controlled. The economy may be booming or experiencing negative growth (as in many African countries). Labor may be well trained and paid above U.S. wage levels or paid less than $1 per day. Terrorism and kidnapping may be a concern in countries such as Iraq and Colombia. There may be very little private enterprise. Industry may be concentrated in one sector, such as mining (as in Zambia). The society may be highly agricultural (Nepal) or totally urban (Singapore). Crime may be a serious concern, and bribery may be demanded for routine government approvals. The people may be of numerous nationalities and may be accepting or suspicious of outsiders. The weather may be extremely hot, frigid, humid, or dry.

Governments are dependent on their local constituencies (if democratic) or on themselves and the military (if totalitarian). The allocation of power, as well as the government's regulation of access to resources and opportunities in the country, may be determined by what best serves the government, not necessarily what serves the citizens or local or foreign corporations. Economic policies that might be best for the economy may not be best for the people who wield power. Business opportunities may require ingratiating one's firm with the family in power (e.g., Indonesia) or abiding with strict religious customs (e.g., Saudi Arabia).

Governments both shape and are shaped by culture. There are historical, religious, and cultural reasons that citizens believe in or accept a certain political, governmental, or legal system. Governments exclude or include specific groups on the basis of ethnicity, gender, age, and/or economic status and may decide the legality of certain practices according to religious beliefs (e.g., Islamic banks cannot charge interest). Regulations governing who may be hired and fired and the status of unions, the role of government, and the party or faction in power are all factors that can change overnight (as by a coup, for example), altering a particular government's position regarding an industry or a corporation from support to opposition.

7. *Roles of trainers:* The roles of and expectations placed on trainers in the United States are significantly different from those of trainers in most other cultures. Much of the world places educators/trainers on a pedestal based on various customs and other cultural factors (e.g., the writings of Muhammad or Confucius, a paucity of highly educated or degree-holding people, a high value placed on degrees conferred by U.S. universities). Trainers in these cultures, however, are expected to act and behave in a disciplined, nearly omniscient, and authoritative manner. As in all cultural situations, one rarely gets a first chance to make a first impression because learners have preconceptions of what Americans are like—individualistic, friendly but perhaps superficial, hardworking but perhaps selfish, honest but not very religious. Trainees from non–U.S. cultures may see American women as competent and professional but, as American television and movies would suggest, loose in sexual morality.

8. *Language:* Language may have an impact in a variety of ways:

- The HRD practitioner's language may be different from the language spoken by the trainees, cotrainers, and/or administrative staff in the country and at corporate headquarters.
- The HRD practitioner may be training in a language that is not his or her native tongue but rather that of the trainees, cotrainers, and administrative staff.

- The HRD practitioner and the other parties may all communicate in a non-native language that is understood by everyone. A native English-speaking trainer working in a French West African country might train in French, which could be the second (or third or fourth) language of the trainees.

In any of these three situations, using a second language presents a number of difficulties for the HRD practitioner:

- One's fluency in and comfort with the language will affect interactions with the trainees, producing varying degrees of stiffness and unnaturalness.
- Translation, if used, will slow the process and the spontaneity of the learning.
- Certain words, meanings, connotations, and even feelings cannot be conveyed across languages.

9. *In-country HRD partners:* The global HRD practitioner often works with HRD staff from local or third-country cultures in the design, delivery, and/or administration of HRD activities. These coworkers often think and operate differently from each other and have different directives from their superiors. For example, they may believe that training should consist primarily of lecture or open discussion, that more time should be devoted to religious or official functions, that theory or practice is more important, that women should be separated from or intermixed with men, or that the foreign trainers should stay in the background or be included as equals.

Major Challenges of Global HRD

In working in the global arena, global HRD practitioners face a number of significant challenges, all of which intensify the need for high-level skills and well-planned strategies.

Working with Cultural Diversity and Conflicts

Working in different cultures creates complexities and confusions that pose a formidable but exciting challenge to global HRD. Members of each cultural group believe that their perception of reality is the correct one, the "only rational" way of thinking, acting, and doing. To therefore suggest or impose one's own way of seeing things and doing things may strike someone of another culture as strange, ridiculous, and/or unfair. Thus a host of acrimonious and seemingly unsolvable problems may arise because of mistrust, miscommunication, and lack of cohesion stemming from these cultural differences among the various groups within the global HRD activity. The challenge facing global trainers is to achieve a balance between fostering healthy conflict among ideas and opinions and controlling cultural differences. Naturally, these different ways of thinking and acting affect how team members from different cultures participate in various group activities and processes.

Different Styles of Leadership and Decisionmaking

Leadership and decisionmaking styles are different among the various cultures, and thus determining a course of action can become an interminable process. Western managers are taught to employ a participative, democratic style of leadership, encouraging all participants to express their opinions in order to achieve the organization's goals. Westerners prefer the impersonal authority of mutually agreed-upon goals and objectives rather than the arbitrary power of a superior. Disagreeing with a manager is not uncommon, and followers are expected to take the initiative. Attempts are made to minimize inequality through legal and political means. Western organizations tend to be flatter than many non-Western ones, and power is more decentralized. Managers must earn respect from employees as it is not automatically granted.

In the non-Western world, however, leadership is more hierarchical, and leaders are respected because of their status. Managers are expected to make decisions rather than work out problems with subordinates. Workers may not easily bypass the chain of command. A clear hierarchy based on status—age, sex, family, and/or title—may discourage lower-level workers from airing their views freely lest they be considered disrespectful or be seen as the nail that sticks out. Power and authority are centralized, and organizational structure's highly demarcated levels are tightly controlled. A leader may need to act in a certain formal way to avoid losing credibility.

In Arab cultures the leader may consult with others for advice but will then make the decision on his own. Leaders strongly influenced by Islam would be intensely aware and respectful of the role of Allah in making decisions. Many African cultures, partly because of their education systems, encourage people to be more imitative than creative. Thus African managers may regard their authority, professional competence, and knowledge as personal possessions rather than parts of their organizational role. They may be reluctant to delegate authority, share information, or involve subordinates in the decision-making process.

Many Asian cultures follow more circuitous courses in selecting a course of action than are generally found in the West. Social and political sensitivity may influence the choice of a solution, and that choice must not cause someone to lose face. To save a member from embarrassment, a group might abandon or disavow a decision it previously determined to be proper.

Working with Culturally Diverse Groups

A major challenge for global teams is the building of trust among team members from different countries and even different organizations. How can team members share information, become motivated, work collaboratively, and get things done on time when they come from numerous functional, corporate, and national cultures, many of which may clash with one another?

When establishing and working with global teams, one must recognize that these cultural differences impact every activity of every team. Some of these values and behaviors may need to be transformed, while others may provide an opportunity for synergy.

Handling Geographic Distances

The physical and psychological separation caused by geographic distance presents another challenge to working in global HRD. Although technology enables organizations to be both centralized and decentralized, numerous limitations accrue when face-to-face contact among members of organizations is sporadic. In many cultures, personal contact is essential to the transaction of important business and to progress in partnerships and promotions. Geographic distance can cause people to feel cut off or left out of the loop or to have a diminished sense of importance. Headquarters culture is often misunderstood or denigrated from afar.

Geographic distance has a clear and direct impact on all forms of communication among team members. Distance is an impediment to building relationships of trust. As Handy (1995) puts it, "Trust needs touch." Even among colocated global team members who benefit from formal and informal face-to-face meetings, trust takes time to develop. Distance makes building trust and communication much more difficult as people will tend to be less direct and more constrained in their personal interactions. Distance frustrates trust and communication, while (no surprise) colocation fosters them. Additionally, the generally shorter project timelines of colocated projects provide the opportunity to give feedback quickly.

Distance also affects coordination and control. Problem-solving is more complicated for the team whose members have more difficulty knowing and understanding one another's decisionmaking styles. In addition, it becomes much harder to develop cohesiveness, to share a common vision of the team's work and its products. Working remotely can also bring feelings of isolation. On the other hand, frequent and/or long-term absences from home required of a member to participate in team activities can sap motivation and harm family life. Global teams may operate twenty-four hours a day around the world, requiring some team members to be available well into the early morning hours. Workdays in some countries (e.g., Saturdays and Sundays in the Persian Gulf region) may be days that another team member would prefer to spend with his or her family. Poorly planned and supported global teams can quickly burn out group members.

Finally, distance may lessen the level of interest and commitment on the part of senior organizational staff regarding one's work and career. In summary, the challenges that face distant and dispersed global HRD professionals revolve around the issues of integration and separation, collaboration and necessary independence, inclusion and exclusion—everywhere and at the same time.

Coordination and Control

The coordination and management of global HRD programs involves numerous administrative issues such as transportation, relocation, cultural orientation, language translation, host government relations, housing, facilities, and support services. Chapter 6, Administration of Global HRD Programs, discusses these issues in greater detail.

Coordination (which involves the integration of tasks and organizational units so that team efforts contribute to overall objectives) and control (the process of adhering to goals, policies, or standards) are even more important for global teams than for intraorganizational teams. Yet global teams face greater difficulties and challenges because of the complexities caused by cultural, linguistic, and technological issues (Carmel, 1999).

Distributed, dispersed teams create burdens on coordination and control mechanisms—primarily informal ones. Managers cannot peek around the cubicle wall or informally bring the distance team together. Because of time differences, they cannot make a quick phone call to check on progress, direct activities, or provide advice. Members' distance and different cultural patterns increase potential for conflict and may spawn an unwillingness to accept coordination and control. Team members may feel torn between loyalty to the global team and to their local manager. Thus, there is a delicate balance between avoiding duplication and inefficiencies and allowing enough autonomy to promote innovation.

The complexity of coordinating a team's work increases as interdependence within and between teams increases and as the task becomes more difficult, new, and/or uncertain. All of these factors are common with global teams. Thompson (1981) identified three types of interdependence and proposed general coordination mechanisms for each: (1) pooled interdependence can be coordinated by standardization; (2) sequential interdependence can be coordinated by plan; and (3) reciprocal interdependence needs to be coordinated by mutual adjustment.

The size of global teams may also complicate their coordination, as global teams in multiple sites are generally larger per task than colocated teams. The more people and the more roles involved, the more challenging are the coordination/control issues.

A final challenge with respect to coordination and control of global HRD relates to the management and followership styles of the organization and team members. Different cultures have different protocols and action chains for reporting to managers, especially foreign managers. Managers who usually work with people of their own culture may not understand how other cultures accept direction.

Maintaining Communication Richness over Distances

Global HRD programs cannot succeed without clear, effective communication. Yet much of this communication may necessarily be indirect (people communicating at different times to each other from different places). The "richness of context"—that fullness of meaning which relies so heavily on one's having been there, having witnessed body language, having understood the emotional commitment made to some parts of the message but not others—is missing.

Allen (1997), who developed a correlation between distance and communication, discovered that communication drops precipitously when offices are far away from one another (the "out of sight, out of mind" syndrome). The informal oral communication created by distance tends to promote sloppiness in documentation and procedures, such as passing along a half finished task with the tacit understanding that it will be fully fixed and documented later. Such communication may also contribute to inbreeding, groupthink, and other group pathologies.

Technology, although very powerful and helpful to global teams, conveys only limited context and can complicate people's efforts to understand one another. Team members of lesser-represented nationalities may be more likely to have poor access to or backup for the technology being used.

Asynchronous communications can also exacerbate the pressures on global teams. When members have no overlap of working hours for voice or video conversations, one side always has to compromise. Developing sensitivity to others' time and responsibilities is almost impossible. When there are constraints, we tend to focus on the work at hand.

Low context

Regular mail
Express mail
Electronic mail
Fax
Voice mail
Electronic chat
One-way broadcast audio
One-way broadcast video
Telephone
Live board with point-to-point audio
One-way broadcast video with audio back channel
Point-to-point videoconference
Virtual reality meeting
Face-to-face meeting

High context

FIGURE 1.1   Levels of contextual interaction

Most of the commonly used media are linear. These may be appropriate for certain types of information sharing, such as logical stream-progress reports, data, and logistical information. However, linear modes cannot communicate the collage of information one encounters by walking into the office of a person who lives and thinks differently because of culture. Managing and meeting over distances results, unfortunately, in managing by charts and sacrificing important cultural context and nuances.

Teams and individuals in most cultures prefer to do many of their tasks via face-to-face communication since it is much richer in context. When we channel communication into any electronic form, the communication loses richness. In some cross-cultural business settings, using technology for communications may actually be counterproductive. Figure 1.1 shows the varying levels of communications media, ranging from high (rich) to low (poor) context. Few global companies have grappled successfully with the context of their communication; most don't even recognize its existence. Many of us are unaware of the tremendous amount of relevant, needed information we casually obtain from our work environment.

Communications, both text and context, are vitally important to global HRD professionals and the global teams they work with. Together the challenges discussed above create difficulty in getting accurate information from distant sites, especially the bad news. And in many cultures people find it difficult to report things that are going wrong. Global teams must nurture and maintain context that promotes full, open communication, or they will suffer the consequences of weak team interactions and less-than-satisfactory team results.

Key Capabilities and Roles for Global HRD Professionals

The challenges of a rapidly changing workplace within a global environment necessitates competencies and knowledge on the part of the global HRD practitioner in a number of crucial areas, all of which will be explored in the remaining chapters of this book:

- Understanding cultural differences and how they impact every aspect of workplace learning, including leadership, motivation, communications, organizational structure, and decisionmaking. These differences and the factors that create these differences are the focus of chapter 2.
- Preparing leaders and HRD professionals to design, deliver, assess, and implement training solutions for a global, culturally diverse audience. Skills, such as identifying culturally appropriate resources, methodologies, technologies, methods, theories, and packaged programs for HRD and adapting HRD roles and processes to fit global and local environments, are highlighted in chapters 3 and 4.
- Serving as technical consultants and change agents to build and globalize organizations so that they are both globally and locally focused is explored in chapter 5.
- Assisting administrators and leaders to develop their cultural sensitivities and abilities so that they can produce, market, and sell products and services in other cultures is discussed in chapter 6.
- Providing cultural orientation and training programs to enable individuals to enter and flourish in multicultural situations and global organizations is the focus of chapter 7.
- Building global teams that can overcome the challenges of distance and cultural diversity is the aim of chapter 8.
- Assisting global public organizations and private corporations in providing a lifelong learning environment and support for employees to keep pace with globalization; in understanding the evolutionary stages of the global corporation; and in demonstrating the power of improved workforce productivity, performance, cost effectiveness, and efficiency is discussed in chapters 9 and 10.

- Optimizing the role of HRD in developing the political, economic, social, environmental, and educational sectors of communities and nations is treated in chapter 11.
- Understanding and appreciating the influence culture has on performing any HRD role in any region of the world are critical for the global HRD practitioner. In chapters 12–23 the specific cultural influences and their impact in twelve different regions or countries are explored.
- Understanding the global HRD megatrends of the 21st century (chapter 24) will enable global HRD practitioners to understand and successfully negotiate the future global workplace environment.
- Learning from the best HRD programs around the world is highlighted in chapters throughout the book.

Globalization has significantly impacted the world of work and the work of HRD. Increasingly, leaders are seeing HRD as the key lever for success in the global arena at individual, group, organizational, community, and national levels; in public and private sectors; and across all industries, boundaries, and cultures.

Culture and HRD

Globalization lies at the heart of modern culture; cultural practices lie at the heart of globalization.
John Tomlinson, *Globalization and Culture*

Introduction

Culture influences every aspect of HRD. Diagnosing and understanding learners' cultural values is as important as understanding their training needs. Hofstede (1980, 1991) believes that national culture is the strongest influence on the behavior of employers and employees, customers and citizens— stronger than differences in professional roles, education, age, or gender. And these cultural differences do not go away if one is employed in a global corporation. Laurant (1983) discovered that the impact of culture was greater in global companies than in domestic ones, that a multinational environment causes people to cling even more strongly to their own cultural values.

Components and Characteristics of Culture

Although culture can be defined and described in many ways, most definitions contain three elements: (1) culture is a way of life shared by all or almost all members of the group; (2) older members of the group pass this way of life on to younger members; and (3) it shapes the way one behaves and structures the way one perceives the world.

16

Bierstadt (1963), building on writings of the seminal anthropologists Geertz and Kluckholm, defines culture as consisting of a system of explicit and implicit guidelines for guiding a group's *thinking, doing,* and *living.* Thinking (ideas) encompasses values, beliefs, myths, and folklore. Doing (norms) includes laws, customs, regulations, ceremonies, fashions, and etiquette. Living (materials) refers to the use of machines, tools, natural resources, food, and clothing.

Hofstede (1991) defines culture as the "collective programming of the mind . . . it is learned, not inherited. Culture derives from one's social environment, not from one's genes" (p. 5). Hofstede distinguishes culture from human nature and personality in the following ways: Human nature is what all human beings have in common and is inherited with one's genes. The human ability to feel anger, fear, love, joy, sadness and our need to associate with others, to play, and to learn are all part of this level of human program. However, what one does with these feelings, how one expresses fear and joy or seeks to view reality, is modified by culture. As an individual, each of us has "personness," a unique programming not shared with any other human being. It is partly based on our heredity and is partly learned; that is, this personness is modified both by the influence of culture as well as our unique personal experiences (see Figure 2.1).

A simple example demonstrates the differences between these three realities of the individual person, culture, and human nature. It is part of everyone's human nature to eat. However, different cultural groups eat different foods at different times and in different ways. And, of course, an individual from a specific cultural group may choose to eat in total accord with his cultural group or choose to eat very differently (e.g., an American may eat Chinese food with chopsticks).

Schein (1997) noted that culture has three layers (see Figure 2.2): the innermost layer consists of one's basic assumptions or deeply held convictions, which may elude consciousness. The next layer comprises our values, and the third, most visible layer (to an outsider) represents our behaviors and practices, symbols, rituals, and artifacts. These are more easily influenced and changed than the core of culture, which is formed by values and underlying assumptions not easily recognized or understood by outsiders. Values and basic assumptions are among the first things that children learn—usually implicitly, not consciously. Most children have their basic value systems firmly in place before the age of eight. Teachers, managers, friends, and others of influence may be able to change our practices, but changing our values is much more difficult, and changing basic assumptions is almost impossible.

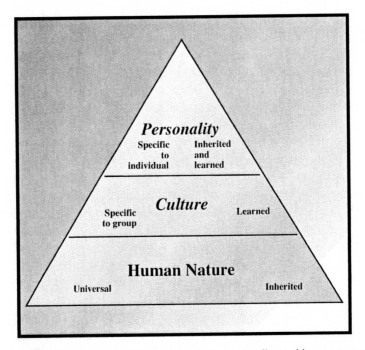

FIGURE 2.1   Culture as distinguished from personality and human nature

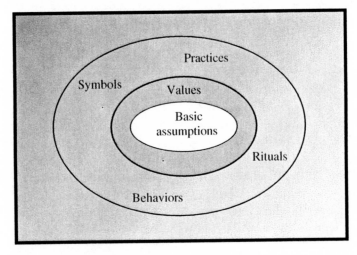

FIGURE 2.2   Layers of culture

Factors Influencing
the Cultural Environment

Nine interacting factors create and reinforce group cultures (see Table 2.1). One culture is distinguished from another by the elements within each of these factors and the power of those elements. Each of these factors can significantly impact every aspect of HRD.

Religion

Religion—the belief in a particular view of the supernatural, with accompanying rituals and rules—is probably the single most influential factor in cultural thinking, living, and doing. Religion helps to establish beliefs and norms; to determine whether a people see themselves as basically good or evil, in control of or controlled by the environment; and to define what is truly important in life. Many religious writings even describe how one should eat, dress, relate to others, and work.

Language

Language, the second most influential dimension of culture, is both the carrier and conditioner of culture. The words and structures available in a language strongly influence a speaker's way of thinking, values, beliefs, relationships, feelings, and concepts. English, for example, is a very direct and active language. An English speaker who reads and enjoys a new book might say, "I think it's a good book," clearly defining himself as a person entitled to, and capable of making, such a judgment. In Japanese, a less direct language, one

TABLE 2.1   Factors Influencing the Cultural Environment

1. **Religion**
2. **Language**
3. **Education**
4. **Economics**
5. **Politics**
6. **Family**
7. **Class structure**
8. **History**
9. **Natural resources/geography**

might say the equivalent of "With regard to me, the book is good." The assumption of authority and objectivity is less present.

English is less formal than many other languages. For example, modern English offers only one form of the second person for both singular and plural, *you.* In Vietnamese, by contrast, there are over forty words for *you,* the choice depending on the age, gender, relationship, number, and status of the addressor(s) and the addressee(s). It is thus much more natural for an American to be informal and egalitarian than for a Vietnamese. English assumes much more power and responsibility on the part of the speaker, whereas Spanish, for example, is more passive and fate oriented. Thus "I dropped the pen" in English becomes "The pen dropped."

Education

Education is a society's means of transmitting the knowledge, skills, and attitudes necessary for common existence. Education may be formal (primary, secondary, higher, vocational), nonformal (learning is structured but occurs outside the academic system—e.g., workplace learning or HRD), or informal (unstructured such as learning from one's parents as a child).

Some cultures encourage inductive learning (experiential, case by case, open-ended), while others are more deductive (general to specific, theoretical). Many societies encourage rote learning in an environment where absolute respect for and obedience to the instructor is expected, while other societies support open, participative learning with a more egalitarian relationship between teacher and student.

Economics

Economics encompasses the activities concerned with the production and distribution of goods. A society's economy may be (a) free market and capitalistic, (b) centrally planned and socialistic, or (c) a mixture of the two. Since the end of the Cold War, the percentage of the world's population living in market-driven economies has grown. Even so, the mindsets of people who lived for so many years in formerly communist countries continue to be influenced by those managed economies.

Politics

The political dimension of culture encompasses structures and activities related to the allocation and use of power as well as the regulation of access to resources and opportunities. Political systems may range from totalitarian to democratic and may exclude specific groups on the basis of ethnicity, gender, age, or economic status.

Family

The concept of family varies among cultures from nuclear families (parents and children only) to extended families (including grandparents, cousins, aunts, and uncles). The nuclear family has limited interaction with the larger kin group, and its members often feel free to ignore expectations of the extended family or even of their immediate family in choosing marriage partners, professions, homes, and so forth. In the extended family, obligations to family members override the desires and wishes of the individual. The son especially is expected to remain with the family to support it in whatever way he can. Most of Asia, Africa, and Latin America place a high emphasis on the extended family structure.

Class Structure

Class structure ranges from open to closed. In open class structures, an individual has the ability to move up, down, or laterally in the system without major difficulty. What one *does* is the important criterion. In closed class structures one's position is determined and limited by *who one is*—that is, by birth rather than by individual achievement. The United States, for example, has a very open class structure compared to rural India, where the class system is very closed.

History

A society's history has a significant impact on its culture. China's long, glorious history has created a culture in which one's perspective of time is very different than it would be in a newly formed nation in, say, Africa. Colonized countries of Africa and Asia often exhibit values derived from their colonizers, as well as their own traditions. The Arab world identifies with the military achievements of Muhammad and his successors. The United States' brief history includes the rugged frontier people, rapid industrialization and expansion, and pride—seen by some as arrogance—in being the "last, best hope of mankind."

Natural Resources/Geography

Obviously, the land on which a society lives influences its culture. The vast spaces, minerals, forests, and farmlands of the United States helped form a culture that exhibited optimism, materialism, and confidence. In contrast, societies regularly faced with hurricanes, flooding, drought, lack of minerals, or scarcity of arable land tend to be more fatalistic. The oil and sand of Saudi Arabia have certainly had an impact on its culture, as have forests and heavy rains on Liberian culture.

Variables of Culture

The nine cultural factors discussed above influence every aspect of our lives and cause peoples in every culture to think and act in very different ways. Our ways of thinking and acting are affected by how we relate to the ten variables shown in Table 2.2.

Environment

People tend to believe and act in three different ways relative to the environment. The people of some cultures, such as that of the United States, believe that they *control* the environment and that the environment can be changed to fit their needs. Others, particularly in Buddhist-based cultures, believe that people should strive to achieve *harmony* with the environment. And the people of still other cultures (e.g., Bangladeshis, who receive annual unwanted floods) believe themselves to be *constrained* by the environment and accept/expect that the environment and fate will control their lives.

Problem solving and solution selection are also dependent on how cultures relate to the environment around them, ranging from a belief of being "in control" to being "controlled." In *in-control* cultures, people believe that they can dominate their environment, that the environment can be changed to fit human needs. Problems are merely opportunities waiting for solutions. In cultures that value *harmony*, people seek to live in harmony with the world around them; this includes harmony with nature as well as with fellow group members. People in *controlled* cultures feel constrained by the world around them; fate, luck, and supernatural forces play a significant role. Everything happens because it is God's will. One takes what life gives.

Time

Cultures have widely differing perspectives regarding the importance of the *past, present,* and *future.* Some cultures value the past and the continuance of traditions; other cultures focus on the *present,* with an emphasis on short-

TABLE 2.2   Cultural Variables

Environment		
Control _____ Harmony _____		Constraint
Time		
Past _____ Present _____		Future
Single focus _____		Multifocus
Fixed _____		Fluid
Action		
Being _____		Doing
Communication		
High context _____		Low context
Direct _____		Indirect
Expressive _____		Instrumental
Formal _____		Informal
Space		
Private _____		Public
Power		
Hierarchy _____		Equality
Personal Behavior		
Individualistic _____		Collectivistic
Universalistic _____		Particularistic
Social Behavior		
Competitive _____		Cooperative
Structure		
Order _____		Flexibility
Thinking		
Deductive _____		Inductive
Linear _____		Systemic

term orientations and quick results; still other cultures emphasize the *future*, with a willingness to trade short-term gain for long-term results.

Time focus also varies across cultures. Time can be viewed as *polychronic* (multifocused) or *monochronic* (single focused). Monochronic cultures, such as that of the United States, prefer to concentrate on one task at a time. Plans and schedules tend to be detailed, followed quite strictly, and changed infrequently. In multifocused cultures people feel comfortable undertaking multiple tasks simultaneously, with a high commitment to relationship building rather than just task completion or meeting arbitrary deadlines.

Finally, cultures vary in the ways their members see and use time. Some cultures see time as *fixed* and important and define punctuality precisely, while other cultures perceive and practice time in a more *fluid* fashion, with punctuality defined somewhat loosely. In the United States, time is very important. "Time is money" and "Don't waste time" are dictums heard from early childhood onwards. Americans see time as a precious resource they can and should control. This concept of time is fixed. A sense of urgency is pervasive; being punctual and meeting deadlines are valued. Meetings begin on time and schedules are taken seriously. This attitude toward punctuality is less prevalent in many other societies, especially in Latin America and the Middle East. In these regions of the world, time is a resource that allows relationships to develop and promotes an environment in which people are more important than promptness. Things happen in "the fullness of time," not "on schedule." Time is more fluid; things can wait. And "soon" may mean three months or when we are ready. Thus, delays are expected.

Action

Cultures can be distinguished emphasizing *doing* (a task orientation and achievement centeredness—e.g., U.S. culture) or *being* (relationship centeredness, which values contemplation and reflection—e.g., Burmese culture). Many Western cultures are concerned with keeping busy and accomplishing things, whereas Eastern and African cultures tend to be more concerned with character and relationships.

Communication

Communications may be viewed culturally in four different ways:

a. *High and low context.* High- or *rich-context* communication cultures have the ability to share experiences and make certain things understood without their needing to be stated explicitly. Rules for speaking and behaving are implicit in the context. In such cultures a great deal of contextual information is needed about an individual or a company before business can be transacted. Transmission of meaning relies not merely on words but heavily on the group's understanding of voice tone, body language, facial expressions, eye contact, speech patterns, use of silence, past interactions, status, and common friends. Meaning tends to be implicit rather than direct, and less literal. For example, in various Asian cultures, "Yes" may mean "Yes," "Maybe," "I don't know," "If you say so," or even "No," as determined from the speaker's level of enthusiasm. The precise meaning depends on the context, not just the words. Silence designates thought, not disengagement. Rushing to fill a silence may be considered pushy or impulsive or even overly emotional. One's background, family, political and social connections, philosophical beliefs, affiliations, and experience are important in how one communicates.

Low-context cultures, on the other hand, emphasize the exchange of facts and information. The message is more important than the medium, the setting, or environment through which the message is delivered. Information is given primarily in words, and meaning is expressed explicitly. Impersonal, task-centered business transactions, common in America, are good examples of low-context communications. Relatively little information is needed about an individual or a company before business can be transacted because trust and compatibility are not primary considerations when doing business. The primary function of communication in low-context cultures is to exchange information, facts, and opinions. Performance appraisals, for example, are impersonal and direct. In such cultures a videoconference or an e-mail is usually accepted as an efficient substitute for meeting in person.

b. *Directness or indirectness.* Cultures can range from those in which people are very *direct*—they "say what they mean, and mean what they say"—to those in which people are very *indirect,* sacrificing frankness, avoiding potential conflict, and allowing others to "save face."

North Americans tend to be *direct* or *explicit* and frank when negotiating and dealing with conflict. Americans encourage the airing of individual opinions and view conflict as natural. They say "Let's deal with this now" or "Give it to me straight." Conflict is often handled by means of power and force.

In contrast, many cultures of the world encourage much more *indirectness* in conveying disagreement or criticism (see Table 2.3). In these cultures people prefer implicit communication and avoid conflict. Indirect cultures use a mix of conflict avoidance and third-party intervention to handle conflict. Indirectness in communication serves the desire to save face, protect honor, and avoid shame. In such cultures to say "no" directly, whether in negotiations or in rejecting ideas and advice from a consultant, is very difficult if not impossible. The desire to avoid direct refusal is a cultural trait rooted in courtesy and respect.

c. *Emotionally expressive or instrumental.* People in some cultures are very *expressive* in displaying emotions and demonstrating charisma, eloquence, and style in their communications and interactions, while people from other

TABLE 2.3 Indirect Communication Strategies

	Description
Mediation	A third person is used as a go-between.
Refraction	Statements intended for person A are made to person B while person A is present.
Covert revelation	Person portrays self as messenger for someone else or allows notes to fall into hands of another party.
Correspondence	Written communication is used so as to avoid direct interaction.
Anticipation	One is understated, unobtrusive, and empathetic so as to accommodate the unspoken needs of the other person.
Ritual	Rituals help maintain control of uncertain situations.

cultures are more *instrumental* in communicating, favoring accuracy, control, and discipline in their interactions.

Expressive communication styles—as found in Latin American, Middle Eastern, and Southern and Eastern European cultures—are considered a highly valued art form. People from these countries are less concerned with the precision of communication than with the establishment and maintenance of personal and social connections. People hiding emotions are seen as dead fish. People raise their voices in joy, anger, and other intense emotions. There is much hugging and touching.

The *instrumental* style of communication found in some other parts of the world is problem centered, impersonal, and goal oriented. *What* is said overshadows *how* something is said. It is more important for communication to be accurate than stylistically appropriate. The primary objective is to reach a factual, objective, unemotional conclusion that leads to action. Displays of emotion are seen as a lack professionalism and rationality; they signal a loss of control and are embarrassing. People from expressive cultures, on the other hand, are more direct and candid and want to do business in a friendly, relaxed atmosphere. They place minimal value on custom and hierarchical status.

d. *Degree of formality.* Communications can range from very *formal*, emphasizing adherence to protocol and social customs, to *informal*, dispensing with ceremony and protocol. *Informal* communication, as in the United States and Germany, is sparser, contains less flowery interactions, and gives less importance to tradition. *Formal*-communication cultures, such as Egypt and Thailand, place high value on etiquette, proper channels, and ritualistic exchanges.

Space

One's personal space can be construed as *private,* so that a defined distance is maintained between individuals when communicating and interacting (e.g., Thais or Indians, who prefer a bow), or as *public,* so that close proximity is preferred (people from Latin and Arabic cultures prefer to embrace each other in greetings).

Power

Some cultures establish *distance* or *hierarchy* (e.g., Japan, France) within power structures, while others (e.g., Scandinavian cultures) minimize the distance between leaders and subordinates and prize *egalitarian* relationships between people.

Personal Behavior

In *individualistic* cultures, the "I" predominates over the "we," and an individual's independence is highly valued. *Collectivistic* cultures, on the other hand, subordinate the interests and needs of the individual to those of the group. Cultures also differ in the way solutions are applied. People in *universalistic* cultures apply generalizations, rules, and procedures consistent with underlying laws and principles. Solutions are more impersonal, and models are developed to explain and predict behavior outcomes. *Particularistic* cultures, on the other hand, emphasize differences, relativism, and uniqueness. The resolution of problems depends entirely on the situation and context.

Social Behavior

Competitive cultures emphasize assertiveness, results, success, and achievements, especially as they relate to tasks and rewards. Work is highly valued and determines one's worth, value, and importance. *Cooperative* cultures highly value consensual decisionmaking. Employees are hired not only for their skills but also for their ability to fit into the group, to promote its shared values, to facilitate communication, demonstrate loyalty, and contribute to the overall work environment.

Structure

People of some cultures value *order*, emphasizing rules, regulations, and procedures; the unexpected or uncertain is not desirable. They seek clear roles and responsibilities as well as work processes that are precise and consistent. Other cultures are more *flexible*, have a greater tolerance for change, and are receptive to new people and ideas. They are more tolerant of deviations from the norm and display a greater willingness to take risks. What works is what counts. These cultures show a preference for broad guidelines rather than specific methodologies. Thus job and task descriptions are broadly interpreted.

Thinking

Cultures tend toward *deductive* reasoning (based on theory and logic, going from the general to the specific) or *inductive* reasoning (based on experience and experimentation, going from the specific to the general). Some cultures are more *linear* in their thinking (using straightforward analysis, focusing on points rather than an in-depth analysis of the whole), while other cultures are more *systemic* in their thinking and focus on the big picture.

Levels of Culture

We tend to link culture to nations, as in "Thai culture" or "Samoan culture." However, the definitions and characteristics discussed in the previous sections can relate to five different levels or types of culture—corporate, ethnic, regional, national, and global.

Corporate Culture

Organizations have distinct cultures, passed on from present members to newcomers, that determine organizational ways of thinking and acting. Schein (1997) points out that organizations have three levels of culture—basic assumptions, values, and behaviors. Deal and Kennedy (1982) note that every organization functions in a way that is distinct from every other organization. The customs, language, folklore, and way of living at IBM, for example, are unique and different from those of all other corporations.

Ethnic Culture

Most nations have many ethnic cultures within their borders. For example, Sri Lanka has two distinct ethnic groups—Tamils and Sinhalese. Cameroon, in contrast, has over one hundred ethnic groups within its national borders. Los Angeles County has over 150 cultural groups. Also, some ethnic groups (e.g., Indian, Chinese) may be found in many different countries.

Regional Culture

There are some cultural characteristics that are "many-nationed" since the cultural factors influencing the various national cultures are powerful and similar. For example, there are many common characteristics of the peoples within the various Latin American countries and within Middle Eastern countries.

National Culture

National culture exists in a country that has within its national borders a distinct manner of thinking and acting. While a number of ethnic subcultures may exist within the country, transcending them are a number of common values and behaviors.

Global Culture

The impact of global business (food, clothing, corporate systems) and worldwide communications (television, radio, music) has created a growing overlap of values, norms, and beliefs common to people located or working in countries around the world. Economists and anthropologists regard this global culture as the first sign of an emerging borderless world with a greater worldwide sharing of lifestyles and behaviors.

Culture's Impact on HRD Practice

As discussed in chapter 1, there are generally approved principles that can be applied to the sequencing and components of HRD design and delivery, the roles of the trainer and trainees, and the general administration and environment of the project or program. However, the implementation of these HRD principles is significantly affected by the cultural environment in which the activity occurs. Culture is like a filter through which training must pass, as shown in Figure 2.3. As we can see, cultural factors and environment have an impact on:

- Roles of the trainer and learners
- Program analysis and design
- Program development and delivery
- Program administration and environment

HRD Principles	Cultural Environment	HRD Implementation
Roles of trainers and learners	Factors	Roles of trainers and learners
Analysis and design	and	Analysis and design
Development and delivery	Characteristics	Development and delivery
Administration and environment		Administration and environment

FIGURE 2.3   Impact of culture on implementation of HRD

Let's now explore how the cultures of four different global regions will significantly influence these four organizational activities.

United States and Canada

Cultural Factors

1. *Religion:* The dominant religious influence is that of Protestantism, with its emphasis on individualism, personal salvation, and the work ethic.
2. *Language:* English is an active, direct, clear, and analytical language with a precise but abundant vocabulary. It is a language that patterns in linear structures and lends itself to detailed, observation-based, scientific analysis.
3. *Education:* Educational opportunities are universal, with a strong public education system from kindergarten through graduate schools. Emphasis is on learning that is practical, utilitarian, and applicable. The inductive approach of thinking is encouraged. Experiences tend to be evaluated in terms of dichotomies (right/wrong, do/don't, successful/unsuccessful, good/evil, work/play, winner/loser, subjective/objective).
4. *Economics:* The economies are market driven and capitalistic. Competition is seen as healthy and essential to economic development.
5. *Politics:* Extensive democracy is preached and practiced with universal suffrage. Government should serve the people, without becoming too powerful. Individual rights are paramount.
6. *Family:* Families are nuclear, and children are responsible primarily to themselves for career choices and education.

7. *Class structure:* There is an open class structure with opportunities for nearly all to advance. Initiative is respected and rewarded, and equality of opportunity is the norm.
8. *History:* Compared to the cultures of Asia, the history of these countries is relatively short. They have generally been economically and militarily successful.
9. *Natural resources/geography:* As a result of the vast arable land and temperate climates, farmlands are abundant and fruitful. Both countries have enjoyed vast frontiers and open spaces that have encouraged rugged individualism and independence.

Impact on HRD Implementation

Each of the nine factors of culture has an impact on the implementation of HRD in the United States and Canada. In the following section we identify some of the these HRD practices and what cultural factors account for them.

1. *HRD roles:* The relationship between the trainer and the learner is much more equal than in Asian, Latin, or Arab cultures. Trainers must prove their competency. They can and will be challenged by learners, and their credibility must be earned. Trainers can be more informal and casual. Such cultural factors as *class structure, politics,* and *language* support these types of roles and relationships between trainers and trainees.
2. *Analysis and design of learning programs:* The trainer collaborates with the trainees and/or their organizational managers to jointly determine learning objectives. Participants are expected to state their needs openly, because it is believed that everyone can improve and learn. Learners generally want to achieve success and want to be involved in setting learning objectives. Clear, measurable objectives are established, and learners can achieve them if they make the effort. The factors of *religion* and *history* encourage this cultural approach to needs analysis and objective setting.
3. *Development and delivery of learning programs:* Training programs should be practical and relevant. Behavior can be changed and skills can be developed. A wide variety of methodologies are offered. Both inductive and deductive learning are desired. Methodologies built on analysis, problem solving, and learning from fellow trainees and by oneself are appropriate. Lecturing by the instructor is tolerated in short doses. Cultural factors, such as *natural resources, education,* and *economics,* favor this approach to development and delivery of HRD programs.

4. *HRD program administration and environment:* The venue should be comfortable and economical. Fancy ceremonies and speeches from dignitaries are not necessary. Learners are selected based on the needs of the organization and the perceived benefits of training the selected individuals, not on their family or class. Beliefs about *politics, education,* and the *family* drive these approaches to HRD administration and environment.

East Asia

Cultural Factors

Global HRD professionals who work in the countries of East Asia—Thailand, Malaysia, Singapore, Korea, China, and others—but come from other cultures know they must modify their HRD practices if they wish to succeed. Here are some of the cultural factors that influence HRD and learning in this region of the world:

1. *Religion:* Buddhism and Hinduism are the dominant religions. Both preach the importance of harmony with nature and one's fellow human beings, of accepting the world as it is, of seeking collaborative means to resolve problems. Humility is a prime virtue.
2. *Language:* Languages in this region are "high context"—that is, environment, context, or nonverbal language may be more important than the words people speak. The languages have numerous forms of "you" to better distinguish the myriad relationships and levels of respect for one another. Some languages, such as Mandarin, are very rich and complex, while others, like Bahasa Indonesian, are very simple and have a relatively small number of words.
3. *Education:* The influence of Confucianism, with its emphasis on learning and respect for the educator, permeates these cultures. Since opportunities may be limited, one should seek to learn whatever one can. Instruction is primarily by lecture and students learn by rote.
4. *Economics:* In recent years, the economies of East Asia have moved from state control toward free-market capitalism. Small family businesses are numerous and entrepreneurship is highly valued.
5. *Politics:* Although democracy is beginning to emerge in some countries, for the most part, power is still concentrated in the hands of a few.
6. *Family:* An extended-family structure dominates, and one is expected to respect and obey parents and grandparents in the selection of one's

profession, domicile, and spouse. The needs of the extended family and even the village are more important than those of the individual. *Guanxi* (Chinese for "relationships") are central to accomplishing results.

7. *Class structure:* Class structures have traditionally been closed and remain so in rural areas. However, the trend in cities is to be judged by one's achievement and hard work.

8. *History:* The Chinese, Japanese, Korean, and Thai cultures and histories are thousands of years old, with much past power and glory. Time frames are long term, and people appreciate the past.

9. *Natural resources/geography:* Huge populations strain the food and mineral resources of these societies. Floods and earthquakes create a sense of the inevitability of nature's power.

Impact on HRD Implementation

Due to the impact of these cultural factors, the global HRD practitioner needs to adapt her training activities in East Asia in the following ways:

1. *HRD roles:* Learners have the utmost respect for all educators and treat them reverently. They expect the HRD practitioner to behave, dress, and relate to them in a highly professional, formal way. They also hope to be treated with sensitivity. The trainer is expected to know the answers. Assignments must be carried out without questioning or disagreement. *Religion, education, politics, family, class structure,* and *language* all contribute to these views of the roles of trainer and trainee.

2. *Analysis and design of learning programs:* Since the trainer is considered omniscient and thus should know what the trainees need to learn, it is not necessary to undertake a needs analysis. Moreover, it would represent a loss of face and be embarrassing for learners to admit weaknesses to an outsider. Questioning of Asians can result in ritualized behavior, withdrawal, or even resentment of the trainer. Asking for self-analysis may be fine for Americans who value frankness and openness, but it is potentially disastrous in East Asia, where a much higher value is placed on hiding one's own feelings and thoughts and not prying into the feelings and thoughts of others.

3. *Development and delivery of learning programs:* East Asians, as a result of their rigid and rigorous education system, are accustomed to listening to lectures, note taking, and limited and respectful questioning of the teacher. Students attempt to soak up information like a sponge and repeat it back verbatim. Learners from these societies

also tend to place a high value on orderliness, conformity, and clear, specific instructions. Therefore, training materials should be orderly, well organized, and unambiguous. Designing a workplace learning program that includes role plays and structured experiences will be difficult due to a variety of cultural factors. Asians are uncomfortable placing themselves in the shoes of others because of their respect for hierarchical and social differences. Role plays that feature confrontation or innovation are hard to initiate in a culture whose *religion, education, politics, language,* and *history* value compromise, conformity, clear authority relations, and conflict avoidance. Most learners believe that it is much better for the trainer to demonstrate what is the best knowledge, skill, and/or attitude. Mixing learners of different ages, genders, and/or professional ranks (thereby ignoring status differences) may be viewed as undermining authority and power in the workplace. Exercises that strip the learners of status tend to cause embarrassment, confusion, and loss of face at the expense of learning.

4. *HRD program administration and environment:* East Asians place high value on visible signs of status and worth. An HRD professional's authority is determined to a great extent by who and how many people report to him, the location and decor of the HRD office, and so forth. The aesthetics of the training room, quality of training materials and announcements, and the number and quality educational resources available are indications of how important a training program is and greatly influence attendance. Ceremonies with important dignitaries in attendance, certificates, plaques, and speeches are taken as signs of the training program's value and importance.

Middle East and North Africa

Cultural Factors

The Arab world, stretching from Morocco in North Africa to the Gulf States of the United Arab Emirates and Oman, include more than 400 million people, bonded together by a common religion (Islam) and language (Arabic)—both powerful factors connecting the peoples of these countries.

1. *Religion:* Islam permeates the daily life of the region. The five pillars of Islam—the one God (Allah), prayer, charity, Ramadan (the holy month of fasting), and pilgrimage to Mecca—guide all, rich and poor, Egyptian and Saudi, young and old. The teachings of

Muhammad in the Koran (for example, the brotherhood of all Muslims), the status of women, Islamic rituals, and mosques deeply affect the educational, political, and family life of these societies. Trust and acceptance of fate is so ingrained that the most common phrase in this region is *Insha'Allah* (if God wills), since only that which Allah chooses or allows will occur.

2. *Language:* Arabic, the language of the Koran, is for Arabs a language to be spoken and heard. Arabs enjoy listening for hours to Arabic poetry, speeches, and songs. How one says something is as important as what one says. Arabs are generally much better at speaking their language and the language of others than they are at writing them.

3. *Education:* The key learning experience for most Arab people involves the memorizing of the Koran. Education systems emphasize an imitative, rather than a creative, approach to learning. One learns from memorization rather than from independent research and original work. In most places, girls are educated separately from boys and learn different subjects and roles in society.

4. *Economics:* The region includes some of the richest countries in the world (Saudi Arabia, Bahrain, United Arab Emirates) and some of the poorest (Yemen, Egypt). Oil is the primary source of wealth, and foreign workers in the rich countries who send their remittance back to their families represent a major source of income for their own, poorer countries. Social relations and loyalty are as important as getting the work done. Misfortune may be attributed to outside influence—that is, what Allah wills.

5. *Politics:* While increasing numbers of people seek democratic expression, most countries in the region are oligarchical, run by benevolent royal families and military dictators. The mullahs (church leaders) are powerful and influential among the people and in some governments. Decisions are made by consensus among ruling councils and by families.

6. *Family:* The extended family is the foundation of Arab life, with the Koran spelling out proper roles and relationships. There are social distances between persons based on age and gender: Men have a higher status than women; age is valued over youth; those who are married outrank those who are not. A parent's word is final, and great respect for one's elders is expected and given. The family is the primary determinant of individual behavior in such areas as choice of occupation, spouse, and living site, as well as of numerous social obligations. Families are paternalistic and male centered. Many

homes will have a special meeting room, a *diwaniah,* where neighboring men spend time socializing each evening.

7. *Class structure:* Social structure is highly stratified; labor is divided primarily on a class basis, and social mobility is difficult. Social morality prevails over individual morality. Thus the concepts of right/wrong, reward/shame derive not from an individual's determination of appropriate behavior but from what society in general dictates as the social norm. People retain a formality of manners, particularly in initial social relationships.

8. *History:* Within a hundred years of the death of Muhammad, the Arabs were masters of an empire extending from the shores of the Atlantic to the Chinese border. While the Western world was experiencing the Dark Ages, Islamic culture was flourishing in the arts and sciences. More recent history, however, saw much of the Arab world colonized by the British, French, and Ottoman (Turkish) empires. Most Arab countries achieved independence in the 20th century.

9. *Natural resources/geography:* Much of the region is desert with hot, dry weather. The Bedouin traditions of hospitality and generosity to people traveling from oasis to oasis remain strong. Elaborate greetings and close physical contact while communicating also derive from these traditions. Rich deposits of oil are the main natural resource, but they have enriched relatively small segments of the population.

Impact on HRD Implementation

1. *HRD roles:* Muhammad declared that education was the highest of the professions and therefore teachers and trainers must be highly respected by trainees. At the same time, trainees should be respected and should seek to develop a friendly relationship with the instructor. Formality is important, and even casual encounters with a colleague begin with traditional and elaborately formal words of greeting. In more traditional societies males (including trainers) are not to touch or shake hands with female trainees, especially those wearing a scarf. In some countries men are not allowed to be in the same room as women. Religion, family, and class structure are important cultural determinants for HRD roles.

2. *Analysis and design of learning programs:* Identifying needs and weaknesses in an individual or organization may be difficult since people are not expected to speak negatively of others even if they dislike them. "Allah loveth not the speaking ill of anyone," according to

the Koran. The frankness of Americans regarding others' faults is regarded as highly improper. In designing the training program, it is important to allow considerable time for socializing and building of relationships. Prayer time should also be built into the schedule. Things should not be rushed, for, as the Koran teaches, "haste is of the devil."

3. *Development and delivery of learning programs:* A number of strategies and structures, based on the factors of culture, can enhance the effective delivery of training programs in Arab societies:

- Provide ample opportunities for interactions between the trainer and learners and among the learners themselves
- Rely more on oral than written demonstrations of knowledge or skills acquired
- Avoid paper exercises and role-playing since they are thought to be games for school children

4. *HRD program administration and environment:* The Arabs, reflecting their language, prefer the learning process to be permeated with flourishes and ceremonies. Training should be moderated during Ramadan, the month of fasting. Do not expect quick decisions from a singe person, since the culture is very consultative and time is flexible. (One of the authors was told that the Arabic word *bukra* [tomorrow] had a similar connotation as *mañana* but that it lacked the urgency of that Spanish word.)

Latin America

Cultural Factors

The countries of South and Central America share many common cultural characteristics.

1. *Religion:* The Catholic religion—with its historical emphasis on hierarchy, patriarchy, and fatalism—permeates Latin culture. Spanish missionaries established a highly structured social and economic system. Women are much more active in religion than men.
2. *Language:* Spanish and Portuguese, both Romance languages, employ the passive voice more broadly than does English, thereby implying less active personal control of or responsibility for the world around the speaker.

3. *Education:* Latin American education systems tend to emphasize the theoretical and the humanities and place less emphasis on the practical. Upper classes send their children to private schools and universities, most of which are under the auspices of the Catholic Church. Illiteracy is high, and limited vocational education is available.

4. *Economics:* Free-market capitalism is practiced in most countries (Cuba being the exception), although economic power still remains in the hands of small numbers of families in most countries. Only a small middle class exists.

5. *Politics:* The Spanish tradition of monarchy and authoritative government dominated in Latin America until independence from Spain was achieved in the 19th century. Most countries, however, maintained the tradition of strong, decisive rulers and have had a succession of military dictatorships. Bolivia, for example, has experienced more than 150 coups in its 150 years of independence. A democratic form of government has begun to emerge throughout the Latin American countries, yet people still tend to elect powerful, decisive leaders with strong charisma and *personalismo* (personality).

6. *Family:* Latin American culture has extended-family structures, with a high respect for the family. Women are placed on a pedestal, and a men's *machismo* protects and seeks to impress them. Authority is centered in the father and is often extended to the strong ruler, who is considered the "father of the nation."

7. *Class structure:* In most of these countries there is a closed class structure in which one is born high or low. Throughout Latin America there are three distinct classes: (1) rich European families, whose wealth was earned from the coffee plantations and haciendas, and the new corporate leaders; (2) workers, Latinos, who are mostly of mixed Spanish and Indian descent; and (3) native Indians, at the very bottom economically and politically.

8. *History:* Many Latin American countries identify with the long and glorious history of Spain or Portugal, which colonized the region for over three hundred years. The native Indian population has been decimated or assimilated except in Bolivia, Peru, and Guatemala. The phrase "Rich today—gone tomorrow" captures the Latin American attitude that chance guided their past and now guides their destiny.

9. *Natural resources/geography:* Many of us continue to visualize Latin America as a land of large cattle ranches, coffee plantations, the Andes, and the Amazon. However, Latin America has become the

world's most urbanized regions; two of the largest metropolitan areas in the world are São Paulo in Brazil and Mexico City.

Impact on HRD Implementation

1. *HRD roles:* As might be surmised from the cultural factors of *politics, economics, class structure,* and *family,* Latin American societies prefer trainers who are decisive, clear, and charismatic leaders. Learners like to be identified with a successful trainer and will be loyal to him or her as a person.
2. *Analysis and design of learning programs:* In many ways, Latin and Arabic cultures are similar (the two cultures did coexist for over five centuries in Spain during the Middle Ages), and there are similar cautions in conducting needs analyses and designing training programs. The macho and *personalismo* qualities make it difficult for learners to express their weaknesses and faults in a needs analysis. Opportunities for affiliating and socializing are important. Class structure and family factors, however, can cause tension if Latinos and Indians are trained together.
3. *Development and delivery of learning programs:* In developing the curriculum, the trainer needs to be aware of the Latin American educational tradition of lectures and more theoretical emphases. Most organizations will expect training to be conducted in Spanish.
4. *HRD program administration and environment:* The value and importance of training are indicated largely by venue (to which dignitaries are invited for the ceremonies) and the trainer's academic affiliation. Time is very flexible, and beginning or ending at a certain time is not important. A single person at the top of the organization often makes key decisions.

Summary

Culture is a powerful influence on the way a group of people live and act, think and learn. It shapes each group member's behavior and perception of the world. As we can see in chapter 3, culture is vitally important in the design, delivery, and administration of HRD programs and in consulting. Simply put, HRD efforts cannot succeed if cultural factors are ignored. Just as form (structure) impacts function (operations), so culture significantly influences training and learning.

Part 2

Roles of HRD

Design and Development of
Global HRD Programs

Two roads diverged in a wood, and I—
I took the one less traveled by,
And that has made all the difference.

Robert Frost

Introduction

Like the traveler in the Robert Frost poem, global HRD practitioners may choose between (a) the easy road of simply transposing a successful domestic training program from one cultural setting to another or (b) the difficult, time-consuming road of "acculturizing" the program to fit the culture of the learners.

We strongly advocate the second path, since it is critical that the HRD professional provide not only the instructional content but also a learning environment that is culturally appropriate with as few barriers to learning as possible. Each of the seven steps of the Global Training Model presented in this chapter should be acculturized—that is, adapted and modified to suit the culture of the target audience. Relevant cultural factors must be identified and then applied as an integral part of the design and delivery of the training program. Informants native to the target culture are invaluable as consultants during this process to ensure that cultural nuances are respected and effectively incorporated. While this approach can be time-consuming and difficult, attention to cultural differences will increase the likelihood of success and positive long-term results.

Global Training Model

Models facilitate the development of any type of training program as they obviate having to start from scratch every time. When designing programs for international use, however, one must not only follow logical steps of development but also analyze the cross-cultural aspects involved throughout the process.

The seven steps of the Global Training Model are similar to those followed to develop domestic training programs. The addition of acculturization at each step, however, differentiates this model from previous ones. Figure 3.1 presents the seven steps and illustrates the central role that acculturization plays in the model. Note that each step involves an integrated acculturization component. Since this is a systems model, after evaluating results in step 7, the cycle starts again with a needs analysis to identify new and changing needs of the organization and the learners.

What Is Acculturization, and Why Is It Important?

Before examining each of the steps of the model and how acculturization works at each step, we need to define what we mean by *acculturization*. Acculturization is the conveying of a program (including its objectives, methodologies, materials, and content) across cultural boundaries to ensure that the training program is user-friendly.

By taking cross-cultural differences into account, an acculturized training program includes as few roadblocks to learning as possible, enhances the learner's experience, and helps him or her accomplish the learning objectives. The goal for the HRD practitioner is to ensure that the program succeeds within the trainees' cultural milieu. Cultural adaptation is as crucial to achieving results as is language translation (where that is necessary). Without this cultural sensitivity, little or no learning will occur.

When designing training programs for use in other countries and delivering them, HRD practitioners must identify the relevant cultural factors and their impact and then synergistically involve the culture throughout the training design, development, and delivery. Such efforts can be time-consuming and complex but are critical to achieving the objectives of the initiative. Merely injecting a few references to another culture into an existing domestic program will seldom result in a culturally meaningful learning experience.

Since we all encounter difficulties when trying to fully understand and apply another's culture, the HRD professional should involve local people in the acculturization aspect of each step in the Global Training Model, to test for cultural relevance, accuracy, and effectiveness.

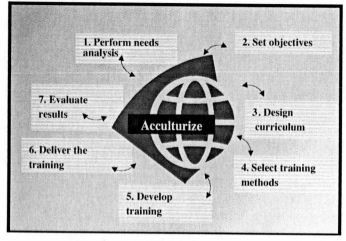

FIGURE 3.1   Global HRD training model

Global Training Model and Acculturization Strategies

Step 1: Conducting a Needs Analysis

Needs analysis is the collection, organization, and assessment of information pertinent to diagnosing the training and development needs of an organization. These needs are identified by analyzing the gaps between the organization's desired capabilities and its staff's current competencies. Organizational performance improves when individuals develop the skills and knowledge to perform their jobs correctly and more efficiently. Often a job analysis is performed to determine the duties, responsibilities, and tasks included in a job, or competency studies are used to uncover the skills and knowledge needed to perform effectively.

Numerous methods can be used to gather needs analysis data, including:

- Observation
- Questionnaires
- Consultations
- Focus groups
- Interviews
- Analysis of reports and records
- Review of work samples

One can gather this data from supervisors, managers, and current and former employees, as well as outside people who work directly with the organization such as customers, vendors, and consultants.

Step-1 Acculturization.   An important element of needs analysis is the identification of gaps, weaknesses, and areas for improvement in the skills and knowledge of individual job performers. In many cultures the client may find admitting such a need difficult, since disclosing some degree of incompetence or weakness would cause the person to lose face. The HRD practitioner may not be allowed access to information that would cause a loss of face. In addition, the client may assume that the "expert" HRD professionals have this information already since they are in a position of authority. They may be perceived as incompetent if they, as the experts, must ask for such information.

Another difficulty arises in cultures that place a high value on agreement and politeness. If individuals from such cultures are asked to provide information about what skills and knowledge are needed, they may try to guess what the HRD practitioner is looking for and provide that response, even if inaccurate. Accordingly, the HRD practitioner must strike a delicate balance between discovering and predetermining learning needs.

For these and other reasons—such as language, unfamiliar organizational environments, different educational systems, cultural and corporate customs and rituals—it is critical to allow much more time and attention to conducting needs analyses when working in different cultural settings than in single-culture settings. The participation of local HRD staff can be invaluable at this stage of instructional design and may also provide the local staff with a greater sense of ownership of the program. A needs analysis can build relationships and credibility when conducted appropriately.

Step 2: Setting Objectives

American instructional designers strive to set clear, competency-based objectives, mastery of which learners will be able to demonstrate at the end of the program. Objectives should state exactly what learners will do (performance), under what circumstances (conditions) they will be able to perform, and the level of accomplishment expected (quality).

Step-2 Acculturization.   For some cultural groups such clearly defined objectives may be seen as:

- Presumptuous—the learners may question how the trainer can know beforehand what the learners will be able to do, since only God knows
- Threatening—if the learners are unable to achieve these objectives, they will have failed. Therefore, training that begins with asking for expectations or personal goals is unlikely to be met with comfortable or enthusiastic responses.
- Foreordained—if God (Allah) wills the learners to have these competencies, then it will happen with or without the trainer's and learners' efforts

Another cultural fact to consider is that for learners in some cultures, the primary objective is the acquisition of a certificate or degree, not the learning. In such cultures credentials are much more important than competency for career advancement. In other cultures learners may value the building of relationships and the development of friendship as much as or more than learning. For them a key training objective may be the opportunity to practice and apply the learning together during and after the training.

Another critical factor in establishing goals and objectives in other countries is the consideration of standards and testing requirements. Labor ministries and other governmental agencies often have specific regulations that apply to various occupations and positions. When working across national boundaries, HRD professionals should be sure to research and be familiar with the requirements of relevant laws and regulations.

Step 3: Designing the Curriculum

The next step in the Global Training Model involves two important tasks: (1) determining the content and structure of the learning plan and (2) sequencing the instructional elements within the plan.

1. *Structure the learning plan.* Structure consists of the relationships among skills and topics and provides a framework for learning. Types of structure the instructional developer may use to organize programs include:

   A. Task-centered structure, which arranges training topics to be learned by their relationships to job tasks
   B. Topic-centered structure, which arranges training topics by the topics to be covered

C.Problem-centered structure, which orients the training program to problems the learners will face on the job

2. *Sequence the learning plan.* Basic ways to sequence learning elements include:

A.Inductive, or step-by-step—going from the specific to the general, from the known to the unknown, from the simple to the complex. This sequence is generally more concrete and practical.
B. Deductive—moving from the general to the specific, from an overview to the individual point. This sequence is generally more philosophical and generic.

Based on the performance objectives, the interplay of the learning tasks, and the characteristics of the participants and their environment, the curriculum designer chooses the most appropriate training structure and sequence.

Step-3 Acculturization. Developing curriculum requires analyzing cultural learning styles in order to determine how the trainees learn best and what structure and sequence they expect. These styles are influenced by the cultural factors discussed in chapter 2 and differ from country to country and even from locality to locality. Fundamental differences exist between the learning styles and expectations of Americans and members of other cultures.

Global HRD professionals may find in comparing curriculum designs that northern Europeans feel comfortable with training developed in the United States since American curricula tend to be very structured, have a tight logical flow, and proceed at a rapid pace. By comparison, the French may also favor a logical flow but often prefer more time to discuss or argue various aspects of a topic, requiring a more relaxed time schedule.

According to Brake, Walker, and Walker (1995), American, northern European, and some other cultures tend to exhibit a problem-centered approach to learning. In these cultures principles and theories are derived from data analysis, and the goal is verification through an empirical method. Much of the rest of the world, however, prefers a deductive, topic-centered learning approach, emphasizing abstract thinking and the principles that can be obtained from ideas, moral values, and theories. When developing curriculum for cultures that prefer a more deductive approach, the designer should plan to present first a more general, big-picture overview and then more specific information. When using a more inductive, experiential approach in this type of culture, the instructor needs to clearly introduce this structure and its purpose and assist learners in becoming familiar and comfortable with new systems of learning.

Since the concept of time varies dramatically across cultures, scheduling and pacing are critical considerations in curriculum development. Recommendations include the following:

- Do not schedule too tightly. The session may not start punctually, and breaks and meals in some cultures are expected to be much longer than in others.
- Allow time for discussion and exploration, as some groups prefer much more than others.
- Allow for flexibility in content. For example, you may build in time for interaction only to discover that the culture in which you are working is not comfortable with this style of instruction and remains silent.
- Take into account the values, styles, and attitudes of the learners. Team activities may take more time if the cultural understanding of agreement is harmony and consensus, rather than decisions made by majority rule.
- Remember that when working with an interpreter, the presentation of content takes much longer because each point must be made in two languages.
- If English is the learners' second language, schedule more frequent breaks to allow rest and absorption of knowledge. Working in a nonnative language can be mentally exhausting.

Step 4: Selecting Instructional Methodologies

In choosing among the dozens of instructional methodologies, global HRD practitioners need to consider which ones work best within a given cultural context. One way to classify such methodologies is to place them on a continuum from those that require little participant involvement and are most didactic and instructor centered to those that require maximal participant involvement and are more experiential and learner centered. Figure 3.2 illustrates the placement of commonly used methods on this continuum.

Step-4 Acculturization. Global HRD professionals understand that the effectiveness of any methodology depends on the specific culture of the learners. American HRD practitioners generally have come to accept interactive, experiential, and process-oriented learning as more effective and enjoyable for learners than other approaches. This instructional approach runs counter

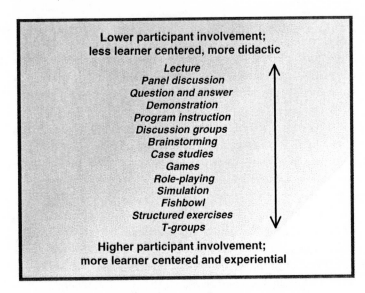

FIGURE 3.2   Continuum of instructional methodologies

to cultural norms in many cultures, however, and will detract from learning if the participants are uncomfortable. Participants from Asian and Arab cultures, for example, often are more accustomed to rote learning and may prefer to observe an instructor demonstrating a skill rather than risk appearing foolish through learning-by-doing methodologies.

In cultures that expect instructors to teach with authority and to provide absolute truths as experts, learners prefer instructional methods that are more teacher centered, such as lectures. In cultures that are more egalitarian and participative and that seek less structure, people respond more positively to more learner-centered approaches. When working in Russia and Eastern Europe, for example, instructors often encounter learners who are accustomed to an authoritarian, nonparticipative style of instruction. Instructors may lose credibility and respect if they ask for the learners' ideas and suggestions, since this may be perceived as a sign that the instructor does not really know the subject.

Similarly, in some cultures games and activities may seem frivolous and be attributed to a lack of seriousness on the instructor's part. Although younger participants may be more open to new learning methodologies, older ones, who have always learned through more didactic approaches, may perceive playing games as childish. Instructional games in Asian cultures are often ineffective, since they are perceived as detracting from the serious business of learning.

Participative activities involving interpersonal confrontation are also ill-suited to Asian and other cultures that tend to place a high value on conflict avoidance and authority relationships. In Asia small-group discussions and case studies can often be effective interactive instructional methodologies if carried out among participants of similar age and status. Representatives of each team should be asked to report their respective team's results to the larger group, so that each small group may discuss topics freely without any member having to take individual responsibility for the results.

When selecting instructional strategies for learners in some cultures, the designer should avoid role plays or interactive exercises that reverse the participants' normal social and power positions. Asians, for example, attach great value to their social positions and status differences. Any activity that removes these contextual differences may cause loss of face and confusion for all participants, thus distracting them from learning. Similar concerns about power differences, status, loss of face, and conflict avoidance are also common in cultures outside Asia and have a critical impact on the effectiveness of instructional methodologies.

Step 5: Developing Instructional Materials

During this step all necessary instructional materials are produced, including workbooks, handouts, instructor guides, visual aids, audio- and videotapes, Web sites, and computer programs. These materials provide learning content and enable learners to achieve the training objectives. Beware of corporate ethnocentrism, a sign of which is that the company wants training to be presented in exactly the same way all over the world. While some standardization may be necessary, our first consideration should be facilitating learning.

Step-5 Acculturization.   Creating new materials or adapting existing programs for use in another culture is a challenging task. Translation of materials into another language may be needed, and even in English-speaking countries some terminology and spelling may require changes to suit local idioms. Common American terminology is often confusing to British speakers, and vice versa. Communicating with individuals from another culture goes far beyond the translation of language, however; culture permeates every aspect of our lives. In many cases, words commonly used in one culture may not exist in another culture and language, requiring that we explain the entire concept to a translator so that the term can then be represented as correctly as possible in the instruction. The entire style—including format, graphical support, examples, and analogies, to name just a few elements—must be reviewed and adjusted so as to be meaningful and acceptable in another culture. Because content developers need to treat each cultural environment as different, they require culturally appropriate learning materials that do not confuse or offend the learners.

When creating training materials for use in another culture, local instructors and stakeholders and the translator should all be involved in the instructional design process from the very beginning. They should critically review all parts of the program—language, structure, objectives, sequence, examples, stories, visuals, length, evaluation, and so on—and work closely with the designer to tailor the program as much to the local culture as possible. The designer and instructor should, whenever feasible, hold a pilot test of the program, elicit feedback from all stakeholders, and then revise accordingly. Be aware, however, that in some cultures it will be difficult to obtain honest feedback, as criticisms or comments may be viewed as impolite or disrespectful.

The following tips are offered to help the global instructional designer think through some of the many issues that he or she may encounter when developing materials across cultures.

- Use pictures and illustrations carefully. For example, inclusion of a picture of a woman in a short skirt or driving a car would reveal ignorance of cultural norms in some Arab countries.
- Use plenty of appropriate graphics, visuals, and demonstrations if the trainees are learning in a second language.
- Provide extensive handouts and instructional materials. Supplementary materials can help learners experiencing language difficulties fill in any gaps. Some learners may value handouts highly, even displaying them at their offices.
- Ensure that materials are well organized and unambiguous. Participants in some cultures are accustomed to highly structured, formal instruction and feel uncomfortable without very specific direction.
- Provide explicit written instructions for any exercise and written examples of worksheets or other assignments to be completed by participants. Participants who are uncertain of an assignment's purpose or exact instructions may become upset and even blame the instructor for any negative outcomes of the instructional program.
- Consider entirely redoing videos so as to fine-tune their culture-specific verbal, nonverbal, and environmental components.

Step 6: Delivering Instruction

In the sixth step of the Global Training Model, delivery, the HRD program is conducted and facilitated as planned in the previous steps. Cultural considerations when delivering training will be discussed in greater depth in the next chapter.

Step-6 Acculturization.   Briefly, some key areas to consider when delivering include:

- Use of language that is clear, unambiguous, easy to understand, and free of slang and idiomatic expressions;
- Attention to nonverbal communication, which varies considerably across cultures;
- Respect for the culture's expectations regarding the roles of instructor and learner; and
- Recognition of differences in learning styles and appropriate learning activities.

Step 7: Evaluating Results

The seventh step in the model is evaluation, both formative and summative. Formative evaluation involves the data collection and analysis that occurs throughout each of the first five steps and during training delivery. This evaluation process enables the training designer to modify and revise the content and process of the program as it takes shape. A summative evaluation is completed at the conclusion of the training program in order to measure the course's effectiveness and impact.

Evaluation most often measures learners' reactions to the course design and materials and instructor materials and identifies ways to improve future training efforts. Additional measurements of the knowledge and skills that learners have acquired during the course, the extent to which they apply the learning once they are back on the job, and the impact of the training on the organization's effectiveness provide a more complete picture of program success.

Step-7 Acculturization. When planning the evaluation process, the designer should keep in mind that significant cultural differences exist as far as who conducts the evaluation, what is evaluated, and how and when evaluation is done. The U.S. style of evaluation is based on values of frankness and openness, whereas in the many cultures that value keeping one's feelings and thoughts private, people may refrain from prying into the feelings and thoughts of others.

Depending on the circumstances, American learners are generally comfortable providing information about their progress and the instructor's performance, especially when this can be done anonymously. However, people from most other cultures would be uncomfortable with such a process. In many cases, any suggestions or criticisms might imply a lack of confidence in the instructor's authority and expertise, so learners respond with only positive comments. They may be too polite to embarrass the instructor and program designers, even if the program is not going well, in order to respect the instructor or save his or her face. Likewise, direct, critical evaluation offered by the facilitator will cause individuals to lose face and may lead to a significant decline in, or even cessation of, learners' performance.

Experienced HRD practitioners recommend the following strategies when designing the evaluation component:

- Appoint a steering committee to meet on the last day of a multiday training program. Encourage learners to give feedback and suggestions to this committee, which forwards these comments to the trainer.
- Designate a person to whom individuals can at any time provide feedback on the program's progress. Be sure that the designated person is a leader based on position, age, status, or other culturally appropriate criteria.
- Use training team member(s) from the local culture to gather data.
- Design the evaluation instrument to focus more on the positive than on the negative; ask for suggestions to improve what is already going well.

When developing evaluation measures, the HRD practitioner should use culturally appropriate norms for particular behaviors. Consider, for example, a case in which the instructor measures the warmth, approachability, and friendliness of a sales associate. It would be inappropriate to evaluate an Italian salesperson against British norms, since the Italian might be rated as overly emotional. Similarly, an American salesperson might be judged inappropriately informal by French norms.

To develop evaluation measures, one organization reported using fifteen different databases that allowed it to measure German behavior against German norms, French behavior against French norms, and so on. Database development takes time: this organization tested about five hundred people in each culture. Developing these databases revealed the value of comparing one culture's ratings to other cultures'. For example, Japanese respondents seldom rate anyone at the top of the scale, so a rating of 4 out of 10 in Japan was found to equal a rating of 7 in the United States.

Special Areas of Consideration

Adaptation of Existing Materials

When adapting existing materials, one should avoid using those portions that represent one's own culture or that imply, even subtly, that the way of one's culture is the best or only way. Although learners may appreciate knowing the approach to a particular task or problem that the instructor's culture would take, they are usually more focused on learning how to apply knowledge and skills in their own environments.

A number of years ago, a literacy training organization was working in India and using pictures of different objects—cattle, rice, insects, houses—to help the local village women learn the written forms of words. The materials developer had acculturized all the materials, but since the insect picture was the same size as the house, the villagers had problems identifying it—they had never seen such a gigantic insect!

Illustrating concepts with examples that are familiar and acceptable to the learners makes learning more productive and enjoyable and shows that the instructor has tried to anticipate the learners' needs. Exercises and case studies should be tailored to the local culture through the use of local names, titles, situations, and the general environment.

The degree of adaptation required depends to some extent on what is being taught. Generally speaking, the more technical the topic, the less need there is for change. For example, to teach someone to operate a particular machine, one would probably go through the same specific, logical steps regardless of the culture, so little adaptation is required. Materials involving other topics such as performance management and supervisory skills will need extensive reworking.

Translation

As mentioned previously, translation involves much more than merely converting the content word for word from one language to another. Language necessarily includes assumptions, values, feelings, and experience connotations that must be interpreted according to local values and applicability. Words in some languages convey very specific nuances that cannot be readily expressed in another language, and all languages include words that are not directly translatable into some other languages. According to Boyce, the German *Schlimmbesserung* refers to a "so-called improvement that makes things worse." The Arabic *alam al-mithral* conveys the idea that language and imagery are a part of reality, particularly that reality which can be approached through dreams, visualization, and imagination. The common Japanese term *genki* encompasses the meanings of both *happy* and *healthy.*

Concepts may also be unclear. In some countries the field of "human resource development," for example, does not exist as we know it in English (recognizing of course that this term remains somewhat ambiguous among native English speakers as well), and in many cultures little distinction is made between human resource management and human resource development.

Common business concepts also may not be clear in transition economies. A few years ago in a small town in Russia, it became obvious during a small-business seminar that the participants understood little about marketing because such capitalistic concepts and approaches were irrelevant under the previous regime.

Working closely with bilingual individuals will help the instructor clarify all words and their meanings. Glossaries can also help clarify terminology for learners. An excellent source is the International Labor Office (http://www.ilo.org), which has published, and also loans, dozens of glossaries of specific terminologies translated into a variety of languages.

During the needs analysis step of training development, it is important to assess the level of language skills—including speaking, reading, writing, and oral comprehension—of the trainees. Instructional materials should be prepared according to their language capabilities. An HRD practitioner working with translators must recognize that the quality of translation can make or break the program.

Following are more tips to help facilitate the development and translation of global training materials:

- When writing English materials that may need to be translated later on, keep language simple and concise.
- Avoid buzzwords, slang, and idioms. A "home run" makes no sense to cultures without baseball, a "rat race" sounds like a strange new sport, "bleeding-edge technology" sounds downright dangerous, and "raining cats and dogs" suggests a meteorological disaster.
- Avoid acronyms and abbreviations. They are difficult enough in one's own language and are often untranslatable into another language. For example, in French HR becomes RH, the UN is the ONU, AIDS is SIDA, and the USA is the EU. For frequently used acronyms be sure to provide definitions.
- Allow for expansion. Most translations are longer than the original text.
- Make the translation fit the culture. Beyond the text be sure that illustrations, charts, examples, and other components fit the culture.

Web-Based and Computer-Based Instruction

More and more organizations are taking advantage of the benefits of technology, particularly through Web-based strategies, to support their training efforts (Marquardt and Kearsley, 1998). This is particularly true for global programs, as a time- and cost-saving approach. However, experts in global training have recognized that the need for Web-based programs to be acculturized is even higher than for other training materials because few if any instructors can acculturize or rework the Web on the spot. Much of Web- and computer-based instruction depends on written and graphic communications between the program and the learners.

One main difference between classroom training and many technology-based instructional strategies is the absence of the nonverbal components of communication that supply much of the meaning when learners work with someone face-to-face or even video screen to video screen. When working across cultures through e-mail, discussion groups, chat rooms, and other approaches, one person's intentions and meanings are often misinterpreted by the other. The sender of the information is often completely unaware that the message has not been received or has been misunderstood and that the intended receiver is hurt, angry, or offended.

Rice et al. (2001) suggest considering the following elements when using Web- or computer-based instruction:

- Degree of comfort with "impersonal media": Due to culture and individual preferences, people vary in their reactions to working on a computer without human contact. Personal photos, audio, video, and other additions may make Web-based instruction more acceptable, but if the learners strongly dislike the medium, they may also dislike the content being conveyed.
- Visual format: The effective use of visual elements, such as the placement of navigation tools and the amount of white space used, differs among cultures. For example, when working with languages such as Arabic that are read from right to left, the directional arrow to point to the next page should be placed at the bottom left, not the bottom right as in English.
- Use of colors: Colors have widely different connotations in different cultures. White, for example, is associated with weddings in some cultures and with funerals and mourning in others.
- Use of icons: Icons seem so obvious to the native user that they are easily overlooked in acculturization, but they may cause considerable confusion. Calendars in Europe often show the weeks as columns and the rows as weekdays, the opposite of American calendars. People from the many countries that use door handles would not recognize a round doorknob symbol. Animals also have many connotations. Owls are seen as wise birds in the United States but are symbols of pessimism and bad luck to many Arabs. Pointing fingers and other

hand gestures, human eyes, and footprints have numerous interpretations.

- Use of illustrations: Learners in the tropics may not relate to snow skiing, and few countries understand American football and baseball. A "piggy bank" is a place to save money to Americans, but to devout Muslims and Jews, who consider pigs unholy, the metaphor would be unclear if not offensive.
- Humor: One culture's humor is one of the hardest elements to translate for another culture. Humor should be used sparingly and only with careful review by representatives of the target culture.
- Technology differences: It is critical that the instructional designer research the learners' hardware, software, and/or Internet capabilities before planning to use technology-based approaches.

Summary

Designing and developing HRD programs for use in different cultural settings requires acculturization of each component of the program. Acculturization occurs in each of the seven steps of the Global Training Model: (1) doing a needs analysis, (2) setting objectives, (3) designing the curriculum, (4) selecting instructional methodologies, (5) developing instructional materials, (6) delivering instruction, and (7) evaluating results. The HRD program developer must address issues involved in adapting existing materials, translating from one language to another, and developing Web-based and computer-based instruction. The success of the HRD program depends on culturally sensitive design and development processes.

Delivery and Assessment of
Global HRD Programs

Blessed are the flexible, for they shall not be bent out of shape.

Anonymous

Introduction

Cynthia Kemper (1998), an international business writer, describes an American HRD professional she observed instructing a group in Sweden. Although clearly possessing an intellectual understanding of the two cultures and how they differ, his behaviors indicated little effort at acculturization. His assertive, in-your-face techniques were offensive to most of his Swedish audience, distracting them from the content he presented.

This chapter focuses on guidelines and strategies that can help avoid scenarios such as the one described above. Designing an effective, culturally appropriate training program is only the beginning; implementing the program presents its own unique challenges. Global instructors need to draw on all their creativity and sensitivity as well as interpersonal and technical skills to make programs successful. This chapter looks at instructor roles and expectations, learner differences, general guidelines for global HRD program delivery, examples of specific cultural differences that affect delivery, scheduling issues, tips for certain types of activities and methodologies, and evaluation and feedback approaches.

Global Instructors/Facilitators

Role and Expectations

In the United States' egalitarian culture, instructors tend to create an informal, often casual atmosphere and relationship with the learners. They may walk around the room, lean on a desk, and call participants by their first names. Learners are expected to participate in discussions and are permitted to disagree with and debate the instructor's views.

How different this image of the instructor is from that found in most of the rest of the world! Most cultures perceive teachers/trainers as high-level experts in their fields and fountains of knowledge. A Chinese proverb, for example, says, "A teacher for a day is a father for a lifetime." In India teaching is generally viewed as one of the most honorable and societally important professions. In Russia Teacher's Day is a national holiday. Former students return to their schools to honor their teachers by giving them flowers and chocolates. Recent reports indicate that many of these countries are experiencing a decline in respect for teachers, although variations across cultures are still quite common. In countries where people hold instructors in high esteem, the instructor may disappoint trainees or damage his or her credibility with a more egalitarian and informal approach.

Global instructors should also realize that as outsiders and members of another culture, they will be viewed not only as an individual but also as a representative of South Africa or Argentina or whatever nation they call home. If coming from the United States, the HRD professional usually represents the "typical American," along with the stereotypes associated with that culture. Americans are often described as impatient, individualistic, hardworking, self-centered, outgoing, open, and wealthy and will be expected to act and teach in the American way as the learners perceive it. One of the authors was providing training and consulting in a small town in Russia and was graciously invited to stay in the home of a local English teacher. While chatting, the host explained to the author that she had been very surprised by the author's appearance and personality because she had been expecting what she termed a typical American—overweight, unaware of the local culture, and arrogant.

An HRD practitioner needs to be conscious of stereotypical expectations. She does not assume that foreign participants will see her as learners in her own country do. She makes additional, conscious efforts to show that she is interested in the learners' country, language, and customs and that she respects their history, religion, culture, and ways of learning.

Working with Local HRD Practitioners

As an outsider who can never fully grasp all of the nuances of a local culture, the HRD professional must, when possible, identify, develop, and utilize the services of local HRD practitioners. In cultures that do not have a history of an HRD profession, individuals who have related jobs and experience may be able to serve the same function. Local staff should be involved in the design, delivery, evaluation, and follow-up of the training program and should be given the opportunity to share their expertise as well as their knowledge of the local cultural environment, traditions, norms of behavior and learning, and expectations.

Global and local HRD practitioners also find it helpful to develop professional, collegial working relationships so that progress and information on the training program can be shared and understood. Also, proper credit and recognition should be given to local staff for their efforts, in a style that is culturally appropriate. In some cultures visible tokens of appreciation are highly valued. Finally, developing the capabilities of local HRD practitioners enables them to work with the global instructor and to conduct the training programs independently after his departure.

Learning Habits, Styles, and Beliefs

Cultures shape the way people learn, their beliefs about learning, and their learning habits from an early age. They do this by means of school, home, parents' behaviors and beliefs, teachers' methods, community and organizational norms, religious experiences, and so on. Thus, ways of learning vary considerably from culture to culture and even between regions within a country.

American culture and the U.S. educational system tend to be more practical and seek not only to provide knowledge but to change attitudes and behaviors and develop skills. Our open, egalitarian values encourage students to speak up in front of groups of fellow students and to learn to critically think through issues and discuss them openly in class.

In many other cultures the role of students and trainees is to listen to lectures, take notes, soak up information like a sponge, and demonstrate their learning by repeating the information back to the instructor on exams or in papers. Contradicting or criticizing the instructor is not encouraged—in some cultures not even tolerated. Silence is a sign of respect, not a lack of interest or low motivation. Learners are often expected to stand up when the instructor enters the room and address him or her in a formal manner. An instructor who does not meet learners' exalted expectations may be seen as undermining accepted authority structures in the society. If this occurs, the program will lose its effectiveness, and the transfer of learning to the workplace will be blocked or diminished.

General Guidelines for Delivering an HRD Program

Following are general guidelines to consider when delivering an HRD program in another culture.

Language

- Speak more slowly and distinctly than usual when learners are working in a second language, but not so much that the learners are offended or embarrassed.
- To avoid confusion, use correct grammar.
- Avoid humor unless you are sure that it "translates," and do not use sarcasm.
- Use correct salutations. In many cultures, using first names when speaking to participants is disrespectful, and participants will often insist on using your title, even though you may indicate that using your first name is acceptable.
- Use the simplest, most common terms, and avoid idioms, slang, and other culturally specific terminology. Sports terms often have no meaning in other countries, and our growing use of jargon in the business world can be very confusing. "Going postal" or "getting to first base" mean little outside the United States. A colleague of one of the authors quickly found that learners in another culture had difficulty grasping the meaning of his western Virginia mountain vernacular.
- Remember that some cultures use a more formal language in business and the public arena and may be offended by very informal, casual language.
- Use appropriate currencies and measures. Most of the world has no idea how far a mile is or how hot ninety-five degrees Fahrenheit feels.
- Learn a few phrases in the local language, such as "Hello," "How are you?" and "Thank you." Try to open with a local welcome. Despite any mistakes, participants will appreciate the effort.

- Be aware of how language is used in other cultures. In Asian cultures, for example, the word *no* is considered impolite.
- Learn the country's body language and nonverbal cues. In some Asian countries, avoid patting a child on the head; the top of the head is considered holy and not to be touched. The common American thumbs-up sign and "OK" gesture are inappropriate or obscene in many cultures, and the meaning of nodding or shaking the head varies from culture to culture.
- Use examples and visuals as much as possible, but be sure they are appropriate and understandable.
- Repeat and summarize important points.
- Expect that the training program will probably take longer than it does in its home culture.
- When participants use English to speak, reassure them of their abilities and show appreciation for their willingness to use your language, but without any hint of condescension.
- When participants ask questions, listen very carefully and ask for clarification before you jump into an answer.
- Be patient and respect the learners' efforts to convey meaning and feelings in a language and cultural context other than their own.
- When appropriate, distribute training materials in advance. This will allow learners time to prepare and gain a better understanding if materials are in a second language.
- Remember that everything, from standard paper sizes to keyboards to electrical plugs, varies throughout the world.

Culture

- At the beginning of the program, address the issue of cultural differences and request the audience's indulgence for any blunders.
- Emphasize your desire to learn more about their culture.
- Explain expectations of yourself as facilitator, of the participants, and of the interactions between you and them. Specify behaviors such as how you wish to be addressed, how you will address the participants, and how you will handle questions. Make it clear that trainees can ask you questions without offending you or appearing foolish if they make mistakes.
- Be sensitive to the local educational system and business environment. Avoid ascribing motivations or meanings to behaviors. Timidity by American standards may be viewed as quite assertive in the local culture.

- Remain calm during silences. Learners may need time to process the language and content, and their culture may be more accustomed to periods of silence than Americans are.
- Recognize that in some cultures participants are likely to base their responses on what they think the instructor wants to hear, not what they actually believe or feel.

Selected Culture-Specific Guidelines

HRD professionals who do not respect local cultural norms may lose credibility. In some regions of the globe, it is common practice for presenters to sit, whereas Americans typically stand and move about the room. Conservative business attire is generally expected in most countries; casual business clothes may be seen as disrespectful or sloppy. Although manager trainees may need to made aware of misconceptions or outdated information, confrontation by the presenter in front of others may cause loss of face and resistance. Because at some sites presentation equipment may not be available, one must be prepared to present information using more than one approach. Electric power and heat or air conditioning may be unreliable or nonexistent.

Keys to Success in Transition Economies

Since the fall of the Soviet communist system in 1991, many HRD professionals have been working in what are commonly called "transition economies" as centrally planned economic systems gradually adopt more market-driven approaches. Many such societies have changed a great deal over the years, but others remain in various stages of transition. Drawing on their experiences training in Uzbekistan, Schrage and Jedlicka (1999) suggest the following tips for working in similar transition economies:

- Meet with the sponsoring organization's training staff to identify the learners' specific needs and to verify commitment to the training process.
- Clarify with your interpreter ahead of time unfamiliar concepts and vocabulary, so that he or she can accurately translate your points.
- Provide trainees with handouts, including copies of overhead slides.
- To illustrate your points, use videos with relevant examples from a market economy perspective;
- Use real-life business examples that participants can relate to and that draw on their realm of experience.

- Respect participants' viewpoints, and explain that you are broadening their understanding, not forcing them to accept that your way is always the best way to operate.
- Research training styles and methods that will be comfortable for the group.
- Dress and act in accordance with local culture.
- If possible, avoid conducting sessions at the company site (to avoid interruptions) or late in the day (when participants are tired from working).
- Plan for almost anything to go wrong, and when it does, be very patient, flexible, and adaptable.

Additional Culture-Specific Guidelines

Each culture has specific expectations regarding the manner in which a trainer should present the training program. Following are a few examples of cultural nuances.

Japan.   The HRD professional should begin in a humble vein and show respect for the learners by honoring them in some small way. Conservative dress is the norm. Sincerity is important. Avoid exaggerations, and be prepared to give specific information. Speak to the trainees as a group, without singling out any particular participant or subgroup.

France.   HRD professionals in France will be expected to prove themselves. Any opinions must be supported with facts and logic. Since the French tend to separate their public and private lives, be reserved when mentioning the latter. Dress in business attire and avoid flamboyant colors. Like many other nationalities, the French do not wish to see their language and culture swallowed up by English and American culture. Individuals who speak some French and admire French history and culture will be appreciated, as long as their grammar and pronunciation are reasonably correct.

China.   While working in China, avoid acknowledging another person's emotions. Such a public recognition of feelings would be embarrassing. Be respectful of and avoid physical contact with any stranger you meet. Make a point of greeting any Chinese VIPs, beginning with the highest in rank and working down the hierarchy.

United Kingdom.   The British may see American HRD professionals as too forward, too informal, and too open. Like many cultural groups, they are often uncomfortable with what they perceive as premature informality and familiarity.

Activities and Methodologies

In many cultures HRD professionals should be prepared to begin instructing in a didactic manner, with lectures and formal presentations. They may then gradually shift to more learner-centered strategies if the participants seem comfortable and willing to participate in interactive and experiential activities. Whenever possible, the instructor should find out as much as possible ahead of time about the audience's preferences and comfort levels with planned activities.

An instructor considering the use of experiential instructional strategies should gauge in advance which individual participants would be most comfortable and successful with them. When looking for a volunteer to critique a role play, for example, one might choose the most senior person as the observer, since he or she may be more accustomed to providing performance feedback.

Experiential exercises require flexibility and extra time. Participants usually take longer to absorb a case study and prepare responses or to become familiar with roles for a role play than they do to listen and take notes.

Working in Groups

As the trainer is conducting a program, she may find she needs to break the class into smaller groups for activities and discussion. In the United States, groups are often formed randomly by counting off, drawing numbers, and so on. In other countries this random approach could result in some very uncomfortable, ineffective groupings—even in some offended members—especially in the early stages of the program, when participants have not yet become comfortable with the instructor and her unfamiliar approaches to learning.

When creating groups, one needs to be aware of the cultural significance of mixing by gender, status, age, or ethnicity. Harris and Moran (1996) suggest that, in many ways, teams or groups in any culture form a microculture that mirrors the macroculture. In some cultures, for example, learning would be next to impossible in groups of mixed gender because gender mixing is strictly controlled in the larger society. In many places, individuals' status in the organization or community determines the degree to which they can state their opinions even in a learning environment. Throughout much of Asia young people hesitate to speak out if older people are in the group. Mixing people from cultures with a history of antipathy toward each other will usually be counterproductive, if not impossible.

The instructor should schedule frequent breaks, especially if participants are learning in a nonnative language. If he rushes the group, he will merely waste time later restating and explaining information already covered. While working in small groups, participants may prefer to discuss the case or problem in their native language. They may even prepare a flip-chart summary in their own language, but when presenting to the whole group, they should then translate their points into the shared language of the instructor and the group.

Distributing Materials and Returning Assignments

Many societies show greater respect for written materials and an individual's own writing than U.S. society. Therefore, when distributing participant workbooks and other materials and returning assignments, the trainer should handle them with care. Koreans, for example, expect the instructor to return the manual or completed assignment to each person reverently with both hands, not just leave them in a pile or ask that they be passed around.

Scheduling

Several aspects of scheduling are extremely important for the instructor to consider in scheduling day-to-day activities such as start and finish times and pace, meals, and events.

Time

Different cultures have widely differing perspectives on the use of time. In the United States, time is very important, as admonishments we hear from early childhood onward attest: "Time is money" and "Don't waste time." Americans see time as a precious resource that can and should be controlled. This attitude is less prevalent in many other societies, especially Latin America, the Middle East, and Africa, where time is not only unimportant but is ignored entirely. In these and other regions of the world, relationships are more important than promptness; to fully understand and discuss an interesting point is a higher priority than staying on schedule.

If one is training in another culture, there may be differing expectations regarding a definite starting time. In some settings, if the schedule indicates 9:00 A.M. as the starting time, participants may interpret it to mean that no one arrives until then and that the true starting time will be 10:00 A.M. Participants in other cultures may interpret the 9:00 A.M. start as absolute and, if the instructor is a few minutes late, may feel that he or she is not taking them or the responsibility for instruction seriously. In these situations it is critical for the instructor to determine and make clear to everyone which cultural definition of time will be employed and then stick to it.

Meals

Different societies have different customs regarding the amount of time to set aside for meals. In many countries one hour is a typical lunch break. In France, however, two hours is often the norm, and in Spain this may even expand to three hours, though participants are also accustomed to working later in the evening. In some countries food and conversation are to be savored and appreciated, in contrast to the American habit of "grabbing a bite to eat." If meal times cannot be compressed, the trainer can try to build learning activities, such as topics to be discussed over lunch, into these longer eating times. However, conducting business during meals is not always culturally acceptable.

Events

It is important to allow time in the training program for formal events. Ceremonial time for awarding certificates, listening to speeches from outside dignitaries, and other such formalities demonstrate the program's importance and encourage greater group motivation, participation, and learning.

Transfer and Application

An effectively designed training program should include a variety of support systems that enable learners to apply their new skills and knowledge when they return to the workplace. Trainers, learners, and the learners' superiors may all take steps before, during, and after the training program to transfer and apply the learning.

No matter how well a program is designed, however, the instructor is responsible for sensing whether the training can indeed be applied as designed and modifying it as needed to ensure application. In many cultures the participants expect the trainer to be specific, focused, directive, and knowledgeable about how the learning will apply in their organization(s). It would be foolish to expect time management training based on American models and assumptions to be applied in everyday business life in Mexico or Madrid. Likewise, a train-the-trainer session on interactive and role-playing strategies might fall on deaf ears in Indonesia.

Evaluation and Feedback

In many cultures the HRD professional faces a double dilemma in evaluation and feedback. First, participants may have difficulty critiquing the training designed and delivered by the trainer, whom they may see as an expert and authority figure. Second, the trainer may have difficulty providing participants with constructive criticism that may cause them to lose face. Care must be taken that evaluation and feedback are based on the surrounding culture. Using American norms to judge the success of training in Tanzania or Azerbaijan would not be appropriate or helpful.

One way to help learners is to provide some comparative analysis and assessment procedures so that participants can do self- or peer evaluation of the success of the program in increasing their knowledge and skills. If a given feedback or evaluation technique does not appear to be culturally suitable or effective, invite the participants to suggest adjustments to the feedback process that may be less embarrassing to them.

Summary

Although a well-planned design and careful development are crucial to the success of an HRD program, the individuals delivering the program are ultimately the ones who must apply the program in a culturally sensitive manner and be ready to adjust the program to fit the needs of learners. To be effective across cultures, HRD professionals must be aware of the impact of language, verbal and nonverbal; recognize the cultural aspects that impact the delivery of the program and adjust their delivery accordingly; plan logistics, such as scheduling sessions and meals, around the norms of the local culture; and use the most appropriate methods for evaluating results and providing feedback.

Consulting
Across Cultures

*Advice is like snow—the softer it falls, the longer it
dwells upon, and the deeper it sinks into the mind.*

Samuel Taylor Coleridge

Introduction

Opportunities for worldwide consulting are expected to rapidly expand in
coming years. The trade newsletter *Consultant News* estimates that there
are over 200,000 consultants worldwide earning over $20 billion per year
from corporations and government agencies. Experienced professional
consultants who can manage organizational change, technology-based
projects, and multinational initiatives will be in particular demand, according to management consultant and professor Melissa Gibson (1998).
But they must also be ready to handle the challenges of operating in other
cultures. Those who cannot adapt their processes and interventions to suit
organizations in differing cultures will be ineffective and may even insult
their clients.

Though they may not realize it, most HRD professionals act as consultants.
Many, if not all, of the concepts and guidelines discussed in this chapter hold
true for those working in a consulting role, regardless of whether they work
from within an organization or are hired from outside.

Global Consulting Roles

Growth of International Consulting

Over the past decade, consulting has experienced a global boom that continues today. Several factors account for this significant worldwide increase in the use of consultants.

- In a trend toward privatization, the public sector is contracting out more of its responsibilities to consultants.
- Organizations are retaining and hiring fewer full-time staff, favoring a more flexible, temporary workforce.
- The rapidly changing global economic environment requires higher levels of specialization.
- Organizations often find they must contract with the best talent available from around the world to remain competitive in global markets.

Roles of the Global Consultant

According to noted international consultants Ronald and Gordon Lippitt (1986), HRD consultants may play eight different roles ranging in approach from highly directive to highly nondirective (see Figure 5.1). By *directive* the Lippitts mean that the consultant leads the project, initiating and directing the activities involved. The *nondirective* consultant serves more as a guide, providing data that the client may or may not use. Since the eight roles are not mutually exclusive, the consultant may serve in two capacities at the same time—for example, as both a technical specialist and advocate—and play different roles as a project progresses. The level of client activity increases as the role of the consultant becomes less directive. The role a consultant is expected to play also differs significantly across organizations and cultures and should be clarified early in the consulting process.

Let's take a look at the eight consultant roles and some cross-cultural examples of each.

Advocate.   In this role the consultant attempts to influence the client, often because the client is asking for a specific recommendation. Advocacy may involve *content* (influencing the client to select certain goals, subscribe to particular values, or take certain actions) or *methodology* (influencing the client to use certain methods of problem solving or change management).

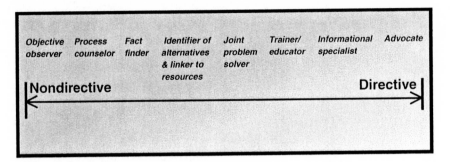

FIGURE 5.1   Roles of a global HRD consultant

A consultant who, after extensive research and data gathering, recommends that a corporation focus its marketing efforts on Eastern Europe would be acting in this role.

Informational Specialist.   In this role the consultant has been called upon because of his or her expertise and knowledge in an area of interest to the client. Examples of this role might include an environmental expert asked to devise a plan for reducing pollution in a lake in Kazakhstan and a World Bank instructor explaining the international funding process to representatives of a nongovernmental organization (NGO).

Trainer/Educator.   Innovative consultation often requires educational initiatives within the client system. In this case the HRD consultant advises what learning methodologies or strategies would best suit the particular client situation. Assisting a client in the design and development of a curriculum that could be used across cultures would be an example of this role.

Joint Problem Solver.   This role utilizes the synergy of the client and consultant working together in solving a problem. The consultant both helps the client maintain objectivity and stimulates the creation of ideas and is a peer in the decisionmaking process. For example, the consultant and a corporate client might determine and agree that the company's distribution strategy in Japan was ineffective and that a new system was necessary.

Identifier of Alternatives and Linker to Resources.   Here the consultant helps to identify various alternatives for the client and provides criteria for evaluating each alternative and its probable impact. The consultant's role also involves linking the client to resources that could be used in solving the problem. A consultant who identifies the benefits, disadvantages, and long-term consequences of several different leadership development strategies for a Malaysian company would be serving in this capacity.

Fact Finder.   In this role, the consultant gathers data through appropriate research methods, such as interviews, observation, and surveys, and then analyzes and synthesizes the results for the client. A consultant who evaluates training programs for a client in Kenya would be carrying out this role.

Process Counselor.   Many global consultants focus on enabling clients to perceive, understand, and act on problems on their own. They provide feedback to help the client improve working processes and to tap resources within and outside the client organization. Consultants who assist global organizations in developing and renewing themselves play this role.

Objective Observer.   The objective observer asks clarifying questions. In this role the consultant serves as a facilitator or catalyst for action, but such action is totally in the hands of the client. A consultant who assists a global corporation in the selection of a new manufacturing site by facilitating discussion of various aspects of alternative sites and posing reflective questions would be operating in this very nondirective role.

When choosing the appropriate consulting role, global professionals must clarify the client's expectations concerning respective roles to avoid misunderstanding and embarrassment. A client in a culture that greatly respects authority and hierarchy might assume that the role of a consultant is to provide expert information. The consultant, however, may come from a culture that embraces egalitarian relationships and views a more collaborative, process counselor role as the ideal approach to consulting. Unless roles are discussed and clarified in the beginning of the process, misunderstandings and conflict may well occur.

Phases of Global Consulting

Consulting, whether in local or global environments, generally passes through five distinct but interrelated phases: entry, assessment, planning, implementation, and evaluation. In international settings, however, the cultural environment significantly impacts each phase.

1. *Entry:* Entry involves establishing a relationship with the client, developing a project proposal, specifying roles for consultant and client, clarifying the project's goals, and contracting. In most situations this phase involves development of a written agreement or contract, a process that is often handled

fairly quickly in the United States and some other countries. In other cultures—such as those found in many Asian, Middle Eastern, and Latin countries—establishing a relationship may take months. Relationships may be more durable and flexible than contracts, which often take a long time to develop and require the approval of numerous levels and individuals within the organization.

Global consultants must be very, very patient. They need to allow plenty of time for laying the groundwork, recognizing that the time required to win the client's trust and acceptance varies considerably across cultures.

2. *Assessment:* The second phase of the consulting process involves assessing the situation through formal and informal data gathering. During this phase the consultant should clearly define the problem and decide what data are needed, who should be involved, and how data will be collected, analyzed, and presented. The choice of methods for gathering the necessary information are affected by the cultural milieu. Cultures vary in their comfort in sharing data, being observed, admitting weaknesses, and stating strengths.

3. *Planning:* The planning phase involves examining the various means of accomplishing the goals of the intervention and developing possible strategies for action. This planning involves varying levels of client input, depending on the role the consultant plays.

In planning, the consultant must be very conscious of cultural context. Certain strategies may be inappropriate because of factors such as religion (too individualistic), class structure (violates status expectations), politics (not socialist), or history (too identified with colonial methods).

4. *Implementation:* Once actions have been planned, the consultant needs to coordinate or manage the implementation. Again, cultural characteristics, such as beliefs about time and space, values, and patterns of thinking and learning, influence the how, when, who, and where of implementation. If, for example, implementation involves providing negative information about another person's behavior or actions, direct and frank feedback to that person in countries such as Indonesia or Thailand would be culturally inappropriate and therefore ineffective.

5. *Evaluation:* The final phase of the consulting process involves assessing the effects of the intervention. How effective has it been? What cultural factors might support or diminish the change? Will the organization revert to its previous mode of operation once the consultant leaves? How could the intervention have been more effective in this culture?

Even gathering this information is much more difficult in some cultures than in others. Clients in many cultures may be uncomfortable telling an outsider that any part of the consulting has not met their expectations.

Challenges Faced by Global Consultants

While HRD consultants working locally often confront complex and challenging situations, when they work globally, these challenges intensify considerably. Culture, HRD strategies, and infrastructure may be contrary to the consultant's assumptions about and understanding of HRD. Consultants may recognize these differences yet not sufficiently adapt strategies and tactics to the culture in which they are working. Directly transplanting HRD tools and interventions from one culture to another, however, is rarely successful.

The following list summarizes some of the challenges facing global HRD consultants as described by Ramchandran (1984) and other experienced professionals.

- *Work ethic differences.* Different cultures view work very differently. Motivation, attendance at work, pride in the work done, and identification of oneself with one's job are a sampling of areas that vary from culture to culture.
- *Concept of time.* Some cultures value punctuality and function with a sense of urgency, while in other cultures the pace is much slower and deadlines are flexible. There are also differences in the emphasis placed on the past, the present, and the future.
- *Acceptance of criticism.* Criticism by the consultant may be taken very personally in a number of cultures, straining client-consultant relationships. Pointing out errors or problems in the organization may cause managers to lose face, a reaction that many cultures avoid at all costs.
- *Expression of agreement or disagreement.* In many cultures it is impolite to say "no" directly to someone. Courtesy and respect demand that refusals and rejections be implied subtly, often by context, not directly stated. Consultants must pay close attention to contextual clues to determine the client's level of agreement or disagreement and should respond to the client in a similarly subtle and tactful manner.
- *Problem-solving approach.* In some cultures mutual problem solving is expected. In others, particularly those in which education tends to involve mostly rote learning, a joint problem-solving approach may cause confusion and be inappropriate. In the latter case, the organization often would expect the outside expert to solve problems without the assistance of others.
- *Management style.* Despite a trend toward more participative management approaches in some cultures, a more authoritative,

hierarchical style is still common in many other cultures. In these cultures, lower-status individuals who share their views may be seen as disrespectful, and open discussions across status levels rarely occur.

- *Efficiency versus employment.* In some cultures organizations commit to retaining high numbers of employees, even those who may be unnecessary to operations or incompetent. High employment is valued more highly than high efficiency. In such cultures a consultant who suggests downsizing the workforce may be seen as culturally and politically inept.
- *Role of women.* As is noted in other chapters, women's roles vary dramatically around the world. Most countries place women at a lower status level, and consultants who ignore these cultural norms may be resented by both men and women.
- *Bureaucracy.* Bureaucracy is a worldwide phenomenon, but in countries with a history of socialism and centralized planning (such as China, Russia and its former satellites, and some countries in Africa), huge governmental bureaucracies require substantial paperwork and delays in decisionmaking, contracting, and other business processes. Rules become ends in themselves, delays drag on, and implementation may be subject to change at the whim of various bureaucrats.
- *Limited resources.* In many countries resources, such as flip-chart paper, markers, computers, work space, and projectors, may be limited or nonexistent. Electricity, phone service, and tap water may be intermittent or nonexistent.
- *Organizational structure and staffing.* In many countries an organization's structure and staffing may have little relationship to the products or services being rendered or to customer needs. Political or family ties may be more important than actual work qualifications and may lead to higher levels of power and authority.
- *Corruption.* The definitions of bribery and corruption vary across cultures. In many countries additional payments to individuals for products and services are common, particularly when salaries are low, forcing individuals to look for additional income to support their families.

Competencies of Successful Global HRD Professionals

Global and cross-cultural experts (including Marquardt, 1999a) have identified the following competencies as essential to success in international HRD work, particularly for consultants.

- *Cultural self-awareness.* Before you can understand other cultures, you need to closely examine your own cultural values and assumptions. Consultants must be aware of their own ethnocentric assumptions and the behaviors that stem from them.
- *Knowledge and appreciation of other cultures.* Explore key elements of other cultures with which you may come in contact—religious beliefs, family structure, governmental structure, history, geographic and demographic information, to name a few.
- *Global perspective and mindset.* Continually expand your knowledge and strive to be sensitive to cultural diversity.
- *Respect for the values and practices of other cultures.* Recognize that your own ways of thinking and behaving are not necessarily superior.
- *Cultural flexibility, adjustment, and resiliency.* While experiencing a new culture may be exciting at first, confusion, disorientation, and frustration sometimes follow. Be patient and tolerant of the ambiguities of new cultural settings.
- *Acculturize learning programs and events.* Be sure that training programs are as comfortable and appropriate as possible for the learners.
- *Communication skills.* Important in other settings, appropriate verbal and nonverbal communication skills are critical to cross-cultural success.
- *Cultural empathy.* Be attuned to other cultures and try to understand meaning from context.
- *Patience and sense of humor.* These competencies help you deal with many cross-cultural differences and ambiguities.
- *Commitment to continuous learning.* Because of the increasingly fast pace of a constantly changing global environment, HRD professionals must constantly and quickly keep up with changes in the field.

Given the countless variations in ethnic and corporate cultures and sub-cultures and the economic, political, and social conditions that an international consultant encounters, it is impossible to devise a list of generally accepted strategies that could be used around the world. Professional consultants should instead rely on sound principles of consulting, a thorough understanding of cross-cultural differences, and research specific to the region and company involved.

Impact of Technology

Technological innovation has had a tremendous impact on organizations worldwide and, consequently, on the consultants who work with them. Improved technology has made videoconferencing, Web meetings, virtual teams, Web-based learning, and many other techniques easier and more commonplace. In response to rapid changes in technology, consultants need to keep up with and use relevant new technologies, as well as recommend the use of relevant technology when working with clients.

Global consultants must also recognize, however, that technological solutions suited to their home business environment often are not appropriate in other conditions. For example, many consultants assume that automation is a cost-effective solution for tasks that most people would not want to do anyway. However, consider the case in which the price of a reasonably powerful computer might equal the annual salaries of seven employees. In this example, and in most countries having very low wages and/or high unemployment, the purchase of equipment is hard to justify from a cost-benefit standpoint, as the laying off of workers would create additional problems.

Virtual Teams

As virtual teams and work groups become more common, global consultants need to be able to collaborate effectively online with clients. Many HRD professionals have assumed that face-to-face interaction, even if limited to an initial meeting, is critical to team effectiveness. However, when virtual team members are scattered around the globe and assigned to short-term projects, such meetings are often just not feasible. The HRD consultant might use periodic videoconferencing, teleconferencing, and synchronous Web-based meetings to help bring such teams together. HRD professionals working internationally must continually find creative solutions of this type to match changing conditions and cultural expectations.

When consulting across borders with groups of various cultures, keep the following recommendations (Saphiere, 1999) in mind:

- Be mindful of your own reactions to people in interactions with them and of the roots of those reactions in your own cultural assumptions.
- Be comfortable with silence: listen, observe, think.
- Encourage differing viewpoints. Allow individual opinions to diverge before trying to come to a common understanding.
- Avoid debates or attempts at persuasion that may stifle some individuals.
- Before actively entering a discussion, observe the dynamics. Who talks? Who takes a leadership role? How do members tend to interact?
- Tell stories and use illustrations to clarify concepts and bring them to life.

- Know yourself. It is much easier to understand others if we first become aware of our own feelings, thoughts, biases, and assumptions.
- Normalize diversity. Choose a topic that will bring out diverse opinions and encourage sharing of different views while confirming that diversity is appreciated and respected.
- Acknowledge that values are part of a system for decisionmaking; work to understand the values that shape decisions made by others.
- Estimate the time you need and then double it. Working across language and cultural barriers and time zones takes extra time and energy, so deadlines should be set accordingly.

Summary

To be successful, consultants need strong interpersonal skills, excellent proficiency and knowledge in their particular area of specialization, and thorough understanding of the roles, phases, and processes involved in consulting as a profession. In addition to these important requirements, the competent global HRD consultant needs a comprehensive knowledge of the challenges and issues to consider when working across national boundaries and across cultures. This chapter provides an overview of consulting roles and stages of consulting, as well as a discussion of the challenges faced by global HRD consultants.

Administration of Global HRD Programs

What managers do is the same around the world; how they do it is determined by tradition and culture.

Peter Drucker

Unless the HR function is seen as a living example of . . . how a global organization recruits, develops, and rewards people; how it stimulates and supports global networks; and how it makes decisions that integrate global and local perspectives, it may be difficult to gain the credibility to influence others.

Vladimir Pucik

Introduction

Managing and administering HRD programs in the United States can be a daunting task, but doing so in another culture often raises even more difficult and perplexing challenges. Expectations concerning the manager's role and responsibilities in another country may be quite different from those in the home country.

This chapter briefly reviews some of the key conditions that can complicate the HRD manager's job when working globally. It then discusses the global HRD manager's main areas of responsibility: administration and management of the HRD staff, management of HRD programs and initiatives, and marketing and contracting for HRD activities. The chapter also looks at the changing role of HRD professionals as the business world continues to globalize and change. A clear understanding of the complexities of management and administration across national and cultural boundaries is critical to the success of a global HRD professional.

Global Dimensions of HRD Management

Although many of the roles and responsibilities of domestic and global HRD managers are the same, the role of global manager is complicated by multiple international dynamics, some of which are discussed below.

Culture

Perceptions of management, authority, and power differ widely across cultures. In a more egalitarian and collegial culture, such as Sweden's, expectations concerning the style, level of involvement, and job tasks appropriate for a manager will be quite different from the more authoritative role generally expected in Mexico, for example. Certainly an American managing Chinese or French employees or a multinational HRD team encounters much more complex dynamics than when managing other Americans.

Political and Economic Systems

The political and economic systems within a country help determine the responsibilities of the HRD manager, as well as the manner in which he or she carries them out. Marketing HRD services, for example, may be unheard of in a country accustomed to central planning and authority but will be essential in a country with a strong capitalist history.

Geographic Distance

Despite the advantages of increasingly advanced Web and telecommunications technology, managing and communicating with people and organizations thousands of miles and many time zones away still poses significant problems.

Resource Limitations

In less-developed countries, in particular, the HRD manager may not easily find the supplies, materials, facilities, or qualified local trainers needed for a successful HRD program.

Government Regulations

In some countries labor laws prescribe in detail much of what employees and employers can and cannot do. Such laws may also govern who provides and who attends certain types of training, what is to be taught, how often training will be offered, and so on. Other governments allow the HRD manager much greater latitude and autonomy in making decisions.

Administration and Management of HRD Staff

When dealing with their staffs, HRD managers often handle both human resource management (HRM) functions—such as recruitment, selection, compensation, and evaluation—and HRD functions—such as training, development, and career counseling. HRD managers should serve as an example to other managers for the way they create a work environment that promotes continuous improvement and learning. They should also encourage staff participation in HRD professional organizations that expand professional networks, update ideas and strategies, and advance the field of HRD.

In a competitive global marketplace HRD managers often are faced with managing two types of staff—full-time employees within the HRD department and temporary independent contractors. With the growth of outsourcing (both domestic and abroad), teleworking, virtual teams, and other nontraditional approaches to work, HRD managers constantly deal with new challenges in staff management and development.

Administrative Tasks

Whether sending domestic employees abroad, bringing foreign employees to a domestic site, or managing employees in other countries, HRD managers must handle a number of very important and often complex issues, including:

- Passports, visas, and other immigration requirements
- Travel details

- Work permits and other paperwork
- Compensation and expense allowances
- Housing, health care, and insurance
- Recreation and schooling
- Family needs
- Safety and security

The manager should research any of these areas that are unfamiliar to her and consult knowledgeable experts if possible so that she is aware of requirements and possible pitfalls.

Orientation and Relocation

Working abroad is more common than ever before, and young professionals often see an overseas assignment as necessary to round out their résumés. Learning how to function in a different cultural environment, however, presents numerous challenges. Whether HRD professionals are going abroad for two weeks or two years, the HRD manager must prepare them to adapt to their new environment and reenter their home environment as successfully as possible. Pretrip preparation can help prevent employee burnout, low motivation, frustration, depression, and failure. Since failed assignments can result in direct financial losses to the organization, the loss of current and future business in the region, damaged relationships with the host country and company, and career difficulties for the employee, it makes good business sense to prepare employees beforehand for overseas work. The amount and intensity of cross-cultural training needed depend on a number of factors, including the extent of cultural differences, planned length of stay in the foreign country, and the employee's level within the organization and previous cross-cultural experiences.

While employees are out of the country, the HRD manager must also provide long-distance support. No matter how interesting and exotic the setting may be, most travelers experience various stages of culture shock. Feeling cut off from their home base can exacerbate their sense of isolation.

Often forgotten but just as important is the employees' transition back into their home country. Returning employees tend to go through a type of "reverse culture shock" if they have been away from home for a long time. Just like immersing oneself in a new culture, coming home requires a great deal of readjustment, often made more difficult because employees do not expect to encounter problems when coming home.

Recruitment and Selection

When recruiting and hiring global HRD staff, it is essential to look for the competencies needed in cross-cultural assignments. Although technical expertise is required and successful international experience is helpful, the key competencies identified by global HRD practitioners are most often related to attitudes and mindset. These characteristics include respect for the values and practices of other cultures, tolerance of ambiguity, initiative and persistence, flexibility, a sense of humor. Behavioral interviews or assessment activities can be used to test applicants' ability to handle unexpected situations and conditions.

Management of Staff

Managing and coaching staff members, whether full-time or temporary, at a distance complicates an already complex task. Despite technological innovations managers still may feel that they need to "be there." Managers must recognize the cultural differences employees are experiencing and provide support and assistance when needed. Furthermore, they should realize that not all trainers who succeed at home will do so abroad.

Managers must also ensure that the staff continue to develop their skills. They must be kept up-to-date on technical information needed to work effectively, as well as news about the organization and other employees, so they maintain a sense of connection to the home workplace.

Evaluations

Evaluation is complicated when a home-country manger is not fully aware of what the staff is experiencing and what is happening abroad. For example, local events and cultural differences may require major adjustments to content and materials, significantly increasing the employees' workload. The demands of working in another culture, particularly in another language, can be exhausting, and results may not always reflect the staff's commitment and efforts. HRD managers having little or no international experience may not be able to provide an adequate, fair evaluation of an employee's performance in another country.

Evaluations of HRD staff should take into account information from coworkers and other knowledgeable individuals in the host country. At the same time, the manager should recognize that local people's perceptions are shaped by their own cultural frames of reference and expectations, which may be quite different from those of the staff's home country.

Following are guidelines—based on research by Gregersen, Hite, and Black (1996) and other experts—for making performance appraisal of overseas employees more effective:

- If you're using standardized forms, be sure that they are customized for local contexts. Criteria for evaluation must reflect the environment and critical abilities and tasks involved in a global assignment.
- Make allowances for the difficulty of the assignment, since working in one country may be more difficult than working in another.
- Conduct performance appraisals more often than you might in the home country.
- Incorporate perspectives from appropriate raters in the host country.
- Balance the participation of raters from within and outside the host country.
- Consider all aspects of the staff members' experiences. Realize that beyond performing a specific job, they are also developing a deeper understanding of the organization's overall operations and their skills in working cross-culturally.

Facilities Management

The HRD manager should arrange an acceptable working environment for the staff, as well as reasonable housing accommodations and meals. Staff will adjust more quickly to comfortable surroundings. In addition, in some areas individuals in the host country judge the staff's importance and credibility based on the home country's investment in a clean, well-equipped, and well-located facility. If employees will be working in a developing country where facilities are generally below the home country's standards, the manager should make the best possible arrangements and prepare the staff for what to expect.

Finance

Management of financial matters—particularly in developing countries, countries with strong hierarchical structures, and the public sector—can take a great deal of time and exasperate the most patient HRD manager. HRD programs may be put on hold for months while appropriate approvals or funds are obtained. Staff members serving abroad may quickly become demoralized if there are holdups in pay or other necessities from home, and staff hired in the host country may leave if pay is delayed, regardless of the problem's source. Strong planning, good negotiating and political skills, and lots of patience are critical to the HRD manager's success.

Management of HRD Programs and Initiatives

Coordination of HRD Teams

Before sending an HRD team abroad, the manager must first select appropriate team members. Their skills and knowledge should be complementary so that they can handle the various aspects of the project and learn from one another. Of course, if only one person is being sent out of the country, then the manger must make sure that the assignment is appropriate and feasible for that individual. In any case, careful plans for logistical and administrative support will ensure that HRD professionals can focus their talents on the task at hand. This includes assistance in preparing and reproducing materials, arranging for translators and interpreters as needed, checking on computer and multimedia equipment availability, scheduling transportation, and hiring clerical support.

Materials

Finding and buying materials in another country can be quite an adventure. Supplies that the HRD professional may take for granted at home may not be available in another setting. Methods of obtaining supplies and equipment may also be quite different in other cultures and may involve delays. One of the authors was working at the headquarters of an international public organization in a European country. While all the requested equipment—overhead projector, VCR and television, and video camera—was available, the items were locked up overnight. The challenge each morning was to find the person with the key to unlock the cabinets, a search made more difficult by the fact that some of the employees came from cultures in which punctuality was not valued.

In developing countries the HRD manager may need employees to take certain resources with them or may have them sent from headquarters. Even the process of sending materials ahead of time, however, may not work in certain countries where parcels are not protected from theft. Handy precautions include the following:

- Find out in advance if you can purchase or borrow necessary materials in the host country.
- When in doubt, take basic supplies with you (handouts, paper, markers, etc.), especially if you have very specific needs or preferences.

- If you're planning to make copies of a document in a foreign country, remember that standard paper sizes vary worldwide, and prepare your original documents accordingly.
- If taking electronic equipment, such as a laptop computer or projector, be sure to take the appropriate voltage adapter(s) and plug(s) with you, as well as extra bulbs and other replacement parts. If planning to use local computer equipment, recognize that keyboards can be laid out quite differently to accommodate other languages and alphabets.
- Recognize that even the best-prepared plans may not work out. Always have backup plans, especially for technology.

Training materials and/or textbooks are often deeply appreciated in developing countries. If you can take extra books or materials to leave in the country, they will be valued long after your departure.

Training Venue

Selecting suitable training facilities is also an important decision for the HRD manager. The venue, surroundings, and technology can enhance or diminish the status of the instructor and the program's content, as well as the learners' receptivity to the instruction.

In countries where facilities for training are limited, the manager will have few choices. In developing countries the trainer may be collaborating with a local organization that has limited funds for facilities. In any location instructors should check out the training site as far in advance of a program as possible to adjust for special conditions. When this is not possible, flexibility is critical to success. In one such case, the instructor walked into a training site on a cold day only to find that the heat was not on and the learners were huddled in coats, scarves, and mittens; there was no audiovisual equipment available, and the electricity was intermittent; even the blackboard was so old and of such poor quality that writing on it could barely be seen from a few feet away.

Participant Accommodations

On occasion the HRD manager may also need to arrange for overnight accommodations for learners. In societies having a distinct class system, trainees usually prefer to have different facilities (rooms or floors) for people of different classes. Mixing them together may alienate all of the participants, of both high and low status. In cultures having strong power distinctions, rooms for management-level people should also be separate from those for lower-level employees.

Ceremonies

In many countries, program participants may expect official opening and closing ceremonies. The program manager should arrange for a respected senior-level person to attend or speak at the opening and/or closing exercises to emphasize the importance of the program. Providing certificates or plaques for program completion is also expected and appreciated in many places. When planning a program, the manager should allow time for such formal procedures and be prepared to adjust training schedules in the event that an invited guest uses more or less time than anticipated.

Ceremonial gestures indicate to learners as well as instructors the importance and prestige of the HRD program. The participants' appreciation also increases their attention to the program and eventual application of the learning.

Food

The selection of food and beverages to be served at training programs requires careful consideration. Hindus do not eat beef, Muslims do not consume pork or alcohol, and many Buddhists are vegetarians. Many Asians expect rice with their meals and often prefer tea to coffee. In the many countries where the midday meal is the largest meal of the day, providing a typical American lunch of sandwiches and side salads would be unacceptable.

Marketing and Contracting for HRD Activities

Marketing Internal Programs

Representing the importance and needs of HRD within the organization can be a frustrating task. Decisionmakers at headquarters may not recognize the problems encountered when providing HRD programs and services in another culture or may be unwilling to provide enough funding to adapt programs to new environments. They also may not be aware of obstacles such as local labor strikes, foreign government regulations, and religious and national holidays. The HRD manager must serve as an active link between the local HRD reality and the members of top management. Emphasizing the strategic importance of high-quality training and evaluating the results of HRD initiatives in cost-benefit terms can help the HRD professional avoid management resistance.

External Marketing, Negotiating, and Contracting

Billions of dollars' worth of training and consulting or technical assistance are marketed and sold each year by HRD professionals worldwide. In fact, training and consulting are huge exports for the United States. Global marketing of HRD products and services requires not only strong sales and negotiating skills but also exceptional cross-cultural communication and political skills.

Marketing. Successful techniques for marketing and selling HRD are unique to each culture, since what is perceived as beneficial to the customer will vary from culture to culture. While American organizations may focus mostly on organizational benefits and other anticipated results of HRD initiatives, firms and learners in other cultures may have entirely different purposes in mind. For example, people in some cultures may value the credentials of the HRD professional or company much more than the content of the programs because of how those credentials serve the individual and his or her family. People in other cultures may analyze the history, size, track record, and other evidence of the HRD organization's capability before evaluating the product itself.

Negotiating and Contracting. Finalizing contracts for the delivery of HRD services often requires much more time and expense than the provider anticipated. Various cultural values and styles influence this process:

- *Establishing rapport and trust.* In most cultures, before getting down to business, the two parties must first develop a trusting relationship, a process that may take days, weeks, or months. Attempts to rush through the process often offend the local stakeholders and lead to failure.
- *Power structure.* In societies having a clear, hierarchical power structure, lower-level officials or managers cannot make final decisions without the approval of higher authorities. Only when the lead person (who must review stacks of documents) has signed off can the contract go forward.
- *Context.* In negotiating and signing agreements, low-context and high-context cultures differ significantly. In low-context cultures, such as Switzerland and Germany, each detail must be agreed to and put in writing. High-context cultures, such as Malaysia, may not require a written contract. After a trusting personal relationship is established, a handshake between the two parties may be enough to finalize an agreement.
- *Communications.* Cultural context can also make it difficult for the HRD manager to carry out communications and may cause

confusion. For example, a local subordinate who has important data related to a project may be quite articulate in early meetings but then become a shadow in a meeting that includes his superiors. A senior official who is open and warm when negotiating alone may become extremely formal and cautious when colleagues are in the room.

- *Language.* Negotiating and contracting become even more challenging when not conducted in the HRD manager's primary language. Much of the tone, meaning, and nuance can be lost in the translation process, especially when one is working with inexperienced translators or dealing with words and concepts unfamiliar within the culture.

Government Relations. In some countries the HRD manager must consult closely with various government ministries and officials before and during HRD activities. Without their approval implementation is unlikely.

In much of Asia, Africa, Europe, and Latin America, a government department, such as a ministry of labor, regulates most aspects of work life. Many European countries have a governmental system for testing standardized skills and achievement, qualifying workers for occupational status and related pay scales. In some regions these systems are in transition. For example, as the individual countries of Europe integrate within the European Union, relinquishing some local control is inevitable.

HRD managers should be up-to-date on relevant regulations during the planning, development, and implementation phases of HRD programs. Understanding the structure of the educational and training systems in the target country helps managers incorporate new programs into the existing system. Germany, for example, has strong vocational programs at the secondary school level, which influences the amount and level of technical training workers may need. In some countries corporations are required to use a certain percentage of their budget on education and training. When working with the public sector, managers should become familiar with the government's funding and administrative arrangements.

Labor Unions. Labor unions play an important, although lately somewhat diminished, role for workers around the world. Since the structure, purposes, and strength of unions vary from country to country and as a result of changes in economic and political systems, HRD managers should be careful not to make assumptions about unions based on experiences and observations at home. For each country and each company it is important to study labor-management agreements and related legislation that may contain clauses regarding training. Are there items concerning increased wages for successful completion of training? Can union members serve as instructors? Must training occur during work hours? Pursuing questions of this type helps the manager avoid embarrassing and potentially costly mistakes.

Strategic Impact of HRD

Although much of the discussion in this chapter relates to training initiatives, HRD as a field has come to represent a great deal more than training and development. To truly contribute to an organization's success, HRD must see the bigger organizational picture and align its initiatives with the overall vision and mission. Systems thinking is critical to long-term individual and organizational improvement. More and more HRD managers and professionals are taking a strategic role within organizations, helping to analyze, improve, and build capacity through people. Ulrich, Losey, and Lake (1997), in their study of large international companies, identify several important roles that HRD professionals are and will be expected to play. These include:

- Creating horizontal teamwork,
- Decentralizing decisionmaking,
- Facilitating communication and learning,
- Managing for high performance,
- Recruiting and retaining key talent, and
- Creating global training and development.

Summary

The role of HRD managers is constantly evolving as the field itself and the environment in which HRD operates continues to change. Global managers must often work on two levels simultaneously, handling the day-to-day administrative work inherent in HRD planning and implementation and, at the same time, providing comprehensive, innovative strategies for individual and organizational performance improvement.

The main tasks of the global HRD manager include administration and management of staff, management of programs and initiatives, and marketing and contracting for HRD initiatives. Certain factors complicate the global HRD manager's work: culture, political and economic systems, geographic distances, resource limitations, and governmental regulations. A final consideration is the importance of HRD's broad, strategic role in building organizational capacity.

Part 3

Levels of Global HRD

Global HRD for Individuals

A handful of patience is worth a bushel of brains.
Dutch proverb

Introduction

Most individuals who have worked abroad would probably agree that one of the key personal characteristics for successful global work is patience, along with the ability to relax and to accept and appreciate the differences and frustrations of life abroad. While living and working in another country can be full of fascinating and exciting experiences, it seldom comes without some frustrations and difficulties.

This chapter discusses a number of characteristics and skills essential for global HRD professionals. An understanding of these competencies will help the HRD practitioner prepare for work in other cultures and also guide him or her in selecting and training individuals best suited to global work. The chapter also discusses the importance of orienting employees and their families before sending them abroad, supporting them while they are gone, and providing readjustment assistance once they return.

General Characteristics and Skills for Overseas Success

How well prepared are you to work in another country? How can one tell if an employee is "right" for an overseas assignment? While the answers to these questions come with no guarantees, a number of tools can help in the analysis. Numerous checklists of general characteristics and skills needed for successful overseas work are available. If adapted to specific needs, a list of this kind can help HR professionals select global employees, coach those who may want to eventually work overseas, and assist employees in analyzing their own potential for working successfully in another culture. The degree to which an individual needs each of the traits and skills for an overseas assignment will vary depending on the location, type of work, and extent of cultural dissimilarity. For example, Americans will probably find that adjusting to life in the UK is much easier than in Turkmenistan.

According to Jean-Marc Hachey (2003), author of *The Canadian Guide to Working and Living Abroad*, some personality traits and skills that typify individuals who work successfully overseas include:

General Traits

- Love of change
- Sense of adventure
- Desire for challenge
- Open mind
- Patience
- Curiosity

Adaptation and Coping Skills

- Emotional stability and ability to deal with stress
- Familiarity with culture shock
- Observation and adaptation skills
- Flexibility
- Humor
- Self-knowledge

Intercultural Communication Skills

- Tolerance
- Sensitivity
- Listening and observing
- Nonverbal communication skills
- Knowledge of a second language

Overseas Work Effectiveness Skills

- Independence and self-discipline
- Training experience
- Resourcefulness
- Versatility
- Persistence
- Organizational and people skills
- Leadership
- Energy
- Project planning skills
- Writing skills
- Verbal communication skills
- Loyalty and tenacity
- Tact
- Philosophical commitment to field of work

Of course, global workers must have very strong technical skills in their areas of expertise, as well, since they are expected to perform successfully abroad while also adjusting to differing terminology, facilities, equipment, and procedures.

Assessing Overseas Effectiveness

Over the past few years, a wide variety of assessments have become available to evaluate different aspects of cross-cultural competency. These instruments can serve several purposes: individuals can assess their readiness and skills to undertake an international assignment; managers can use assessments as part of the selection process; the key points can serve as a framework for planning a selection interview; assessment results can provide needs analysis data for building or revising cross-cultural training programs. Highlights of two typical inventories follow.

The Intercultural Living and Working Inventory

The Intercultural Living and Working Inventory was developed and validated by the Centre for Intercultural Learning of the Canadian Foreign Service Institute, based on research into the behaviors of interculturally effective individuals. Its main scales look at the candidate's:

- Personal situation,
- Interest in other cultures,
- Motivation,
- Positive attitudes,
- Realistic expectations,
- Initiative,
- Flexibility,
- Patience and perseverance,
- Self-confidence,
- Tolerance of ambiguity,
- Relationship building,
- Respect,
- Diplomacy,
- Social insight, and
- Cross-cultural awareness.

The Cultural Orientations Inventory

As the name implies, the Cultural Orientations Inventory, developed by Training Management Company, provides insights into an individual's cultural mindset. It would be particularly useful as a self-assessment for people who are planning to work abroad to help them think through their own beliefs and values. Dimensions of this instrument include:

- *Environment:* beliefs about controlling, living in harmony with, and/or being constrained by the environment
- *Time:* cultural tendencies to feel more comfortable with a single or a multiple focus when dealing with tasks and relationships; the degree to which time is viewed as fluid versus fixed; and the tendency to focus more on the past, present, or future
- *Action:* beliefs about actions and interactions with people and the environment; general orientation toward accomplishment of goals and tasks or toward relationships, reflection, and analysis
- *Communication:* tendencies toward high-context versus low-context, indirect versus direct, instrumental versus expressive, and formal versus informal communications
- *Space:* preferences for a private versus public approach to physical and psychological space
- *Power:* cultural views about power relationships, tending toward either equality or hierarchy

- *Individualism:* whether the individual values a more individualistic or more collectivistic approach and whether more importance is given to adhering to universal concepts or to differences and uniqueness
- *Competitiveness:* whether more importance is given to competition or cooperation
- *Structure:* culture-influenced approaches to change, risk, and uncertainty, whether through more rules, regulations, and procedures that provide order or through a flexible approach to receiving new people and ideas
- *Thinking:* degree to which the individual is culturally more deductive versus inductive, more linear versus systemic in his or her thinking patterns

Given the many different types of assessments available, HRD professionals should review and evaluate these instruments based on the variables they wish to measure, their purposes in using the instrument, validity and reliability data, cost, and other relevant criteria.

Competencies for Global HRD Effectiveness

The previous paragraphs discuss general characteristics and skills that apply to working globally, regardless of the type of assignment. Through personal experience and interviews and discussions with scores of international professionals, the authors have found a number of competencies to be particularly important for global HRD success. These competencies—broadly categorized as attitudes, skills, and knowledge—are discussed below.

Attitudes

Respect for the Values and Practices of Other Cultures.   HRD practitioners, like everyone else, grow up learning what they come to believe is the best way of behaving and communicating; to do otherwise would seem foolhardy. We are "wired" to perceive the world in a particular way, and society reinforces our viewpoint through family, schools, political institutions, religion, media sources, and other cultural influences. We tend to think that we are the best and that we have all the right answers. Americans in particular, perhaps because of their affluence and their country's position of power in the world, assume that their way is the best and that other approaches are inferior and should be changed. The ability to recognize this ethnocentricity and realize that other cultures often do things at least as well, if not better than we do, can help reduce the desire to criticize what is merely different.

Patience and Tolerance. Coping with the unavoidable stresses of an intercultural setting is difficult. Yet the ability to react to new, different, and at times unpredictable situations with little visible discomfort or irritation is important for global HRD professionals. Americans, for example, tend to believe that they can and should control time and that they have some control over their futures. This viewpoint is exactly the opposite of that found in many other places in the world and can lead to impatience and frustration. Adaptation requires a great deal of patience and a willingness to withhold judgment and instead work toward understanding new surroundings and ways of doing things.

Commitment to HRD. A healthy respect for one's profession and a concern for one's image as an individual and as an HRD professional can make a difference in how well a person is received in other cultures and how he or she responds to them. Demonstrating a commitment to high-quality work and believing that HRD provides important tools for developing individuals, organizations, and nations can separate the mediocre from the effective global HRD professionals. This attitude also leads one to thoroughly prepare for all HRD activities, to accept personal responsibility for efforts, and always to show concern for quality and improvement.

Initiative and Persistence. Working abroad requires a great deal of initiative on the part of HRD professionals, particularly in a pleasant climate or a place with numerous interesting distractions. When viewed as experts, however, HRD professionals are expected to take the lead and keep projects on track.

While one should avoid forcing ideas on others, making one's views clear and understood can require a lot of persistence. HRD professionals also must recognize that even with a good deal of prior research, they may have to rework their plans and approaches once they have been in the new culture for a period of time. Such willingness to revise and adapt requires persistence, especially when the professional is faced with a sense of failure or uncertainty.

Sense of Humor. Global HRD professionals should have a sense of humor—that is, the humility and ability to laugh at themselves when dealing with the unexpected and the unknown. Stress can be very high in intercultural situations in which one is unsure of what is expected and has less control over one's interactions or results. As humor specialist Paul McGhee (1999) explains,

> Your sense of humor is one of the most powerful tools you have for coping with any source of stress in your life. When you're able to find a light side of deadlines, conflicts and other aspects of your job—especially on the tough days—

you have a tool for letting go of the frustrations and upsets of the moment. This enables you to sustain a frame of mind conducive to dealing more effectively with the problem of the moment.

Skills and Knowledge

Knowledge of One's Own Culture.   When cross-cultural experts are asked what information is most needed by people working in another culture, they usually rank "knowledge of one's own culture" first. "Know thyself" is the first lesson for global HRD professionals, since our behaviors are influenced by our basic cultural values, beliefs, and assumptions. Unless we become conscious of these values and carefully examine them, we will not be able to understand why we react toward other cultures as we do. Before embarking on an international HRD career, one should consider attending a cross-cultural or cultural awareness program, examples of which are discussed later in this chapter.

Knowledge of Another Culture.   To fully appreciate another culture and to achieve the maximum benefit from the HRD experience, one must learn as much as one can about the culture. Having some prior knowledge allows the practitioner to make sense of unfamiliar situations and events and to provide points of reference, examples, case studies, resources, and cultural values that can be used to make the HRD program more relevant and more effective.

Following are some of the areas that help the HRD professional build an understanding and context for experiences in a new culture:

- Geography and weather
- History
- Politics, laws, and government
- Economics and industry
- Religious beliefs and practices and philosophical tenets
- Family and social structure and norms
- Fine arts and cultural achievements
- Scientific achievements
- Symbols
- Basic language information

HRD Field.   Our knowledge of best practices in HRD is constantly evolving, based on research and experience. Technology applications in the HRD field are also rapidly changing. Effective HRD practitioners should use new information and strategies to work effectively both domestically and globally.

They should also be aware of the key forces influencing HRD around the world, be able to tap into helpful HRD databases, and be familiar with Web-based instruction (WBI) and appropriate applications of technology.

Language. More and more global HRD practitioners are stressing the importance of speaking the target language or, at a minimum, understanding basic phrases and the language's structural content. Learning some basic language skills can demonstrate your interest in the culture and help you feel less dependent on others. Almost everyone appreciates attempts by a nonnative speaker to communicate in his or her local language, and this show of good will is usually more important than the speaker's degree of proficiency. One of the authors recalls a family vacation in which the owner of a small restaurant in the Italian countryside offered complimentary after-dinner drinks and made several toasts to his guests after their halting attempts at conversing with him in Italian throughout the meal.

Some languages also reflect important cultural nuances. For example, Mandarin Chinese provides a sense of hierarchy, place, and order. Thai shows great respect for elders. And in French and German, specific word forms are used to distinguish between formal and informal personal relationships.

In addition to the verbal language, nonverbal meanings are also critical to understanding a culture. Gestures can be meaningful in one culture and obscene in another. In a high-context culture body language and the environment often communicate more clearly and completely than spoken words.

Corporate and Business Culture. A clear understanding of the strategic and cultural dimensions of the corporation or organization in which one is working is important in a domestic setting and crucial in an international environment. Too often HRD practitioners are not very knowledgeable about corporate culture, including the corporation's history, rituals, structure, strategies, communication processes, symbols, and so on. They must also understand financial issues, marketing, and other business processes to project credibility when leading organizational projects.

Global Perspective. Globalization is a fact of life and a key to survival in today's business world. Global HRD professionals must understand the political and economic factors that have led to globalization and the steps necessary for organizations to function effectively in a global context. They should be familiar with models of successful globalization and the resources needed to guide that process. An understanding of customers and competitors around the world, as well as internal employees with diverse cultural backgrounds, is imperative for effective HRD leadership in many organizations. Contributing to success is the ability to create and join in global networks for acquiring information and influencing people worldwide.

Preparation for Global HRD Assignments

Training and preparing a person for any job is important, but they are critical when the person will work globally. Because of increased globalization the process of selecting, training, supporting, rewarding, and learning from expatriates has become much more important to many organizations.

A high percentage of American expatriates fail in their long-term assignments and return home before they complete their project, and even a high percentage of employees on shorter international assignments (as short as two weeks) return early. Inability of the expatriate and/or accompanying family members to adjust to the host culture is cited as the main cause for failure. The cost of failure is high not only to corporations but also to employees, both professionally and psychologically. U.S. corporations spend well over $2 billion each year recalling and replacing employees in other countries. Much has been written about the financial costs of ill-prepared global work, yet many employees and their families are sent overseas each year with little or no preparation for the transitions and stresses they encounter.

Selecting, Preparing, and Retaining Global Professionals

Pucik (1997) distinguishes between *global professionals*—who have a global mindset and the skills and knowledge needed to work comfortably with a wide range of culturally diverse individuals and situations worldwide, even if working domestically—and *expatriates,* who are physically located in a different country. With the growing sophistication and diffusion of global communications, organizations may find they need fewer expatriates and many more global professionals. Most experts agree, however, that actual experience working in another culture is a crucial component in the development of globally competent individuals.

The next few sections look at some of the issues involved in what should be an integrated process of selection, cross-cultural preparation, career development, completion of the global assignment's business objectives, and repatriation of employees assigned abroad.

Global Staffing Strategy

As companies have begun to realize the importance of overseas assignments and the costs of failure, they have been paying closer attention to the selection process. A recent study found that for 70 percent of the companies surveyed, skills or competencies constituted the most important factor in selecting employees for assignments abroad. The second most important was job performance (23 percent). The person best suited for a project in the home country, however, may be the wrong person for a similar project in a country with another culture. What works in New York may be the opposite of what is needed in Seoul. What expatriates often lack are the people skills and the cross-cultural understanding and sensitivity necessary to apply their technical skills successfully. Ways to improve selection include the following:

- Institute a more holistic selection process that includes personal attributes and interpersonal skills in addition to technical skills.
- Devise in advance a long-range development plan that helps prepare people for global assignments and evaluate their capabilities. Experts consistently agree that last-minute training is not as effective. Organizations can begin by conducting general cross-cultural training, even before deciding where an individual will eventually be sent.
- Make a clearer link to strategic business goals. Are you trying to develop the person? Are you simply trying to fill a technical slot in another country? Will the person be expected to manage and lead host-country natives? And so on.
- Take a more strategic approach to deciding whether to hire a local professional rather than send someone on assignment.

Main Reasons for Expatriate Failure

Explanations for the failure of expatriates include

- Selection criteria based on headquarters criteria rather than assignment requirements;
- Inadequate preparation, training, and orientation prior to assignment;
- Alienation or lack of support from headquarters;
- Inability to adapt to the local culture and working environment;
- Problems with spouse and children;
- Insufficient compensation/financial support; and
- Inadequate programs for career support and repatriation.

Predeparture Preparation for HRD Expatriates

Organizations use a variety of approaches to predeparture preparation for global HRD professionals. Companies that work extensively abroad may provide ongoing cross-cultural training to many or all of their employees, regardless of their future plans. After all, it is often just as important to train a domestic customer service representative who regularly handles customers from various countries as it is to prepare a manager for an assignment overseas. Self-assessment tools can be an important part of training, helping learners become aware of their own cultural orientations.

More extensive cross-cultural training, as well as specific host-country training, is needed for expatriates and their families. Several areas should be covered in such training:

- Culture profiles comparing the differences and similarities between home and host cultures, such as the country's geography; history; historical and current political environment, particularly in relation to the home country; religious customs; art; music; crafts; theater
- Logistical information—weather, appropriate wardrobe, suggested items to take that are not available abroad
- Social norms—etiquette, gift giving
- Procedures to follow in an emergency
- Specific information about how to apply cultural information
- Basic language skills, beginning with speaking (level of accomplishment depends on what level is needed for competence)
- Job training, if the job will entail tasks different from the home job

In addition, as part of predeparture preparation, there should be a clear discussion of pay, benefits, communications, and other important HR aspects while the person is abroad. Conversations with others who have had experience working in the area can provide valuable inside information, as can informal briefings by experts in specific countries. Making contact with key people by e-mail and/or phone before arrival can provide a sense of connection and acquaintance. Although less common, some kind of orientation for the host-country employees who will be working with the expatriate can help them deal more effectively with the expatriate and increase both parties' comfort level.

Following is a sample agenda of a predeparture training program:

- Introduction and Establishment of Expectations and Needs
- What We Do (and Don't) Mean by the Word *Culture*

- Classic Models of the Meaning of Culture
- How Others See Americans and How Will Others See Me?
- Host Country 101: Historic and Political Roots of Current Social Issues
- Brief Overview of Host Countries' Cultural Values and Business Approaches (with emphasis on expectations about leadership, negotiation style, conduct of meetings, and business writing)
- Cultural Differences in the Workplace: Data and Application from Around the World
- Communication Styles: The Dangers of Not Understanding the Role of Culture
- Tips for Business Travelers to Host Country
- Application of Training (analysis of trainees' own management approaches in light of their own cultural values, communication styles, and learning styles and in light of current multicultural situations)
- The Surprising Course and Management of Culture Shock
- Eleven Reasons Moving to a New Country Can Be Difficult (and What to Do About It)
- "Ask the Expert" (question-and-answer period)
- Wrap-up and Evaluation

Support During the Project

Another key to maintaining motivated, satisfied expatriates is to provide support throughout the period abroad. A common practice—perhaps even more helpful than predeparture training—is host-country orientation and training after the expatriate arrives. During this period the expatriate and, if applicable, his or her family may obtain a tremendous amount of useful information about local life, including the location of food markets, availability and use of public transportation, rules of the road if a car is provided, tax information, assistance in filling out official forms, banking procedures, day care and school facilities, recreational opportunities and fun things to do, historical and other tourist sites, housing, shopping, and health care. A tour can also provide a big picture of the area.

The expatriate should also participate in a work-related orientation to learn about the layout of the facilities; use of technology; resources available; training opportunities; basic company and specific department information, including contacts; and a clear explanation of job responsibilities. Additional in-country support might include host-country mentors to interpret experiences and perceptions and provide helpful advice, and international clubs for companies with numerous expatriates so that they can socialize and share experiences.

The home office should also stay in frequent touch, providing relevant e-mails, company newsletters, career counseling, assistance in handling difficult situations, magazines from home, and other reminders that the expatriate and family members have not been forgotten.

Planning for Repatriation

According to a 1997 study (expat study identifies policy trends), expatriates cost three or more times their domestic salaries. However, 20 percent of repatriated managers leave their companies within one year after returning home, and as many as 50 percent leave within the first three years. The cost of losing a single repatriated employee has been estimated to be as high as $1.2 million. More than money is lost as talented and experienced employees walk out the door. In some companies, ineffective repatriation has led to a perception of overseas assignments as "the kiss of death," reducing the pool of highly qualified individuals for such assignments.

Allen and Alvarez (1998) cite the following factors as accounting for ineffective repatriation:

- Loss of promotional opportunities and of one's place on the "fast track"
- Career setback rather than enhancement and, in some cases, limited job opportunities for the returning expatriate
- Tendency of some companies to send mediocre employees overseas
- "Out of sight, out of mind, and out of the loop" syndrome, as expatriates return to find drastic changes in their department and their job have occurred during their absence
- Cool reception by fellow colleagues, who may not be interested in the expatriate's experiences or new insights and who have moved on to new concerns and interests

From the expatriate's perspective, repatriation involves fitting back into the job and community and adjusting to reverse culture shock. Long neglected as an important part of the whole expatriate experience, companies are realizing that adjusting to the return home is just as critical as pretrip preparation. During the expatriate's absence, numerous changes may have occurred not only at work but also in politics, sports, television, music, movies, and books. But the expatriate has also changed. Many repatriates are amazed to find that what was once familiar and normal feels strange and unfamiliar upon return. It can also be surprising and disappointing to realize that friends and relatives are not really that interested to hear about the expatriate's experiences and their meaning.

The degree of cultural readjustment needed and the time it takes is usually influenced by how long the assignment lasted, how much the expatriate and family enjoyed the experience, and how much contact was maintained with family and friends while away. Working in a developing country in particular may cause an individual to become more critical of America's consumer society, fast pace of life, and values. Many experts agree that repatriation should start before an individual ever leaves the country. Managing expectations and creating a receptive environment for returning expatriates can make a big difference in the decision to stay with the organization.

Summary

Organizations working globally need associates who have the technical knowledge and skills, as well as the mindset and sensitivity, to work effectively across cultures. Key issues arise in the selection of potentially successful global professionals. Pre-departure preparation, in-country orientation, ongoing support, and effective repatriation of expatriates and their families—all are important to the success of an assignment abroad. Research suggests that many organizations have yet to implement the necessary development and support systems to select and retain global professionals.

Teams and Global HRD

None of us is as smart as all of us.

Japanese proverb

Introduction

A team that works well together is much smarter than any individual leader. Global teams, although much more challenging to build and manage than domestic, face-to-face teams, are becoming a key strength of organizations. With that strength, global teams of all types are being used worldwide to manage cross-functional projects, work on assembly lines, reengineer business processes, develop marketing strategies, and accomplish a host of other tasks essential to the organization.

Global HRD practitioners have an important role in building teams that not only are highly productive but also meet the human, social, and cultural needs of the group members. Although increasingly seen as essential for global prosperity, teams fail far more often than they succeed. The obstacles of cultural differences, distances and time zones, the complexity of global teamwork, language differences, and the costs and time involved in arranging face-to-face meetings have overwhelmed most companies.

Thus building global teams is considered one of the most important business challenges facing global HRD professionals in the 21st century—the *sine qua non* for global success. Devereaux and Johansen (1994, p. xii) note that "the powerful, creative dynamics of teamwork are the electricity that lights up the global economy." More and more every day, thousands of companies around the world need to call on their people to work in global teams, to "communicate and cooperate across radically different cultures, to manage widely dispersed, fragmented organizations, and to hurdle multiple time zones in a single bound" (p. 139).

What Are Global Teams?

Global teams are groups of people of different nationalities working interdependently on a common project across cultures and time zones for extended periods of time. The global team is expected to serve a very widespread set of customers, solve problems in many areas simultaneously, and/or sustain or significantly increase organizational profitability and service. The growing power of technology enables global teams to collaborate both face-to-face and virtually so that members may work at different times and in different locations as well as in the same time and place. Global teams typically work on projects that are highly complex and have considerable impact on company objectives.

Importance and Growth of Teams in the 21st Century

Tom Peters (1992), a noted guru on the future of organizations, sees teams as the foundation for organizational survival in the 21st century. He offers the following predictions about the importance of teams and their composition as we enter the new millennium:

- Most of tomorrow's work will be done in project teams. The life span of a project team might be indeterminate or just a few hours. Dynamic, short-lived project configurations will be commonplace.
- No matter their size—whether 200,000 or 20 employees—organizations will be broken down to work in fast, learning-efficient units of four- to forty-member teams.
- It will not be uncommon for one to work on four or five project teams in a year—but one might never work twice with the same configuration of colleagues.
- The typical project team will include "outsiders" such as vendors, customers, and distributors.

- Who reports to whom will change over time, rotating depending on the task. Thus the ability to lead and guide groups will become an important skill for almost everyone.
- Developing world-class teams with world-class members will be more important than any single business victory.
- Performance appraisals will be based primarily on team skills and success and will be done by fellow team members.
- There will be constant reorganizing, restructuring, and reengineering based on endless reconfigurations of project teams.

Teams, like companies, are now going global. As Davison and Ward (1999) note, global teams are necessary for creating a company's "sustainable global capability." The increasing complexities of scientific, sociological, and commercial issues demand individuals from different cultural backgrounds and different nations to collaborate in order to creatively resolve global problems and take advantage of global opportunities.

Why must global teams be the avenue for organizational responses to these challenges? The simple answer is that today's global problems are too complex, require solutions too quickly, and involve too many resources for local teams, much less individual leaders, to resolve. Global teams have the capability to be much more resourceful and ultimately successful. The power generated by the technology revolution now enables people to participate in meaningful interaction anywhere anytime, for groups to spend as much time working apart as together, and for people to access and share information as never before.

Building Power in Global Teams

Organizations and leaders recognize the necessity and value of high-performing global teams and are increasingly turning to HRD professionals to help build such teams. They understand that global teams' power to link and leverage resources, move and manipulate those resources, and provide superior services and products at low costs can give them a significant competitive advantage. This power will enable them to acquire the best workers, produce the best products, and attract the best customers.

Why do global teams have such power? What is the source of their robust capabilities? How do they link and leverage these overwhelming advantages? Let's examine the ten advantages/benefits of global teams that global executives and leading global HRD theorists have identified most frequently (see Figure 8.1). In conjunction with each power source, an example of how an organization used its global team will be presented.

TABLE 8.1 Power Sources and Benefits of Global Teams

1. **Ability to reduce costs and gain economies of scope**
2. **Ability to get specialized talent from anywhere inside or outside the organization**
3. **Ability to better solve complex 21st-century problems**
4. **Increased ability to go global**
5. **Ability to increase speed of operations**
6. **Proximity to and greater understanding of local customers**
7. **Development of future global leaders and professionals for the organization**
8. **Increased access to knowledge and information resources**
9. **More opportunities to form alliances and partnerships**
10. **Increased ability to become a global learning organization**

Power Sources and Benefits of Global Teams

Ability to Reduce Costs and Gain Economies of Scope

A primary purpose of global teams, according to Bartlett and Ghoshal (1998), is to achieve global efficiency by developing worldwide and regional cost advantages and standardization of designs and operations. Although establishing global teams may require additional costs for travel and technology, global teams can reduce costs in a number of ways:

- Global teams integrate across functions, boundaries, and professional areas.
- They can reduce duplication by eliminating and consolidating identical activities.
- They allow for more efficient and focused use of human resources.
- Companies can enhance the quality and effectiveness of efforts as global teams develop worldwide the best practices and strategies.
- Global teams can lower costs, shorten delivery times, and/or develop broad assortments of standard products.
- The steep learning and experience benefits gained via global teams can ultimately result in higher productivity and profits.
- Team membership can be composed of high-quality talent at a much lower cost because of members' location.

Colgate-Palmolive.   When Colgate-Palmolive entered the global market-place, it faced increased pressures to reduce costs and standardize products and services in order to achieve economies of scale and scope. A global team was established to ensure that employees have access to and properly use the best worldwide technology. As a result of the efforts of the Total Productivity Maintenance (TPM) global team, Colgate now has a global set of tools and standards and is doing quality training against those standards. Colgate has also lowered costs since less equipment is needed and less waste occurs. A number of functions have been eliminated that had required resources and consultants. Finally, production is better organized, thus motivating employees to work more diligently.

Ability to Attract Specialized Talent

Global companies need access to the best people around the world, regardless of nationality, background, or location. These people bring to the organization the experiences and learning from their cultures, their best universities, and their best organizations. Snell, Snow, Davison, and Hambrick (1998) point out that one of the most beneficial byproducts of using global teams is that they force the company's HR department to "seek, motivate and develop superior talent from around the world" (p. 182).

Due to the power of technology, teams can now communicate and work together even though they are separated by great distances and time. Virtuality and asynchronicity allow an organization to find and use the best people from within as well as outside the organization. If accessing and capitalizing on top knowledge and skills lead to greater corporate success, global teams provide that success.

Marriott.   Marriott faced the challenge of quickly integrating the $1 billion Renaissance and New World hotel chains into the Marriott fold. A global team was formed to assess what the current status of the new hotels was, what brand might best fit, what capital expenditures would be necessary to bring the new hotels up to Marriott standards, and what architectural and interior design modifications were needed. Within thirty days the team developed a strategy and written procedures that enabled all the hotels to attain operational status and add to Marriott's global growth and prestige.

Marriott also used a global team to globalize its brand. Marriott has a number of different hotel brands—Ritz, JW Marriott, Courtyard by Marriott—each of which needed to have global standards (reservations, sales, etc.) yet have localized or regionalized touches and maintain the brand requirements of the local owner (e.g., the Courtyard in China with nine-course meals, the fifty-seven-room Ritz in a palace in Berlin). A global team quickly analyzed and developed worldwide standards and implementation procedures.

Ability to Better Solve Complex 21st-Century Problems

The 21st-century workplace will involve rapidly changing socioeconomic trends and markets, overnight innovation by competitors, mergers across disparate corporate cultures and industries, new distribution channels, and globalization of business. Linsky and Heifetz (2002) distinguish the problems more common to the 20th century from those that will be most critical in the 21st—that is, what they term technical versus adaptive problems.

Technical problems (20th century) can be solved with knowledge that already exists in a legitimized form or set of procedures. The challenge is to obtain and apply the knowledge in an efficient and rational way. Technical problems have a linear, logical way of being solved, with precedents within or outside the organization.

For adaptive problems (21st century), such as handling global mergers or retaining knowledge workers, no satisfactory response has yet been developed and no technical expertise is fully adequate. The challenge is to mobilize the people experiencing the problem to make painful adjustments in their attitudes, work habits, and other aspects of their lives while learning their way toward the creation of something that does not yet exist. Adaptive problems have no ready solutions. They require people collectively to *apply their intelligence and skills to the work only they can do*. The responsibility requires unlearning the habits of a managerial lifetime, acquiring new learning to meet challenges for which current skills are insufficient, and developing capacity to explore and understand competing values.

Adaptive challenges are more difficult to define and resolve, precisely because they require efforts of people throughout the organization. As the workplace continues to become more complex, however, strategic and operational problems require more than a technical response. Leaders and teams face learning more adaptive approaches in order to solve problems for which no plan of action has yet been developed and current technical expertise is not fully adequate. Thus, problems are becoming ever more confusing and difficult to identify, much less solve. And solving problems is no longer the domain of any one person or leader—we need to incorporate the information, imagination, perspectives, and talents of many people to find answers to tomorrow's dilemmas. In confronting 21st-century problems, organizations need to create new entities such as global teams that have the internal diversity and complexity required to understand and solve such problems (Schwandt and Marquardt, 2000).

Research by Snow, Snell, Davison, and Hambrick (1996) shows that global teams are much more effective than homogenous teams when the key challenge is to generate a broad array of ideas that will lead to a more powerful solution than has been considered previously. Because global teams are located in and working with numerous cultures, they can "synergize" the strengths of differing cultures. The teams' diversity can be a primary source of new ideas when innovation and creativity are needed. The complex problems of the global marketplace require new ways of thinking and fresh ideas. Mobilizing the diverse energies of various cultures can lead to multiple perspectives and the development of a wider range of options and approaches to problems and challenges.

Royal Dutch Shell.   At Royal Dutch Shell six global teams meet every week at the Exploration and Production divisions in Houston and in the Netherlands to mull over ideas that have been pitched to them by e-mail. The teams (known as GameChangers) have reviewed hundreds of ideas from employees—everything from ways for reducing company paperwork to using laser sensors to discover oil. The results have been outstanding. Of Shell's five top business initiatives in 1999, four emerged from the global GameChanger teams and now are reaping millions of dollars. One successful initiative engendered by the global virtual teams was Shell's new "Light Touch" oil discovery method, which helps explorers by sensing hydrocarbon emissions released naturally into the air from underground reserves. This laser technology recently helped locate some 30 million barrels of oil reserves in Gabon.

Increased Ability to Go Global

Companies around the world are rushing to globalize, recognizing that doing so provides significant competitive and comparative advantages. Most organizations, however, still think and operate in an international or at best multinational mode. They do not know how to link and leverage resources on a single worldwide basis, how to operate without borders, how to go global (see chapter 10).

Global teams are "at the heart of the globalization process" (Snow et al., 1996). Global leaders see the development of global teams as a key to launching and managing the transition to global status. Establishing a global presence and being seen with global players can occur quickly with global teams.

Creating global teams forces the organization to begin to operate in a global fashion. The existence of global teams helps group members develop a global mindset and a greater appreciation of different cultures. It enables people within the organization to think and see the world globally, be more open to exchanging ideas and concepts across borders, and to break down provincial ways of thinking.

MMD.   Two large pharmaceutical companies, Marion Laboratories and Merrell Dow, with combined sales of over $3 billion dollars and several thousand employees around the world, merged in 1999 to become MMD. Thanks to the efforts of the global team composed of members both companies, the merger succeeded, and every MMD site improved production levels, lowered costs, and increased speed.

Ability to Increase Speed of Operations

Team members located in different time zones around the world can maintain round-the-clock efforts and activities. Team members in Singapore may work on a project for eight hours, transmit their efforts to members in London who, in turn, after another eight hours can send their work to team members in Los Angeles. Team members at each site can tap the resources available in their region of the world during that region's normal working hours.

IBM.   IBM created a five-site, five-country global team to work around the clock to develop the VisualAge application development environment. The efforts of the JavaBeans teams (so called because they were working on the small components—or beans—of the application) significantly benefited IBM. The cost of the offshore sites was only 10 percent of the cost of such activities in North America. The teams were able to reduce the time from conception to market from three months to less than a month. In addition, IBM was able to create a strong presence in each of the emerging markets in which members of the team were operating and to develop a strong base of computer expertise.

Proximity to and Greater Understanding of Local Customers

The most successful global corporations are those that are sensitive to local situations, those that have "glocalized," or have developed a global reach but a local touch. Such companies appreciate the value of gathering information through face-to-face interactions and building stronger relationships with suppliers and customers, thereby designing more culturally sensitive products and processes. Since members of global teams are located at the company's various manufacturing and/or marketing sites, decisions are made by people who have greater proximity to and understanding of the organization's customers. Local people who serve as global team members bring an understanding of and sensitivity to workers and customers in their part of the world—buying habits, cultural consumer practices, motivational strategies that are most likely to succeed, and management attributes that are effective in the local environment.

The increased creativity and flexibility generated by multicultural teams can prove invaluable in addressing culturally distinct clients and environments. Thus global teams are able to create global strategies that are more sensitive to local requirements and to the demands of different countries' market structures, consumer preferences, and political and legal systems.

Pfizer. Pfizer has launched twenty new global teams in Canada, Latin America, Asia, Europe, and Africa–Middle East to work on product issues and improve customer service. Plans are underway to establish a Center of Excellence for Global Teams to expand the company's use of global teams and identify new ways to cross-pollinate and leverage resources across country borders and organizational functions. As a result, Pfizer is successfully changing both its infrastructure and its institutional culture.

Development of Future Global Leaders and Professionals for the Organization

Global teams provide a wonderful opportunity to develop the people that global companies need. As Snell et al. (1998) note, "If a company wishes to select, retain, and develop exceptional employees in multiple parts of the world—particularly in professional and managerial ranks—then it must establish vehicles by which the employees' current talents are fully tapped, as well as ways to enhance the employees' capacity for making future contributions to the company" (p. 200).

Such human resource development is especially important for employees located at sites away from headquarters. Few things are as frustrating to a talented, ambitious, midlevel manager as being treated as a "local nobody" who is allowed to make contributions only to operations in his or her own country while the most important strategic or innovative endeavors and matters of global significance remain the purview of people in the headquarters country. With the presence of global teams, however, the company greatly increases opportunities to utilize and develop these talented individuals. Employees with demonstrated aptitudes for working in global teams can work on company-wide issues and be seen as future "shining stars." Hamel and Prahalad (1994) believe that the use of global teams in building the human resources of a company will be among the "critical capabilities needed for companies to prosper" in the 21st century.

Ernst & Young. Ernst & Young is one of many companies (others include General Electric, Unilever, General Motors, and Marriott) that see membership in global teams as a key tool in building future global leaders. Like many global consulting firms, Ernst & Young needs to attract, develop, and retain high-performing leaders. For example, a global team was formed to look at best practices across countries for recruitment and retention in the Ernst & Young community. Members of such teams are quickly becoming new global leaders for Ernst & Young.

Increased Access to Knowledge and Information Resources

Information and knowledge have become the most important part of an organization's competitive advantage (Sveiby, 1997; Stewart, 1997). According to leading futurists and business leaders, we have entered the knowledge era; the new economy is a knowledge economy. Knowledge provides the key raw material for wealth creation and is the fountain of organizational and personal power. Knowledge has become more important for organizations than financial resources, market position, technology, or any other company asset. Knowledge is thus the main resource used in performing work in an organization. The organization's traditions, culture, technology, operations, systems, and procedures are all based on knowledge and expertise.

Organizations with the most information (about new technologies, customers, sources of best employees, political events, etc.) generally make better decisions and produce better products and services.

Global companies, therefore, deliberately establish a presence via global teams in countries that are major sources of industry innovation and have prestigious, high-quality universities. Global companies seek to locate near Cambridge, Silicon Valley, or Singapore so they can gain more direct access to the many sources of innovation present in those locations. Such access includes opportunities for face-to-face contacts with university researchers, participation in technical and professional conferences, quicker access to publications (e.g., many scientific journals are published only in Japanese and circulate little outside the country), and recruitment of the best local minds.

General Motors University.   General Motors University (GMU) is assisted by a global team with members from Singapore, Zurich, São Paulo, and Detroit, allowing the team to be knowledgeable about the latest training and learning resources in all parts of the world. The global team has achieved a number of successes, including the globalization of all courseware. A number of courses have been made available on the GMU intranet, both in English and the local language. A global sourcing process has been developed that includes the bid-soliciting and negotiation process. Training has moved from a North America focus to a global focus, and an increasing number of worldwide distance learning programs are available.

More Opportunities to Form Alliances and Partnerships

Members of global teams may be composed of employees of other organizations, particularly partner companies that contribute to the primary organization's specific activities. Global companies with global teams have greater choices for alliances and partnerships and are more attractive to prospective suitors. Global teams can create opportunities to extend each partner's global reach while contributing to each partner's local competence.

The presence of local team members allows these partners and alliances to better compete in the local market, due to convenience, proximity, and greater levels of trust. Such global alliances and partnerships provide innumerable advantages for the global company, including:

- Combining physical and human resources
- Sharing capital, equipment, and information
- Gaining easier and greater market access

Whirlpool.   Several years ago, Whirlpool acquired the $2 billion appliance division of Philips, headquartered in the Netherlands. In one fell swoop Whirlpool had gone from an almost exclusively domestic company to a 40 percent–global corporation and, in the process, had become the largest household appliances company in the world. Whirlpool quickly perceived the significance of becoming a global company. Impressive amounts of learning would be needed if the company were to adapt and transform itself to compete successfully for customers in the new global environment. And Whirlpool had a long way to go—many of its senior U.S. managers didn't even have passports. Integrating the American and Dutch companies would not be easy.

CEO Dave Whitwam asked the human resources staff to develop global teams to work on policies and programs to help the company globalize.

Within six months of the acquisition, Whirlpool brought 150 of its senior managers from sixteen countries to Montreux, Switzerland, for a one-week global conference.

Encouraging cultural mixing among the 150 managers was deemed crucial for active learning to take place. The typical behavior of international managers gravitating toward their own "cultural cocoons" was avoided by planning activities and events that pushed managers beyond their own national backgrounds and people of their own language. The conference's well-planned structure freed the managers to be creative, reflective, and open to new possibilities. Participants were encouraged to meet, get to know and trust, work with, and learn from their new global colleagues. Together they could better focus on critical, challenging issues such as the Whirlpool vision, strategic planning, and quality.

One element that spurred powerful learning among the global participants was the conference's "ground rules." Attendees were encouraged to be active themselves and to help others participate, as well, in both the meetings and informal activities. The guidelines challenged them to break out of their comfort zones.

During the weeklong event, managers were invited to identify which major areas of the company's operations could be improved. From an original list of two hundred, fifteen key issues were identified. Each issue became one of Whirlpool's One-Company Challenges. The challenges ranged from global management reporting systems, to global quality initiatives, to development of a global corporate talent pool, to consumer product delivery cycles. Fifteen cross-functional global teams, called "Whirlpool One-Company Challenge Teams," were then formed to examine these fifteen topics and present their recommendations at the following global conference in Washington, D.C. Team members met regularly and reported their progress in *The Leading Edge*, the corporate newsletter for Whirlpool's worldwide leaders.

The learning and change that these global teams generated were so significant that Whirlpool executives felt the process vaulted the company ahead by three to five years in the integration of its global management team and also saved the company millions of dollars in the process. It was at this conference that the vision of a global learning company and the values of "commitment to people"—all people—began to emerge at Whirlpool.

Increased Ability to Become a Global Learning Organization

Global companies have greater requirements, opportunities, and resources for acquiring, creating, storing, transferring, applying, and testing knowledge—

the essence of a learning organization. The cultural synergy, demands of global customers, and challenges of global competition compel the organization to learn faster and continuously. Every employee needs to be a learner; every occasion needs to be a learning opportunity. Learning is necessary on an organization-wide basis and is tied closely with the company's business goals. High-quality learners, customer demand for constant innovation, and cultural diversity all push global companies to become learning organizations.

Global teams offer the richest resource for organizations to acquire the ability to learn how to learn, to gather and store knowledge about the global market, and to distribute that information to people in all parts of the company so that they may use it—in short, to become a global learning organization (Marquardt and Reynolds, 1994).

British Petroleum.   British Petroleum CEO Sir John Browne has long recognized that competition in the global marketplace has made efficiency and innovation necessary for continuing company success. BP needed to become a global learning organization. Browne has therefore sought to help BP combine the agility of a small company with the resources of a large one. Browne quickly determined that a key strategy for building the new BP was to use technology and global teams. In 1994, he launched the Global Virtual Teamwork Program, whose purpose was to develop effective ways for team members in different locations around the world to collaborate. The primary aim of the initiative was to let knowledgeable people talk to each other and to capture their expertise. BP wanted to build a network of learning people, not just a storehouse of data, information, or knowledge.

The global teams were taught how to use the technology to further their work. Members communicated with each other using virtual teamwork (VT) stations, an ongoing real-life demonstration of the system's value as a tool for collaborative work and knowledge exchange. Project team members were encouraged to discover untapped potential in themselves and the system and to build organization-wide learning. Only 20 percent of the technology coach's time was designated for assisting the team in how to use the system. The rest was devoted to helping team members link their business objectives to the capabilities of the system and challenging them to consider the new ways of working that the VT system made possible (Davenport and Prusa, 1998).

One of the numerous team successes occurred one day in 1995 when equipment failure brought operations to a halt on a North Sea mobile drilling ship. The ship's drilling engineers hauled the faulty hardware in front of a tiny video camera connected to one of BP's virtual teamwork stations. Using a satellite link, they dialed up the Aberdeen office of a drilling equipment expert, who visually examined the malfunctioning part while talking to the shipboard engineers. He quickly diagnosed the problem and guided them through the necessary repairs. In the past, a shutdown of this kind would have necessitated flying an expert out by helicopter or sending the ships back to port and out of commission for several days (costing $150,000 per day). This shutdown lasted only a few hours.

Another success is Andrew Project, a joint endeavor among BP, Brown and Root (a Houston-based design and engineering firm), and Trafalgar House (a construction company based in Scotland) to build a new oil platform in the North Sea. Andrew Project team members took advantage of the application-sharing feature of the VT clients to write joint memos in just ten or fifteen minutes that previously had involved hours or days by mail. Virtual meetings and virtual work sharing led to quantifiable benefits on the Andrew Project, including significant reductions in travel costs and expenses associated with bringing vendors on site. There were also measurable productivity improvements related to more efficient information searches and issue resolution and reductions in duplication of effort and wasted travel time. Virtual teamwork contributed significantly to the project's meeting its target date, lowering offshore costs, and greatly reducing the total cost to bring forward first oil, a key milestone in the development of a new field.

BP uses global teams not only to increase incremental efficiencies but also to improve the way work is done in the organization. The company is using teams to build its knowledge base and develop a repository of solutions to frequently encountered problems. The company believes that the combination of technology and coaching will lead to an ever more collaborative culture of executive decisionmaking across the organization and will help build a successful global learning organization.

Challenges for Global Teams

The impact and value of these ten sources of power attained via global teams should compel every organization to quickly and systematically establish global teams. The company's future success, if not survival, depends on building effective global teams. However, creating and maintaining global teams is a difficult, complex task that requires the assistance of global HRD professionals.

HRD in Public and Nonprofit Global Organizations

Education is a human right with immense power to transform. On its foundation rest the cornerstones of freedom, democracy, and sustainable human development. . . . Knowledge is power. Information is liberating. Education is the premise of progress, in every society, in every family.

Kofi Annan,
secretary-general of the United Nations

Introduction

Kofi Annan delivers a powerful message about the primary importance of learning opportunities for all people. A major purpose of HRD is to increase the capacity of people to lead productive, complete, and fulfilling lives, regardless of where they live and work. As a result of globalization HRD professionals play an even more critical role than before in global nonprofit and public development organizations. The challenges we face in an interconnected world are testing the limits of our HRD skills and expertise, and HRD professionals have more and more opportunities to make valuable contributions to world development. This chapter explores HRD initiatives in several prominent organizations in the global public and non-profit sectors.

Value

Learning about the HRD activities of international public and nonprofit development organizations can increase the HRD practitioner's understanding of the vital contributions of these organizations to the economic and social growth of developing nations. An understanding of the resources of global associations enables one to identify those that might benefit one's professional development most, as well as provide opportunities to contribute to human development worldwide.

Goals of Global Public and Nonprofit Organizations

The first truly global organizations were the public ones that emerged after the devastation of World Wars I and II, such as the League of Nations, created in 1920, the precursor to the United Nations. In general terms the focus of these organizations was to accomplish one or more of the following goals:

- Build a more peaceful, secure world
- Strengthen international law
- Exchange information to better implement the programs of national and local organizations
- Share both human and financial resources to solve international problems and provide relief

These public organizations, both governmental and nongovernmental, have continued their focus on the development of people and nations around the world, especially in developing countries and those recovering from natural disasters or wars. This chapter discusses three categories of global organizations: public intergovernmental organizations, private voluntary organizations, and professional associations related to HRD.

Global Intergovernmental Organizations

United Nations Development Programme (UNDP)

Most United Nations agencies and departments use training as an important tool in international development. As the UN's global development network, the United Nations Development Programme works on the ground in 166 countries to develop and share solutions in a variety of problem areas.

At the UN Millennium Summit in 2000, world leaders agreed on specific targets for worldwide development, known as the UN Millennium Development Goals (MDG). These include eight main priorities:

- Eradicate extreme poverty and hunger
- Achieve universal primary education
- Promote gender equality and empower women
- Reduce child mortality
- Improve maternal health
- Combat HIV/AIDS, malaria, and other diseases
- Ensure environmental sustainability
- Develop a global partnership for development

UNDP is charged with leading joint aid and assistance efforts within the UN system to raise awareness of, track, and meet these goals. At the same time, it connects countries to the knowledge and resources they need to achieve these goals. UNDP works with thousands of development projects around the globe, focusing on democratic governance, poverty reduction, crisis prevention and recovery, energy and environment, information and communications technology, and HIV/AIDS. Some examples of its projects include:

Democratic governance: In Bangladesh UNDP trained 1.8 million election officials and law enforcement officers; educated voters through posters, interviews, and news bulletins on television and radio; and trained women and other marginalized groups about elections.

Information and communications technology: In Guyana, one of the last South American countries to connect to the Internet, UNDP trained and assisted public officials to use e-mail and the Internet and helped build Web sites to allow quicker and easier public access to governmental information.

Crisis prevention and recovery: UNDP, in partnership with UK-based Cranfield University, implemented training courses to develop the management skills of senior and midlevel managers for the national land mine action program, a small part of UNDP's larger land mine initiative.

Energy and environment: UNDP established the Dryland Development Knowledge and Learning Network, a Web site using a variety of formats to share best practices and ideas and increase the number of partnerships and encourage innovation in the sustainable development of desert and drought-stricken regions.

HIV/AIDS: UNDP implemented leadership development training programs for key leaders in government, civil society, and the private sector in Cambodia, Ethiopia, South Africa, Swaziland, and Ukraine.

World Bank Institute (WBI)

The World Bank Institute, the learning branch of the World Bank, is the world's largest source of development assistance. WBI reinforces the bank's anti-poverty efforts in the developing world by providing access to the bank's worldwide expertise and experience. Its services include learning programs, policy consultations, knowledge networks, and scholarship programs.

The institute trains leaders, decisionmakers, and others to develop and implement policies on poverty reduction, trade, environment, AIDS, corruption, education, health, and other important issues. WBI delivers nearly six hundred learning programs each year to 48,000 clients in more than 150 countries, awards about two hundred scholarships annually, and recruits more than one hundred interns annually for the World Bank's Knowledge Intern Program. Clients include government officials and policymakers, staff from nongovernmental organizations, journalists, academics, and other development specialists, as well as secondary school teachers and children and World Bank staff. The WBI also supports and utilizes the Global Development Learning Network, launched in 2000. Using high-speed communications technologies, this network links nearly fifty distance learning centers equipped with interactive videoconferencing and e-learning facilities.

International Labor Organization (ILO)

Created in 1919 and headquartered in Geneva, Switzerland, the International Labor Organization has over 160 member nations. Its main purpose is to seek the promotion of social justice and internationally recognized human and labor rights. Within this mandate the ILO sets minimal international labor standards and provides technical assistance in fields such as vocational training and rehabilitation, employment policy, labor administration, labor law and industrial relations, working conditions, management development, social security, labor statistics, and occupational safety and health.

The training arm of the ILO is the International Training Center (ITC) in Turin, Italy. Working toward the ILO's goals, the ITC develops and delivers instruction in a variety of formats on global workforce issues. During the past four decades, it has trained over 80,000 people from 172 countries. Course topics include international labor standards and human rights, enterprise development, management of development, distance education and learning technology applications, and many more. In addition to training courses the ITC produces a wide variety of print, online, and multimedia training materials. Its Documentation Center lends materials from its collections, which include over 14,000 books, reports, and documents, as well as videos, microfilm articles, and CD-ROMS.

Through the InFocus Programme on Skills, Knowledge and Employability, the ILO seeks to promote investment in skills and training so that both men and women have better and more equal opportunities to find productive, decent work. In many regions this assistance is critical to improving and sustaining individuals' productivity and income earning at work. The program helps improve training policies and programs, with special emphasis on training approaches that support the integration of groups disadvantaged in the labor market.

United Nations Industrial Development Organization (UNIDO)

The United Nations Industrial Development Organization, headquartered in Vienna, Austria, provides technical assistance and promotes the industrial development of developing countries, newly industrialized countries, and countries with economies in transition. For more than thirty years, UNIDO has worked with governments, business associations, and individual companies to solve industrial problems and to better equip them to be self-sustaining. Its member states include more than 170 nations.

One of UNIDO's main objectives is to generate and disseminate knowledge about a variety of industrial development issues. In this role, it serves as a global forum for enhancing cooperation and dialogue and encouraging partnerships across public, private, governmental, and policymaking sectors worldwide. UNIDO's second objective is to serve as a technical cooperation agency, designing and implementing programs to support its clients' industrial development efforts. Integrated solutions including training, technical assistance, and other components are the main vehicle for providing technical assistance.

UNIDO provides a variety of information services—including publications such as its *Industrial Development Report*, a weekly electronic newsletter; *UNIDOScope*; and the *UNIDO Exchange*, a business intelligence network tool. UNIDO's contributions are considerable—during 2002 UNIDO's technical cooperation programs and projects, found in every region of the world, totaled about US$81.8 million.

International Project on Technical and Vocational Education (UNEVOC)

Established in 2000, the International Project on Technical and Vocational Education (UNEVOC) of UNESCO (UN Educational, Social, and Cultural Organization) is committed to the development of technical and vocational education and training within UNESCO's member states. UNESCO-UNEVOC focuses on networking, exchanging information, and improving international cooperation. Its base of operations is the International Centre for Technical and Vocational Education and Training, in Bonn, Germany.

UNEVOC's first major focus was to improve technical and vocational education and training in southern Africa. This effort was launched with a conference in Gaborone, Botswana, entitled "Learning for Life, Work and the Future: Stimulating Reform in Southern Africa through Sub-regional Cooperation," which resulted in eight subregional project proposals in technical and vocational education and training in southern Africa. Similar workshops were held in 2002 in the Middle East and Asia. In addition, UNESCO-UNEVOC has sponsored focus groups, outreach programs, conferences, and workshops in Wales, Canada, Thailand, Finland, Tanzania, Germany, South Korea, Mauritius, Lebanon, and other global sites.

UNEVOC also has developed and sponsors an e-mail forum, *E-Forum*, to provide a place for the virtual exchange of information and experience in technical and vocational education worldwide. This forum is a free service to educators, researchers, and practitioners with an interest in international technical and vocational education and training, and its archives are also available free on the UNEVOC Web site. Additional news and information are disseminated through its periodic electronic *Bulletin*, also available at the UNEVOC Web site.

Private Global Voluntary Organizations

World Education

For over five decades World Education has provided training and technical assistance in a variety of sectors to more than fifty countries in Asia, Africa, and Latin America, as well as in the United States, often in partnership with other international organizations. To increase local autonomy, World Education partners with local stakeholders to plan and implement their programs. The organization strives to build and enhance the assets of individuals, communities, local institutions, and societies, including health, verbal, and mathematical literacy; business and civic participation skills; and access to credit.

Recent World Education training projects have included:

- Train-the-trainer programs in Cambodia in various technical sectors such as health education, sustainable agriculture, human rights work, community development, and project and organizational management;
- Vocational training in Tibet in order to provide participants with new, employable skills;
- Integrated reproductive health and literacy activities in Egypt designed to train and mentor literacy facilitators and supervisors who in turn teach an estimated 8,850 women learners throughout Egypt;
- Building the capacity of local microfinance and microenterprise organizations in Guineau-Bissau through technical assistance and training.

International Federation of Red Cross and Red Crescent Societies

The International Federation of Red Cross and Red Crescent Societies was founded in 1919 in Paris in the aftermath of World War I to coordinate the work of various Red Cross societies in order to provide humanitarian relief for prisoners of war and combatants. Since that time the federation has grown from the five founding member societies to 178 recognized national societies. Its programs focus on three main priorities: promotion of humanitarian principles and values, disaster preparedness and response, and community health education and services.

HRD-related initiatives are vital to accomplishing the federation's goals. One of its tasks is to encourage cooperation and learning among the member societies through regional meetings, workshops, specialized networks, and other learning strategies. Building the capacities of volunteers, trainers, and managers is also vital to strengthening national societies, as illustrated by the following examples of recent projects:

- Training in logistics, water sanitation, and other critical relief techniques for thirty-one English-speaking national members of West African regional disaster response teams
- Training for emergency preparedness and response teams in Argentina and Panama
- Distribution of informational brochures, cards, videos, and billboards, as well as providing training programs for volunteers and trainers to help prevent SARS throughout East Asia

World Rehabilitation Fund (WRF)

Founded in 1955, the World Rehabilitation Fund was one of the earliest organizations to develop and implement rehabilitation programs worldwide for people with disabilities. WRF focuses on all aspects of rehabilitation, from time of injury through the individual's socioeconomic reintegration. Training and education activities are among its priorities, including:

- Improving the skills of rehabilitation service providers (physicians, therapists, health promoters, nurses, social workers, and vocational rehabilitation specialists);
- Training professionals throughout the world in the fabrication and fitting of artificial limbs, braces, and other assistive technologies;
- Partnering with industry to enhance vocational training, job readiness, and job placement programs.

An issue of special interest to WRF is the rehabilitation of victims of land mines throughout the world.

Lebanon.   Since the 1970s, WRF has helped improve rehabilitation services in Lebanon. Examples of its projects include land mine awareness programs, assistance to individuals with disabilities in developing small businesses, and aid to land mine survivors and others with disabilities in South Lebanon through the development of small-business and agribusiness enterprises to increase economic independence. WRF also offers basic education, counseling, and mentoring to adolescents, especially girls, who have been affected by land mines.

Cambodia.   In partnership with the UNDP and ILO, the WRF has introduced a Business Advisory Council model to help employers in placing and training people with disabilities. This effort has resulted in at least 150 job placements for land mine survivors and others with disabilities as accountants, customer service representatives, garment factory workers, administrative assistants, and computer operators.

Sierra Leone.   In this war-torn nation the UNDP and WRF are focusing on the rehabilitation and reintegration of women and girls abused during wars. Efforts include counseling combined with vocational training in day care management, the vanishing skill of fish salting, hat and logo design, and agricultural methods.

ProLiteracy Worldwide

Formed in 2002 with the merger of Laubach Literacy International and Literacy Volunteers of America, Inc., ProLiteracy Worldwide is active in forty-two countries and supports a global network of eighty-two local partner programs. Its programs serve more than 350,000 new adult learners around the world each year. The organization's purpose is to sponsor educational programs and services to help adults and their families gain the literacy skills they need to function more effectively in their daily lives while participating in societal transformation. In addition to providing educational programs, ProLiteracy works to raise public awareness of adult literacy issues and to influence public policy and funding.

ProLiteracy provides training, technical assistance, and grants to communities to create programs that combine literacy and other social issues such as sustainable development, human rights, health, peace, and education. For example, ProLiteracy is partnering with corporate and nonprofit organizations to expand a literacy and AIDS campaign in Africa designed to train individuals in local schools, churches, and other community institutions in Uganda, Tanzania, Kenya, Ethiopia, Malawi, South Africa, Zimbabwe, and Ghana. Its programs focus on information, prevention, treatment, and control of AIDS through training in literacy, family planning, health education, civil and political rights education, and other important topics. ProLiteracy's methodology of using literacy for social change is also the foundation for projects in China, Cambodia, the Philippines, Afghanistan, and other locations.

Global HRD Associations

*International Federation of Training
and Development Organizations (IFTDO)*

Founded in Switzerland in 1972, the International Federation of Training and Development Organizations now consists of 150 member organizations representing 500,000 training and development professionals in fifty countries. IFTDO members include national HRD and training and development organizations, human resource management (HRM) associations, government agencies, universities, consulting firms, nongovernmental organizations (NGOs), and other nonprofit associations. A brief sampling of the member organizations includes the Bahrain International Retail Development Center, Korea Labor Education Institute, Dutch Training and

Development Association, Australian Institute of Training and Development, Finnish Association for HRM, and Industrial and Vocational Training Development Board of Mauritius. IFTDO has special consultative status with the Economic and Social Council of the United Nations and is an accredited NGO with the UN Department of Public Information in New York and the ILO in Geneva, thus enabling members' voices to be heard by international policymakers influencing outcomes in human development.

IFTDO's general purpose is to improve the field of HRD throughout the world, as by assisting the formation of new national HRD organizations and sponsoring an annual training and development conference. Past conferences have been held in Geneva, Dublin, Rio de Janeiro, Manila, Mexico City, Sydney, Amsterdam, Stockholm, Madrid, and New Delhi.

International Society for Intercultural Education, Training, and Research (SIETAR)

Founded in 1974, the International Society for Intercultural Education, Training, and Research is a global organization with more than 3,000 members worldwide. It is made up of a network of regional and local SIETAR groups with an administrative "hub" in Brussels, Belgium. Its main purpose is to "encourage and support the development and application of values, knowledge, and skills that promote and reinforce beneficial and long-lasting intercultural and inter-ethnic relations at the individual, group, organization, and community levels."

SIETAR is affiliated with the Council of Europe and holds NGO status with the United Nations. Its members can attend the annual UN-NGO conference in New York City as both a learning opportunity and a chance to voice their views. Regional groups also hold annual conferences to provide members the opportunity to network and share the latest information and research in HRD.

International Council for Open and Distance Education (ICDE)

Founded in 1938 to help provide education for students and children living far away from schools, the International Council for Open and Distance Education has developed into a global membership organization consisting of educational institutions, national and regional associations, corporations, educational authorities, and agencies in the fields of open learning, distance education, and flexible, lifelong learning. Although supported by the government of Norway, it now comprises members in 142 countries and represents the world's leading network of expertise and experience in distance education.

ICDE embraces research as a powerful tool for informing practice. The organization considers research and engagement a critical factor in developing quality open and distance learning institutions and products and a focus that distinguishes this organization from many online or virtual institutions that have little understanding of pedagogy, andragogy (adult learning), or inquiry.

The results of ICDE activities are most evident during its world conferences. Almost every two years since 1938, ICDE has been organizing World Conferences on Open and Distance Education. These conferences are major events, offering diverse presentations on issues related to open and distance education in all parts of the world.

ICDE is officially recognized by the United Nations as the global NGO responsible for the field of open and distance learning and is affiliated with the UN through UNESCO. ICDE is also an affiliate member of Southeast Asian Ministers of Education Organization (SEAMEO) and is a World Bank partner organization.

International Council for Educational Media (ICEM)

A nonprofit nongovernmental organization, ICEM has been active in the field of educational technology for over fifty years. Its members include both individuals and organizations representing over thirty nations, and it is an NGO affiliate of UNESCO. Among its objectives is to facilitate an international exchange and evaluation of information, experience, and materials about educational media for all levels, preschool through adult education. ICEM also cooperates with other international organizations to develop and apply educational technology.

ICEM's activities include an annual international conference, sponsorship of an annual international student media development contest, and publication of a quarterly journal, *Educational Media International (EMI)*, that publishes academic papers and articles about a wide range of educational media topics.

Summary

In the past sixty years, global public and nonprofit organizations have taken on an increasingly important role in supporting the social, economic, political, and educational growth of people around the world, particularly in less developed regions. Three types of public and nonprofit organizations support HRD initiatives globally: (1) global intergovernmental organizations, (2) private voluntary organizations working worldwide, and (3) global HRD associations.

Major public intergovernmental organizations include the United Nations Development Programme (UNDP); the World Bank Institute (WBI); the International Labor Organization (ILO); and the International Centre for Technical and Vocational Education and Training (UNEVOC), which is a part of the United Nations Educational, Scientific, and Cultural Organization (UNESCO). These and many other institutions provide direct government-to-government support of efforts to strengthen the structures of developing nations, establish labor standards, and transfer knowledge and technologies needed in the development process.

In addition, hundreds of private voluntary organizations operate worldwide to improve the lives of millions of people. The International Federation of Red Cross and Red Crescent Societies, the World Rehabilitation Fund (WRF), and ProLiteracy Worldwide are examples of organizations providing successful HRD programs.

Global HRD associations include the International Federation of Training and Development Organizations (IFTDO); International Society for Intercultural Education, Training, and Research (SIETAR); International Council for Open and Distance Education (ICDE); and International Council for Educational Media (ICEM). These organizations provide a means for HRD professionals around the world to communicate information and best practices as they respond to new challenges and responsibilities.

HRD in Global Corporations

Whatever cause you champion, the cure does not lie in protesting against globalization itself. I believe the poor are poor not because of too much globalization, but because of too little.

Kofi Annan,
secretary-general of the United Nations

Global Companies—Forces for Good or Evil?

Global corporations are highly controversial. Proponents of globalization believe that global companies have made the world a better place, a world that will eventually lead to economic prosperity, political freedom, and world peace. Friedman (2001) argues that globalization is the result of the "democratization of finance, technology, and information, but what is driving all three of these is the basic human desire for a better life—a life with more freedom to choose how to prosper, what to eat, what to wear, where to live, where to travel, how to work, what to read, what to write, and what to learn." In a globalized world ideas, people, values, and systems move freely across the globe.

Opponents of global companies, on the other hand, look at these organizations with hostility, even fear, believing that they increase inequality within and between nations, threaten living standards, and thwart social progress; that the benefits of globalization are reaped by only a few organizations from the richest countries in the West; and that there is no accountability in the

process. Scarce natural resources are being exploited for the benefit of the industrialized economies and at the expense of future generations.

Critical Need for HRD in Global Companies

Although there may exist vast differences of opinion as to the benefits or
detriments generated by global companies, there appears to be very little dispute on the inevitability of the forward growth of global companies. Thus
human resource development professionals have a responsibility to step in
and take the leadership role to ensure that globalization has a human face
with long-term benefits for all of humanity. The ultimate success of global
companies depends upon utilizing the resources and diverse talents and capabilities of the broadest possible spectrum of humanity.

The key attraction created by global companies, according to Micklethwait
and Wooldridge (2000), is freedom. People bemoan restrictions on where
they can go, what they can buy, where they can invest, and what they can
read, hear, or see. Humanized global companies can bring down these barriers and help to hand the power to choose to the individual. Global markets
create competition that yields better goods and services at better prices. People all over the world can have opportunities and better-paying jobs that
never existed in economies closed to global organizations.

Corporate Evolution to Global Status

Organizations typically go through four distinct, progressively more complex phases as they evolve toward global status: (1) domestic, (2) international, (3) multinational/multiregional, and (4) global. Each of these stages
(and types of companies in these stages) has a particular philosophy and way
of operating (see Table 10.1).

Domestic

Historically, all companies were domestic—producing and selling their products and services within a single country. Going outside the domestic market
was neither necessary nor, in most cases, even possible because of costs, vastly
different consumer values and needs in other countries, the limited availability
of appropriate currency, and so forth. Many companies remain in phase I. Such
companies operate on domestic terms and focus solely on domestic markets.
They emphasize either product or service, and technology they use is highly
proprietary and protected. The companies perceive themselves as having rela-

TABLE 10.1   Journey from Domestic to Global Status

Corporate activities	Phase I: Domestic	Phase II: International	Phase III: Multinational	Phase IV: Global
Competitive strategy	Domestic	Multidomestic	Multinational	Global
Product/ service	New, unique	More standardization	Completely standardized (commodity)	Mass-customized
	Product engineering emphasized	Process engineering emphasized	Engineering not emphasized	Product & process engineering
Competitors	None	Few	Many	Significant (few or many)
Market	Small, domestic	Large, multidomestic	Larger, Multinational	Largest, global
Production location	Domestic	Domestic & primary markets	Multinational, least cost	Global, least cost
Structure	Functional divisions	Functional with international division	Multinational lines of business	Global alliance
	Centralized	Decentralized	Centralized	Centralized & decentralized
Cultural Sensitivity	Unimportant	Very important	Somewhat important	Critically important
With whom	No one	Clients	Employees	Employees & clients
Level	No one	Workers & Clients	Managers	Executives

tively few competitors and are structurally centralized. As their perspective is generally ethnocentric, cultural sensitivity is relatively unimportant.

International

International, or phase II, companies export their products or services abroad or import raw materials needed for manufacturing. Usually in such companies only a small group of expatriate managers are involved directly in foreign operations. Structurally, the company is decentralized and often forms a single international division for its foreign operations. The corporate strategy is multidomestic. Cultural sensitivity begins to be more important. International organizations are typically ethnocentric, or home-country oriented. Operations center around a domestic headquarters, and home-country nationals are recruited, trained, and transported for international positions. Foreign managers and employees are typically overlooked and underestimated. Ethnocentrism may be due to biases of owners and stockholders, the influence of labor unions, or government emphasis on domestic markets. International companies have difficulty communicating in different languages or accepting cultural differences.

Multinational/Multiregional

In phase III, the multinational/multiregional stage, companies focus on least-cost production with sourcing, manufacturing, and marketing worldwide. The parent company operates with a centralized view of strategy, technology, and resource allocation, but decisionmaking and customer service shift to the national level for marketing, selling, manufacturing, and competitive tactics. There are many competitors, and profit margins are low. Products and services are standardized, and the primary orientation is price.

The headquarters is run by home-country nationals, while local nationals run their respective local subsidiaries. The organization recognizes profit potential in foreign markets, but because it does not understand how they function, it leaves local managers to run the operations. These local foreign nationals have little to no chance of receiving senior positions at headquarters.

The multinational enterprise shows more diversity in culture and organizational structure. Its headquarters is less important than a phase II organization's, and each national/regional operation has more autonomy for operational decisions. Business processes and technology are based less on a "one size fits all" approach than on local standards or optimization of local cost drivers. Headquarters provides guidance regarding policies but permits great local discretion. At the multinational phase, the company usually functions on the idea that "local people know what is best for them."

The multiregional organization is very similar to the multinational company but implements some of the linking and leverage characteristics of a global company. Multiregional companies capitalize on the synergistic benefits of sharing common functions across regions. Each region has a headquarters, which organizes collaborative efforts among local subsidiaries and is responsible for implementing the plan provided by the world headquarters, as well as pursuing regionwide research and development (R&D), product innovation, executive selection and training, cash management, public relations, and so on. The world headquarters is in charge of world strategy, country analysis, basic R&D, foreign exchange, selection of top management, technology transfer, and establishing corporate culture.

Global

In the global phase (IV), the corporation operates without geographic boundaries. Global thinking and global competencies become critical for survival. The company is constantly scanning, organizing, and reorganizing its resources and capabilities, so that national or regional boundaries are not barriers to potential products, business opportunities, or manufacturing locations.

Companies send their best, fast-track managers and senior executives for global assignments. Cultural sensitivity and language skills become critically important. Products are mass-customized. Imports as well as exports are part of the company's operations for manufacturing and sales. There are globally coordinated strategies, global structures, and a global corporate culture. Global learning becomes essential to remain competitive. Developing a "think global, act local" mindset is integral to operations and interactions (Adler, 1991; Marquardt and Engel, 1993).

The truly global enterprise operates very differently from both the international and the multinational enterprise. While it may have roots in one culture, it has created an organizational culture that values diversity. A few core values are its major unifying force. Although it has a "headquarters," the global enterprise is often managed by a team of managers from diverse locations. Its business processes, policies, and technologies are often diverse, with the exception of a few rigidly standardized policies, often centered around communications technologies and training of the workforce. Examples of global enterprises can be found in the pharmaceutical industry, management consulting, and consumer packaged-goods industry.

Global organizations are geocentric, or world oriented, and maintain a highly interdependent system. *Their ultimate goal is creation of an integrated system with a worldwide approach.* The organization simultaneously focuses on both worldwide and local objectives, with collaboration between headquarters and subsidiaries to achieve universal standards with local variations. The leaders are diverse, as the most competent people are sought to fill positions regardless of nationality and are rewarded for meeting worldwide objectives. Unhindered by any geographical borders, resources and ideas flow through the organization freely. The global firm also overcomes political barriers by *turning its subsidiaries into good citizens of the host nations.* These companies also provide base countries with more hard currency, new skills, and the knowledge of advanced technology.

Global companies have globalized not only their operations and strategies but, equally important, their corporate culture and structure. They have also globalized their people and their learning. How companies globalize each of these areas will be explored in the remaining chapters of this book. Let us first look at how companies can determine their present status on the globalization curve.

Power of Global Companies

Companies that globalize link, leverage, move, and manipulate resources and provide superior services and products at low cost; such companies overwhelm their nonglobal competitors. Global firms increase exponentially their competitive edge as they acquire the best workers, produce the best products, and attract the best customers. Why do companies wish to globalize? And what benefits can an HRD professional provide to global companies? There are fifteen benefits that accrue to global organizations (see Table 10.2).

Ability to Reduce Costs

Global companies reduce the cost of their products and services as a result of (a) economies of scale, (b) economies of scope, and (c) focused production.

Economies of scale. A global approach to activity location can help exploit economies of scale by pooling production or other value-adding activities. Global benefits of manufacturing, for example, are generally greater in the commercial aircraft business than in the apparel business. Why? Because the minimum efficient production scale requires a much higher share of the global market in aircraft than it does in apparel (Yip, 1992, p. 16). Unlike multinational firms, global companies integrate production, marketing, and other activities from several countries or regions. The production of large volumes of computers, cars, or fruits can result in economies of scale, lowering the cost per item.

Economies of scope. A global concentration of activities can exploit economies of scope by spreading activities across multiple product lines or businesses. Such concentration also reduces duplication of activities by eliminating and consolidating identical activities from many countries into one or two globally centralized locations. For example, Unilever reduced the

TABLE 10.2   Power Sources of Global Organizations

1. **Ability to reduce costs**
2. **Ability to provide higher quality**
3. **Enhanced customer awareness and loyalty**
4. **Increased competitive leverage**
5. **Greater access to human skills and knowledge**
6. **Increased access to capital and other financial resources**
7. **Increased availability of information resources**
8. **Longer and more diversified use of equipment and technology**
9. **Broader customer base**
10. **Geographic flexibility**
11. **Enhanced bargaining power**
12. **Cultural synergies**
13. **Opportunity for alliances and partnerships**
14. **Enhanced image and reputation**
15. **Power as a global learning organization**

number of its soap factories in Europe from thirteen to three. Philips closed eighty factories to consolidate and reduce duplication. While a global approach to activity location results in fewer locations than a multinational approach, it may sometimes involve more locations and duplication than a purely export, or international, approach.

Global organizations can gain economies of scope over local competitors through lower costs, shorter delivery times, and/or broad assortments of standard products. Economies of scope are also obtained by:

- Gaining access to local, immobile factors of production and technological resources;
- Reducing transportation costs;
- Avoiding tariff and nontariff barriers;
- Satisfying demands of and gaining benefits from local governments;
- Hedging against country-specific risks;
- Preempting competition;
- Operating at full capacity in the various global locations; and
- Gaining steep learning and experience benefits.

Focused production.   Reducing the number of products manufactured from many local models/brands to a few global ones is another way global companies can reduce costs. Typically, unit costs drop as the number of different products made in a factory declines. This reduces duplication of development efforts as well as the costs of purchasing, production, and inventory. A company can gain cost advantages by increasing volume through globalization—achieving lower unit costs by running fewer plants worldwide, buying inputs from fewer suppliers, and reducing duplication in engineering.

Ability to Provide Higher Quality

Global companies are able to focus on a smaller number of products and programs than are multinational companies, especially in R&D and production. Concentration in R&D, for example, allows a company to devote greater resources to the projects undertaken. At the same time, a concerted R&D function can also be the center of a global network that taps selected skills and knowledge available in particular countries.

Global concentration of production allows investment in better facilities and equipment than can be afforded under a multinational approach. These superior assets can then produce higher-quality, lower-cost products. In highly globalized industries, combining high quality and low cost is particularly important because buyers have more choice as to what they can buy.

Another reason for superior quality in global companies is that they are forced to improve quality via exposure to worldwide customer demand and worldwide innovative competitors. Global focus on quality is one of the reasons for Japanese success in automobile manufacturing. Toyota markets a far smaller number of models around the world than does General Motors, even allowing for its unit sales being half those of General Motors. Toyota has concentrated on moving its few models, while General Motors has fragmented its development funds.

Enhanced Customer Awareness and Loyalty

The three complementary forces of global availability, global serviceability, and global recognition can enhance customer preference for a product by reinforcing its image. Yip (1992) refers to this global factor as "exposing customers to the same mix in different countries." Coca-Cola, McDonald's, and Pizza Hut are leading examples of how to build worldwide customer loyalty.

Financial service companies (via credit cards, ATM machines) and hotels also use this approach as they seek to reach the growing number of global travelers. Likewise, manufacturers of industrial products can provide supplies to a global customer (e.g., AMP supplying General Motors) with a standard product around the world.

Increased Competitive Leverage

Global companies achieve leverage over competitors by bringing the resources of the worldwide network to bear on the competitive situation in individual countries. Competitors that operate under an international or multinational approach are forced to deliver products and/or services that are provided by local facilities. Thus each subsidiary's competitive position depends on that subsidiary's own market share and revenues. A subsidiary that loses market share under competitive attack also loses the operating scale needed to maintain the best cost and quality advantages needed to defend its market position (as happened to Philips when its highly independent subsidiaries faced Japanese global strategies).

Greater Access to Human Skills and Knowledge

Global companies have access to the best people around the world, regardless of nationality. These people bring to the organization experiences and learning from their cultures, their best universities, and their best organizations. Often this high level of skill and knowledge is available at a much lower cost than in the United States or Western Europe. Russia, Eastern Europe, the Philippines, and India are sources of highly skilled, low-cost R&D workers for many global organizations. A local presence creates better opportunities to compete in the local job market.

Local people also bring an understanding and sensitivity to workers and customers in their part of the world—buying habits, cultural consumer practices, motivational factors that are most likely to succeed, and management attributes that are effective in the local environment. Global firms, such as Microsoft and General Electric, pride themselves on obtaining the highest-quality people from and for each country in which they operate.

Increased Access to Capital and Other Financial Resources

Global companies have much greater access to capital and other financial resources. They can be listed on multiple stock exchanges around the world— Hong Kong, Singapore, London, São Paulo, to name a few. This provides the opportunity to sell stock and raise capital from a greater array of sources. Operating on a global scale allows the company to hold several currencies and to buy, sell, and leverage with financial institutions around the world. It is able to deal more forcefully with global as well as local banks.

Increased Availability of Information Resources

Information is often an organization's competitive advantage. The organization with the most information (about new technologies, customers, sources of best employees, political happenings, etc.) generally makes better decisions and produces better products and/or services.

Global companies often deliberately establish a presence in countries that are a major source of industry innovation and have prestigious, high-quality universities. Such companies try to locate near Oxford, Silicon Valley, or Tokyo so they can gain more direct access to the many sources of innovation present in those locations, including face-to-face contact with university researchers, participation in technical and professional conferences, quicker access to publications (e.g., many Japanese scientific journals are published only in Japanese and circulate little outside the country), and a chance to hire the best local minds.

Longer and More Diversified Use of Equipment and Technology

Equipment and technology can be prohibitive in cost unless amortized over long periods of time and put to a wide array of uses. Global companies have the ability to earn additional income on existing technology and equipment due to their wider and greater possibilities for application. Technology, equipment, and products can be reused as additional countries and/or companies seek to benefit from the product or service created by the technology. (An analogy is the "format painter" in Microsoft Word that allows one to reapply in many other places what works well in one place.)

Flexible manufacturing via computer-assisted design and manufacturing (CAD/CAM) also make globalizing operations more feasible. Telecommunications technology, once the initial investments are made, often requires little or no additional expenditure as it is utilized at sites worldwide.

Broader Customer Base

Global companies have larger customer bases than other companies. They see the entire world as their marketplace. With the opening up of the economies of China, India, and Russia, another 2.5 billion people have become potential customers. Global companies are not heavily dependent on any one market. If the economy in one region falls or collapses (as happened in several Asian countries in 1997–1998), the organization can divert marketing efforts, subsidize prices or losses, and ameliorate expenses.

The broader customer base serves another important purpose for global firms: Having a larger multitude of consumers generally expands the number of consumers demanding improved and customized products and services. These demands force companies (especially their R&D units) to better understand present and future customer needs. For example, many firms have referred to the predictive advantage of attempting to meet the present demands of customers in California, who often are forerunners of what the rest of the United States will be expecting in the near future.

Geographic Flexibility

Global firms have much more geographic flexibility in determining where they will manufacture, carry out R&D, store supplies and products, and so on. They make choices based on a variety of factors such as the level of political stability, government policies toward foreign investment, trade policies, tax policies, legal factors, the macroeconomic environment, and policies on international payments. They choose locations that put them close to major global markets (thereby incurring lower costs for trans-shipment of raw materials and for intermediate and final products) or where costs of raw materials and highly skilled labor are low. A global manufacturing network also provides opportunities to set transfer prices and subsidiary remittances so as to minimize total tax liability.

Enhanced Bargaining Power

Global companies have the ability to switch production among multiple manufacturing sites and therefore enjoy enhanced bargaining power with suppliers, workers, and host governments. Global firms can also gain offensive and defensive advantages by having a presence in many markets, enabling them to retaliate against an attacker on its home ground. They also have more options to attack and counterattack competitors. Becton Dickinson, for example, a major American medical products company, decided to enter three markets in its Japanese competitor's backyard.

Cultural Synergies

Since global companies are located in and working with numerous cultures, they are able to "synergize" the strengths of these differing cultures. This diversity becomes a primary source of new ideas when innovation is needed.

Mobilizing the divergent energies of these various cultures can yield multiple perspectives and a wider range of options for and approaches to problems and challenges. This increased creativity and flexibility proves invaluable in addressing culturally distinct clients and partners.

Opportunity for Alliances and Partnerships

Global companies not only have greater choices for alliances and partnerships but also are much more attractive to prospective suitors. As Rosabeth Kanter (1995) eloquently states, "Globalization extends each partner's global reach while each contributes its local competence." Such global alliances and partnerships provide innumerable advantages for the global company, such as combining physical and human resources; sharing capital, equipment, and information; and gaining easier and greater market access.

Enhanced Image and Reputation

Global companies are perceived, deservedly or not, by the public as having better products and services because of their globality. The authors believe that they must be superior, or they would not be playing in the global arena. People who work for global enterprises are similarly perceived as "the cream of the crop" in terms of capability, compensation, opportunities, and fun (traveling to all those exciting places). An exalted reputation attracts a high caliber of worker that, in turn, creates high quality in products and services. In many countries products sell because of their global image—witness McDonald's in Moscow, Tommy Hilfiger in China, or Nike in urban America.

Power as a Global Learning Organization

Global companies have greater requirements, opportunities, and resources for acquiring, creating, storing, transferring, applying, and testing knowledge—the essence of a learning organization. The synergy of cultures, the demand of global customers, and the challenges of global competition compel the organization to learn faster and continuously. Every employee becomes a learner and every occasion a learning opportunity. Learning is mandated on an organization-wide basis and is tied closely with the company's business goals. High-quality learners, customer demand for constant innovation, and cultural diversity, all push global companies toward becoming learning organizations.

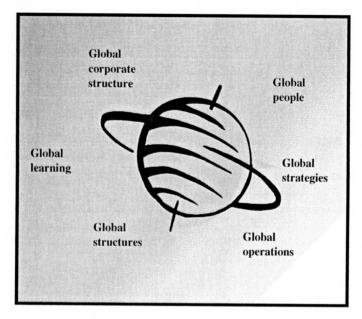

FIGURE 10.1   Global success model

How HRD Can Build Global Corporations

Despite the urgency and benefits of becoming a global organization, very few companies have succeeded thus far. Many may have globalized their structure and some of their corporate activities, but most firms are still far from making the changes necessary to create a true global organization—one with a global corporate culture, global people, global strategies, global operations, global structure, and global learning.

Marquardt (1999a) developed the GlobalSuccess Model, which has guided many HRD professionals in assisting companies as they move from national, to international, to multinational, to global status (see Figure 10.1). The GlobalSuccess Model enables organizations to develop six components.

Global Corporate Culture

Many global leaders as well as leading global theorists (Rhinesmith, 1996; Adler, 2002; Marquardt and Snyder, 1997; among others) believe creating a global corporate culture is both the most important and the most difficult aspect of globalization. Changing external factors (structure and operations) is easier than changing internal factors (people's values; the way they think, act, and react). Trying to transform someone's image of reality, helping someone to be a world citizen in spite of having a national identity, and persuading someone to adopt new heroes, another ideology, and new behaviors, all are immensely difficult. Yet a company must undergo these cultural changes if it is to incorporate and implement the other five dimensions of globality. The new corporate culture, like any culture—national, ethnic, or corporate—involves a new mindset, new values, new rituals and practices, new heroes and leaders. The GlobalSuccess Model's corporate culture component includes five dimensions: vision, mindset, values, activities, and heroes (see Figure 10.2).

Global vision.   A vision captures the organization's hopes, goals, and direction for the future. It is the image and dream that is transmitted inside and outside the organization. A global vision is borderless and multicultural, with links and leverages worldwide.

Global mindset.   A mindset is a predisposition that directs people to see the world in a particular way. It establishes boundaries and provides explanations for why things are the way they are while offering guidance for behavior; it is a filter through which we look at the world. With a global mindset one thinks and sees the world globally, is open to exchanging ideas and concepts across borders, is able to break down one's provincial ways of thinking. The global mindset balances global and local needs and operates cross-functionally, cross-divisionally, and cross-culturally around the world.

Global values.   Values are the deep, often subconscious part of culture, passed from present members to new members of a group. Values provide purpose and meaning for what one does. Global values include:

- Global thinking,
- Cultural sensitivity,
- Continuous learning,
- Cultural customization,
- Quality and continuous improvement,
- Speed and timeliness,
- Empowered global people,
- Meaningful work life.

Global activities.   All cultures comprise a variety of actions, rituals, events, activities, and norms that externalize and reinforce desired internal values,

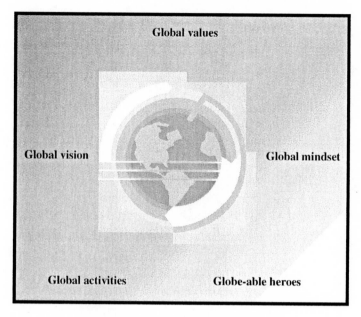

FIGURE 10.2   Global corporate culture

mindsets, and basic assumptions. Global companies undertake activities, such as global conferences and seminars, use of a global language (usually English), policies and procedures, and reward systems, to build the desired corporate culture.

Globe-able heroes.   Every culture has heroes, whose qualities and successes group members are encouraged to emulate. Global companies seek to identify existing heroes (mentors) and to build future heroes via mentoring, training, development, and teams (Marquardt and Berger, 2000).

Global People

The second component of the GlobalSuccess Model relates to the people in the organization. Global companies seek to identify, recruit, train, develop, provide global experiences for, celebrate, and retain the best people from around the world, no matter their location or cultural background. Employing the top global people and benefiting from their capabilities and their learning will result in better products and services and greater success. The GlobalSuccess Model contains six dimensions under the category of global people (see Figure 10.3).

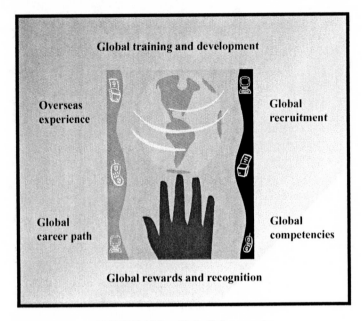

FIGURE 10.3   Globalizing people

Global competencies.   Organizations need to identify the capabilities, attitudes, and skills necessary for implementing their mission and goals. There are a number of special competencies for workers of global companies, including cultural self-awareness, global perspectives, language, tolerance for ambiguity and differences, cultural flexibility, and strong communication skills.

Global recruitment.   Global companies search worldwide for the best people, using global and local recruiting firms. Recruitment and hiring policies reflect local customs and laws and are sensitive to the appropriateness of questions. Local and third-country nationals as well as expatriates are welcomed in the applicant pool.

Global training and development.   A company's ability to compete globally depends heavily on the quality and level of global training in the organization. Training and career development strategies include the following:

- Connection of business goals to training
- Creation of a global training mission
- Examination of internal and external factors and resources related to global training

- Identification of training goals and objectives
- Identification of action steps to accomplish the organization's learning needs
- Development of an evaluation system to assess the impact of and needed changes to training and development strategies

Overseas experience. In global companies overseas experience is essential to the development of global employees. Ideally such experience should:

- Be seen as an integral part of career development and a valued assignment,
- Be built upon solid selection criteria,
- Include extensive predeparture as well as ongoing training,
- Recognize the importance of the employee's family,
- Ensure ongoing communications and support, and
- Include a plan for repatriation.

Global career path. Retention of high-quality global workers and managers is much more difficult in the global arena. Yet globality requires identifying future leaders and providing them the career opportunities and experiences needed for individual and corporate success. Employees should have career tracks that feature planned sequences of global career assignments, linked to the company's global business needs.

Global rewards and recognition. Global companies need to expand their capacity for recognizing workers' achievements and successes. Performance appraisal systems and reward mechanisms must be globalized as well as localized to accommodate corporate and cultural differences among employees.

Global Strategies

Global strategy goes beyond developing a core business strategy (products, customers, geographic markets served, major sources of sustainable competitive advantage). The company must also organize and manage for worldwide business leverage and competitive advantage. Strategy encompasses the whole picture; it determines when, where, and how to act; it includes logistics, tactics, and policy. Global strategy in the GlobalSuccess Model includes the following seven steps:

1. Develop global mission and philosophy
2. Undertake analysis and diagnosis of global opportunities

3. Develop specific global goals and objectives
4. Adopt strategic alternatives and choices
5. Form strategic contingencies and plans
6. Implement strategy through alignment and integration of resources and organizational units
7. Evaluate, modify, and reapply global strategy

Operations

All functions and operations of the global company should be globalized to maximize the complementary linkages and leverages between them. The GlobalSuccess Model includes twelve operations (see Figure 10.4).

Global research and development.   R&D is a growing endeavor of companies in the highly competitive marketplace, where innovative new products and services are critical for survival. Companies such as 3M and Rubbermaid recognize that 30 percent of their products need to be invented and developed each year. Global R&D consumes major resources, is centralized or regionalized to serve the entire global market, and is located where the world's top research is being conducted in that industry.

Global manufacturing.   Flexible manufacturing systems, self-directed work teams, and statistical controls are part and parcel of global manufacturing. Global manufacturing allows for greater access to local factors of production, reduces transportation costs, avoids tariff and nontariff barriers, creates efficiencies of scale, and hedges against country-specific risks.

Global product development.   To compete globally, companies must develop a product development strategy relative to diversity, innovation, scope, and design. Cultural awareness and customer values and buying habits are part of the product development mix.

Global quality.   Global quality means the ability to compete with and be benchmarked against the world's best. Quality should be based on local and global aspects of conformance, aesthetics, perception, reliability, durability, performance, features, and serviceability.

Global finance.   Global finance is more than just acquiring access to cash. Identifying financial resources with expertise and success on the local as well as global scale is equally important. Global companies need to know the currency conditions and regulations of the countries and regions in which they

1. Global research and development
2. Global manufacturing
3. Global product development
4. Global product and service quality
5. Global finance, purchasing, and procurement
6. Global materials management, inventory systems, and sourcing
7. Global marketing, advertising, and pricing
8. Global distribution
9. Global sales and services
10. World-class technology
11. Global telecommunication and information systems
12. Global administration

FIGURE 10.4   Global operations

operate. Global finance involves understanding tax policies and currency exposure issues worldwide, knowing best locations for investment, and following procedures for obtaining listing on multiple stock exchanges. Flexibility and speed, as well as rigid measurement and reporting systems, are a must in global finance.

Global materials and inventory management.   Global inventory management enables the global company to adequately and appropriately respond to the following key questions:

- Do we have a consortium of suppliers who can deliver materials just-in-time?
- Do we have capital to invest in needed technology?
- Can inventory be shared across plants/regions/countries?
- Do we have software capabilities to access inventory data from centralized databases?
- Does global sourcing consider price, quality, delivery, dependability, and service?

Global marketing and advertising.   Global marketing and advertising carefully consider the cultural and global dimensions of appropriate customization and differentiation, global product strategies and pricing, culture-based advertising, world-class standards for quality and service, global sales and promotion strategies, and global customer education.

Global distribution.   In designing a global distribution system, one examines the mix of global and indigenous distribution channels. The channels are chosen or developed based on appropriate cultural, political, economic, and distance factors between and within countries.

Global sales and services. Promotion and sales strategies include worldwide world-class standards that are tailored to provide local, decentralized customer service geared to the needs and expectations of the local culture.

Global technology systems. Technology includes both process and product technology. Technological systems should exhibit global quality standards and be integrated with all the other eleven operations and with value-added networks. Issues include cost, speed, quality, space, obsolescence, maintenance costs, customer service, dependability, and ease of use.

Global telecommunications and information systems. Global telecommunications and information systems involve standardization of gathering, processing, and distributing information through a variety of necessary yet culturally appropriate mechanisms.

Global administration. Administration of global companies includes coordinating a wide array of concerns, such as immigration, transportation, work permits, pay differentials, family needs, schooling, safety and security, insurance, health care, and labor relations.

Global Structures

The fifth component of the GlobalSuccess Model addresses the structures of the organization (see Figure 10.5). Globalization changes the spatial dimension of enterprises and creates the need for a more flexible organization. New structures are required to cross both the aisle and the oceans. Since knowledge is rapidly becoming the most important advantage of global companies, this new global structure must enable companies to act more quickly and transparently to collect, store, analyze, distribute, apply, and test knowledge. Global structures are affected, both organizationally and physically, by the dimensions of culture and distance. Three elements are included in the structures component of the GlobalSuccess Model.

Global integration of functions, operations, and units. Global firms are matrixed and projectized, global yet local, seamless and streamlined, boundaryless and networked, flat and unbureaucratic.

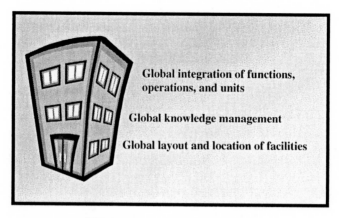

FIGURE 10.5   Global structures

Global knowledge management.   Structures, technology, and policies are critical to facilitating and enhancing the flow of knowledge to, within, and out of global organizations.

Global layout and location of facilities.   Where to locate manufacturing and other facilities and how to arrange the layout are important management decisions that relate directly and indirectly to corporate success, worker satisfaction, and customer confidence in the organization. Cultural elements, such as feng shui, play significant roles in how local and global players participate in the company's day-to-day operations.

Global Learning

Increased speed and quality of learning enable global companies to continuously improve the quality and speed of products and services demanded by global customers. The sixth and final component of the GlobalSuccess Model, global learning, involves the company's status as a learning organization, the process by which its learning programs are acculturated, and globalization of its learning curriculum (see Figure 10.6).

Global learning organization.   The learning organization includes five subsystems:

- Learning dynamics: levels of learning (individual, group, and organization-wide), skills of learning, and types of learning

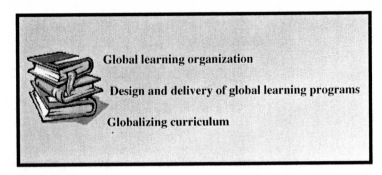

FIGURE 10.6   Global learning

- Organizational transformation: vision, culture, strategy, and structures for learning
- People empowerment: leaders, employees, customers, partners, and the community as learners
- Knowledge management: acquisition, creation, storage, and transferral of knowledge
- Technology application: information and learning technologies

Design and delivery of global learning programs.   Designing, delivering, and evaluating organizational learning programs require acculturization and globalization of each step and process to effectively reach the target learners.

Globalizing curriculum.   Learning materials—written materials, computer software, videotapes, and the like—need to be adapted to fit users' language and culture.

Organizational Approaches for Delivering Global HRD Programs

A global organization can follow either of two basic approaches in delivering its HRD programs—centralized and decentralized.

Centralized

Many companies take a centralized approach to HRD programs, sending trainers from headquarters to sites around the world to deliver the training, though it is adapted as much as possible to each local area. For example, at McGraw-Hill, trainers based at headquarters deliver training programs in their specialty areas to their field offices throughout Europe and Asia. Likewise, the corporate director of training for Johnson Wax designs and delivers training for its subsidiaries around the world.

Decentralized

The other approach is to develop and deliver training regionally and/or locally. IBM, for example, organizes its education functions in 150 countries into five geographic units. Within each country, there is a training division. 3M is even more decentralized in its approach to global training. Each of its subsidiaries in sixty countries is responsible for its own training. Often the subsidiaries develop and deliver their own courses. Sometimes, however, they will ask for consulting help from the headquarters training staff. This is also the case with BP's worldwide language training programs.

Importance of HRD and Ethics in Building Global Companies

Human resource development truly has the power to build and lead global companies that are people-centered and concerned about environmental sustainability. We must be on guard so that damage to ecosystems can be prevented, biological diversity and productivity are conserved, the entropy of energy and matter is moderated, and the economy is converted to reliance on perpetual resources and resilient technologies.

HRD for Development of Communities and Nations

A crisis is an opportunity riding the dangerous wind.

Chinese proverb

Role of HRD in the Global Arena

Because of the inequities and tensions created during these early stages of globalization, at no time in history has HRD been more central to solving critical economic and social problems faced by a wide array of groups, communities, organizations, and nations. Human resource development professionals have an important responsibility to assist national governments and the global community in endowing globalization with a human face and to ensure that it provides long-term benefits for all of humanity.

According to McLean (2001) and Bates (2003), the HRD profession should not only focus on economic development and workplace learning but also commit to the political, social, environmental, cultural, and spiritual development of people around the world. A positive future depends upon utilizing the resources and diverse talents and capabilities of the broadest possible spectrum of humanity.

A growing number of people, companies, and countries are looking to HRD professionals for strategic thinking and for help in succeeding in the global arena. In response, HRD practitioners can serve a mediating function, negotiating and resolving value and goal conflicts between work systems and sustainable human development needs at both micro- and macrolevels. HRD should be concerned about all humans and thus become a key broker in developing a world that serves the interests of all. Unless we act, the world could face increased exposure to external risks of all kinds, including economic disruption, forced migrations, ethnic strife, cross-border health crises, famine, fundamentalism, regional conflicts over resource use, weakened states, and ecoterrorism (Marquardt, 2003).

Eight Areas in Which HRD Can Positively Impact the Forces of Globalization

There are a number of key areas in which HRD can maximize the beneficial elements of globalization and limit its dehumanizing forces. However, the most significant value and greatest leveraging emerges from focusing on the following eight areas:

1. Political development
2. Economic development
3. Human and social development
4. Organizational and workplace learning
5. Education and vocational training
6. Global leadership development
7. Technology and knowledge
8. Environmental sustainability

Let's examine why each of these areas is so crucial for initiating and sustaining long-term and community-wide human development and what are the most strategic and effective roles the HRD profession can play.

HRD and Political Development

HRD professionals are rarely involved in political development—in promoting democracies; creating clean and transparent governments; propounding fair, nondiscriminatory legal practices. Yet government, more than any other institution, impacts human development on a local, national, and global scale. The failed efforts of public, private, bilateral, and multilateral development assistance programs over the past fifty years demonstrate conclusively that good government is essential for technical or financial assistance to have any impact. National governments, the World Bank, UN agencies, and religious groups have spent hundreds of billions of dollars on development programs for people living under dictatorships and closed governmental systems, and without exception, the conditions and development of people in many of these nations are worse today than before the aid was first offered. The training, technical support, and financial assistance have resulted in many cases only in supporting, strengthening, and maintaining corrupt and immoral governments. The people have remained poor, powerless, and threatened.

Ethical, free, transparent government is the sine qua non of human development. Friedman (1999) notes that the key to societies and organizations capturing the positive benefits of globalization is "all about the fundamentals. It's about . . . good governance, institutions, free press, and a process of democratization. If you get the fundamentals right, the [benefits] . . . will find you, and globalization will basically work. You get them wrong, and nothing will save you." Thus, without political freedom, democracy, and good governance, there will be little or no improvement in the lives of citizens.

Political development involves the collective development of institutions such as schools and corporations and of legal, banking, and health care systems. There is a symbiotic relationship between governmental development and human development. For example, the literacy rate, mortality rate, and gross domestic product (GDP) are indicators of both economic and human development in a country. In a society in which personal development is a priority (high literacy, low mortality rates), the chances of finding developed institutions (producing high GDP and employment rates) are higher.

HRD can help governments create expansive policies and avoid raising reactive barriers against globalization that ultimately hurt their citizens. HRD should encourage and train political leaders and government officials to adopt policies that encourage country integration into the global economy while assisting those adversely affected by the changes. Such policies fall into several important categories:

- Strong institutions and an effective government, to foster good governance without corruption
- Structural reform, to encourage domestic competition
- Macroeconomic stability, to create the right conditions for investment and saving
- Outward oriented policies, to promote efficiency through increased trade and investment

- Education and vocational training, to ensure to workers the opportunity to acquire the right skills in dynamic economies
- Well-targeted social safety nets, to assist people who are displaced

HRD and Economic Development

The living standards in many poor countries are not catching up with those of richer countries. Today nearly half of the world's 6 billion people survive on less than two dollars a day. Thus, a prime goal for HRD worldwide must be the elimination of such abject poverty. Poverty is an important HRD issue because it deprives people of choices and significantly reduces their level of well-being, limits their participation in political and development processes, and is associated with unemployment; underproductivity; poor health, nutrition, and housing; and lack of personal security.

Recent history shows that successfully developing countries have shared an openness to trade (Bhagwati, 2002). When governments try to protect particular groups, such as low-paid workers or old industries, by restricting trade or capital flows, they may help some people in the short term but ultimately harm the living standards of the population at large. The economy as a whole benefits more from policies that embrace globalization and promote an open economy and, at the same time, directly help to ensure that benefits are widely shared.

Traditionally, most HRD efforts have focused on improving the economic lives of workers, and this focus remains important in the mix of benefits that globalization brings. The experience of the countries that have increased output most rapidly shows the importance of creating conditions that are conducive to long-term income growth for increasing numbers of citizens. Economic stability, institution building, and structural reform are at least as important for long-term development as financial transfers. What matters is the whole package of policies, financial and technical assistance, and if necessary, debt relief.

HRD is an essential tool for building and maintaining the reservoir of skills needed for economic and social development. Singapore, Korea, China, Ghana, and Chile provide examples where HRD has been a key part of the national strategy to foster sustainable economic development.

HRD and Human and Social Development

A number of human and social development indicators have slowly improved over the past several decades. Infant mortality and maternal mortality rates have declined, as has the percentage of people suffering from hunger and malnutrition. Food production per capita has grown by 25 percent during the past decade. Access to education has been broadened worldwide, as reflected in a 12 percent increase in the adult literacy rate since 1990 (up to 76 percent worldwide). Eighty-four countries (including forty-nine in the developing world) now have life expectancies of seventy years or more.

Despite significant progress in many parts of the world, notably East Asia and China, the current overall development situation remains troubled. The new millennium began with over 1.2 billion people in extreme poverty, over 100 million school-age children not in school, and nearly one of every three countries in the world poorer than it was at the beginning of the previous decade. Over 9 million people starve to death each year, 75 percent of whom are children under the age of five. (It should be noted, however, that twenty years ago, nearly twice as many children died each year from starvation.) Health conditions are much worse in poorer countries. Half of pregnant women in less developed countries are malnourished during pregnancy, resulting in weakened babies with lower IQs. Women in poor countries generally receive lower wages, have low life expectancies, work longer for less, and suffer a higher level of illiteracy (Marquardt and Berger, 2003).

Thus, much more needs to be done in all *basic human needs* areas as defined by the United Nations Development Programme (the lower two rungs of Maslow's hierarchy). Some strategic HRD roles could include the following:

Health.   Needed efforts include development of national health policies; training of health aides, especially for rural areas; intensification of population and family planning programs by strengthening all aspects of service delivery; perhaps of highest priority, provision of safe drinking water and proper sanitation; expansion and strengthening of the quality of health services at all levels; consolidation and strengthening of basic health care services through synchronized measures; unified actions for the prevention and control of HIV/AIDS.

Housing.   HRD practitioners could assist in generating safe affordable shelter for all citizens; encouraging simple but culturally appropriate housing; educating governments in recognizing that decent, energy-efficient homes contribute to social cohesion, improved health, and better use of fuel and other resources.

Nutrition.   The Green Revolution has generated dramatic increases in agricultural production. Some former breadbasket countries have become food importing countries, however, because of corrupt or shortsighted economic policies. Training is needed for agricultural extension agents as well as senior agricultural officials.

Transportation.   Jobs as well as the distribution of foods and services require effective transportation and mass transit systems; thus HRD should assist in the transfer of best practices from around the world.

Organizational and Workplace Learning

Organizations increasingly need to operate and compete for customers on a worldwide scale. They rely increasingly on global sourcing of human resources, capital, technology, facilities, resources, and raw materials. Global capabilities as well as cultural sensitivity to local employees, customers, and life patterns are increasingly critical to organizations' success.

Specific HRD roles in this include the following:

- Preparing employees for overseas assignments: cross-cultural training, expatriation and repatriation support, language training
- Building global teams and enhancing their ability to work virtually across time and distance
- Creating systems for continuous quality improvement to meet global customer expectations
- Developing cross-cultural communication skills
- Employing active learning processes
- Building capabilities in knowledge management and technology systems

Organizations need individuals who can operate effectively in diverse cultural environments, use increasingly complex organizational structures and communications patterns, and manage change using multiple integrative business strategies with an embedded global perspective. Sustainable development is possible only when human beings are properly educated and trained.

Education and Vocational Training

Changes in global market dynamics, technology, and the structure of labor have created work that is much more complex, abstract, and knowledge based, thereby increasing the number of jobs that require higher levels of reading, math, problem-solving, interpersonal, and other workplace skills.

McLean (2001) notes that as unskilled and semiskilled workers become less needed, countries must put greater effort into developing high-quality education systems so that students can be prepared for the more skilled jobs of the future. This requires that HRD professionals train teachers and administrators at local levels and policymakers at local, state, and national levels. We should also utilize our organizational development skills to sustain an environment in which professional education can work effectively and students can learn successfully.

The UN's Agenda 21 Forum declared that "education, including formal education, public awareness and training should be recognized as a process by which human beings and societies can reach their fullest potential. Education is critical for promoting sustainable development and improving the capacity of the people to address environment and development issues." Societies must rely on both formal and nonformal education to change people's attitudes and increase their capacity to assess and address their sustainable development concerns; to achieve environmental and ethical awareness, values and attitudes, skills, and behavior consistent with sustainable development; and to participate effectively in public decisionmaking. Environmental and development education must address dynamics of both the physical/biological and socioeconomic environments; and human development (including spiritual development) should be integrated in all disciplines.

Demand for learning and performance improvement grows exponentially. Periods of rapid change place a premium on learning—for both individuals and organizations. Prosperity and growth are the rewards for those who learn and apply their learning the quickest; stagnation and decline are the penalties for delay. When knowledge rather than physical assets defines competitive advantage, the process of managing knowledge becomes a central part of the learning process.

As societies transition from the industrial era to the global knowledge era, job requirements are becoming more challenging (Drucker, 2001). Employees are moving from needing repetitive skills to having to deal with surprises and exceptions, from depending on memory and facts to creating spontaneously, from avoiding risk to risk taking, from focusing on policies and procedures to collaborating with people. Work will require "higher order" cognitive skills—the ability to analyze problems and find the right resources for solving them, even with limited and conflicting information.

Most of the world's potential workers, however, lack these new basic skills. HRD should assist vocational education programs to develop competencies in trainees that fill these emerging gaps. HRD professionals should also help to:

- Establish or strengthen vocational training programs that meet the needs of the natural environment and of economic development, with ensured access to training opportunities, regardless of social status, age, gender, race, or religion;
- Promote a flexible and adaptable workforce of various ages, equipped to meet growing environmental and development problems and changes arising from the transition to a sustainable society;
- Strengthen national capacities, particularly in scientific education and training, to enable governments, employers, and workers to meet their environmental and development objectives and to facilitate the transfer and assimilation of new, environmentally sound, socially acceptable, and appropriate technology and know-how; and
- Ensure that environmental and human ecological considerations are integrated at all managerial levels and in all functional management areas, including marketing, production, and finance.

Global Leadership Development

HRD professionals can help in shaping global leaders who possess the following key capabilities:

- Skills for understanding global business opportunities, including the ability to recognize and connect trends, technological innovation, and business strategy
- Skills for setting an organization's direction—creating vision, mission, and purpose
- Skills for implementing this direction in an ethically and culturally sensitive way
- Skills for mutual personal understanding and effectiveness with multicultural teams and alliances in a global context
- Ability to think with a global mindset

Leaders with global mindsets, according to Rhinesmith (1996), continually seek to expand their knowledge, have a highly developed conceptual capacity to deal with the complexity of global organizations, are extremely flexible, are sensitive to cultural diversity, are able to intuitively make decisions with inadequate information, and have a strong capacity for reflection. A leader with a global mindset thinks and sees the world globally, is open to exchanging ideas and concepts across borders, and is able to break down provincial ways of thinking. Global leaders are able to balance global and local needs as well as operate cross-functionally, cross-divisionally, and cross-culturally around the world (Dalton, Ernst, Deal, and Leslie, 2002).

HRD should also instill in global leaders a strong sense of ethics and a concern for global sustainability. Twentieth-century cost cutting, downsizing, and reengineering have cut out the soul of many companies. Many workers worldwide feel unfulfilled, unmotivated, and find little meaning in their work. Too often people have been treated as disposable. Global leaders must help their companies create a sense of meaning and purpose at work, establish connections between the company and the community, and recognize that the combination of head and heart yields a competitive advantage.

HRD professionals should therefore encourage leaders to:

- Institutionalize a proactive ethics program throughout the organization;
- Set the organization's ethical tone by tying ethics to shared company values and goals (employees are more likely to embrace corporate ethics programs and policies when senior management proactively endorses and practices them);
- Adhere to high ethical standards as an example for all employees;
- Create an ethical climate in the organization that accommodates differences in cultures worldwide;
- Develop a reward system that encourages good ethical behavior, empowers employees, equates ethical behavior with success in business, and treats ethics programs as a continuous learning process.

HRD should encourage leaders to look beyond economic growth and their shareholders' expectations to all the company's stakeholders by improving lives, sharing wealth, and shaping the future of the global communities in which they operate. Businesses exercise their economic and social responsibilities by contributing to the social advancement, protection of human rights, education, and vitalization of host nations and the world community. They should protect and improve the world environment and avoid participating in or condoning unethical or illegal business practices. HRD can thus serve as the organization's conscience.

Technology and Knowledge

Technology has the power to propel peoples and nations past slower intermediate routes of development. Its increasingly lower costs and wider accessibility make its resources available to the poor as well as the rich.

Technology's most valuable contribution to the development of people around the world lies in its ability to spread knowledge, for inequalities in access to information and in the capacity to create knowledge exceed even in-equalities of income among people around the world. The recent World Bank report "Knowledge for Development" begins:

> Knowledge is like light. Weightless and intangible, it can easily travel the world, enlightening the lives of people everywhere. Yet billions of people everywhere still live in the darkness of poverty—unnecessarily. Knowledge about how to treat such a simple ailment as diarrhea has existed for centuries—but millions of children continue to die from it because their parents do not know how to save them. (World Bank, 1999, p. 1)

Poor countries and poor people not only have less capital than rich ones but also have less knowledge. Forty years ago Ghana and the Republic of Korea had virtually the same income per capita. By the early 1990s, Korea, which had enjoyed greater success in acquiring and using knowledge, generated a per capita income six times greater than Ghana's.

HRD professionals should help nations and people in the following areas:

1. *Acquire knowledge:* encourage the creation of knowledge locally through research and development as well as tapping into and adapting knowledge available elsewhere in the world
2. *Absorb knowledge:* ensure universal basic education, with special emphasis on extending education to girls and other traditionally disadvantaged groups; create opportunities for lifelong learning; support tertiary education, especially in science and engineering
3. *Communicate knowledge:* take advantage of new information and communications technology—through increased competition, private sector provision, and appropriate regulation—to ensure the poor access

HRD and Environmental Sustainability

Globalization has already harmed the environment and continues to threaten its future. Protecting the environment is one way the HRD profession can help develop the lives of and provide equity for future generations. As Arnold and Day (1998) suggest, we can undertake a number of activities, including:

- Advocating that governments and national professional associations develop and review their codes of ethics and conduct so as to strengthen environmental connections and commitment;
- Ensuring the incorporation of sustainable development skills and information at all points of policy- and decisionmaking;

- Encouraging national and educational institutions to integrate environmental and developmental issues into existing training curricula and promote the exchange of their methodologies and evaluations;
- Encouraging all sectors of society—industry, universities, government officials and employees, nongovernmental organizations, and community organizations—to include an environmental management component in all relevant training activities, with emphasis on meeting immediate skill requirements through short-term formal and in-plant vocational and management training;
- Strengthening environmental management training capacities;
- Establishing specialized train-the-trainer programs to support training at the national and enterprise levels;
- Developing new training approaches for existing environmentally sound practices that create employment opportunities and make maximum use of local resource–based methods;
- Encouraging nations to develop a service of locally trained and recruited environmental technicians able to provide local people and communities with the services they require, starting from primary environmental care;
- Enhancing the ability to access, analyze, and effectively use available information and knowledge on and economic development and the environment;
- Preparing environmental and development training resource guides with information on training programs, curricula, methodologies, and evaluation results at the local, national, regional, and international levels;
- Assisting governments, industry, trade unions, and consumers in promoting an understanding of the interrelationship between environment-friendly and good-business practices.

Planning and Implementing HRD Programs for a Global Future

HRD professionals should be concerned with societies' overall human needs. This mindset begins with how we assess the needs of the global workplace and community, including political, economic, social, and cultural perspectives. We must develop a holistic, systems approach that recognizes how the worker and learner are part of an entire human development chain.

A number of useful strategies, both traditional and new, are available for developing and implementing programs for improving people's lives. Perhaps the most important trend in human resource development today involves changes in the traditional relationship between the trainer and learner, the donor and recipient, the manager and worker. New methods of participation and association should emphasize joint action throughout the development cycle. The recipients (whether governments, workers, students, or citizens) should have much greater input into programs and projects and should help determine the needs as well as the means. Basic development objectives should be changed to reflect the increased capacity of communities to be the actors and craftsmen of their own sustainable development.

Establishing Societal Objectives in the Global Environment

HRD must move beyond its traditional individual- and organization-centered foci to consider broader issues related to improving and sustaining socioeconomic progress. These include organizing educational systems to meet sustainable social and economic development, using education and training interventions to enhance political participation, and addressing issues of health, nutrition, population growth, urbanization, and environmental degradation.

Including sustainable human development as a fundamental HRD objective can make explicit the normative component inherent in all human resource development activities. The process of developing human resources is action oriented, practical, and aimed at solving problems in ways that enable work systems to reach their goals. HRD is concerned not only with what is but, equally important, with what should be.

From a global perspective, HRD also must extend and expand its levels of objectives. At the *individual level*, HRD addresses the needs of individuals performing in a work system so as to enable them to improve and maximize their contribution to overall work system performance. These objectives are oriented toward acquisition of individual expertise or potential. At the *performance level*, objectives derive from and contribute to the mission of the overall work system—teams, production units, divisions or departments. *Process-level* objectives focus on customer-related, administrative, and management processes and improvements in the way work gets done. *Mission-level* objectives are more universal and examine the relationship between HRD, long-term performance, and work system goals on one hand and the work system's external environment on the other. These highest-level objectives seek to enhance learning, human potential, and performance in work systems in ways that contribute to sustainable human development. HRD goals must bring about both (1) intergenerational equity (work system goals and activities carried out in ways that preserve development for future generations) and (2) intragenerational equity (conduct of work systems in one community should not undermine the ecological, social, economic, or political ability of other communities to meet their needs or improve their quality of life) (Bates, 2003).

A number of elements essential to planning for HRD yield benefits sustainable global development. The most important element of HRD planning is that individuals and organizations learn while they implement plans so they can optimize outcomes (i.e., active learning). Planning in HRD contains the essence of global citizenship for it maintains the vital element of redefining and improving the processes of work and living. HRD planning involves strategies for bringing out the full potential of people across the world as global citizens.

HRD and the Future: Enriching the Quality of Human Life Around the World

Humanity stands at a defining moment in history. We are confronted with a perpetuation of disparities between and within nations; worsening poverty, hunger, ill health, and illiteracy; and the continuing deterioration of the ecosystems on which we depend for our well-being. Without the development of human resources in societies around the world, the degradation of natural resources will continue, as more humans lack access to the resources and skills necessary for them to become productive constituents of and contributors to world progress. Friedman (2001) warns that globalization is monumentally empowering but can also be monumentally disempowering. It can be both incredibly enriching and incredibly impoverishing. It can enhance environmental preservation and can wreak turbocharged environmental degradation.

HRD is fundamentally concerned with the enrichment of the quality of human life. It can be instrumental in breaking the cycle of poverty and can lead humankind to an era of global development and peace, thus meeting its primary goal of increasing the capacity of people to lead productive, complete, and fulfilling lives. HRD professionals must commit themselves to assisting people everywhere to secure:

- Access to educational opportunities and lifelong learning,
- Respectful, socially equitable treatment that preserves their dignity,
- The ability to participate in governance decisions that affect their lives and the community in which they live, and
- The opportunity to earn sufficient income to supply themselves with ample nutrition, shelter, and other material and esthetic needs.

Human resource development truly has the power to lead to global development in which economic and technological advances are people centered and nature based. We must be on guard to prevent damage to ecosystems, to conserve biological diversity and productivity, to moderate the entropy of physical energy and matter, and to convert to economic reliance on perpetual resources and resilient technologies. A developed and sustainable society equalizes the benefits and burdens of its civic order and decisionmaking in a collaborative manner, democratizes its capital creation and work, and vitalizes basic human need fulfillment, ensuring sufficiency. This is what human resource development, properly designed and implemented, can do for the betterment of people around the world.

Part 4

HRD Best Practices
and Programs
Around the World

Europe

The safety of the world ... requires a unity in Europe, from which no nation should be permanently outcast. It is from the quarrels of the strong parent races in Europe that the world wars we have witnessed, or which occurred in former times, have sprung.

Winston Churchill, Iron Curtain Speech,
March 5, 1946.

Introduction

For over forty years the continent of Europe was divided by the "Iron Curtain" into two parts: a free, relatively prosperous Western Europe and an impoverished Eastern Europe dominated by the USSR. Since the collapse of the Soviet system, Europe has faced the challenge of shaping a single entity despite numerous and powerful political, social, and cultural differences. Starting from the original six members of the European Economic Community, or Common Market, in 1958, Europe has grown into the European Union with twenty-five member states and additional applicant states being considered over the next several years. As the redefinition of Europe continues, human resource development will undoubtedly be one of the keys to economic unity and growth.

This chapter examines various aspects of Europe's culture and environment for HRD, discusses key points about HRD in Europe, and describes some successful HRD responses to the unique characteristics of life and business in this region.

Cultural Factors Impacting HRD

Geography, Demographics, and Language

Because of numerous transitions in the area, the term *Europe* has several meanings. For some, Europe is limited to the current members of the European Union, while for others it includes all countries on the continental landmass. From a geographic perspective, Europe is the sixth largest continent and comprises only about 7 percent of the earth's landmass, or about 4 million square miles. Geographically, the continent is bounded by the Atlantic Ocean and North Sea to the west and northwest, the Mediterranean Sea in the south, and the Arctic Ocean in the north. The boundary with Asia is generally considered to be defined by the Ural Mountains and Ural River in the east, the Caspian Sea and Caucasus to the southeast, and the Black Sea in the south. Climate zones in Europe range from the dry, warm Mediterranean area to the subarctic and tundra regions of the northeast. Prevailing westerly winds from the Atlantic Ocean tend to moderate much of Europe's climate.

While Europe is about the same size as Canada, it is home to more than twenty times the number of people. About 730 million people live in Europe, and around three-quarters of the population live in urban areas, with the densest populations occurring in Belgium and the Netherlands. Among the largest cities are London, Moscow, Paris, Essen, St. Petersburg, Madrid, and Berlin. Among European Union (EU) countries population distribution varies widely, from about 15 inhabitants per square kilometer in Finland to 372 in the Netherlands. As a result of increasing affluence and the desire to limit family size, annual population growth rates in Europe are some of the lowest in the world. A long tradition of respect for education has contributed to very high literacy rates throughout most of the region.

As might be expected in an industrialized region, the amount of land devoted to agriculture has steadily declined since the early 1960s. Farm properties continue to be replaced by homes, businesses, and infrastructure. In Europe's most heavily populated countries, built-up areas increase by 2 percent or more every ten years. Heavy industry has declined over the past three decades, although not as quickly in the eastern countries as in the western.

The diversity of ethnic and cultural groups in Europe is reflected in the large number of relatively small countries. Even within countries having a strong ethnic majority, a variety of minority ethnic groups are found as a result of wars, invasions, migration patterns, and constant changes in empires over the centuries. Arab, Celtic, Croat, French, German, Greek, Italian, Roman, Scandinavian, Serb, Slavic, Slovene, Spanish, Turkic, and dozens of other ethnic groups are represented across the continent. Most of the region's languages fall into the Germanic, Romance, or Slavic families, although small pockets of indigenous languages exist, including Basque, spoken along the French–Spanish border; Celtic languages, spoken in parts of Brittany, Wales, Ireland, and Scotland; and a group of Finno-Ugric languages spoken in Hungary, Scandinavia, and parts of Russia.

Religion

Christianity has by far the most adherents among Europeans. Protestantism dominates the United Kingdom, Scandinavia, and northern Europe, while Roman Catholicism is predominant in Southern and Western Europe, and Orthodox Christians are concentrated more in Eastern and Southeastern Europe. Islam is the fastest-growing religion in the region. According to UN statistics, the Islamic population grew by more than 100 percent in Europe from 1989 to 1998, to approximately 14 million. Large Muslim populations have existed for centuries in the Balkan countries and other eastern and southeastern areas of Europe; however, in Western Europe most of the Muslim growth has occurred since the 1950s, as a result of postcolonial immigration, family reunification programs, worker recruitment, and immigration of asylum seekers, professionals, and students. Judaism is also present, particularly in France. And there are sizable communities of believers of Hinduism, Buddhism, and other world religions.

History

Europe is the birthplace of what is commonly called Western civilization. From the time of the ancient Greeks and Romans, Europe's religious beliefs, philosophies, arts, scientific advances, and political theories have spread to other parts of the world. Large colonial empires established and administered by France, Spain, Great Britain, and Portugal from the 17th through the 19th centuries drew Europeans to the far corners of the globe. During the 19th and 20th centuries, millions more migrated to the United States, Canada, Australia, New Zealand, South America, and Africa. In each of these migrations, immigrants brought their languages, cultures, and belief systems with them. As a result, many of the world's social, political, and economic systems; philosophies; and values stem from European roots.

Throughout history Europe has experienced numerous large-scale wars and invasions that have devastated both rural and urban areas. Although once controlled by massive empires and kingdoms, Europe was divided into many sovereign nations as a result of nationalistic uprisings, particularly during the 19th century. During the 20th century, the continent endured two enormously destructive world wars and separation of the eastern Soviet bloc from the western area. Postwar recovery in Western Europe, assisted by substantial infusions of aid from its military ally, the United States, led to renewed economic and political leadership position in the world. The states of the Soviet bloc remained isolated and stagnant until the 1990s but are gradually regaining some of their former political and economic strength.

In response to a need for a more unified political and economic system in the region, the European Economic Community, or Common Market, was founded in 1958 and was expanded into the European Community in 1967. The Treaty of Maastricht in 1992 broke down many remaining barriers within the community and created the European Union. Founding EU members include Austria, Belgium, Denmark, Finland, France, Germany, Greece, Spain, Ireland, Italy, Luxembourg, the Netherlands, Portugal, Sweden, and the UK. Cyprus, the Czech Republic, Estonia, Hungary, Latvia, Lithuania, Malta, Poland, Slovenia, and Slovakia joined in 2004, increasing the area of the EU by almost one-quarter and its population by one-fifth. The EU became much poorer at that time, since the average GDP per capita of the newcomers was just 40 percent of existing EU levels. Some concerns have been raised that the increased number of states will make decisionmaking more difficult and that the EU will find it even harder to present a unified face to the rest of the world. Bulgaria, Romania, and Turkey are presently seeking membership as applicant states.

Values and Customs

Europeans are proud of their long and distinguished history and place special emphasis on the arts and culture. They generally respect education and appreciate culture. Some of the principal cultural influences in much of Europe have their roots in historically Christian values such as faith in God; responsibility to family, church, and community; modesty, charity, and tolerance.

The 2001 European Values Survey of thirty-two countries provides some insights into broad European values:

- Europeans are increasingly protective of their individual freedoms, but they also continue to value solidarity.

- Although church attendance has dropped, belief in God remains relatively stable.
- Despite European unification, only about 3 percent identify themselves primarily as European, as opposed to identifying with their own nationality.
- Most Europeans voice their solidarity with the elderly, sick, and disabled.
- As for tolerance, while the Netherlands, Germany, and the UK report greater tolerance for ethnic minorities, there has been an increase in intolerance toward foreigners in other countries.

Life in the southern countries of Europe tends to be somewhat slower paced and more relaxed, with an emphasis on family and community and the need to balance work and other responsibilities with the enjoyment of life. The northern populations tend to place greater importance on industry, punctuality, orderliness, and thrift. In most European countries, there is greater concern for family reputation, educational background, and financial standing than is found in countries such as the United States. For the most part, family matters are considered private and not open for general discussion. Even in the more outgoing cultures, people are reserved with strangers and take time to establish friendships.

Family

Family remains a priority for most Europeans. Although there is greater support for newer family structures, most people still prefer the traditional family unit and middle-class values. Denmark, Norway, Sweden, Iceland, Hungary, France, Belgium, and Germany legally recognize same-sex partnerships, and single-parent families are becoming more common, but statistics vary according to religious preferences and legal statutes. Women commonly work outside the home, and in many countries traditional gender roles have broken down. In southern countries, such as Spain, Portugal, Italy, and Greece, however, extended families are more common, and men and women tend to take on more traditional roles and responsibilities. In these countries individuals are also expected to protect the family's reputation and not bring shame or dishonor to the family name.

Divorce rates have generally increased, with a European average of 1.8 per 1,000 people, but rates vary from country to country. At 2.7 divorces per 1,000, Britain has the highest divorce rate, while Italy has the lowest at 0.6. Compared to divorce rates in the United States, however, most European countries have considerably lower rates.

Economic Environment for HRD

Despite inevitable economic upturns and downturns, Europe remains one of the main drivers of the world economy. One of the foremost purposes of the European Union (EU) is to build a single Europe-wide market, using the euro as a common currency among member states, and strengthen Europe's voice in world affairs. The EU does not replace existing nations; however, member states have set up common institutions to which they have agreed to delegate some of their sovereignty. This system allows decisions on issues of joint interest to be made democratically at a European level.

The last few years have seen numerous changes in the European business environment. European companies have worked to cut costs and sell less profitable operations and have combined in numerous mergers, some more successful than others. Governments in some areas have deregulated select state-controlled industries, such as telecommunications, banking and finance, and media.

As might be expected, the countries of Central and Eastern Europe have experienced wide variations in transitioning from previous regimes to market-oriented economies and more democratic governments. Since the transformation process involves both macro- and microeconomic systems and social, political, and psychological processes, transition of some processes has been quick, while that of others has lagged.

Farther to the east, Russia's economic and political systems remain in transition. Despite some moves toward democracy—or "managed democracy," as President Vladimir Putin describes it—strong central control of and state intervention in business activity continues. Russia is still struggling to establish a modern market economy and sustain strong economic growth. The Russian economy has grown over the past few years, reaching a 6.9 percent rate of growth in GDP in 2003, due mainly to rising oil costs. Oil, natural gas, metals, and timber make up 80 percent of its exports, which makes the economy susceptible to swings in world market prices. The countries of Central and Eastern Europe and Russia continue to experience significant corruption, clearly a detriment to investment and growth.

Western European Model of Management

Despite the wide diversity in cultures across the continent, top executives from major Western European firms suggest that the Western European approach to management is distinctive, particularly when compared to American and Japanese models. Common characteristics noted by researchers Calori and Dufour (1995) include:

A greater orientation toward people than U.S. or Japanese companies. As one European executive notes, "We work for profit, but also for people." From a European perspective in the United States, profit dictates just about everything, and people are merely a resource in accomplishing profit goals. As Vittorelli, a former deputy chairman of Pirelli, explains it, "If you have to close a plant in Italy, in France, in Spain, or in Germany, you have to discuss the possibility with the State, the local communities, with the trade unions, everybody feels entitled to intervene . . . Even the Church!"

A higher level of internal negotiation. In Europe top management is powerful, but it must consult, discuss, and negotiate with lower-level workers, unions, and others to arrive at decisions. In different countries, however, dialogue between management and employees may play out in different ways. For example, in France and Italy there may be more confrontation, in Germany more consensus building; in Scandinavia a naturally egalitarian view of society shapes the dynamics.

Greater skill at managing international diversity. European managers generally demonstrate greater experience and skill in managing diversity and seem to respect and appreciate international diversity more than U.S. and Japanese managers do. The European perspective suggests that, on average, European companies are more accepting of the risks of intercultural management and are less imperialistic than U.S. and Japanese organizations, which tend to export their own models with less adaptation.

Greater capability to manage between the extremes. If the United States and Japan represent two ends of a continuum, from the United States' short-term profit orientation to Japan's long-term growth orientation, Europe falls somewhere in the middle. European managers seem to balance the individual with the organization, individualism with collectivism in the workplace, and the short term with the long term.

Business Guidelines

As in any region, the HRD professional conducts business in Europe more effectively by keeping in mind a few guidelines concerning customary practices.

Dress. Although casual dress has become acceptable in many U.S. companies, business dress tends to be more formal in Europe. Conservative suits are a safe choice unless the particular organization displays a more casual approach. Informal dress may be perceived as a sign that the individual does not take business seriously enough or does not respect the people of the organization enough to dress appropriately.

Titles and introductions. Although it is common in the United States to use first names, courtesy demands that titles and last names be used in Europe. When introductions are made, all parties normally stand up and shake hands.

Meetings. In the United States it is not uncommon for the group to dive immediately into the business at hand according to an established agenda. Long discussions may be cut off and taken off-line so that the meeting can proceed. Meetings in many European companies tend to be more relaxed, and participation and discussion are expected. The U.S. habit of multitasking, such as working on e-mail or handling cell phone and pager messages during a meeting, would be viewed as impolite in most settings.

Meals. Meals are generally relaxed in Europe, with time allowed to savor the food and wine. Business often is not discussed until the end of the meal. It is not unusual to be served wine or other alcohol at the midday meal as well as at dinner.

HRD in Europe

Many European professionals regard HRD as an American creation that serves as an umbrella to bring many different activities together. Although Americans generally find the definition of HRD fuzzy at best, European HRD has fewer boundaries and its disciplinary bases are even more diverse. Europeans seem to appreciate the openness of the field rather than searching for a unifying definition or theory of HRD, and they tend to include within HRD a wider variety of activities than Americans typically do. In many European countries HRD remains under the human resource management (HRM) umbrella and may not be clearly defined as a separate field of study. Among European countries the United Kingdom currently is the dominant player in both research in and practice of HRD. This leading role has resulted in part from having a common language and some cultural similarities with the United States.

According to Tjepkema, Horst, Mulder, and Scheerens (2000), five objectives dominate the practice of HRD in Western Europe.

- Support of the business
- Support for (informal) learning
- Support of knowledge sharing (as a special form of supporting informal learning)
- Development and coordination of training
- Changing HRD practices

HRD has been slower to spread in Russia, in part because of the many challenges involved in its continuing transition from an entrenched, centrally planned and governed system to a more democratic, market-oriented society. As new businesses emerge, they must first deal with surviving, making a profit, and dealing with the more technical aspects of their work. With greater stability comes a recognition that issues, such as organizational structures, management and employee training, interpersonal communications, and other people-related matters, require attention. Unfortunately, after the communist era, many businesspeople and consultants from the West attempted to introduce their organizational development and HRD concepts and strategies to Russian organizations without sufficient adaptation to local conditions. Despite these Western advisers' best intentions, their interventions often created confusion as the Russian clients tried to apply foreign concepts and ideas in a completely different social and economic environment and culture.

Management development appears to be one of the key needs of Russian organizations. In a recent study, about a third of Russian CEOs conveyed their dissatisfaction with the abilities of key executives and managers and noted that key individuals in marketing, research and development, and accounting must also be trained to deal with new concepts and systems. The study also indicated dissatisfaction with subordinates' low levels of initiative and ability to take responsibility. While training and development can play a key role in developing organizations, deficiencies are unlikely to improve unless root causes, such as unsatisfactory performance management and inconsistent compensation systems, are revamped. Culture-specific organization analysis, diagnosis, and intervention can provide lasting improvement in Russian companies' long-term viability and stability.

Investment in Training

According to the 2002 ASTD International Comparisons report (Marquardt, King, and Erskine, 2002), European training expenditures as a percentage of payroll are at about 2.5 percent, a decrease from levels in previous years but still higher than that of Canada and the United States. Recognizing that Europe needs a skilled, flexible workforce, several of the European countries have instituted governmental policies to increase training. In France, for example, employers with more than ten employees are required by law to invest specific amounts of their gross yearly wage costs on training, currently 1.4 percent. Organizations have a great deal of control over what types of education and training can be included. This sum is actually a tax, since any amounts not spent on training revert to the government, so most companies spend up to or beyond the limit. As Mathevet of Elf Aquitaine notes, costs for this program are high, but in the long run, this requirement has served France well.

Europe also contracts for a much higher percentage of training conducted by outside companies than any other region reported in Massey (2003), while the United States had the lowest percentage of outsourced training by expenditure.

Vocational Training

European countries have a strong tradition of apprenticeship based on the guild system, vocational education, and self-organized education in the agricultural sector. In many countries this has led to an emphasis on vocational training. Germany, in particular, is recognized for its extensive vocational training system, carried out through a variety of programs and providers. After completing school, many German young people enter a dual system in which they spend about two-thirds of their time training in a workshop, production facility, or service operation in a company while also attending vocational school classes to improve their technical and theoretical knowledge and skills. Continuing training is also provided by many firms and is promoted through the government's social and employment policies and programs.

E-Learning

European organizations, like many of their counterparts around the world, are rethinking workforce training strategies and issues because of rapid changes resulting from Internet and telecommunications innovations, globalization, e-commerce, and a constant stream of innovation. Marquardt, King, and Erskine (2002) show that European learners from a variety of organizations spend about a quarter of their training time using e-learning and blended learning. Although the use of e-learning varies a great deal depending on the country and the type and size of organization surveyed, e-learning expenditures continue to grow. Traditional instructor-led approaches are still widely preferred, and e-learning growth has been somewhat slower in the past several years than predicted. A blend of traditional and technology-based training programs appears to be the best solution for many companies, including corporate university-type programs for some of the larger organizations.

Chapnick (2000) points out, however, that e-learning will continue to grow in Europe because of four main influences: technological infrastructure and adoption, government initiatives, the deeply ingrained value of training, and a history of distance learning and nontraditional education.

Reflecting Europe's growing recognition of technology's importance, an action plan called *e*Europe 2005 was established by the European Council in 2002. Its purpose is to improve the European Union's competitiveness in a changing, knowledge-based economy and includes plans to provide more widespread broadband access at competitive prices, develop a more secure information infrastructure, and make available modern online services such as e-government, e-learning, and e-health services.

Corporate Universities

Since 1999, the number of corporate universities has steadily grown in Europe, mostly in Western Europe, in response to the need to develop staff in order to attract, motivate, and retain employees and to improve organizational performance. Some European corporate universities provide training solely to internal employees. Some are limited to top management, while others include all employees. Some corporate universities have expanded to become profit centers offering instruction to external clients. Corporate universities frequently work in combination with academic universities, an arrangement benefiting both parties and facilitated by the use of Internet technologies. The Lufthansa School of Business in Germany, for example, partners with the London Business School, INSEAD in France, McGill in Canada, and the Indian Institute of Management in Bangalore.

HRD Programs in Europe

Nestlé and Global E-Learning

The world's largest food company, Nestlé employs about 225,000 people at 479 facilities worldwide. Providing consistent high-quality training to all of its workforce is a priority for Nestlé but presents challenges for a company with so many employees so widely distributed. In the late 1990s, realizing the advantages of distance learning, the company decided to add e-learning to its training mix, while still retaining classroom learning as its primary approach. Nestlé now has more than nine hundred distance learning courses in a variety of languages. Courseware is available through central servers on the intranet, through a Web-hosted service for those sites unable to connect to the intranet, and via CD for those locations with limited IT infrastructure.

Two-thirds of Nestlé's courses are IT/IS-related, while about one-third are soft-skills training modules. Courses are provided through short modules (five to seven minutes in length) and focused on a particular skill or topic. This approach makes the courses more flexible to allow employees to more easily fit learning into their busy schedules and to better provide just-in-time training needs. The widespread use of these courses illustrates the company's belief that training is not a one-time event but rather a continual process. Nestlé plans to continue its development with a blended approach, using e-learning, classroom, and other methods according to what is most cost-effective and appropriate for the learning content.

Isvor Fiat, Corporate University for the Fiat Group

Fiat (Fabbrica Italiana Automobili Torino) was founded in 1899 in Turin, Italy, by a group of investors that included Giovanni Agnelli. In addition to cars Fiat has manufactured agricultural, construction, and aviation equipment and buses, streetcars, marine engines, railcars, and other vehicles. With revenues of more than Euro 57 billion, Fiat is one of the world's largest industrial groups, with 1,063 companies employing 223,000 people at 242 manufacturing plants and 131 research and development centers in sixty-one countries.

Isvor Fiat serves as the Fiat Group corporate university, providing training, assistance, and consulting services. Formed in 1978 by combining all of the training departments within the Fiat Group, Isvor Fiat has since been augmented to include the Isvor Knowledge System and Isvor Dealer Net, which handle specific client needs more effectively. The organization has its own network of professional trainers and consultants, who specialize in various fields including economics, HR, manufacturing, product development, marketing and sales, change management, e-business, service management, information and communication technology, and production and maintenance processes.

The learning specialists at Isvor Fiat take a systems approach to training, from needs assessment to macro- and microplanning to evaluation. Numerous learning methodologies are incorporated into its programs, including on-the-job training, coaching, counseling, and classroom and online courses; instruction is learner centered. To make technology-based learning more accessible, learning facilities known as "learning centers" and "learning points" are set up at the users' work sites. These centers use an "assisted self-instruction" training approach, combining support from tutors with modular courses and materials presented through the Web, satellite television, videoconferencing, and a video library. These centers also provide a place for experts, tutors, and learners to meet and share ideas, a key strategy to avoid the sense of isolation that many distance learners' experiences.

Polkomtel: Meeting the Telecommunications Needs of Poland

Polkomtel is a relatively new but important company to the mobile communications market in Poland. When the company started, Poland had among the fewest telephone lines per citizen in Europe, yet with 38 million inhabitants, the country is one of the largest telecommunications markets in Europe. The World Bank has estimated that development of the telecommunications network could add 1 to 2 percent growth to the economy each year. Given this environment, Polkomtel faced exciting opportunities but huge challenges as it jumped into the mobile communications business.

Polkomtel found that a large new sales force had to be recruited and trained, most of whom had sales experience but little knowledge of telecommunications. Training also was needed to provide a common language among employees coming from other industries. The company chose to work with a generic sales program designed by AG Learning Systems Polska to rapidly launch training. This collaboration involved translating the original program, adapting it to business needs in Poland, and reworking portions that did not fit with Polish culture. Role plays about selling insurance, for example, were changed because the concept of insurance did not exist in Poland. The program helped to create quickly a sales culture focused on client needs and satisfaction.

As competition has grown in Poland, the company has also recognized that training is an important strategy for attracting, motivating, and retaining the best people. As salespeople rise through the managerial ranks, they also receive management training in order to continue building the organization's capabilities. Coaching skills are developed for retail outlet staff. A seminar for dealers focuses on product benefits and essentials of communicating with customers. Technical training classes are available, as are English classes. In all, each employee participates in an average of eleven days of training per year, some of which is required safety training. Recognizing that they have a relatively young workforce in a rapidly changing industry, Polkomtel sees cutting-edge training and development as a key to gaining and retaining competitive advantage.

Summary

With the integration of Eastern and Western Europe over the past twenty years, the development of the European Union, and the growing power of the euro, Europe has become a dynamic player in the global economy. Innovative and exciting HRD programs are emerging throughout Europe. Vocational training and active learning continue to be among the strengths within the European HRD community. Top workplace learning programs, such as Fiat, Nestlé, Novartis, and Polkomtel, serve as benchmarks for the rest of the world.

Middle East and North Africa

Live together like brothers and do business like strangers.
Arab proverb

Introduction

The countries of the Middle East and North Africa, although in many ways diverse, share similarities in culture and beliefs that have a strong impact on business and HRD practices. However, those unfamiliar with the region should avoid the common practice of considering the entire region as a homogenous entity and should carefully research the organization and the specific country in which it operates before working with it. This chapter explores the HRD environment in this important region of the world and considers the evolving practice of HRD in a business setting defined by culture and religion.

Cultural Factors Impacting HRD

Geography, Demographics, and Language

Stretching from the Atlantic Ocean through North Africa to Western Asia, the former Arab-Muslim Empire is a region bound more by a common culture and language than by geography, economics, or politics. The region is an elusive one to define, but for our purposes, the authors have included those countries that represent the mainstream of the area both culturally and in terms of business. This chapter focuses on some, not all, of the countries of three geographic regions: North Africa (Algeria, Libya, Morocco, and Tunisia); the Middle East (Egypt, Jordan, Lebanon, Syria, and the West Bank); and the Gulf States (Bahrain, Kuwait, Oman, Qatar, Saudi Arabia, the United Arab Emirates, and Yemen). Omitted here are Iran, Iraq, Israel, Sudan, Turkey, and other countries that the authors would have considered had they addressed different factors.

With a population of more than 300 million and relatively high birth rates, the region is expected to grow to nearly 450 million people by 2020. Birth rates have declined significantly in many Arab countries but are still high by international standards. A large proportion of the region's population is under fifteen years of age—48 percent of Yemen's population and 46 percent of Palestinians. In contrast, in Kuwait, the United Arab Emirates, and Qatar, about one-quarter of the population is younger than fifteen.

Although the majority of residents speak one of the many dialects of Arabic, there are also substantial communities speaking Berber dialects, as well as Farsi, Armenian, Kurdish, and modern Aramaic. Even in those communities, however, written Arabic, which is considerably more standardized than the spoken forms, is usually the choice for written communications in education and government. Despite the use of Arabic in daily life, English and French are strong second languages in the region and are often used as the primary business language, particularly in those countries that were at one time colonized or governed by Britain or France. The region is overwhelmingly Islamic, with percentages ranging from 70 percent in Lebanon to virtually 100 percent in Algeria, Tunisia, Saudi Arabia, and Libya. Among believers in Islam numerous sects exist, including the Sunni, Shi'ite, Ibadhi, Alawhi, and Wahhabi. What may appear to be a surface Muslim unanimity masks a more diverse foundation, and relations among various sects are at times quarrelsome.

History

It was the Muslims from Arabia who, during a series of invasions in the 7th and 8th centuries, carried Islam and Arabic to the shores of the Atlantic on the west and into Central Asia on the east, forming an enormous empire from Spain to Samarkand. Although many of its cultural leaders were not ethnically Arabs, the growing civilization reflected Arab values, tastes, and traditions. Education and philosophy flourished, as did medicine, the arts, and literature. Modern science and mathematics were in part derived from the early Arab civilization and are still reflected in terminology such as *algebra*, from the word *al-jabr* in the title of a treatise on equations from the 9th century. *Alchemy, alcohol, nadir,* and *azimuth* are just a few of the scientific terms with Arabic origins. Although this powerful civilization began a gradual decline in the 12th century that marked the end of political unity, it left an enduring legacy of culture and language.

Religion

Islam plays a prominent role in family life as well as in the affairs of community, state, and business. Islamic principles are very much in evidence in the region's laws, business relations, and social customs. The Koran is believed to be the last of the sacred books and is the final and complete word of God (Allah). Friday is the Islamic day of worship, but religion is practiced daily through dress and dietary codes as well as prayer. Alcohol, pork, games of chance, and usury are all forbidden by the Koran. Muslims are called to prayer five times a day by muezzins (callers), or recordings of them, and they pray facing the sacred mosque in Mecca, Saudi Arabia. One of the basic pillars of Islam is the pilgrimage to Mecca, or Hajj, at least once in one's lifetime (Aziz, 1993).

During the month-long period of Ramadan, devout Muslims abstain from food, drink, and smoking from dawn until sunset. The end of the fast is marked by the major, three-day Islamic holiday *Eid-al-Fitr*. A visitor to an Islamic culture should avoid criticizing or questioning Islamic beliefs and refrain from attempting to proselytize in any way, as this is illegal in some countries.

In many of the countries of the region, the body of religious law known as "sharia" stands alongside civil codes, and most countries of the Middle East and North Africa maintain a dual system of secular courts and religious courts (Aziz, 1993). The Arabic word *shari'ah* refers to the laws and way of life prescribed by Allah to his followers. These laws and prescriptions deal with ideology and faith, behavior and manners, and practical daily matters. In more conservative societies, such as Saudi Arabia, Islamic law and civil law are closely intertwined. In fact in true Islamic law, there is no separation of church and state. The religion of Islam and the government are one. In more traditional societies religious beliefs about the prohibition of alcohol and the possession of books, magazines, videos, CDs, or other materials that are sexually suggestive or explicit are strictly enforced by local authorities with little consideration given to cultural differences or ignorance of local standards.

Family

In Islamic culture the traditional extended family—parents, siblings, aunts and uncles, cousins, and grand- and great grandparents—still forms the basic unit of society and is the center of an individual's life. Individuals are considered subordinate to the larger family unit. One's family is the source of reputation and honor, and any personal achievement reflects on the entire family. Likewise, it is to the extended family, not to the government or others, that a person first goes to seek help. Extended families with two or three generations living in the same household are not unusual, and even when urbanization results in nuclear family units, a son and his family will generally live close to his father's home. Children are cherished and indulged by the entire family. Elder members are respected by the entire family, and grown children are expected to provide for their parents in old age.

The Role of Women

Much has been said about the role of women in Islamic society. As a general rule women are subservient to men. Traditionally, men and women are seen as having very different identities and roles based on their natural biological states, with men normally working outside the home as providers and women taking care of the home and family. However, these roles are beginning to blur in some cases, with more women seeking outside employment and more men taking on some home responsibilities—unheard of only a few years ago. According to a report published by the United Nations Development Programme (Prusher, 2000), female participation in the labor force in Lebanon is the highest in the Arab world, at 28 percent, followed by 27 percent in Yemen, 25 percent in Syria, and 21 percent in Jordan.

In countries such as Saudi Arabia, where women cannot drive and must be properly clothed and veiled, some agitation is surfacing for more freedom and equality. Although the family is primarily a male-dominated unit, women exercise considerable influence in the home, especially in educating and socializing their children. In several countries men and women remain separated in public places, such as restaurants, public events, and the workplace. In addition, although the practice is dying out, polygamy is still found in some communities. However, by tradition, husbands must be able to provide equally for all their wives, and earlier wives must agree to later marriages. Infidelity and adultery are illegal and often are severely punished. Divorce, which can only be instigated by the husband, is frowned upon.

Business Meetings and Hospitality

Since Islamic culture is more relaxed and slower paced than many Western cultures, patience is essential, and more importance is given to relationships than to time. In business situations trust and confidence must first be established between the parties involved before anything can be accomplished. Several meetings may be required before any real business is conducted. Meetings often have no clear beginning and ending times, and punctuality has little value, although it is best as a visitor to be on time. A strong sense of fatalism imbues much of Islamic society, as illustrated by two common expressions: *Insha'allah* ("If God Wills") and *Ma'alesh* ("Don't worry" or "Never mind"). Saving face and avoiding shame are extremely important, and compromises are sometimes necessary to protect a person's dignity.

Despite wars and disputes that have disrupted the region for the past fifty years and throughout history, the people of this region are renowned for their generosity and hospitality to family, friends, and strangers alike. Hospitality is a virtue, and how well one treats guests is often seen as a direct measurement of what kind of person one is. Although men enjoy lively conversation and socializing in public places, they consider their family a matter of privacy. To be invited into the home is an honor, and the occasion will likely be formal. Following a few rules of etiquette helps avoid embarrassing or insulting the hosts. One should eat with the right hand; food (and other items) may be passed with either the right hand only or with both hands, but never with the left alone. One avoids sitting at any time with the sole of the foot pointed at the host or other guest and refrains from crossing one's legs. Shoes are sometimes removed before entering a home. In more conservative countries, an invitation may be extended to men only; if women are invited, they will likely dine with the host's wife in a separate area.

Idealism is a prevalent value within the Arab culture, according to Ali (1995a). Despite current setbacks, many Arabs still long for the glorious past and hope for a bright future. While this penchant for idealism can be a powerful force, it may also lead to dealing ineffectively with world events from day to day.

Economic Environment for HRD

Income in Middle Eastern countries varies widely, partly due to differences in oil resources. Per capita income in 2001 ranged from about $800 in Yemen (whose oil production began in the 1990s) to $13,000, $21,000 and $21,000, in the oil-rich nations of Bahrain, Qatar, and the UAE, respectively. The wealth of oil-producing states has attracted large numbers of immigrants, particularly from surrounding countries and from South Asia. Overseas workers represent 61 percent of the total labor force in Oman, 82 percent in Kuwait, 83 percent in Qatar, 69 percent in Saudi Arabia, 60 percent in Bahrain, and 91 percent in the UAE. The presence of numerous and diverse nonnationals, many from non-Arab countries, has created cultural, religious, and language barriers among the workers and their Arab managers.

After the Gulf War in 1991 and the war in Iraq in 2003, many foreign workers left, causing disruptions in the region's economy. As a result, a number of countries have instituted "indigenization" campaigns to decrease dependence on foreign labor and are also promoting diversification of their economies to avoid the frequent economic and social disruptions caused by fluctuating oil prices. In Oman, for example, where the majority of Omanis are employed in the public sector and the majority of private sector jobs are held by nonnationals, the government's Omanisation program encourages employment of Omani nationals in the private sector. A major part of this effort has been to develop human resources and upgrade the skills of the workforce in all sectors through education and training.

Education

In an increasingly global economic environment, with an emphasis on developing knowledge economies, educated and skilled human resources—both men and women—are needed. This region, however, has the lowest female participation in the labor force (28 percent) in the world, and 46 percent of women are illiterate. The disparity between male and female literacy is striking. The largest difference is in Syria, where about 86 percent of men are literate, while only 56 percent of women can read and write. In contrast, the gender gap in the UAE and Qatar remains around 1 percent. Similar gender disparities exist in secondary school enrollment. In 2000, 53 percent of Yemeni males attended secondary school, but only 17 percent of Yemeni females did. In comparison, over 95 percent of women in Libya and Bahrain attend secondary schools.

Although most Arab countries have excellent universities, many of the top political and business leaders and leading engineers and technicians attend universities in the United Kingdom or United States. By thus experiencing two cultures, these key employees can more easily understand and utilize the services of outside trainers and consultants and more effectively deal with cross-cultural relations.

Challenges

A special challenge for the region is the lack of water. The region is lowest of all regions in available water and second lowest in the amount of arable land per capita. Disputes over water rights erupt periodically, and the lack of water is a serious deterrent to development in some areas.

Wars and terrorism have also directly or indirectly depleted the energy and resources of many of the region's countries. The Gulf War in 1991, the Iraq War of 2003, the ongoing conflict between Palestinians and Israelis, terrorist attacks, and other clashes in the region affect not only the countries involved but neighboring countries as well. Millions of workers from Egypt, Jordan, Yemen, and other Arab states left Kuwait and Iraq after these wars, decreasing productivity in the host countries and also putting tremendous strain on the workers' home countries, which had benefited from wages the workers sent back to their families. Even in relatively stable Jordan, the presence of war and unrest in the region, although outside Jordan's borders, discourages new investors and businesses. In addition, sanctions and embargoes against countries believed to be harboring terrorists have hampered trade and left some countries without export dollars and vital imported goods.

A dependable, qualified workforce will be increasingly important to the region's remaining competitive, attracting investors, and developing both private and public organizations. Stronger education and training programs linked more closely to labor market needs and expanded research and knowledge generation would support this effort.

Cultural Characteristics of Arab Management and Organizations

Arab culture plays a major role in shaping organizational structure, management, and decisionmaking throughout the region. Mahmoud Al-Faleh (1987) has identified the following characteristics of Arab organizations and managers:

- Within an organization status, position, and seniority significantly outweigh ability and performance.
- Organizations are centrally controlled with a low level of delegation. Subordinates act with deference and obedience to the formal hierarchy of authority.
- An authoritarian management style is predominant. Decisionmaking is pushed upward in the organization.

- Most decisions and commitments are considered renegotiable at a later time.
- Consultative styles of decisionmaking dominate. Consultation is usually carried out on a person-to-person basis, thus avoiding group meetings. Moreover, decisions are often made in an informal and unstructured manner.
- Organization members are motivated by affiliation and power needs rather than by performance objectives. Social formalities are extremely important.
- Innovation and risk taking may be punished rather than rewarded.
- A strong preference exists for a person-oriented rather than task-oriented approach in managerial activities.
- Nepotism is regarded as natural and acceptable. Arab managers view their organizations as family units and often assume a paternal role in them. They value loyalty over efficiency.
- The open-door tradition is an integral part of the informal or unwritten organizational structure.
- Punctuality and time constraints are of much less concern than in Western cultures.

Strategies for Improving Management Development

Although demand for management development has significantly increased in the Middle East and North Africa, effective, high-quality programs have not been available in many areas. Factors accounting for this shortage include inadequate library systems, a lack of strong professional networks and associations, a private sector that undervalues management research and education, and government control of publications and programs are just a few of the reasons. As a result, educators often rely on Western management theories and practices without evaluating their relevance to Arab cultures.

Ali (1995b) suggests that Arab scholars should scrutinize their own culture and its constraints while reflecting on foreign intellectual contributions so as to arrive at more appropriate models of management in the region. Management education could then focus on topics applicable to the Arab environment, the global marketplace, and Arab and other cultures. Case studies should be used that highlight the successes and failures of Arab organizations and that deal with managerial issues in the Arab business environment.

HRD Programs in Middle Eastern and North African Organizations

Kuwait Institute for Scientific Research (KISR)

The Kuwait Institute for Scientific Research conducts applied research related to environmental preservation, natural resources and their discovery, sources of water and energy, agricultural exploitation, petrochemicals, and other important issues. Research divisions include Environment & Urban Development, Water Resources, Food Resources & Marine Sciences, the Petroleum Research and Studies Center, and Techno Economics.

KISR is also one of the more important training institutions in the Middle East, attracting participants from KISR as well as other organizations. KISR provides a wide range of technical/scientific, computer, and administrative and managerial courses. In addition, special training is available to intermediate and secondary school students, students of the Public Authority for Applied Education and Training, and university students from throughout the Gulf region. Other offerings include multimedia resources, videoconferencing, and scientific publications and conferences.

During the Gulf War, the Iraqi army dismantled the institute and took many of the institute's books and materials, computers, and other equipment. KISR has rapidly rebuilt itself since that time and once again offers some of the more impressive training programs in the Middle East.

Abu Dhabi National Oil Company (ADNOC)

The Abu Dhabi National Oil Company is one of the world's leading oil companies, located in the emirate of Abu Dhabi. To maximize the number of UAE nationals in its workforce, ADNOC is implementing plans to train and develop UAE nationals through its Human Resources and Administration Directorate. This directorate regularly conducts internal training courses and arranges for external ones in various disciplines for its national employees. The number of scholars studying in the UAE and abroad has increased tenfold in the last ten years. The training department offers both in-house and public courses in personal development, including supervisory and management training, technical and functional areas, and computer applications. In 1999 alone, 166 training courses were offered. ADNOC Technical Institute (ATI), established in 1978, has been expanded to accommodate four times more trainees in the last five years. It is now training and qualifying young UAE nationals as entry-level technicians in process plant operations, mechanical and electrical maintenance, and instrumentation control technology. During its "preparatory program" the ATI also offers English, mathematics, and Arabic and Islamic studies.

The AIT Learning Resources Center is equipped with a variety of educational and recreational resources. It has computers with educational and general-interest software, including geography and word games, as well as programs to develop trainees' grammar, spelling, and reading skills. It also provides trainees with books, VCRs, and videos on natural history, energy, and the oil industry.

America-Mideast Educational and Training Services, Inc. (AMIDEAST)

A private nonprofit organization, AMIDEAST was founded in 1951 to strengthen understanding and cooperation between North America and the Middle East and North Africa through education. It is headquartered in Washington, D.C., with a network of field offices in Egypt, Iraq, Jordan, Kuwait, Lebanon, Morocco, Syria, Tunisia, the United Arab Emirates, the West Bank and Gaza, and Yemen. AMIDEAST provides English language skills training, professional training and development, educational advising, and testing services (TOEFL and GRE) to hundreds of thousands of students and professionals in the region each year, as well as administering academic exchange programs and supporting institutional development projects.

Business and professional training programs include:

- Basic skills acquisition for young professionals to upgrade their English, computer, and job entry skills;
- Professional interpersonal training in the international business environment;
- Business writing and formal report writing;
- Public speaking and conference training;
- English HRD Language Management Performance Workshops for improving the knowledge base of managers and executives; and
- Human Resources Management Performance Workshops to aid managers and trainers in designing appropriate and effective training programs.

Programs for Americans include study-abroad opportunities in the Middle East and North Africa, educational exchange programs, and a variety of books, videos, and other educational resources about the region.

Aramco

Aramco operates one of the largest industrial training programs in the world and was one of the first companies in the region to offer training. Employees have the opportunity to upgrade their skills through online courses or at company training facilities. The company frequently sends employees for advanced training at top-ranked training institutes overseas and on short-term learning assignments at other leading companies around the world. Training programs range from programs for nonemployees to internal professional and management programs.

Among the nonemployee programs are apprenticeships, cooperative study, student summer programs, and college degree programs for potential employees. For internal employees self-development is becoming increasingly important. Thousands of employees have taken e-learning courses in corporate learning centers and on the intranet and Internet. Tools available for self-development include:

- Corporate Learning Centers located in the company's various areas of operation,
- Online technical training courses,
- Online management training courses,
- Online libraries, and
- Membership in professional societies.

For managers the company offers leadership and competency development programs and processes, which are designed to provide a logical development sequence for employees from the supervisory level to the ranks of upper management. The higher-level programs and processes are clustered into three distinct series: The Management Development and Organization Committee series is chaired by the president and CEO and includes the Executive Leadership Development Process, which is more of a self-development process than a structured program. The University Executive Program allows eight to ten managers per year to attend executive development programs throughout the world. The Challenge Series is made up of two action learning programs: The President's Leadership Challenge gives participants a chance to apply new concepts, such as systems thinking, organizational learning, and vision building, to real corporate problems. The Global Series is designed to create an understanding of the global business environment. Additional programs provide skill building in dozens of areas from business writing and time management to gravity and magnetic oil exploration techniques. In addition, the Saudi

Aramco Leadership Forum (SALF) provides a series of structured, guided discussions involving members of middle management and senior professionals from a broad range of administrative areas, plus key members of Saudi Aramco's senior management. During these five-and-a-half-day forums, sixteen participants address a topic of importance to Saudi Aramco such as thinking strategically, managing innovation, ethics, and leadership. Both participants and guest discussion leaders from senior management have the opportunity to identify, question, and examine the business challenges that face Saudi Aramco. Feedback from both participants and management on SALF experiences has been very positive.

Aramco also supports numerous advanced training opportunities, including advanced degrees in technical areas, advanced medical and dental training, attendance at conferences worldwide, mentoring programs, and international field experience.

Arab Air Carriers Organization (AACO)

The Arab Air Carriers Organization in Amman, Jordan, was founded in 1965 as a regional association of airlines. Among its objectives it strives to "provide a high-quality and cost-effective framework for human resource development." AACO has become an important center for aviation training in the Middle East and has earned a reputation that attracts aviation professionals from other areas of the world, as well. Courses are conducted year-round in Amman, Beirut, and Cairo using a multidisciplinary and multimedia approach. Instructional strategies include lectures, discussions, case studies, role plays, and video and computer training, as appropriate. In addition to its regular schedule of courses, AACO offers customized training programs and consultancy services.

Courses include the following:

- Managing a Customer Service Organization
- Advanced Training Techniques for Instructors
- Airline Marketing and Sales
- Airline Industry Management for Executives
- Scheduling Skills
- Staff Loyalty
- Fraud Prevention
- Professional Telephone Reservation and Sales Techniques
- Airline Economics and Fleet Planning

Summary

The HRD environment in the Middle East and North Africa is defined by the region's geography, demographics, languages, history, religions, cultural beliefs, and economics. Challenges include the scarcity of water and the low percentage of women in the workplace. Arab organizations and managers share unique cultural characteristics and behaviors. Successful HRD programs can be found at the Kuwait Institute for Scientific Research (KISR), Abu Dhabi National Oil Company (ADNOC), America-Mideast Educational and Training Services, Inc. (AMIDEAST), ARAMCO, and the Arab Air Carriers Organization (AAOC).

Africa

We must run while others walk.

Julius K. Nyerere (1922–1999)

Introduction

African long-distance runners, who have come to dominate world-class marathon events, offer a poignant symbol of Nyerere's prescient words. If African nations seek individually to emulate the West, they will run without ceasing. But insofar as efforts succeed to create and strengthen pan-African economic and cultural structures, Africans will run together in graceful easy strides toward a bright future. This chapter explores the cultural factors impacting HRD in Africa and the economic and HRD environments of Africa and then considers the evolving practice of HRD as African peoples strive to gain the skills and technology to survive and prosper in the age of globalization.

Cultural Factors Impacting HRD

Geography and Demographics

The second largest continent, with 22 percent of the world's land surface area, Africa is certainly the most culturally diverse by almost any measure. Its 750 million people, one-eighth of the world's population, are citizens of fifty-three independent countries and several island dependencies. The number of ethnic, cultural, and linguistic divisions is uncertain but is much larger than the number of political entities.

The population is unevenly distributed, with the highest densities along the coast of the Gulf of Guinea, where one person in five lives in Nigeria; in the fertile lower reaches of the Nile; in the temperate highlands of East Africa and Madagascar; and in the urban and mining areas of South Africa, Zimbabwe, Zambia, and the Democratic Republic of the Congo (DRC). The Sahara Desert forms a great divide between ethnic groups, with Caucasoid peoples— among them Arabs, Berbers, and Tuaregs—to the north and a large number of Negroid peoples—among them Hausa, Wolof, Somali, Dinka, Yoruba, Ibo, Kikuyu, and Masai—in the forty-eight countries to the south. Indians, whose ancestors were brought to Africa by the British to fill civil service positions, are an important minority in many coastal towns of southern and East Africa.

Language

The peoples of Africa speak more than eight hundred languages; five major divisions are generally recognized: Afro-Asiatic, Khoisan, Niger-Congo, Sudanic, and Malayo-Polynesian. Some fifty of these tongues have a half million speakers each, and unlike those of the Americas, these indigenous spoken languages are very much alive. Some languages spread with commerce far beyond their original environments. Swahili, for example, originally a language of the people of the East African coast, spread inland with Arab and African traders. Today more than 40 million Swahili speakers live throughout East Africa and the Great Lakes region.

Most African languages did not have a written form before contact with Europeans. This, along with their large diversity, has resulted in much of the written mass media being produced in French or English. Both Arabic and Roman letters are used increasingly to represent native African languages.

English is one of the official languages, if not the only one, in all the former British colonies except Tanzania, where Swahili has been adopted. French is the official language in most former French possessions south of the Sahara, and Arabic is the official language of the seven Saharan states. Numerous lingua francas, such as Lingala in the DRC and Mandingo in West Africa, are used for commerce in mixed-language areas.

Religion

With an estimated 155 million believers, Islam is the dominant faith in northern Africa and the fastest-growing religion on the continent. Some 140 million Africans are Christian, 55 percent of whom are affiliated with Protestant churches. Forty percent of the population practices traditional religions and animism.

History

Africa is the site of the earliest known protohuman fossils, as well as the home of one of the world's oldest known civilizations, that of ancient Egypt. North Africa first engaged in significant commercial and cultural exchanges with Europeans at the time of the Roman Empire. In the 7th century, Arab culture and Muslim faith spread across the Sahara. A number of African kingdoms flourished during the period of the Middle Ages in Europe, including Ghana, Mali, Ashanti, Benin, and Dahomey.

European colonization of African territory was begun by the Portuguese, who established trading posts on African coasts during the 15th and 16th centuries. European explorers began to venture into the interior of the continent in the 19th century, and by the early 20th century, nearly all of Africa was subject to European rule, which divided African territory into "nations," not to preserve traditional culture and civilization, but to facilitate the extraction of raw materials. Since World War II, forty-eight of these nations have gained independence, but the colonial experience left a legacy of arbitrarily defined borders, a diversity of political systems and problems, and economies dependent on the industrial world. The exploitation of African minerals, timber, and fishing stocks has transferred from colonial governments to global corporations in the 20th and 21st centuries.

Given the ethnic, cultural, and linguistic diversity outlined above, it would be unwise to make cultural generalizations about Africans. Yet we can identify some characteristics that, if not universal, are certainly evident in many of the continent's societies.

Africans tend to identify themselves first as members of a group, usually defined in terms of village, region, ethnicity, race, or language. Group members include both the living and the dead, those ancestors who retain influence in the people's affairs. Intense pride in ethnic/language groups has, at times, led to conflict, especially when land became overpopulated or when access to food or water became difficult. Colonial rule and creation of artificial borders exacerbated a complicated land-sharing situation. For example, scholars note how the Belgian definition of *Tutsi* and *Hutu* in economic terms contributed to an increased hostility among the two groups that populate Rwanda, Burundi, and eastern portions of the Democratic Republic of the Congo.

As the peoples of Africa struggle with 20th-century economic and political realities, nationalism has been added to the ways of defining group membership. In the same way that Africans are proud of their village or ethnic heritage, they are, for the most part, proud of their national identities. The victories in Kenya of the Rainbow Coalition in the 2000 presidential and parliamentary elections provide a recent example of this pride in national identity. Hundreds of thousands of Kenyans from ethnic groups with histories of conflict with each other agreed on a multiethnic slate that opposed corruption and promoted national development.

Class

Africans are sensitive to differences in prestige or status and take for granted perquisites and powers that are connected with class differences. The less privileged accept their lot for the most part passively, while the more blessed are not shy about wielding their authority. This is but one aspect of the fatalism that has marked many African cultures. In some cases it is the fruit of religion; in others, of history, environment, and circumstance. In any case, there is an acceptance of one's lot that to the Western mind is remarkably passive.

Economic Environment for HRD

Sub-Saharan Africa is the poorest region in the world. According to the *Human Development Report 2000* (Fukuda-Parr, 2000), 80 percent of sub-Saharan countries fall within the "low development" measure on the United Nations human development scale, with an average gross domestic product per capita of US$1,690—one-twentieth that of the United States. Rapid population growth, political dictatorships, exploitation by wealthy countries, corruption, droughts, and huge bureaucracies have caused these countries to become even poorer over the past twenty years.

Particularly difficult for African countries, according to Hassett and Shapiro (2003), have been the agricultural policies of Europe and the United States that have subsidized Western farmers to produce excess crops and the accompanying tariffs, which effectively block export of African agricultural products.

Because they are poor, African countries also face daunting challenges to health. Diseases that most other counties have overcome through the application of human and financial resources continue to plague many African nations. Malaria, diarrhea, polio, and HIV/AIDS take a high toll on the human resources African nations struggle to develop. HIV/AIDS has weakened the workforces and the economies of many countries, particularly in the southern part of the continent, by afflicting significant numbers of people in the twenty-to-forty age range. A resulting shortage of critically needed professional engineers, educators, and managers has led to lower industrial output and a worsening socioeconomic situation.

Despite these challenges, recent political changes in Africa are beginning to bear economic fruit. Western firms are showing new interest in Africa, drawn by widespread moves toward democracy and economic reforms. Furthermore, pan-African economic and technical collaboration continues to grow. With the institution in 2001 of the New Partnership for Africa's Development (NEPAD), African leaders have pledged to eradicate poverty and place their countries on a path to sustainable development.

A brief examination of the five major sectors of employment in Africa facilitates an understanding of HRD issues on the continent.

Government and the Public Sector

Central and local governments in Africa employ from 30 percent to 75 percent of all employees in the formal sector. A public sector job is the career goal of many educated Africans because such jobs offer both prestige and relative security. Today civil service administration in many African countries is bloated and inefficient, much as were many city governments in the United States during the era of the big-city mayors. Increasingly, however, state enterprises are being cut back or privatized, although they remain, according to Roberts (1990), a substantial provider of jobs and HRD in Africa.

Industry

Industry provides less than 10 percent of Africa's gross domestic product, with most manufacturing focusing on import substitution. As in the West, African government policies tend to hinder the free market economy, and the difficulties in international financial and trading markets have created additional obstacles.

Agriculture

Subsistence agriculture remains the basic work and livelihood for more than 60 percent of Africans. Food crises are common as regional drought and flooding, regional and civil wars, and poor distribution and transportation systems inhibit cross-continent growth in agricultural production and transportation.

Commerce and Finance

With rapid urban growth and the global integration of many enterprises, Africa's commercial and financial sectors are expanding rapidly. The quality and sophistication of these institutions vary greatly and, in many cases, are still dependent on expatriate financial firms and management. HRD is critically important to Africanize this sector.

The Informal Sector

Much of Africa's economy lies beyond formal government control and in the hands of "millions of small manufacturers, traders, service providers and self-employed business people who make up the informal sector" (Roberts, 1990, p. 6). As the governments of African nations have struggled to apply sound development policies, the informal sector has assumed even more importance. Building on the spirit of entrepreneurship widespread on the continent, national and international nongovernmental organizations (NGOs) offer technical assistance and microfinancing to strengthen and grow this sector. Apprenticeships and on-the-job training in small enterprises will continue to be critical for economic growth in sub-Saharan Africa.

Cultural Characteristics of African Organizations

Much of African business life has been influenced by the Western colonial experience (primarily British and French), by tribal customs, and by the region's poverty. Jones (1991) lists the following attributes of African organizations:

1. Organizations function in an environment of acute resource scarcity, economic uncertainty, and highly centralized political power.
2. These organizations tend to retain the major characteristics of structure developed in the colonial era—rather rigid, bureaucratic, rule-bound hierarchies.
3. The local people view organizations as having a wider mission than is generally understood in the West, in that they expect them to provide socially desirable benefits such as employment, housing, transportation, and assistance with social rituals and ceremonies. Profit maximization and efficiency may be viewed as secondary or incidental.
4. Workers have high expectations of organizational benefits to themselves and their families.

5. Many African societies place great emphasis on prestige and status differences, creating relationships of dependency, wide differentials between managers and workers, extreme deference to and dependence on one's boss, and a paternal but strict style of management.

6. Managers have a high regard for their subordinates as human beings (not as human "resources"). They emphasize maintaining relationships rather than providing opportunities for individual development, and ritualized interpersonal interactions rather than accomplishment of work-related tasks.

7. Managers regard their authority, professional competence, and information as personal possessions rather than as parts of their organizational roles. They are, therefore, reluctant to delegate authority, share information, or involve subordinates in decisionmaking processes.

8. The management style tends to push decisions upward in the organizational hierarchy, involve managers in trivial activities, limit information sharing, encourage highly dependent subordinate behavior, and create dissatisfying relationships between managers and employees.

9. African managers require highly developed political skills and well-developed diplomatic skills.

HRD in Africa

African governments place a high priority on HRD for developing skills for the workplace. Roberts (1990) asserts that "mobilizing professional, managerial and technical skills was seen as vital to replace foreign experts and turn independence into a reality. . . . Developing the workforce was akin to nation-building" (p. 7). Soon after independence, most governments established vocational education centers, which produced well-trained workers, but the creation of skilled jobs did not keep pace. Now governments and international donors are turning their HRD efforts to the informal sector, especially the development of small-scale entrepreneurs. Ministries of education in most African countries coordinate national training systems and adult vocational centers. Many governments have also set up centers to train small entrepreneurs in bookkeeping, marketing, and other essential skills.

According to Roberts (1990), there are thousands of nonformal HRD centers throughout Africa, mainly in the small craft industries. One example is the Kenya Village Polytechnics, in which two hundred low-cost, village-managed centers teach technical skills to educate school dropouts.

In many African nations umbrella associations have arisen in support of nonformal organizations. These associations, often in partnerships with international organizations such as the United States Agency for International Development (USAID) and the World Bank, provide training, technical assistance, and advocacy for the thousands of local NGOs across the continent.

In Lesotho, for example, the Lesotho Council of Non-governmental Organisations (LCN) was founded in May 1990 to provide support services to the NGO community through networking, leadership, information dissemination, capacity building, coordination, advocacy, and representation when dealing with the international community and with government. The council's mission is to stimulate, promote, and support NGOs in their development efforts.

The Tanzania Association of Nongovernmental Organizations (TANGO) is the largest and longest-standing national umbrella organization serving the Tanzanian NGO community. Founded in 1988, it now has over 580 member organizations. Through regional networks, TANGO supports new and smaller NGOs and provides training to develop members' lobbying and advocacy skills.

In West and southern Africa, the Pan-African Institute for Development (PAID) has supported capacity building among NGOs for nearly forty years. PAID, with numerous training centers in Cameroon, Burkina Faso, and Zambia, offers a diploma in development studies and a wide range of management courses for both government and nongovernment staff.

Africa needs agricultural training. Most of Africa's fifty-seven universities offer agricultural degrees. Kenya, Ethiopia, and other countries have networks of farmers' training centers that offer courses. In many countries training and visits by agricultural extension agents have proved to be highly effective.

Most African countries have established national institutes for public administration to train civil servants in basic management fields and in the complex civil service procedures and rules. Low wages, poor management, and poor prospects for advancement, however, drive many of the better HRD officers from these training centers.

Training African Managers

Acknowledging the cultural and organizational milieu in which African managers operate, HRD professionals should consider several points when training managers in Africa. First, it is important to recognize regional sociocultural values and the fact that Western management practices and techniques might contradict them. For example, performance appraisal and management-by-objectives may not appeal to African organizations since it is a sign of weakness to admit incompetence or ignorance.

Second, many management development and HRD concepts reflect Western but not necessarily African values—for example, individual responsibility for development, the value of self-discovered knowledge as opposed to prescribed knowledge, teacher–learner relationships that involves interdependence as an assumed quality, and development as involving risk and change for learners. Many African learners perceive training as a way to enhance status rather than as a vehicle for personal growth, and as a way to avoid risk by acquiring additional information that can be hoarded and protected as a source of power. These learners have a greater need for clear and unequivocal direction and for regular face-to-face contact.

Jones (1991) suggests the following criteria for management training in Africa:

1. The organizational policy should state that managers have a major responsibility in developing employees and that training does not imply personal inadequacy. The HRD program should be seen as supportive.
2. Learning strategies should reflect the communal nature of African society. This would mean avoidance of methods that focus on individual performance (especially shortcomings) in favor of small-group and other supportive methodologies.
3. Trainers should focus explicitly on continuous learning from experience, thereby developing skills in analyzing successes and failures in a conscious, structured way.
4. Managers should be trained in coaching skills so as to more effectively develop their subordinates.
5. Since organizational structures tend to be rigidly bureaucratic and slow-moving in an environment of accelerating change, all employees, especially managers, should understand the processes of organizational change.

On-the-Job and Apprenticeship Training in Africa

Most African governments do not have sufficient funds to address the investment in human resources that will be needed over the next twenty or thirty years. International donors, such as USAID, the World Bank, and a host of international NGOs, are contributing resources for skill building at local levels in education, health, agriculture, and municipal management.

Many African leaders and HRD professionals are promoting on-the-job training, especially apprenticeships, as cost-effective skills training. The apprenticeship system is firmly rooted in African culture and is particularly well suited to the conditions of African life. The placing of the apprentice is negotiated by a master craftsman and the parents. The small entrepreneur assumes considerable responsibility in relation to the apprentice's family, which pays a fee to place its child with the craftsman. The craftsman must educate his apprentice beyond the requirements of the profession and provide board and lodging during the period of apprenticeship. The apprentice learns not only the technical craft but also skills associated with marketing, public relations, and managing a small business (Bas, 1989).

The principal defect of the traditional apprenticeship system is insufficient theoretical training. This is due both to the limited knowledge of the master craftsmen and to the number of apprentices in relation to the number of skilled workers. Governments have begun to regulate apprenticeships in Africa by providing for alternate periods of theoretical training and by giving entrepreneurs themselves proficiency courses and pedagogical support in their training function. Examples are the 1977 law in Ivory Coast, Togo's 1983 law, and the 1981 law in Algeria creating the National Institute for the Promotion and Development of Vocational Training in the Enterprise and Apprenticeship.

Nonformal Education Programs in Africa

According to Hamilton and Asiedu (1987), nonformal educational programs have a substantial history in most African countries. These programs are designed to handle a number of community problems ranging from literacy to family planning. In recent years the bulk of nonformal education activities have been devoted to skills training for employment. There are three main categories of activities that characterize skill-training approaches—preemployment training for industry, skills upgrading for small business and industry, and training for farmers and craftsmen in rural areas.

A skills-training program that has proven successful is based on the Opportunities Industrialization Center (OIC) model created by the Reverend Leon Sullivan. Established in 1964 and originally designed to provide trade skills for African Americans in Philadelphia, these programs have been replicated in Cameroon, Nigeria, Ghana, Ethiopia, Liberia, Sierra Leone, Togo, Lesotho, Guinea, Ivory Coast, Kenya, the DRC, and the Central African Republic. The OICs offer vocational-technical training in a variety of areas (e.g., accounting, air conditioning, auto mechanics, carpentry, electricity, computer technology, and farm management). The OIC model consists of seven program components: recruitment, counseling, prevocational training, vocational training, job development, placement, and agricultural resettlement.

HRD Programs in African Organizations

ABANTU

Established in 1991, ABANTU for Development is an international NGO providing information and advice on mobilizing resources toward sustainable development in Africa. ABANTU's approach to development is participatory and people centered, paying particular attention to gender issues in development. ABANTU's mission is to empower African people, particularly women, through various types of training for development.

ABANTU's objectives include:

- Supporting African people to empower themselves through a participatory and people-centered method of training to develop skills in the areas of policy analysis, economics, health care, media, and the environment;
- Developing and supporting a core group of trainers and NGOs;
- Providing support and networking opportunities for trainers and consultants to create an increased pool of competent Africans skilled in participatory training and gender-sensitive policy analysis; and
- Capitalizing on the resources available in the Northern and Southern Hemispheres to benefit African people.

Recognizing the dominant role that women play in local African economies, ABANTU trains African women and their NGOs in policy analysis, economics, health care, and other areas of expertise to equip these women with the knowledge and skills to help shape development policy. ABANTU also helps African women acquire advocacy and negotiation skills to make their voices heard by international agencies and organizations as well as at the national level.

Since 1998, ABANTU has trained more than 1,000 men and women in strategic planning, policy analysis and policymaking, lobbying and advocacy, management and fund-raising, and conflict management within organizations. According to Irving (1999), ABANTU considers strong north–south links among its main assets. With offices in Kenya, Tanzania, Ghana, Nigeria, and the United Kingdom, ABANTU encourages a two-way flow of knowledge and experience between its own organization and organizations in Europe and North America, and it plans programs to explore new networks and ideas for cooperation with European NGOs.

The African Virtual University (AVU)

The African Virtual University is a first-of-its-kind interactive-instructional telecommunications network established to serve the countries of Africa. AVU's objective is to build capacity and support economic development by leveraging the power of modern telecommunications technology to provide world-class quality education and training programs to students and professionals in Africa. AVU is based in Nairobi, Kenya, and has thirty-four learning centers in seventeen African countries.

Initiated in 1997 with assistance from the World Bank, AVU aims by 2007 to be a reputable, independent African organization contributing to the continent's capacity-building efforts and harnessing the power of information communication and technology (ICT) to expand access to quality and affordable education at the tertiary level throughout Africa. AVU's mission is:

- To increase access to education at the tertiary level in Africa by reaching large numbers of students and professionals simultaneously in multiple learning centers;
- To provide opportunities for life-long learning;
- To conceive and implement a delivery strategy that can provide quality education in Africa at affordable rates;
- To improve the connectivity and computing capacity of African educational institutions that host AVU learning centers;
- To increase access to higher education in subject areas critical to economic development, such as engineering, computer science, information technology, business studies, health, and teacher training;
- To improve the quality of education by accessing the best academic resources, both in Africa and worldwide, and by offering training to lecturers in African universities toward the preparation of adequate teaching materials for the AVU network;
- To bring African faculty members, students, and professionals to closer dialogue and to offer them an opportunity to play an active role in the global knowledge age and to share educational resources developed in Africa with the rest of the world; and
- To serve as a catalyst for new investments and economic development by offering skills training and upgrading for professionals.

Already, AVU has:

- Created a network of partner institutions in seventeen francophone, anglophone, and lusophone African countries, with learning centers hosted mainly in public universities;
- Affiliated with a global network of leading universities;
- Established thirty-four sites in seventeen African countries;
- Delivered more than 3,000 hours of instructional programs, sourced from leading universities in North America and Europe;
- Registered over 23,000 students in its semester-long courses;
- Enrolled close to 2,500 professionals in executive business seminars;
- Provided 1,000 PCs to learning centers,
- Set up a network of 45,000 e-mail account holders and a digital library of more than 1,000 journals; and
- Achieved over 40 percent participation of women in AVU's preuniversity courses at the most active learning centers.

In 2002, nearly two hundred students from eight sub-Saharan countries took a Massachusetts Institute of Technology (MIT) course without leaving their countries, thanks to a joint initiative of MIT's Center for Advanced Educational Services (CAES) and AVU. The course was beamed via satellite from a central uplink facility in Clarksburg, Maryland, to AVU e-learning centers across Africa. Besides MIT, AVU has partnered with universities in Europe and the United States, including New Jersey Institute of Technology, Indiana University, and Georgetown University.

SABMiller

The South African Brewery (SAB) was established in 1895 and for fifty years succeeded as a local brewery that expanded slowly into neighboring territories. After World War II, SAB moved its headquarters from London to Johannesburg, and the company grew rapidly over the next twenty-five years, expanding and diversifying its holdings from beer to soft drinks, glassmaking, furniture, food distribution, footwear, real estate development, retail apparel, and textile manufacturing.

In 1997, SAB returned to its core operations, selling off all but its hotel, gaming, brewing, and bottling businesses. In 2001, SAB became the first international brewer to enter Central America, and in 2002 it wholly acquired Miller Brewing Company and changed its name to SABMiller. SABMiller has

72,835 employees and operates in Africa, Asia, North and Central America, and Europe; it is the largest brewer in the developing world.

Since for many years the company employed a multinational/multicultural workforce in an environment of apartheid, it became accustomed to managing in turbulent social environments, and this experience helped to shape the development of its HRD policies and practices. In 1978, SAB developed the first code of nondiscriminatory employment in South Africa.

When apartheid laws were abolished in 1991 and global sanctions were lifted from South Africa, SAB required a virtual overhaul of its HRD policies and practices. SAB was guided by principles that respect the freedom and equal dignity of all people without distinction of any kind, including race, color, gender, or religion. The principles pledge equal pay for equal work and fair remuneration, with adequate protection for health and well-being. They provide for reasonable working hours and periodic holidays with pay.

SABMiller's position is that there is no longer space in organizations for huge, highly populated HR departments with lots of people doing lots of administrative tasks that don't really add value to the organization. Rather HR must focus on and apply its resources to those activities and components within the organization that leverage the most strategic success (Doke, 1993).

In 2002, Beer South Africa's Newlands Brewery, an operation of SAB, became one of the first organizations in the country to be recognized as an "Investor in People." This recognition program, funded by the European Union, celebrates organizations that align people management and training processes with the goals of the business and offers a certifiable standard to achieve. In addition to this recognition, Beer South Africa was judged, by the annual awards program run by the *Financial Mail,* to be one of the best places to work in the country. The company achieved second place, behind ABSA, the bank; in 2001 it had won the top spot.

In 2003, SABMiller, as part of a major focus on corporate accountability, produced a grading system to judge its management approach to key human resource issues. After careful consideration and consultation with stakeholders, the company chose twelve priority human resource issues. Local operations assess these issues by placing each in one of four precisely defined stages of development and then set a target for progress over the next year. Following are the four stages:

1. *Advanced:* A systematic approach to competency acquisition is applied, and growth in competency is tracked. Development needs

and training address current and future business needs. Appropriate curricula and learning solutions exist for technical, shop floor, management, and executive development. Development plans are in place for more than 75 percent of employees and are aligned to their personal performance management and to their future career direction. Training evaluations as to the effectiveness of the training are conducted regularly. Employees drive their own development.

2. *Developed:* A systematic approach to training, based on individual and business needs, is in place. Development of individuals is tracked. Curricula and learning solutions exist for key skills. Development plans are in place for at least 50 percent of employees. Delegates are required to provide satisfactory ratings for the training. From time to time training is evaluated for effectiveness.

3. *Established:* A systematic approach to training, based on business needs, is in place. Curricula and learning solutions exist for key skills. Development plans are in place for at least 25 percent of employees. From time to time training is evaluated for effectiveness.

4. *Emerging:* Ad hoc training and development occurs, based on business needs. Training plans exist for a few key individuals, where these plans are budgeted and audited.

SABMiller's current aggregate scores for each of the twelve priority issues and planned performance levels are given in Table 14.1.

Summary

The cultural factors of geography, demographics, language, religion, history, and class have all had an impact on HRD capacity in Africa. African governments have always placed a high priority on HRD, which has been seen as critical to nation building. Unfortunately, few skilled jobs have existed for trained Africans. In many African countries HRD has been refocused on apprenticeship and other on-the-job forms of training. Nonformal education programs, based on the Opportunities Industrialization Centers in the United States, have become popular in Africa. Distance learning, particularly e-learning, is having a growing influence on HRD in Africa. As sub-Saharan Africa continues to develop, companies like SABMiller increasingly shoulder the task of human resources development. Three successful HRD programs in Africa are ABANTU, the African Virtual University, and SABMiller.

TABLE 14.1   SABMiller's Priority HR Approach to Management Issues

Priority issue	Current performance level	Planned performance level
Primary health care	B–	B
Labor turnover	B+	A
Training and development	C+	B
Performance appraisal and career management	C	B
Diversity and localization	C+	B
Health and safety	B–	B+
HIV/AIDS	B–	A–
Internal communication	B–	B+
Negotiation and consultation	B+	A
Staff attitude surveys	C	B–
Market-related salaries	B	A
Retirement benefits	B+	A

China

Better a diamond with a flaw than a pebble without.

Confucius

Introduction

Although China enters the 21st century with flaws and difficulties, the country has quickly emerged as an economic diamond in the world of nations, and HRD is playing a central role in developing a trained workforce with the skills required for quality and speed in product development and production. Chinese workers are excited about the new emphasis on workplace learning and seek improved and expanded HRD programs.

Cultural Factors Impacting HRD

Geography, Demographics, and Language

The population of China exceeds 1.25 billion, 70 percent (870 million) of which is rural. About 94 percent of the people are Han Chinese; the remaining 6 percent is distributed among some sixty ethnic groups, the largest being His, Mongols, Uighurs, Chuangs, Yis, and Tibetans. The primary language of China is Mandarin, and standard spoken Chinese is based on the Mandarin dialect, native to 70 percent of the population. Cantonese is the language of Hong Kong. The languages and dialects of China share a single writing system.

History

China's written history began during the 16th century B.C. with the Shang dynasty. Ruled by a series of dynasties following the Shang, China became a republic after the fall of the Ch'ing, or Manchu, dynasty in 1912. From 1921 until 1949, a bitter civil war raged in China between communist forces led by Mao Tse-tung and those of the nationalists, led by Chang Kai-shek. Following their defeat, the nationalists fled to the island of Taiwan and established the independent Republic of China. The United Nations recognized Taiwan as the legitimate government of China until 1971, when the People's Republic assumed the UN seat. The sovereignty of Taiwan is still in dispute. Hong Kong, administered by Great Britain after 1841, became a part of the People's Republic of China in 1997.

Religion

After many years under communism, nearly 60 percent of the population considers itself to be nonreligious. However, an interest in religion has been renewed. Confucianism (considered by some as a philosophy rather than a religion) is the major religious influence on Chinese people. Christianity and Buddhism are growing in influence.

Economy

After a half century of communism China has in recent years undertaken a major directional shift toward capitalism. In 2003, China joined the World Trade Organization (WTO). Assuming that China continues its economic growth rate of 8 to 10 percent per annum, it is expected to be the world's largest economy by 2025.

Family and Education

Chinese people hold a strong loyalty and attachment to their families. An individual exists primarily as a member of a family. The young are expected to take care of the elderly. Elders are respected, and the word of the father is usually law.

Family members are expected to cooperate among themselves and assist one another in times of need. Businesses often are family based, if not family owned. Most medium-sized businesses in China are family affairs. Recently, families have come under stress as the national government, seeking to limit population growth, has promoted a policy of one child per family. The influence of Confucianism encourages families and individuals to revere education and academic credentials. There is very high respect for teachers and for the learning process.

Guanxi and Doing Business in China

Chinese culture is distinguished from Western culture in many ways, including how business is conducted. For example, the Chinese prefer to deal with people they know and trust. On the surface, this may seem little different from doing business in the Western world. But in reality, the heavy reliance on relationships means that Western companies have to make themselves known to the Chinese before any business can proceed. Furthermore, these relationships are not simply between companies but also between individuals at a personal level. The relationship is ongoing and does not end after a sale takes place. The company must maintain the relationship if it wants to continue doing business with its Chinese associates.

Businesses intending to invest in China may fare poorly unless they get good advice. Getting good advice has a lot to do with *guanxi*, which literally means "relationship(s)." It is a concept essential to one's effective functioning in Chinese society. By getting the right *guanxi*, an organization can minimize the risks, frustrations, and disappointments of operating in China. Often acquiring the right *guanxi* with the relevant authorities determines the long-term competitive standing of an organization in China.

How is *guanxi* established? First, it does not have to be based on money. Treating someone with decency while others treat him or her unfairly could create a good relationship. Second, *guanxi* begins with and builds on the trustworthiness of the individual or the company. A company that promises certain things and delivers them shows trustworthiness, and the Chinese would be inclined to deal with them again. Third, dependability strengthens a business relationship in China. In this sense *guanxi* is analogous to a friendship between two who can count on each other in both good and bad times. For example, companies that stayed in China during the period of political instability in 1989 found their relationship with the Chinese strengthened. They were viewed by the Chinese as friends who did not abandon the Chinese when they needed friends. Fourth, frequent contacts with each other foster understanding and emotional bonds, and the Chinese often feel obligated to do business with their friends first.

China's Commitment to HRD

With China's entry into the WTO, vocational education plays an increasingly vital role in boosting the rate of employment and making better use of human resources. Membership in the WTO will require China to adapt to international performance standards. Well-trained and skillful people will be essential to attract investment.

Zhang Xiaoji, head of the Foreign Economic Relations Department of the State Council's Development and Research Center, notes that China is facing increasing challenges in developing its human resources but that the country is determined to turn its large population into an advantage in human resources. Cheap labor is one of China's advantages in competing with foreign countries, but it will play a less significant role in the future. "The boom in China's high-tech industries," Zhang observes, "plus the country's fast economic growth demand a large number of well-trained workers, which poses challenges as well as opportunities to China's vocational education."

World Bank statistics show that in 2002 China's population was about 4.5 times that of the United States, but it has only 45 percent of the number of skilled workers in the United States. There is a large gap in average productivity between the two countries. Over the past two decades, about 60 percent of foreign investment in China went to the manufacturing sector. Currently, however, investment in high-tech sectors, such as telecommunication and electronic industries, is increasing.

To ensure social and economic development, China is integrating education, science, technology, and talent into its national development strategy. It is combining its human resource restructuring with ongoing industrial restructuring, rural economic development, and urbanization. China's recently adopted tenth five-year plan for national economic and social development places strategic importance on attracting, training, and making the best use of human talent.

China promotes HRD in the context of economic restructuring. For example, it focuses on training management personnel for new and high-tech enterprises and other urgently needed capacities. A recent project of the International Labor Organization promoted effective HRD and HRM, train-the-trainer programs, and material development in assisting the Chinese government to improve its economic productivity and competitiveness in the global economy.

China is also intensifying institutional reform and creating an environment that recognizes and celebrates talented and capable employees. Moves in this direction include reforming personnel management and recruitment systems as well as the income distribution system. China also plans to open itself wider to the outside world and promote international HRD exchanges.

Chinese Employees Seek More Training

Keeley (2003) notes that most Chinese employees believe they cannot get enough HRD, that their appetite for learning, training, and personal development is "insatiable." Employers, driven in turn by an urgent need to boost knowledge and skill levels, provide sixty hours of HRD per year to each employee. Still, indications are that employees are not satisfied. According to Hewitt's study of 2003 Best Employers in Asia (cited in Keeley, 2003), satisfaction scores in China for development and career advancement (including training opportunities) are only about 40 percent.

The main reason for this dissatisfaction, according to Keeley, is that employees have expectations beyond what most companies' training and development programs can deliver. Fueling employees' appetite for training is their goal to "get ahead" in the race for the best opportunities, the best jobs, the next promotion, and the highest pay. Conditioned by China's extraordinary growth over the past ten years, many expect that the "next" or "best" accomplishment is just around the corner. Training is seen as an important, if not the most important, means of positioning oneself in that race and preparing for that next job.

When trainees perceive that a training course does not meet their expectations because it is "too simple" or does not equip them to work better today and do better tomorrow, they are disappointed. Some are apt to vote with their feet and walk away from the session or fail to return after the break or the next day. Those who stay rate the training program low.

Chinese companies must do more than just offer training, according to Keeley (2003). First, they tell people "why they are being trained in a topic"; second, employees must recognize that development comes not merely by sitting in a classroom but primarily from within as a matter of choice, focus, experiences, and reflection. The change in employers and employees' mindsets will take time. Employers are still learning about the importance of mentoring, transfer of training, networking, action learning, and other HRD programs.

China's Top 500 Firms: The Gap with the World Remains Wide

Every year, the U.S. magazine *Fortune* releases its "*Fortune* 500" list of the world's top firms. In 2003, for the first time ever, a Chinese version of this list was released by the China Enterprise Confederation and the China Enterprise Directors Association in *A Report on the Development of Chinese Enterprises*. The combined revenue of the top five hundred Chinese firms amounts to more than 60 percent of China's gross domestic product, and these firms now form the core of the nation's economy. However, a wide gap still separates the top five hundred firms in China from their global counterparts, and a number of serious problems plague the Chinese firms.

First, although the top five hundred Chinese companies are growing fast, they are still small compared to the top global firms, and their labor productivity remains very low. The average assets and average revenue of the top "Chinese 500" in fiscal 2002 were a scant 6.5 percent and 5.3 percent, respectively, of those of the global 500. On a per employee basis, revenue, profits, and assets at the Chinese companies were only 13 percent, 29.6 percent, and 15.9 percent of the corresponding figures for the world's top five hundred firms.

Second, there is a huge gap in companies' abilities to create profits and innovate. The average profit of the top five hundred Chinese firms in fiscal 2002 was only 12.1 percent that of the global 500. Furthermore, because Chinese firms lack a system of incentives to encourage technological innovation, they invest relatively little in this area. Whereas many of the top five hundred companies in the world pump the equivalent of more than 10 percent of their business profits into research and development, the corresponding figure for the Chinese 500 is only 3.8 percent. As a result, technological innovations at Chinese firms are limited, and they lack core technology, making it difficult to further develop, or increase the value added to, their products.

Third, there is a great gap in the extent to which companies are internationalized. Most major corporations in China have penetrated overseas markets by exporting; only a handful have set up production bases overseas through direct investment or secured global distribution channels for their products. In other words, very few companies have organizational structures and management strategies befitting transnational corporations.

Finally, state-owned enterprises constitute 60 percent of the Chinese 500 and account for more than 80 percent of their total revenue, profit, assets, and workforce. The top twelve Chinese firms (State Power Corporation of China, China Petrochemical Corporation, China National Petroleum Corporation, Industrial and Commercial Bank of China, Bank of China, China Mobile Communications Corporation, China National Chemicals Import and Export Corporation, China Telecommunications Corporation, China National Cereals, Oils and Foodstuffs Import and Export Corporation, China Construction Bank, and the Agricultural Bank of China) also count among the global 500, but they are all state-owned firms operating in highly monopolized sectors that are protected through government regulations. Furthermore, among them are four major banks saddled with massive nonperforming loans, raising doubts about their actual strength. In fact, state-owned enterprises are huge, but the productivity of their capital and workforce lags far behind that of other forms of ownership. In contrast, most of the companies that are not state owned and have shown rapid growth in recent years have not yet reached the top of this list.

HRD Best Practices

Mass Transit Railway Corporation, Hong Kong

In 2003, Mass Transit Railway Corporation (MTR) received the BEST award from the American Society for Training and Development in recognition of its world-class HRD programs. Serving over 2.3 million passengers daily, MTR is one of the most intensively utilized mass transit railway systems in the world, transporting one in three people in Hong Kong per day. MTR has been recognized by recent benchmarking studies as one of the world's finest railways for reliability, customer service, and cost efficiency. In addition to railway operation and development and associated businesses, MTR also engages in the development, sale, and management of residential and commercial properties above and adjacent to its railway stations.

MTR is considered a pioneer and world leader in the area of knowledge management, having initiated in the early 1990s a mechanism for storing, transmitting, and sharing critical business information. In recent years the organization has introduced sophisticated knowledge management tools such as its Knowledge Library and Virtual Team. These tools allow project teams to share information and communicate in virtual workspaces. Any unique knowledge or experiences can be shared with the entire organization with the click of a button.

Defining successful learning initiatives as "training and development activities that bring [positive] impact to the business," MTR's Management Training and Development Department evaluates and leverages learning effectiveness using Kirkpatrick's four levels of evaluation. To evaluate level-4 results, MTR uses an HR balanced scorecard system in which quantitative and qualitative measures are tied to business objectives. As part of its succession plan and talent management strategy, MTR created an accelerated development program, a 12- to 18-month leadership development program for senior managers, middle managers, and senior supervisory staff. Benefits to the organization include more timely and successful placement of candidates in managerial positions, recruitment cost savings, and increased individual and organizational performance. Action learning has become an important HRD methodology utilized by MTR for developing leaders, building teams, solving problems, and changing the company into a learning organization.

Vocational Training and Employment in China

Vocational education is an important part of China's educational undertakings. The country today has 18,000 vocational schools nationwide with 9.5 million learners enrolled. To initiate the massive task of preparing the Chinese workforce, nearly 500,000 vocational training teachers are involved in vocational training. China emphasizes developing vocational education in rural areas, especially among ethnic minority groups and in poverty-stricken areas.

The Chinese government has recently implemented a system of job qualification certification based on the principle that workers should, whenever possible, receive necessary training before being hired or taking up their jobs. In accordance with the Labor Law, the Ministry of Labor and Social Security has formulated rules and regulations to implement this principle.

The principle of "integrating training, testing and assessment with application and remuneration" is a part of this premise. Vocational training is financed through various sources, including government budget allocations, funds raised by enterprises themselves, tuition fees charged to trainees, income creation by training entities, social financial assistance, donations, and grants. State regulations stipulate that 1.5 percent of the total payroll of enterprise workers be used for workers' training and that a certain proportion (usually 15 percent) of local governments' employment and unemployment insurance funds be used for preemployment training and retraining programs for the unemployed.

In response to the challenges in the field of human resources, says Chen Zhili, minister of education, China plans to reform its middle and higher vocational educational systems with a focus on training professional workers to meet the demands of the market. Experts suggest that besides improving the school training system, China should also upgrade its preemployment, on-the-job, and retraining programs to increase the mobility of China's workforce.

The number of secondary students enrolled in specialized technical and vocational schools has risen dramatically for the past thirty years. China's vocational training system has three components:

1. *Specialized secondary schools:* Nearly 3,000 of these schools train over 1 million students, emphasizing engineering, agronomy, forestry, health services, and finance.

2. *Workers' training schools:* These schools provide part-time training to secondary students and include technical theory and production practice for numerous trades. Politics and physical education are also part of the curriculum.
3. *Vocational schools:* These trade and agricultural schools currently enroll nearly 3 million students for a period of three to four years. The major specializations are agronomy, agricultural machinery, accounting, garment making, preschool education, textile skills, architecture, chemical industry, electricity and electronics, and machine making.

Full-time vocational training instructors generally teach five one-hour classes per day, six days per week. Each class has thirty to forty students. The State Education Commission compiles the training materials. Instructors may supplement the state-provided materials. The government assigns jobs to graduates based on the needs of the national economy and the skills of the trainees.

China's vocational training system is composed of three key elements: (1) occupational classification and vocational skill standards, (2) vocational skills testing and qualification certification, and (3) skill competitions and awards for skill talents.

Occupational Classification and Vocational Skill Standards

In 1992, the People's Republic of China published its first Directory of Job Classifications, including more than 3,200 occupational skill standards. Vocational training incorporates prejob, job transfer, apprentice, and on-the-job training. According to vocational skill standards the levels of training are categorized into low-, medium-, and senior-level vocational training; technician and senior technician training; and other adaptation training. Training programs are primarily provided by technical schools, which are the main base for training skilled workers, and by employment training centers, which train unemployed workers. Both focus on practical skills and adaptability training. In addition, there are enterprise-sponsored training centers and training providers run by various organizations or individuals who deliver on-the-job training and other training programs.

Comprehensive training bases are the results of reforming the existing technical schools and enterprise-based training entities. They have a wide range of functions, including job demand forecasts, vocational skills testing, and vocational guidance and are closely linked to job match. Comprehensive training bases provide trainees with integrated services including training, testing, and job placement.

The vocational skill development group is a new model of training alliances. Various kinds of training providers based in urban communities seek to carry out joint operations among training, testing, and employment service agencies and aim to improve economies of scale in training and employment promotion.

The Labor Preparatory System was initiated in urban areas in 1999 to enhance the qualifications of workers. New entrants into the labor force and other job seekers are organized to receive vocational training and vocational education ranging from one to three years. After having acquired vocational qualifications or mastering certain vocational skills with the assistance and guidance of government policies, trainees are employed through the labor market.

The Chinese vocational system recently began implementation of the program known as "Helping 10 Million People Get Reemployment in Three Years." This program aims at promoting reemployment of workers laid off from state-owned enterprises and maintaining basic living standards among them. The government has mobilized all types of training providers and has established a close link between enterprises, reemployment service centers, and vocational training institutions. Another effective program, government-purchased training, encourages laid-off workers to participate in reemployment training.

Vocational programs now also include more entrepreneurial training and probe into new ways to promote employment. Over thirty cities throughout China have carried out such entrepreneurial training.

Vocational Skill Testing and Qualification Certification

China has established a testing system for low-, medium-, and senior-level skills and a testing and assessment system for technicians and senior technicians in order to measure and assess the vocational skills of workers and publicize the vocational skill certification system. Occupational skill testing and certification have been adopted for the graduates of technical schools and vocational training institutions. For all types of skilled jobs, workers are required to obtain certificates through training and testing before starting work. The practice of certifying employees is also being adopted for self-employed persons and private enterprises.

Skill Competitions and Awarding of Skill Talent

Since 1995, the winners of "Grand China Skills Award" and "National Skilled Hands" have been selected and commended based on merit. Vocational skill competitions in all industries in the nation have been organized, involving millions of workers in on-the-job experience and significantly improving vocational skills.

HRD in Global Firms

China is attracting more and more direct foreign investment. This economic activity is affecting the way local and global companies operate in China. The flourishing of capitalism and market-based reforms has enhanced the role played by training and development.

Although about 60 percent of the foreign investment streaming into China over the past two decades has gone to manufacturing, an increasing amount is now being directed to high-tech sectors such as telecommunications and electronics. The so-called knowledge worker is the key asset in these industries. As information becomes the world's "currency," not only are more people gathering knowledge, but they are also required to generate it. This requires a major shift in thinking, knowing, and doing business in China. Companies must build innovation into daily operations, make work a continual learning process, and recognize that knowledge sharing is essential to the continued growth of these companies and to China as a country.

While global firms are one step ahead of local Chinese companies in training and development, the latter acknowledge their own limitations and readily seek external expertise. Most of the global five hundred firms operate in China and recognize the importance of upgrading the skills and competencies of the local workforce. Such global firms and their workforce development programs in China include the following.

Caterpillar

In January 2004, Heilongjiang Engineering University in northwest China and Caterpillar signed an agreement to establish a gray-collar worker training base. Under the agreement, Heilongjiang Engineering University will train skilled technicians in engineering fields such as mechanical engineering. "Gray-collar worker" refers to skilled technicians, whose expertise is desperately needed in China due to a lack of professional skills among the labor force.

Microsoft

China's Ministry of Education and Microsoft co-announced the recent start of a "Microsoft Academic Courses Program," designed specifically for Chinese students. The program is directed mainly to vocational education in China. Presently, China needs 200,000 software developers, a goal far from being realized. The program pays special attention to training students in software applications. Microsoft has organized forty courses and blended them into various training programs. As part of the training process, an interactive teaching method will provide a simulated working environment and process for trainees. Teachers, too, will be trained. Specialists will answer questions that teachers ask in a specially designed forum on the Internet. Microsoft already trains about 2,000 core teachers per year. The program was given a trial run in Fujian Province in 2004, followed shortly thereafter by programs in Sichuan, Jiangxi, Jilin, Hunan, and Jiangsu Province.

Oracle

In 2002, Oracle launched a training plan with China's International Talents Exchange Foundation known as the Oracle Workforce Development Program. It will train software engineers for eleven National Software Industry Bases in Beijing, Shanghai, and Chengdu by taking advantage of the experiences of the International Talents Exchange Foundation. Oracle will provide the foundation with software products, teaching materials from Oracle University, and preferences in certification, teachers, and funds. Oracle has advanced software technology and teachers that will help students to improve their research and application abilities.

Siemens

Siemens has recently expanded its training and investment in China, seeking to be a long-term, committed, and trustworthy business partner and contributing state-of-the-art technology and expertise to foster development in China. The company recognizes that to safeguard its employees' future, it must provide extensive training and continuing education, build up local competencies through extensive technology and management know-how transfer, and foster innovation through building up local research and development activities.

Importance of HRD in China

Chinese organizations and leaders recognize the importance of knowledge, talent, and HRD for promoting sustained economic and social development. The government of China recently put forth a four-point proposal for human resources development:

1. HRD should be guided by the principle of being centered on and benefiting people, and its goal must be the overall enhancement of people's quality of life.
2. HRD should contribute to improving people's health. A system of health coverage for all that ensures the health of all citizens is the key to breaking the vicious circle of poverty leading to illness, which in turn leads to further poverty.
3. HRD should facilitate the creation of an educational system for continuous learning and a learning-based society.
4. HRD should promote international exchange and cooperation; it must be regarded as an important means of assisting countries to achieve economic growth, narrow the digital divide, speedily build information and communication networks, and improve the quality of the workforce.

As a result of China's commitment to HRD, the country is witnessing unprecedented economic prosperity, social harmony and progress, and increasing development of human resources.

Japan

*Though we cannot live one hundred years, we should be
concerned about one thousand years hence.*
Namihei Odaira, founder of Hitachi

Introduction

Just since World War II Japan has become the second largest economic power in
the world. As a result, Japanese business practices—group consensus, long-term
planning, quality orientation, organizational learning—are highly respected in
the global economy. This chapter examines the cultural and economic environments that impact HRD practice, the place of HRD in Japanese corporate culture, and ways HRD is practiced in the Japanese workplace.

Cultural Factors Impacting HRD

Geography and Demographics

Japan consists of more than 3,000 islands extending some 1,300 miles northeast to southwest in eastern Asia between the Pacific Ocean and the Sea of
Japan. Four large islands—Honshu, Hokkaido, Shikoku, and Kyushu—account
for 98 percent of the land area and hold virtually all of the population.

By the year 1700, Edo (now Tokyo) was the largest city in the world; by
2003, it was home to an estimated 12.3 million people. Although Japan's total

territory is comparable to California's, its 127 million residents are concentrated in an area about the size of Indiana. Eighty percent of the population lives in urban areas, with most of the rest living on the scant 11 percent of the land that is arable. It is estimated that Japan's population has peaked and will begin slowly to decline over the next twenty-five years. The country's population growth rate from 1975 to 2000 was 0.5 percent; its projected rate between 2000 and 2015 is zero.

The people are 99.4 percent ethnic Japanese, with a small number of Koreans and Chinese constituting almost all of the remainder. The native Ainu, thought to be descendants of Caucasoid people who once lived in north Asia, live mainly on the northern island of Hokkaido.

Language

Japanese is the official language. Its remoteness from other world languages, the complexity of its written form, and the fact that there are relatively few speakers of Japanese as a second language have combined to make it a domestic rather than an international language. English is taught universally in the public schools and is seen as a basic requirement at the university level. Although the many spoken dialects of Japanese are more or less mutually intelligible, the Tokyo dialect is the standard for textbooks and media. The written language, initially borrowed from the Chinese and augmented by two native phonetic alphabets and a third based on Roman letters, has been standardized and is accessible to the 99 percent of the population that is literate.

History and Religion

Modern Japanese culture has its roots in migrations from Northeast Asia beginning in the 4th century B.C. Evidence of the earlier Jomon civilization can still be seen in the traditional beliefs, rituals, and customs known by their Chinese name, Shinto. A religion without a recognized founder or basic scriptures, Shinto—with its emphasis on honor, courage, politeness, and reserve—has been an important influence in the development of Japanese social values. By the 10th century, Japanese culture had also woven in threads of Buddhism—with its emphasis on harmony, flexibility, adaptation, and compromise—as well as of Confucianism, with its virtues of frugality, hard work, and respect for elders. More recently, the simplicity and austerity so valued in Zen philosophy were adapted to the Japanese culture.

Historically, geographically, and culturally, Japan has been first and foremost an island, but it was never more so than during the period from the beginning of the 17th through the mid-19th centuries. For those 250 years, Japan's rulers effectively isolated the country from all but a handful of Dutch traders, who were limited to a small trading station in Nagasaki, and occasional visitors from mainland Asia. Japan's emergence from this self-imposed isolation began in 1854, when Commodore Matthew Perry sailed his "black ships" into lower Tokyo Bay and pressured the Japanese into establishing commercial and diplomatic relations with the United States. The next century saw Japan's rise as an industrial, commercial, military, and finally, imperial power; and since its utter military defeat in 1945 Japan has risen from the ashes of war to become one of the major players in global business and economics.

Family

The family, and by extension the company, community, and nation, is the foundation of Japanese society. The Japanese are bound together by a strong sense of obligation to and responsibility for the group. Historically, their identity, their honor, and in some ways, their survival have depended on membership in, and protection by, the groups that define them. The Western notions of independence, self-determination, and individualism are alien and largely misunderstood by the Japanese, who have historically seen family, class, village, and ethnic identity as both determining their fate in life and as- suring their livelihood. In return for lifelong loyalty and obedience to the group, the individual expects and receives protection against forces that would otherwise certainly overwhelm him or her.

This role as a benevolent protector, historically assumed by family and vil- lage elders and, by extension, the emperor or shogun, is largely taken on to- day by the company. Since employees have traditionally stayed with a single company for life, there is a mutual commitment between employer and em- ployee that is seldom seen in the West. Length of tenure is often valued over specific contribution. Until recently, employees were neither hired nor fired on the basis of their ability to produce short-term results; in fact, laying off an employee was seen as a disgrace for all parties concerned. Japanese man- agement practices tend to focus on process improvement and long-term human resource development rather than short-term numbers and results.

Lack of Privacy

The practice of individual subordination to group needs, together with the extreme population density, has resulted in an absence of individual privacy. The Japanese have learned to live as if those around them are not there. Paper walls are somehow soundproof, and close neighbors focus on their miniature gardens and overlook the proximity of their houses. In business the "open" office, so much disliked by Americans, is a natural extension of this ability to ignore one's surroundings.

Consensus and Organizational Design

In a society that anticipates long and close relationships, both planning and conflict resolution are best accomplished through consensus gathering. If people are going to stay together for the duration, and if they are going to do so in close proximity, it would make sense for them to come to consensus on the conditions under which they will do so.

The organizational structure of modern Japanese companies reflects the historical relationship between the great feudal landholders of Japan (the daimyo) and their advisers, samurai, and other vassals. Such companies have relatively flat organizational structures as compared to their Western counterparts but, more important, are organized into groups or clusters of individuals rather than along the more familiar Western management lines. Each group, in turn, has a leader who is responsible for communicating on behalf of the group to other peer groups and to the leaders of groups above and below.

The result is that, while strategic planning and policymaking certainly take into consideration the wishes and desires of upper management, in a very real way, decisions evolve and are influenced from the bottom up. Ideally, they are then articulated and implemented, with resources provided from the top down. Cooperation, flexibility, and polite acquiescence to the will of the group are necessary enabling requirements for this process. "No" is hardly ever an acceptable response to a request from a superior or group, and when unavoidable, it comes in the form of an apparent "yes."

Communication Styles

Japanese communication styles tend to be implicit, nonverbal, and highly contextual. The language is characterized by vagueness and ambiguity; this is why Japanese haiku most often fails in English and other Western languages, as the translator must render a single reading from the many contained within the characters of the original text. Japanese are reluctant to be too direct or blunt. Movement in a conversation often takes the form of a slow spiraling toward the main idea or conclusion. This strategy works well with the process of consensus gathering; it is likely that the will of the group will be developed and understood through indirect reference long before it is stated for all to hear.

Economic Environment for HRD

During the past half century, Japan has risen from destruction to become an economic global giant. With modest beginnings in the late 1940s, Japan quickly began shifting its industrial base. It centered on the textile industry in the late fifties, on steel and shipbuilding in the sixties, and began moving toward automobiles, electronics, and cameras in the seventies. The eighties and early nineties saw Japanese industry diversify to other high-tech industries such as semiconductors, computers, and robotics. Japan now enjoys global dominance in videocassette recorders (95 percent), copiers (85 percent), and fax machines (70 percent).

Japan is the second largest supporter of research and development (R&D) after the United States. In 1997, the public and private sectors in Japan invested $90.3 billion in R&D. For many companies R&D expenditures are now greater than capital spending on plant and equipment. Hitachi's R&D goals are typical of many Japanese corporations: "to perform long-term continuous research to meet social needs and corporate policy in the next decades through development of original science and significant patents" (Kelly, 1995, chapter 3).

Japan experienced an economic downturn between 1990 and 2003, when the growth rate fell to 1.1 percent. Between 1999 and 2000, the price index fell by 0.7 percent. Green (2003) notes that Japan's eight largest banks were shaken by losses of $60 billion in 2002 due to stock market declines, uncollectible loans, and some risky accounting practices.

Japan's status as the world's second largest economy was not shaken, however. Its economic influence remains strong as the following statistics indicate:

- Despite a decline in assets during the 1990s, eight Japanese banks were among the ten largest in Southeast Asia and the Pacific in 2000.
- The top twenty Japanese companies were also in the top one hundred worldwide in 2002.
- Forty-one of the world's two hundred largest corporations are Japanese. In 1999, nearly 700 of the 1,000 largest companies in Southeast Asia and the Pacific (including China) were Japanese.
- The Japanese automotive industry has grown from 1.8 percent of the world market in 1953 to over 30 percent by 1997. In 2002, 25 percent

of automobiles purchased in the United States were produced by Japanese motor companies.

- The Japanese trade surplus exceeded $90 billion in 2002.
- The economic interaction between Japan and the United States continues to flourish. Japanese-affiliated companies in the United States now account for 9 percent of the total value of America's exports, for example, and employ about 638,000 Americans.

HRD in Business and Industry

Lindberg (1991), in her comprehensive study on training and development in Japan, suggests that the development of human resources is seen in Japan as "crucial to the nation's survival" (p. 113). Training has been and continues to be necessary to ensure that the small country, devoid of natural resources, can industrialize rapidly and compete with other nations around the world. Given this challenge, Japan recognizes its people as its greatest resource.

To understand Japanese HRD activities and the impact of these activities on Japanese business and industry, one must understand how Japanese culture has shaped HRD assumptions and practices, for these cultural constructs prescribe "who gets the training, who does the training, what the content of training is, how long it lasts, where it occurs and why it occurs at all" (Lindberg, 1991, p. 113). Lindberg identifies eleven cultural constructs that have shaped HRD in Japan.

Philosophy of egalitarianism. Japanese companies strongly value their employees. Employees across widely separated social and economic strata are given the opportunity to advance their positions. Japanese organizations practice a more egalitarian distribution of resources throughout the organization than do organizations in Western countries. Participatory management fits with the Japanese *ringi* system, a form of consensus building and problem solving based on the circulation of data and group decisionmaking processes (Ishida, 1986). This sense of participation is strong even at an organization's lower levels.

Groupism. One of the most noticeable characteristics of the Japanese is their sense of group identity and group loyalty and the belief that the whole is more than the sum of the parts. This belief creates interdependency and group bonds among employees in the workplace so strong that they share a collective sense of responsibility for one another's actions. This groupism leads Japanese to center on how work is divided among groups, in contrast to the United States, where jobs generally embody individual discrete tasks and responsibilities. In this ambiguous, interdependent division of labor, employees need to be able to change roles and assignments as group circumstances change.

Relationships.   Relationships among employees, like all human relations in Japan, are both highly personal and formal. The role of the older, senior-ranking employee toward a junior employee is similar to that of a father who would guide and assist his son in the organization by providing him with protection, securing favorable assignments, and advising him on problems and difficult circumstances.

Leadership.   Whereas in the West, leaders are "individual stars," in Japan they are "group-minded team players." Group harmony comes before competition. "Japanese followers are relatively docile, but the leader must be skillfully unassertive" (Hayashi, 1988, p. 117). The leadership style includes warmth, sociability, and concern for the employee.

Long-Term Orientation.   Japanese managers have a longer-term perspective—ten to twenty years into the future—than American managers. Rewards are given for long-term accomplishments—market share and growth—rather than for short-term profits.

Generalist Orientation in Education.   The Japanese education system is broad based and general, emphasizing theoretical and unspecialized studies. It inspires a lifelong interest in learning and provides a "high learning readiness" for Japanese organizations (Lindberg, 1991, p. 105).

Generalist Orientation in Business and Industry.   Japanese employers have historically paid little attention to prospective or new employees' educational background, for several reasons:

- They are most concerned with their personality, dedication, general ability, and openness to new knowledge.
- School-acquired knowledge will soon be obsolete with the speed of technological change.
- The corporation will teach new employees everything they need to know.
- People are being hired not just for specific positions for this year but for the company for the remainder of their lives.

Government Policy.   The Japanese government has been minimally involved in HRD. Historically, the Japanese school system did not prepare students for the industrial economy. As a result, Japanese businesses were required to develop an internal labor training system. Since the private sector had done such a splendid job in training workers, the government had little incentive to develop public vocational training institutes.

Hierarchy Within a Duel Economy.   There are two distinct groups of organizations in Japan: (1) the large industries that pay better wages and benefits, offer lifetime employment, provide substantial training, and offer employees personal status; and (2) the small and medium-sized organizations (e.g., suppliers, vendors, satellite firms) that cannot guarantee lifetime employment, provide fewer or no chances for training, and are likely to employ women, part-time laborers, and males in job transition.

Lifetime Employment System.   Although only about 25 percent of the workforce is protected by the guarantee of lifelong employment, it does represent "a national ideal, the fullest expression of the company as family" (Smith, 1987, p. 28). This system has served as a major foundation for continuous training for employees in Japan's major enterprises since the early 1900s. The employers' commitment to ongoing training helps to produce the following results:

- High versatility and adaptability of workers
- Employment dependent on length of service rather than on current value
- Upper-level managers and technicians who, knowing they will not be replaced until retirement, are more willing to train and develop their subordinates
- Virtually no turnover

Internal Labor Market.   The final construct within Japanese culture impacting HRD is the internal labor market, which includes all hiring done for entry-level positions, skill hierarchies, internal promotion, continuous training, and lifelong development of careers.

These eleven constructs within Japanese culture have created a "unique environment for learning" in Japan that is intricately woven into Japan's approach to human resource development (Lindberg, 1991, p. 108). They affect the HRD environment in the following ways:

- *Broad scope of training:* Training in Japan tends to be broader and more general, unlike training in Western organizations, which stresses expertise in specialized areas. In Japan the primary goal of HRD is to develop a flexible, multiskilled workforce capable of adapting to technological change at any time.
- *Company-specific training:* The skills and knowledge learned by Japanese employees are company specific. HRD objectives focus on employees (1) gaining a thorough knowledge of the organization; (2) having their behavior, attitudes, and values shaped to suit the organization's needs; and (3) acquiring and developing skills the organization needs.
- *On-the-job training:* This is the major component of all Japanese HRD programs.
- *Employee as trainer:* All staff, especially supervisors and managers, are considered trainers in Japanese organizations.
- *Long-term development:* Just as Japanese organizations have long-term business perspectives, so do they maintain a long-term perspective regarding their employees' training and development. Employers expect skills, knowledge, and abilities to steadily accumulate over the years.
- *Self-development and volunteerism:* Japanese employees are encouraged to volunteer to participate in group activities in order to learn about subjects such as history, English conversation, cooking, and flower arrangement. Companies also encourage employees to seek self-development programs outside of work. Recent studies reveal that, in some companies, up to 70 percent of the employees pursue self-development through correspondence courses, in-house study groups, and television and radio courses.
- *Performance-based training:* In contrast to the West, where the focus is often on the future skills needed for a promotion, HRD in Japan is focused on improving present performance. The reason for the Japanese approach is the fixed, hierarchical progression in an organization based on years of employment. Since promotions are routinely made by seniority, employees can concentrate on improving their performance within their present position with little concern about future promotion.
- *Human relations–based training:* Japanese employers value human relations skills as much or more than talent and technical skills. HRD programs therefore encourage the development of the total person.

Japanese culture impacts HRD learning activities for (1) orienting new employees, (2) training blue-collar workers, and (3) training white-collar workers.

New-Employee Orientation. Japan provides extensive orientation for new employees. This is due to the internal labor market cultural construct mentioned earlier in which companies hire unskilled, inexperienced young recruits for entry-level positions. The orientation program may last for weeks or even months, with a thorough indoctrination in the organization's the culture, including its history, policies, practices, and management philosophy. The orientation discusses how to be "cooperative, committed, and loyal to the employer" (Lindberg, 1991, p. 110). The orientation program may also include theoretical and practical course work in the employee's professional area and industry.

Training of Blue-Collar Workers. After orientation the formal technical training of the employee begins. This may be accomplished through on-the-job training (OJT) and/or attending the company's vocational training center. The vocational training center, which is of very high quality, trains new employees in basic industrial skills and prepares them to take national trade skill tests.

Training of White-Collar Workers. Since they enter the company with little experience and a lack of specific job descriptions, white-collar workers spend their first years in an apprentice-like capacity. The jobs for the new white-collar workers are relatively easy and are assigned not so much by a match of skills as by the worker's personality and relationship to the peer group. The trainee's supervisor serves as a tutor in a wise elder–junior learner relationship. The primary manner in which training is provided and information is shared is the process of consensus building and after-hours socializing. Learning by osmosis is just as important as specific job training.

A major technique used in HRD for Japanese managers is job rotation among the company's departments. Overseas experience is considered important for those working in global organizations. Job rotation provides the prospective manager with a general overview of the organization and provides the employee with the opportunity to practice different technical and managerial skills, as well as to experience the joys and difficulties of the business. Also, by temporarily serving in some of the subordinate positions in the corporation, an employee has a greater sensitivity to the feelings and experiences of his subordinates when he becomes a manager. Job rotation as a training technique for Japanese companies also helps to create more homogeneity and conformity among the company's workers, which would be more difficult to develop if managers and technical staff did not understand the activities and operations of the entire company. Finally, rotating staff throughout the organization improves the communication processes and aids consensus building.

Larger Japanese firms also send white-collar workers to external HRD training programs. In increasing numbers these companies are sending top managerial candidates to the United States to seek advanced degrees and to develop contacts for future business opportunities.

HRD Programs in Japan

Hitachi

Hitachi is a global corporate giant with annual sales of $68.5 billion in 2002. It is one of the world's largest manufacturers of electrical equipment, producing as many as 20,000 different products and systems ranging from nuclear power to microelectronics. By character and tradition, Hitachi considers the training and development of its employees (now numbering over 320,000) as "one of its most important business commitments." The company is strongly committed to the idea that "to respect, develop and make the most of each individual is the basis of employee education and that business, progress and growth cannot be realized without such a philosophy" (Tanaka, 1989, p. 12). Hitachi's principles of education include employees learning the "Hitachi sense of responsibility and performance capability." As can be seen by these principles, Hitachi sees training for its professionals as a means of cultivating the personality of each employee.

The most important of a Hitachi manager's various responsibilities, according to Tanaka (1989), is to "educate, lead and develop subordinates" (p. 17). The manager is to be a mentor in a teacher–student relationship.

In addition to training over 5,000 managers annually in its Institute of Management Development, Hitachi approaches HRD in a farsighted way, in accordance with the vision of its founder. Imagining itself as dependent upon personal relationships and corporate partnerships lasting well into the future, the company has supported a variety of HRD initiatives:

1. *Environmental Education:* The Hitachi Group has an environmental education system that urges employees to think more about environmental issues and encourages specialists to study and implement new environmental technologies. This education system focuses on training internal auditors for environmental management

systems and educating planners and manufacturing departments about ecoproduct development.

2. *Hitachi Young Leaders Initiative (HYLI):* This community service project seeks to nurture the next generation of Asian leaders and promote mutual understanding and harmony among Asian countries by identifying and encouraging young Asian leaders to meet and discuss crucial issues pertaining to the region.

3. *Partnerships in Learning:* In 2002, the Hitachi Institute of Management Development (HIMD), a corporate university and subsidiary of Hitachi Ltd. established a partnership with the University of Maryland University College (UMUC) to offer online courses to qualified Hitachi employees worldwide. UMUC, considered by many analysts the world's leading online course deliverer, entered into its first major agreement with a multinational Japanese corporation.

Hitachi Business International Services (HBI): As a parent company of 1,069 subsidiaries, including 335 overseas companies, Hitachi offers a variety of training and technical support services to its more than 320,000 employees. These include:

- *Permanent seminars:* HBI regularly holds courses graded by level from introductory to advanced. Seminars include training with word processing, spreadsheet, and database software, along with groupware and the Internet.
- *Special seminars:* HBI offers seminars customized according to a company's requirements. These may include continuous support, from planning training to preparing training textbooks, holding training sessions, and operating a help desk for posttraining user support.
- *Seminars at local sites:* HBI provides visiting seminars and visiting help desk service at locations both in Japan and abroad. These may include intensive training on the premises, individual instruction for executives, and training of overseas staffs.
- *Textbook sales:* Original textbooks prepared by instructors are available for those wishing to buy them without attending the classes. They are designed to be easy to understand and are suitable for self-teaching.

In 1999, Hitachi Europe Ltd. was awarded the prestigious Investors in People Standard for demonstrating effective commitment and investment in its

European employees. Hitachi is the first organization to win the award on a pan-European basis. The award is granted only to those companies that demonstrate an ongoing commitment to train and develop all staff to meet the goals of the business.

SANNO Institute of Management

Founded in 1950, SANNO Institute of Management is one of the largest HRD organizations in Japan, training over 500,000 Japanese company employees annually. In addition to a graduate business school and college, SANNO has a General Management and Research Center that provides public training seminars, consulting services, in-house training, and correspondence courses to over 20,000 organizations from Japan and around, the world. In 1992, SANNO established the Graduate School of Management; in 1995, it created a Distance Education Division of SANNO University; and in 2000, it added a School of Management to SANNO University.

To better respond to the needs of Japanese business and public service organizations, SANNO conducts extensive research in the areas of management, business, finance, marketing, sales, interpersonal skills, personnel development, information processing, and computer applications.

In 1990, SANNO helped establish the Japanese Society for Training and Development (JSTD). In addition to an annual conference, JSTD, with SANNO backing, has a monthly forum and publishes the *JSTD Journal,* supports international exchanges with the International Federation of Training and Development Organizations (IFTDO) and various national training associations, and carries out research and study programs. SANNO also coordinates a Euro-Japan cooperative program involving business education in topics such as creativity and group dynamics, HRD administration, production and manufacturing management, executive development, and computer application.

Complementing its academic institutions is SANNO Institute's Business Education and Management Consulting Division, which offers the following services:

Consulting services: To respond to the diverse needs of the business community, the institute draws on the services of experts in such fields as business strategy, organization, personnel, production, sales, distribution, research and development, and office automation.

In-company training: The institute conducts training programs on-site to address in an appropriate and comprehensive fashion the increasingly complex issues confronting corporate managers and provides follow-up service as needed.

Correspondence education: The Correspondence Education Department offers 450 courses and has served over 300,000 students. Many of the courses employ computerized teaching materials and are tailored to meet current needs.

Business seminars: The SANNO Institute has conducted more than 180 business seminars nationwide. Under the direction of facilitators, participants discover and nurture their own potential, gaining confidence and skill in the process.

Toyota

Toyota, Japan's largest industrial corporation and the tenth largest global corporation, employed 66,000 people in 2001, with sales of $67.5 billion. A key reason for Toyota's steady and rapid growth has been its commitment to high-quality training.

College graduates embarking on a Toyota career begin with a nine-month training program. During this time, they spend four weeks working in a factory and three months selling cars. They get lectures from top management and instruction in problem solving. Their supervisors make them keep rewriting solutions until they produce one that is suitable.

Toyota has even gone into community colleges and vocational schools to prepare students for work with the company. According to Robinson (1998), Toyota provides vocational schools, technical training institutes, and community colleges with a Toyota-specific curriculum. It also provides tools, training materials, auto parts, and even entire automobiles to train students who eventually will work in a service department at one of the automaker's U.S. Toyota and Lexus dealerships. Toyota found that the technical curriculum at most educational institutions adequately prepared students as auto repair generalists but did not provide the specific training Toyota really wants. In the twelve years that this program has been in operation, it has produced more than 2,000 trained graduates.

Toyota employees are trained to work with less supervision, accept more responsibility, and move projects along more quickly. Instead of getting up to ten approvals on a new program, in many cases they now need only three. Decisionmaking by consensus and teamwork, however, remain important.

Like most Japanese companies, Toyota uses a godfather system of training managers called the Advisory System. Managerial candidates who enter Toyota are assigned to group leaders who are two ranks above them. These group leaders are responsible for the training of these new managers for the rest of their careers. Training revolves around actual work situations and problems on the job. Approximately five hundred Toyota employees are officially appointed as advisers (DeMente, 1990).

Toyota also conducts ongoing training seminars for its managers. In-house executives as well as outside management specialists serve as trainers. The president and chairman regularly participate as speakers at these training programs. In addition, Toyota teaches foreign languages and provides courses on international issues for these managers. They learn the Toyota management style and how to transfer their technology competencies to their subordinates. Administrative and technical personnel are rotated every three to five years. This constant rotation and new on-the-job training is aimed at "enhancing the individual development of employees and continuously reenergizing the workplace" (DeMente, 1990, p. 29).

A primary objective of Toyota's collective HRD programs is to ensure employees' familiarity with company policies and understanding of performance expectations and responsibilities. Another important aim is to assist employees in developing new skills and learning new technologies. Toyota differs from most Japanese firms in allowing employees who had been recruited as factory workers to be promoted to white-collar management positions.

Summary

Japan has quickly emerged as an economic superpower, and the Japanese cultural factors supporting high-quality HRD are important reasons for this success. According to Lindberg (1991), the cultural constructs positively affect HRD in the following areas—broad scope of training, company-specific training, OJT, employee as trainer, long-term development, self-development and volunteerism, performance-based training, and human relations–based training.

Three globally acclaimed HRD programs are noteworthy. Hitachi's long history as a leader in HRD in Japan includes its Institute of Management Development and Institute of Technology. SANNO Institute of Management, which trains over 500,000 people annually, helped establish the Japanese Society for Training and Development. Toyota, one of the world's largest automakers, successfully uses an extensive advisory system in training its staff.

South Central Asia

17

*What kind of victory is it when someone is left defeated;
you must be the change you wish to see in the world.*
Mohandas Karamchand Gandhi (1869–1948)

Introduction

A subcontinent containing a culture formed by the struggles of diverse peoples over many centuries produced one of the most effective advocates for nonviolent change. The nations of South Central Asia have taken Gandhi's wisdom to heart, undergoing internal change so that none of their citizens might be defeated by hunger, ignorance, or disease. The road is long, but if recent history is an accurate predictor, the countries of South Central Asia are on their way to developing increasingly stable democratic environments, a deepening pool of skilled human resources, and a growing influence in the global family of nations. This chapter outlines the region's cultural, business, and HRD environments; considers its evolving practice of HRD; and describes a mix of HRD programs.

Cultural Factors Impacting HRD

Geography and Demographics

South Central Asia, centering on the Indian subcontinent and stretching from the Himalayas in the north to the Indian Ocean in the south, includes the countries of India, Pakistan, Bangladesh, Nepal, and Sri Lanka. These countries are among the most densely populated in the world; at nearly seven hundred persons per square mile, they are two to three times denser than most European countries. The region's population was, according to a UN estimate, 1.3 billion in 2000 and is expected to expand by 342 million by the year 2015 (Fukuda-Parr, 2000). India, by far the most populous of the five countries (1.1 billion in 2000), is expected to surpass China in total population by the year 2025.

Twenty-seven percent of the region's population lives in urban settings, with Pakistan leading the way at 33 percent. The population aged fifteen years and younger, at 35 percent, is declining, while the population sixty-five and over, currently at 4.6 percent, is increasing. Fifty-two percent of the subcontinent's total population is literate; 67 percent of the population aged fifteen to twenty-four can read and write. Sri Lanka leads in literacy with 92 percent and 99 percent of its adult and youth populations, respectively (Fukuda-Parr, 2000).

South Central Asia is home to more than five hundred languages, nearly three dozen of which claim 1 million or more speakers each. The proliferation of languages has presented challenges to nation building: fifteen languages are recognized in the Indian constitution alone. English enjoys associate status but is the most important language for national, political, and commercial communication and is the only major language that all five countries have in common.

History and Religion

Civilization flourished in the Indus Valley from 4000 B.C. Beginning about 1500 B.C., Aryan invaders swept into India from the northwest and mixed with the local Dravidian population. Over the next 2,000 years, the Aryans developed a religious philosophy and social caste system that has evolved as Hinduism. Buddhism appeared in the 6th century B.C. and reached a golden age under King Ashoka in the 3rd century B.C. From the 4th to the 7th centuries A.D., northern India experienced a golden age under the Gupta dynasty, when Hindu art, science, literature, and theology flourished. Arab, Turk, and Afghan Muslims ruled successively from the 8th to the 18th centuries.

European traders began arriving in the late 15th century, lured by India's fabled riches. From 1746 to 1763, France and Great Britain made the region a battleground, with the latter European power finally emerging as the colonizer under terms of the Treaty of Paris in 1763. By the 19th century, Britain had assumed political control of virtually all of South Central Asia.

Nonviolent resistance to British colonialism led by Mohandas Gandhi and Jawaharlal Nehru resulted in independence in 1947. Initially divided into India and Pakistan, the subcontinent was further divided after war in 1971, when East Pakistan became the separate nation of Bangladesh. Sri Lanka had gained independence from the UK in 1948, while Nepal, influenced but never colonized by Great Britain, created in 1951 a multiparty democracy within the context of a constitutional monarchy.

The structure of the region's governments, like those of many former British colonies, is modeled largely on that of English political institutions. For example, the Indian president is the head of state, and the prime minister is the head of government. As in Great Britain, the Indian prime minister wields more political power than the head of state. India has a supreme court and a common people's assembly (*lok sabha*). The prime minister and president are elected by the people.

The Culture of Hinduism

Hinduism, the most widely practiced religion in the region, dominates the cultures of India and Nepal, where it is the state religion. Hinduism is unique among the world's major religions in that it has no single founder and no well-defined ecclesiastical organization. It has grown over a period of 4,000 years by incorporating and/or living alongside the many religions and cultural movements of the subcontinent. Hinduism is composed of innumerable sects, but its most general features include the caste system; acceptance of the Vedas, the sacred scriptures of Brahmanism; and a belief in karma, according to which an individual reaps the results of his or her good and bad actions through a series of lifetimes.

The Laws of Manu are the basis of an elaborate Hindu social system that applies to every aspect of life, describing in detail the roles of the four classes and four stages of life. The entire system was designed to ensure proper functioning of society as a whole and to fulfill people's needs through their lifetimes. As the universe undergoes an eternally repeated cycle of creation, preservation, and dissolution, a single individual in the midst of one of countless lives is seen as relatively insignificant. In light of the belief in reincarnation and karma, Hindus are strongly fatalistic and see their lot in life as a result of their former actions and as a manifestation of God.

In two other countries of the region, Pakistan and Bangladesh, Islam has been the dominant religion since the arrival of Muslim invaders in the 8th century A.D. The impact of Islam on the family, daily life, and gender issues has been as strong in this region as it has been in the Middle East, North Africa, and Central Asia.

Family

The elaborate Hindu caste system has an enormous impact on family life, dictating everything from eligible marriage partners to food handling and preparation. Hindu families are large and take precedence over the individual. Extended families live under the same roof or close together; sometimes entire villages are made up of several generations of only a few extended families. Social mobility between castes is severely limited; more than 600 million belong to the lowest caste.

Marriages typically pair members of the same caste and subgroup and are arranged by the family. For women premarital chastity is an essential part of the marriage contract. Marriage ceremonies are often elaborate as marriage is considered to be a sacred bond that endures beyond death. The wife manages the affairs of the household and has influence in all family matters. The elderly are accorded deep respect; younger family members often yield to the advice and counsel of their elders. Children are expected to take care of their elderly parents.

Economic Environment for HRD

Economic growth since independence has been slow and somewhat sporadic in the region. Countries whose national governments have made a commitment to universal education have seen economic results. Several of the countries in the region are exporting highly skilled workers, and two, Sri Lanka and Bangladesh, receive a significant contribution to gross domestic product (GDP) from worker remittances. And India, which exports both software workers and services, has grown remarkably since liberalizing its economic policies at the end of the Cold War.

As a whole, the region employs a larger percentage of its people in agriculture than agriculture's percentage contribution to GDP. People living in poverty exceed 25 percent of the region's population and reach 42 percent in Nepal, one of the world's poorest countries. But the region is rich in natural gas, timber, coal, hydropower, minerals, and arable land. Steady improvement in universal education is helping to create more democratic and open societies and more open economic systems. In 2002, four of the five countries experienced economic growth rates between 3.2 percent (Sri Lanka) and 4.8 percent (Bangladesh). Only Nepal experienced a negative growth rate (–0.6 percent).

Economic Development in India

In 1991, India adopted the "New Economic Policy" in order to stabilize and restructure its growing trade deficit and declining economic growth rate. This policy was geared toward neoliberal economics, and markets were opened up to foreign trade. Multinational corporations (MNCs) were allowed free access to India, which, at the time, had no labor regulations and weak environmental regulations. The deficit problem also led to borrowing from the World Bank, whose ideology complements the unrestricted capitalism and policy of deregulation that corporations seek. India's economic policies did result in steady growth in GDP. India's GDP per capita in 2000 was US$2,358, and its GDP growth rate over the past decade has averaged 4.1 percent.

India is gradually emerging as an industrial power. It has already attained self-sufficiency in the manufacture of machinery for its major industries—aircraft, ships, automobiles, heavy vehicles, locomotives, construction machinery, and machine tools. Consumer goods, such as refrigerators, TV sets, and household appliances, are all manufactured domestically. India places particular emphasis on applications of new technologies such as electronics, computer science, telecommunications, and space and ocean development. India's growth in manufactured exports between 1990 and 2000 was 8 percent; its high-tech exports, while low, doubled during the same period.

India's emergence as an economic power has been aided by tremendous HRD efforts within India that have increased the country's capabilities in science and technology. Since independence in 1947, some 120 universities, 150 engineering colleges, five institutes of technology, and 350 polytechnic training centers have been established. Each year, India produces nearly 200,000 qualified technical and professional personnel. As a result, India has the world's third largest pool of trained manpower. Many of these highly trained professionals have left India to work in other countries, as opportunities at home have not kept up with the numbers of trained personnel seeking work. Many have migrated to the United States, where they are that nation's wealthiest minority group.

The Indian government has placed a renewed emphasis on the production of handicrafts in order to broaden employment opportunities and to earn foreign exchange. The government has supported training of artisans in hand-knotted woolen carpets, art metalware, hand-printed textiles, and woodenware—products for which there is a robust export market.

Economic globalization has been a mixed blessing for India. The policy of opening up the economy has yielded many benefits such as a higher rate of growth, increased savings and investment, diversification of the industrial base, and the technological upgrading of transportation, communications, and information technology. But globalization also has had a disruptive impact on the socioeconomic life of India. There is no question that the divide between rich and poor has widened, with as many as 300 million marginalized poor having absolutely no social security. According to Swaminathan (2002), a burgeoning middle class has served not only to stimulate the production of luxury goods but to show in bold relief the contrast between conspicuous consumption and the desperate search for livelihood.

Emerging HRD Trends

As foreign investment is attracted to the region by an increasingly stable economic environment, job opportunities should increase for the growing reservoir of skilled workers in South Central Asia. One growing source of employment for Indians and Pakistanis is a variety of Web support services to users in Europe and the United States. For example, The Resource Group (TRG) operates call centers in Pakistan for American and European clients and utilizes its Pakistan-based infrastructure to provide low-cost IT support. The client needing assistance calls a toll-free number in his or her country, and the call is patched to a technical expert in India or Pakistan. With 300 million English speakers, a booming IT industry, and a vast pool of skilled labor to draw on, these two countries benefit from rising employment while users in Europe and America benefit from low-cost technical assistance.

In 1986, the government of India adopted a new educational policy, coordinated by the Ministry of Human Development, that places special emphasis on vocational training linked closely to workplace needs and specific occupations. The policy emphasizes attitudes, knowledge, and skills for entrepreneurship and self-employment. All students, regardless of caste, creed, location, or sex, are to have access to education and training of comparable quality. The old examination system has been replaced by one that evaluates performance. The new educational policy also has brought about changes in instructional materials and methodology. HRD programs are implemented through various methods and channels including:

- Establishment of centers in rural areas for continuing education;
- Workers' education through employers, trade unions, and concerned government agencies;
- Postsecondary educational institutions;
- Wider promotion of books, libraries, and reading rooms;

- Use of radio, TV, and films as mass and group learning media;
- Creation of learners' groups and organizations;
- Distance learning programs;
- Assistance for self-learning; and
- Need- and interest-based vocational training programs.

According to Frank (1998b), there has been "massive growth in training programs in India. They are offered by all kinds of institutions, from the most prestigious institutes of management and universities to small technical and vocational schools, and by thousands of individuals" (p. 38). India's HRD campaign, conducted on a massive scale with consistent direction and resources, is pushing India toward economic stability, despite the many problems it has yet to overcome.

The Indian government is seeking to improve opportunities for women in the workforce. The Committee on the Status of Women has stated forcefully that the training of women is critical for India's development. Government policy has encouraged women's access to training. The large-scale training undertaken by Rural Youth for Self-Employment reserves a minimum quota of women trainees. As more women take positions of power (female representation in Parliament is 9 percent of the total seats, as compared to 14 percent in the U.S. Congress), the government will be encouraged to enforce its policies regarding women in the workforce.

Similarly, the environment for HRD is changing in each of the other four countries in the region. While geography, natural resources, and religious and cultural attitudes regarding education and the place of women in society are factors that impact the pace of change, the commitment of governments and the private sector to skill building for the benefit of the region's population is clear and positive.

HRD Programs in South Central Asia

With so many people in the region living in poverty, it is not surprising that governments undertake HRD services that might otherwise be provided by private sector organizations. Nevertheless, nongovernmental HRD organizations are growing in number. This section highlights four HRD organizations: The government of Punjab's Directorate of Technical Education and Industrial Training; Bangladesh's National Productivity Council—a semiautonomous body representing government, employers, and workers organizations—and its regional umbrella organization, the Asian Productivity Organization; the Academy of Human Resource Development in India, a private, nonprofit organization; and the Central Bank of Sri Lanka, which is transforming itself into a learning organization.

State Government of Punjab

The government of Punjab's Directorate of Technical Education and Industrial Training oversees eleven engineering colleges, thirty polytechnic and pharmacy institutions, and about 120 industrial training institutes and vocational centers, including those in the private sector. Each year these technical institutes train about 2,800 engineers, 5,300 diploma holders, and 16,800 craftsmen at the certificate level.

The directorate has striven to improve technical education in the state. With the needs of millions of Punjabis as incentive, and consistent with India's policy since the early 1990s of opening its economy to the global marketplace, the state government has developed a comprehensive approach to technical education that includes the following policy objectives:

1. To develop a Technical Education System that responds to new innovations in technology, contemporary industrial culture, globally competitive markets, and liberalized economic environments.
2. To develop the Technical Education System as a self-sustaining, demand-driven—rather than supply-driven—market; any certification must be industry oriented and professionally recognized.
3. To develop specially designed continuing education programs for upgrading skills of existing technical and skilled industrial manpower at all levels.
4. To improve the Technical Education System by strengthening, reorganizing, and reorienting the existing administrative structure and establishing facilities for internal maintenance of equipment, machinery, and buildings.
5. To make the Technical Education System as self-supporting and self-financing as possible by earning revenue through consultancies and other technical services.
6. To encourage private sector participation in technical education on a self-sustaining basis, without government support, by encouraging industry to pay for continuing training programs for their technicians and craftsmen.

To fulfill these policy objectives, the Punjabi state government initiated the following actions:

- Created Punjab Technical University at Jalandhar to respond to new innovations in technology and to be in tune with contemporary industrial culture and economic environments
- Increased industry's involvement in all stages of training in order to bridge the gap between actual requirements and the final product of polytechnic institutes
- Revised and updated curricula at all levels—engineering, polytechnics, and industrial training institutes in consultation with industry and the Confederation of Indian Industries. More than 375 memoranda of understanding have been signed with industry, and about 6,000 students have been trained under the revised curricula.
- Provided practical training for students in industrial settings and shared assessment of the trainees jointly with industry
- Updated training and instructional material at all levels
- Encouraged women to participate in the technical workforce. Five polytechnics have been established exclusively for young women.

National Productivity Organization, Bangladesh

In poor, predominantly agricultural societies, national governments must shoulder the major responsibility for developing the skills of the workforce until private corporations and nongovernmental organizations (NGOs) mature sufficiently to take a major role in nation building. All of the populations in South Central Asian countries have benefited from government-sponsored national productivity organizations (NPOs).

In Bangladesh, the poorest of the three most populous countries in the region, the governmental NPO continues to strengthen the workforce. It was originally set up as the National Centre for Monitoring Labor Productivity in 1983 in the Ministry of Labor and Manpower. In 1989, it was transferred to the Ministry of Industries, renamed the National Productivity Organization, and charged with acting as a catalyst and focal point for promotion of productivity in the country.

The NPO has a multidimensional National Productivity Council (NPC), the highest-level body in the country providing national productivity policy, planning, and programs. The minister of industries chair the council, which has thirty-six members. Nine secretaries of various key ministries, presidents of different chambers, and presidents/secretaries of different workers' federations, as well as representatives of educational, professional, and research institutions constitute the council's membership.

The NPO's activities include:

1. Conducting regular training courses on various productivity issues for management personnel and trade union officials;
2. Organizing seminars, workshops, and discussion meetings for management and worker groups on productivity issues in the manufacturing and service sectors;
3. Collecting and compiling productivity-related information from primary sources through field staff and storing it in centralized data banks for dissemination;
4. Rendering guidance and process consultancy services to persons and enterprises for improvement of productivity;
5. Conducting interfirm comparisons and business clinics for managers in public and private enterprises to enable them to compare their productivity performance and benefit from each other's experience;
6. Providing enterprises with the compositional, functional, and operational methodologies needed to form productivity improvement cells (PICs);
7. Undertaking studies and preparing reports on labor productivity in jute, textile, chemical, and sugar production; engineering; small and cottage industries; and the service sector;
8. Producing and distributing posters, leaflets, brochures, and other materials for promoting productivity-awareness campaigns; and
9. Maintaining liaisons with manufacturer associations, employer associations, labor unions, chambers of commerce and industry, the Consultative Committee on Labor Management Relations, research organizations, economist associations, engineering institutions, teacher associations, doctor and nurse associations, institutions of higher learning, management development institutes, industrial relations institutes, technical and vocational training institutions, and other relevant government and international agencies.

The NPO in Bangladesh is supported by the Asian Productivity Organization (APO), headquartered in Tokyo, which serves member countries as think tank, catalyst, regional adviser, institution builder, and clearinghouse for productivity information. The APO assists member countries through human resource development, technical expert assistance, and dissemination of knowledge and know-how on productivity. The APO's programs cover the industry, service, and agriculture sectors, with special focus on socioeconomic development, small-industry development, human resource management, productivity measurement and analysis, quality management, production and technology management, information technology, development of NPOs, green productivity, integrated community development, agribusiness, agricultural development and policies, resources and technology, and agricultural marketing and institutions.

The APO's activities include basic research studies, surveys, symposia, study meetings, training courses, seminars, fellowships, technical expert services, study missions, publications, and audiovisual training materials. Its program for 2004 includes the following sample of training courses for member countries:

- Training course on development of income-generating business activities for women
- Study meeting on productivity management in public infrastructure
- Seminar on incubators for small- and medium-sized enterprises (SMEs)
- Seminar on outsourcing strategies for SMEs
- Training course on problem-solving techniques for SMEs
- Study meeting on creative entrepreneurship
- Seminar on knowledge management for the service industry
- Training course on balanced scorecard
- Study meeting on innovation and value creation for higher growth

Indian Academy of Human Resource Development

The Indian Academy of Human Resource Development (AHRD) was established by the National HRD Network in the year 1990 with the mission of developing HRD professionals and professionalism. It is an institution exclusively devoted to the pursuit of enhancing HRD expertise and values and making them available for organizational effectiveness and the well-being of people.

AHRD's vision is to be an international center or hub for research and higher learning attracting national and international scholars and practitioners to visit, learn, and contribute to the building of theories and practices in HRD. In India the academy strives to strengthen, develop, and upgrade the role of HRD in all sectors and to promote Indian culture–based HRD.

To realize its vision, AHRD pursues the following objectives:

- Stimulate positive forces for humanizing systems and organizations and enable people to contribute their best to organizations and society as a whole
- Through exploration and experimentation, discover knowledge and skills relevant to HRD, its philosophy, processes, and implementation

- Generate, acquire, and continuously develop new knowledge and skills related to HRD through R&D
- Build a storehouse of HRD-related knowledge and skills by adopting the intellectual rigor of science and philosophy
- Disseminate HRD-related knowledge and skills among HRD professionals and practitioners and share information and experiences
- Strengthen the HRD movement in India
- Pioneer HRD research into and applications to innovative new areas, in keeping with national and social priorities
- Maintain standards of professional excellence in HRD.
- Act as a clearing house for information related to HRD activities in India.

The Central Bank of Sri Lanka

The Central Bank of Sri Lanka (CBSR) was established in 1951, soon after the country achieved independence from Great Britain. As the country has become gradually less reliant on outside resources for development, bank management has recognized the need for a reorientation of training policy toward having the right people with the right skills and having a multiskilled staff to meet future requirements and challenges. This has led, since 2003, to a commitment by CBSR management to transform the bank into a learning organization. CBSR has thus embraced a policy of learning, training, and development:

- *Learning* encompasses activities adopted and followed by individuals on a regular basis to upgrade skills, gain new knowledge, and be prepared for future challenges. It should come as a fulfillment of an inner motive.
- *Training* is the formal mechanism used by the bank to help its staff to attain both learning and development objectives.
- *Development* is concerned with each individual's reaching new heights: a new outlook, a positive mindset, willingness and ability to accept challenges, and maturity and balance displayed in resolving both personal and external problems.

The bank views a learning organization as one where all employees respond quickly and positively to change and actively seek change for the organization's benefit. This requires organizational systems that capture and disseminate learning appropriate to employee needs and create a culture that encourages employees to share ideas and knowledge. The bank recognizes that in a changing environment, unless it keeps pace with change and becomes a learning organization, it will fall short of fulfilling its role in society. The bank is striving to create a learning organization that emphasizes the responsibility of both the management and the staff for learning. CBSR's list of elements critical to becoming a learning organization includes the following:

- Adapt the external environment
- Continuously enhance the capability to change
- Develop collective as well as individual learning
- Use levels of learning to achieve better results
- Develop mechanisms for continuing learning and bringing about innovation

The following constitute the bank's rationale for its new policy:

- To build a strong linkage between training, learning, and development of staff and the bank's main objectives
- To ensure that all employees gain the required skills to keep pace with the changing environment
- To embed continuous learning in employees' work
- To motivate staff to share with others what they learn and to learn from others
- To facilitate and encourage training, learning, and development and to recognize and reward learning achievements

In structuring a learning organization, the bank is guided by these principles:

- Training is not simply about the transfer of technical knowledge and skills to improve competencies, but about bettering performance.
- Training, learning, and development should be continuous processes to meet present as well as future needs.
- Training, learning, and development policies should be linked to the overall requirements of the bank.

As a facilitator the bank is responsible for providing learning opportunities and creating an environment conducive to learning. The staff assumes responsibility for learning that relates to the bank's mission and goals. The effective implementation of its training, learning, and development policy continually directs the bank toward becoming a "learning organization," one that facilitates the learning of all its members and continually transforms itself to meet emerging challenges. It would foster an environment where individual members are encouraged to learn and to develop their future potential, where people are continually expanding their capacity to create the results they truly desire, where new expansive patterns of thinking are nurtured, and where people continually learn how to learn together. The creation of such a learning organization depends on embedding learning in the management process of the bank itself. Practical efforts to establish the bank as a learning organization include:

- Incorporation of learning in all policies and procedures and training for all employees in core competencies, including learning capability, creative thinking and problem solving, self-development, leadership, and vision
- Establishment of centers of excellence, demonstration projects, and a system of job rotation to develop and circulate best practices
- Measurement of learning outcomes in terms of both financial and nonfinancial indicators
- Creation of time and space for learning

Summary

South Central Asia, with a population of nearly 1.3 billion people that is expected to increase by 342 million over the next twelve years, has been shaped by waves of immigrants over thousands of years. Unique for its caste system and the coexistence of Hinduism, Islam, and Buddhism, the region is also marked by poverty that limits the development of nearly one-third of its population. Industry and regional governments have recognized HRD as critical for national economic development.

The region's HRD campaign—conducted by governments, partnerships between government and employee associations, and nongovernmental organizations—is pushing the region toward economic consistency and stability, despite the many problems it has yet to overcome. HRD providers in South Central Asia include the National Productivity Council of Bangladesh, the state government of Punjab's Directorate of Technical Education and Industrial Training, the Academy of Human Resource Development in India, and the Central Bank of Sri Lanka.

Southeast Asia and Korea

Man has three ways of gaining wisdom. Firstly, on medita-
tion, this is the noblest; secondly, on imitation, this is the
easiest; and thirdly, on experience, this is the most difficult.

Confucius

Introduction

Confucianism remains one of the most dominant influences on the values and behaviors of the people of Southeast Asia and Korea. Learning—whether in the home, workplace, or school—is of utmost importance to all the cultures of this region. Confucius and his ideas and ideals have hastened the development of HRD throughout the region. This chapter explores the cultural, business, and social environments of the ten countries of Southeast Asia and Korea; considers the evolving practice of HRD; and presents several of the region's top HRD programs.

Cultural Factors Impacting HRD

Geography, Demographics, and Language

Southeast Asia is composed of ten independent countries: Brunei, Cambodia, Indonesia, Laos, Malaysia, Myanmar (Burma), the Philippines, Singapore,

Thailand, and Vietnam. These countries are home to 450 million people with a staggering diversity of cultural, religious, and ethnic traditions. The hundreds of languages spoken derive principally from the Sino-Tibetan, Malayo-Polynesian, and Mon-Khmer language families; among those that are written, forms vary considerably, ranging from those of Chinese or Indian derivation, through Romanized alphabets adapted from European languages, to the Arabic script imported with the spread of Islam. Most of the people live in small villages, although the area is rapidly becoming urbanized and hosts some of the world's largest cities—Jakarta, Bangkok, Kuala Lumpur, Manila, Ho Chi Minh City, Manila, and Singapore.

Korea is divided between North and South with respective populations of 22.5 million and 48.3 million. The Koreans are ethnically homogenous, Mongoloid people who shared a common history, language, and culture from the 7th century A.D. until their separation in the 1940s. Korean, a member of the Ural-Altaic language family, was brought to the region by early invaders. The writing system, developed in the 15th century, is used in conjunction with borrowed Chinese characters.

History

The ancestors of the people who now occupy Southeast Asia left China and Tibet 2,500 years ago and migrated down fertile valleys and alluvial plains toward the tropics and the sea. Continuing this migration for centuries, they pushed aside or incorporated the small aboriginal cultures they encountered along the way. Many settled on the mainland, becoming the Khmers and Chams of Cambodia and Vietnam, the Pyus and Mons of Burma and western Thailand, and the Malays farther down the peninsula. Others built boats and spread through the Indonesian archipelago, becoming the forebears of the Dyaks of Borneo, the Bataks of Sumatra, and the Filipinos. Agrarian for the most part, they worshipped ancestors and spirits whom they believed inhabited the fields and streams. Their descent and inheritance systems were mainly matrilineal, and over the centuries, they devised a body of social traditions and customs that survives today as an equivalent of Western common law.

After more than 1,000 years of Chinese settlement among the indigenous Korean tribes, the first of several kingdoms arose in northern Korea around 100 A.D. However, Korea was not united until seven hundred years later; its golden age lasted from the 14th to the 17th centuries. For the next 350 years, Korea was dominated politically by either China or Japan. Despite this long history as a cultural bridge between their two neighbors, the Koreans have maintained their identity as a separate and distinct people. Partition of the country after World War II into two zones occupied by the Russians and the Americans was followed by the establishment of the separate states of North and South Korea in 1948.

Religion

The principal religions of East Asia include (in order of historical importance) Hinduism, Buddhism, Taoism, Confucianism, Islam, and Christianity. The governments of the area subscribe to the notion of freedom of religion, but among the people, there are periodic hostilities and disagreements. Islam is the predominant religion in Indonesia, Malaysia, and Brunei, while Myanmar, Thailand, Laos, Vietnam, and Cambodia all have Buddhist majorities. Although close to 30 percent of South Koreans are Christian, the Philippines remains the only East Asian country that is predominantly so.

Family

Common to all these countries is the high value placed on the family. Whether in Manila or Kuala Lumpur, city or country, rich or poor, all Southeast Asians have a strong sense of loyalty and attachment to their families. The rules and regulations vary somewhat depending on local history and religious influences, but an individual is perceived as existing principally as a member of a family. Families are becoming smaller, but often three or more generations may live together, particularly in rural areas. The young are expected to take care of the elderly, who are highly respected. The word of the father is usually law in most countries, although in the Philippines, a mother's advice is also taken very seriously. Cooperation among family members and assistance in times of need are enlisted and expected.

Importance of Correct Behavior

Loyalty to family extends also to community, ethnic group, and nation. To speak badly of another brings shame on the speaker's family. To refuse the request of a friend brings shame on one's own family. Southeast Asians are mostly reserved in public, discreet in their social relations, and reluctant to make pronouncements about others. They are often shocked by the ease with which Westerners voice opinions about others and also by how seriously they take these opinions and, for that matter, themselves. They appreciate a quiet voice, an unassuming manner, and a sense of discretion.

Problems will be handled in time. Conflict must be addressed quietly by the appropriate people at the right moment. Family and friends are always more important than being on time or resolving a conflict immediately. Southeast Asians rarely disagree in public, seldom say "no," and generally have time for others.

Best HRD Programs in Korea and Southeast Asia

Samsung—Korea

Samsung, one of the world's leading companies, had nearly $150 billion in sales in 2003 and more than 175,000 employees in 285 offices around the world. Ever since it was founded in 1938, Samsung has recognized the importance of developing its human resources as the way to national and then global success.

To achieve the mission of "contributing to a better global society," the company has enhanced its human resources and technology to create superior products and services. Samsung considers its success to be contingent upon its own people, who dedicate their talent and creativity to doing their best at all times. Technology also plays an important role in achieving higher standards of living. The linking of talented people and technology results in superior products and services, in fulfillment of Samsung's mission.

Samsung believes that educating employees is at the core of the company's success. Thus, the company invests heavily in employee training and development so as to attract bright and innovative individuals who can lead the digital era. Special emphasis is placed on training new employees so that they gain insight into Samsung's corporate culture and the contribution of their performances to the company's overall success. This initial training and orientation is followed by on-the-job training (OJT) to help new employees develop functional skills. OJT programs are managed by each site's training department.

Human resource and training departments work closely with the rest of the organization to develop strategies that enhance Samsung's mission. Training and development programs are developed in-house and are outsourced, with collaboration of local and overseas universities. Samsung also has a Local Expert Program that enables employees to better understand the international business environment. Samsung's training programs are designed to link directly with the company's performance. They are learner oriented, site oriented, and task oriented. In addition, training departments are divided according to function, and some of the business sites have their own training programs.

Key training is conducted at the following three centers:

1. *Samsung Leadership Development Center (SLDC).* Samsung links its survival in a rapidly changing world to an imperative to transform the organization into a flat, process-oriented structure that can make decisions quickly. The Leadership Development Center trains employees to become change agents who can adapt to shifting environments, accelerate innovations, and disseminate the most advanced organizational culture.

2. *Samsung Institute of Global Marketing (SIGM).* The mission of SIGM is to develop a customer-oriented mindset in marketing specialists in order to create new value-added businesses. The institute's activities include:

- Developing distinguished training content in order to increase customer satisfaction and improve marketing practices;
- Using case studies, sharing of best practices, and Web-based learning;
- Developing cases for Samsung and other companies in order to provide alternative solutions to on-site problems;
- Researching new marketing techniques and customer-oriented management practices; and
- Diagnosing and researching Samsung's marketing activities.

3. *Samsung Advanced Technology Training Institute (SATTI).* Since 1990, SATTI has been charged with technology research and development for Samsung Electronics. In 1998, SATTI was reorganized in accordance with the company's long-term strategic goals. Reorganization put training on site and recentered it on problem solving and trainees' needs. SATTI has systematically trained the company's core engineers and now focuses on training engineers in the areas of "3S" (software, system, and service) and basic technology—common to all products manufactured by Samsung.

Singapore Institute of Management

The Singapore Institute of Management (SIM) is an independent professional membership organization founded in 1964 with the mission of helping to enhance managerial and organizational effectiveness in Singapore. Over the years, SIM has expanded its role and scope beyond management development to become the leading HRD organization in all of Southeast Asia.

Quality and excellence have always been at the top of SIM's agenda. In 1993, SIM was the first educational and training institute in Asia to be awarded the PSB ISO 9002 certification for its management and delivery of programs and services. The institute scored another significant milestone in

1999, when it became the first educational and training institute in Singapore to achieve the People Developer Standard, an award that recognizes its commitment to staff development. This achievement affirms SIM's reputation as a people development organization.

Now forty years old, SIM is the largest private professional educational and training institution in Singapore. Apart from conducting various qualification-based training courses to meet the needs of local industries, SIM also collaborates with more than ten foreign higher-learning institutions to provide certificate, diploma, degree, and postgraduate programs.

Currently, SIM has more than 19,000 corporate and individual members, over 3,000 full-time students, and almost 12,500 part-time students. Since 2000, SIM has seen an increase in the number of students from China who come to pursue or further their studies. The institute has also responded to the Singapore government's call to participate in China's growing economy by actively seeking opportunities to conduct exchange programs and otherwise collaborate with educational institutions in China, thereby helping provide Chinese institutions with diversified and quality HRD training programs.

Through its partnership with prestigious overseas universities and institutions, SIM provides a comprehensive range of degree courses and senior executive programs. SIM currently offers two doctoral, ten master's, and forty-five bachelor's degrees, as well as over thirty graduate diplomas and certificate programs. Enrollment in these programs exceeds 15,500 to date.

Each year, SIM trains more than 11,500 executives through five hundred executive seminars, workshops, and annual conferences. In addition, SIM's well-established organizational training and consultancy unit provides a tailored approach to helping companies achieve effectiveness in various fields of management. The institute offers a wide range of activities, such as workshops, talks, and company visits, enabling its large membership base of 19,000 corporations and individual members to build contacts and stay in tune with industry developments. Members also have privileged access to SIM's management library resources, research, and other information materials.

To promote lifelong learning, the institute offers scholarships to outstanding students enrolling for studies at certificate, diploma, undergraduate, and postgraduate levels. The SIM scholarship program aims to provide suitable candidates with educational opportunities to develop their potential and equip them with the skills needed for tomorrow. Scholarships cover tuition fees, examination fees, and other compulsory fees, as well as book allowances for required textbooks. There is no bond attached to the scholarships, and they are open to SIM members or staff of corporate members.

SIM provides an extensive range of services for individual and corporate development needs. These include consultancy services in implementing management systems for organizations, in-house training programs, and readily available information through management research, books, and magazines. SIM's comprehensive management libraries contain one of the most complete collections of management-related publications in Singapore.

HRD in Vietnam

George Surya Kencana

In the past fifteen years, Vietnam has made tremendous progress in developing its economy. The country's growth rate has been nearly as high as any in the world. Concurrently, HR has grown and improved, especially in the corporate sector. Progress in HRD has been remarkable, especially since the inauguration of the *doi moi* and *mo cua* (open door) policies.

As late as the early 1990s, HR had no role in Vietnam's corporate sector. When PricewaterhouseCoopers (PWC—now IBM Consultant Services) inaugurated an HR role in 1995, it initially served the company's recruitment needs. As soon as 1998, HR's role broadened to consulting for the company, and by 2004 it had taken on the important role of training in the corporate sector. In 1988, only thirty people worked as HR managers in PWC, but by 1998 there were more than five hundred, and HR had taken on the role of supporting information technology (IT) and business operations.

PricewaterhouseCoopers, which has the country's longest running HR function, has adopted an electronic employee-management system to elevate the role of its HR staff to "business partner." The E-HR software package allows all employees to perform tasks online that previously needed the involvement of the company's HR division, such as applying for salary certificates and checking leave days.

By eliminating routine administrative activities, HR staff can concentrate on more pressing work such as policy and planning initiatives. When PWC started to implement its HR system in 1995, the role of HR was limited to administrative areas such as procedures and policies, paperwork, and pensions. Today its role includes training and development and manpower planning in support of its technical operations. Moreover, HR plays an important role developing strategic direction for the company.

Yen Trinh, manager of human resources for PWC, has noted that HR duties have evolved into responsibilities more associated with "business partners," requiring HR personnel to improve their skills and raise their understanding of business, management, and HR tools. Networking to share best practices among HR professionals has assumed greater importance.

Warrick Cleine, a partner of the Tax and Corporate Service for KPMG in Vietnam, said that successful HR staff need to believe that people are the most valuable assets in the organization. A company needs to be a "learning organization" to survive in the rapidly changing and globalized world. "Factories and computers are peripherals. The people do the business and solve the problems," he said. "If the people are finely tuned, the bottom line can be achieved. But it's difficult in the long term, because staff loyalty is the important factor."

Staff loyalty and development is also important to Unilever, another multinational corporation operating in the region. According to the head of the learning department for Unilever in Ho Chi Minh City, Unilever's success depends on its employees. The company strives to create a work environment that challenges people by increasing employee empowerment, welcoming a diversity of views, bringing together a wide variety of people, and giving them space to think in new ways. Within Unilever the following aphorism, well known in Ho Chi Minh City, accurately reflects HR strategy and applies to its practice: For the sake of 10 years, plant trees; for the sake of one hundred years, grow people.

While Vietnam has shown tremendous progress in developing its economy, much of its growth may be attributed to the catch-up effect. That is to say, Vietnam started from a very low level of economic output, so while its growth rate has been very high, in real terms, GDP remains small. Moreover, barriers to HRD persist in Vietnam. There are still monopolies in many industries involving incompetent state-owned enterprises (SOEs). As long as the government chooses to grant monopoly or preferential treatment to SOEs, there is little motivation for them to improve their performance and competitiveness. The SOEs' monopoly is so comprehensive that the small entrepreneur has no chance of competing with them.

Vietnamese companies are very friendly toward outsiders and quick to learn new ideas but hesitate to share too much information or have too much interaction with other Vietnamese companies. This behavior is related to the notion that knowledge equals power: To share knowledge with other companies is to lose power to them. If companies fail to develop a higher level of trust, they may experience the negative consequence of losing business to foreigners. One of the authors knows of a Vietnamese company that had an opportunity to land a very large American contract. But by refusing to cooperate with other manufacturers to put together the goods to fill the order, the company forced the American customer to leave. The customer went to China.

Building social capital is a high priority in Vietnam. To do this, corporate management must create an environment where more than just profit is valued. Companies must employ innovative means when exploring socially acceptable solutions to business problems. Some companies in Vietnam are running social programs, involving their employees in community affairs, or making donations to social or charitable organizations. By so doing, they are building business goodwill as well as social capital. Achieving business prosperity is increasingly about building both economic and social capital.

The history of major economic and business collapses often reveals that a deficiency of ethical and social capital precedes the commercial collapse. A recent fraud survey carried out by KPMG in Ho Chi Minh City found that the key factor in unethical behavior was the moral tone and conduct displayed by senior management.

Distance Training Programs in Indonesia

The Indonesia archipelago consists of over 5,000 islands spanning nearly 3,000 miles of ocean. This combination of great distances and vast expanses of water has resulted in isolation and limited access to learning opportunities for much of the nation's population. Soon after gaining independence in 1949, the government of Indonesia began to search for ways to link its peoples and provide training and education to its vast rural population. Indonesia was well aware of the inability of its existing training institutions and universities to meet the country's growing need for trained manpower. Less than 20 percent of those who apply for entrance into higher education are accepted due to shortages of staff, materials, and infrastructure. With the development of satellite technology in the 1960s, however, the government recognized that a satellite system might solve the problem of reaching its scattered citizens in a relatively inexpensive way. By placing earth stations at remote sites, the entire country could be reached, and from an HRD standpoint, this network would allow for a comprehensive two-way delivery system.

In 1976, the government installed a national satellite system with forty-two earth stations and two satellites. The satellites were named Palapa A-1 and Palapa A-2. (the name *Palapa* was chosen because of its connection with a quote by a famous Indonesian leader, Prime Minister Gadjah Mada, who vowed that he would not eat *palapa*—a popular food dish of that era—until the islands of Indonesia were united into one nation.) The HRD impact of these new Palapas has served to fulfill that vow of making Indonesia one nation. Indonesia became the first developing nation to have its own domestic satellite system. Over the next twenty years, the Palapa system was expanded to three satellites and 120 earth stations that provide telephone, telex, facsimile, and television coverage to all the provinces of Indonesia.

In 1982, with initiation of the Indonesian Distance Education Satellite System (SISDIKSAT), the resources of the Palapa telecommunications system were employed to meet the challenges of increasing opportunities for quality university education in Indonesia. SISDIKSAT was designed to maximize the scarce professional and teaching resources of the Eastern Islands Association, a group of fairly new universities and teacher training colleges in eastern Indonesia. Isolated by vast stretches of ocean, each university depended on its own limited resources to achieve the growth required of Indonesia's higher education system. Alone, these institutions could not offer the quality of instruction and full curricula expected of universities or serve the overwhelming number of students requesting admission. Multisite communications were critical to their development.

SISDIKSAT's main activities are course sharing, enrichment seminars, training programs, information exchange, and message services. Through its teleconferencing network, SISDIKSAT provides academic courses, otherwise rarely available, to university students and improves faculty knowledge and teaching skills through in-service training programs and seminars. SISDIKSAT makes the expert resources of a university widely available, thus multiplying the outreach and impact of these resources.

With fifteen sites SISDIKSAT is the largest teleconferencing network in the developing world, connecting twelve widely separated universities, the Ministry of Education and Open Learning University headquarters in Jakarta, and the Agricultural Institute in Bogor. The most technically complex and ambitious of the three government teleconferencing networks, SISDIKSAT posed a tremendous challenge for the government in the use of satellite communication for development.

All SISDIKSAT sites rely on the existing telephone system; access to the satellite is provided through dedicated lines from the universities to the nearest earth station. The landlines and satellite capacity are leased on a twenty-four-hour basis, bypassing the noisy local telephone switches and controlling circuit quality. Technical management of the SISDIKSAT network is shared by the user, SISDIKSAT, and the telecommunications company PT TELKOM. The SISDIKSAT electronic classroom consists of an audio-conferencing channel for two-way voice communications. A second channel is used for graphics, hard-copy transfer, private telephone conversations, and as a backup. Each site is equipped with auxiliary power supply units.

All learners are tuned into the same satellite channel at all times; thus anything said at one location is heard at all locations simultaneously. The second channel provides (a) graphics in support of the audio via facsimile and telewriting machines, (b) private conferencing telephone facilities, and (c) emergency backup in case of the audio channel's failure.

Courses taught in the Distance Training Program include adult education, agriculture, forestry, animal husbandry, fisheries management, nutrition, management and organizational behavior, poultry management, telecommunications, and entrepreneurship.

Development did not stop with the Palapa system for fixed telephone service and TV distribution: Digital global system for mobile communication (GSM) service was rolled out in the 1990s to allow tiny hand phones to be operated throughout the country. Extension of GSM to areas outside the developed islands of Java and Sumatra was made possible by way of satellite links. Although this was a phenomenal advancement, people are now taking it for granted, because the old generation has already forgotten and the new generation has never experienced the painfully poor communications of the past. Side-by-side with the phenomenal growth of PCs, practically every part of the country is able to enjoy colorful Internet connections, either from their homes or from Internet cafés, surfing a thousand times faster than the old telex system might deliver. Due to the reliability of data communication within Indonesia, people are comfortable with electronic banking from their homes and transfer large amounts of money throughout the islands.

The telecommunication needs of Indonesia will continue to be served by a mix of digital microwave, digital terrestrial, and undersea fiber-optic cable, as well as digital satellite links. Each of these technologies is applied according to its respective characteristics and economics. Together, they form a digital backbone with ever increasing speed, capacity, mobility, and affordability for delivery of multimedia communications throughout the sprawling equatorial belt of islands. Satellite communications have truly helped this country cross a digital divide.

Summary

Many of the top HRD programs in the world are being developed and implemented in the rapidly growing and culturally diverse economies of Southeast Asia and Korea. The Singapore Institute of Management is one of the top centers for learning in the world. Samsung's HRD programs have become a benchmark for many companies across the globe. Indonesia has made extensive use of technology to provide learning opportunities for its citizens on its more than five hundred islands. And countries emerging from poverty and war, such as Vietnam, recognize the critical importance of HRD for national development.

Central Asia

Whoever travels without a guide needs two hundred years for a two-day journey.

Rumi, Sufi poet

Introduction

Although the poet Rumi was referring to spiritual guidance, his words could just as well apply to HRD professionals trying to understand the Central Asian region. For many in the West, the region is exotic but poorly understood, perhaps best known for its ancient caravan routes, known as the Silk and Spice roads. For the purposes of this study, the chapter first discusses five states of the former Soviet Union that form the heart of Central Asia: Kazakhstan, Kyrgyzstan, Tajikistan, Turkmenistan, and Uzbekistan. It then takes a look at the Caucasus region, Afghanistan, Iran, and Iraq. Also discussed is Turkey, which bridges Europe, the Middle East, and Central Asia.

Kazakhstan, Kyrgyzstan, Tajikistan, Turkmenistan, and Uzbekistan

Geography, Demographics, and Language

Geographically, these five countries of Central Asia represent a region of contrasts, from towering snowy mountains to vast stretches of parched desert and grassy steppes. The region's climate zones range from subtropical desert to

271

polar conditions. The five countries cover an area of about 1.5 million square miles, or a quarter of the land area of Russia. Kazakhstan, the largest, is almost four times as large as Texas. Turkmenistan and Uzbekistan are each slightly larger than California, while Kyrgyzstan is about half and Tajikistan about one-third as large. The region is one of great natural wealth in the form of oil, gas, and minerals. Agriculture is the basis for much of the area's economic life, and cotton, wool, silk, grain, and livestock are common products. Even though Turkmenistan, Kazakhstan, and Uzbekistan have significant amounts of natural gas and oil to export, they have been limited by the fact that their only export pipelines run through Russia, which has led to disputes over prices and access. As landlocked countries, they are dependent on surrounding states for transportation routes—whether by road, rail, or pipeline—to export their products.

The Central Asian nations are a recent geopolitical creation, drawn up by Soviet rulers during the 20th century. Prior to that time, populations, dialects, and cultures intermingled, without clear separations between ethnic groups. As a result, there was not a historical relationship between ethnicity and statehood in Central Asia. States were instead formed around Muslim dynasties ruling over multiethnic populations. The commonly accepted idea that an ethnic group would naturally include a common language, territory, and descent did not apply in this region. This intermixing of populations caused problems for the Soviet Union in trying to divide the region into individual states based on the assumption that each would represent some ethnic or cultural heritage.

Population statistics in the area are commonly reported by the number of Kazakhs, Russians, Uzbeks, Tajiks, Turkmen, Tartars, and others groups. Alternative sources, such as kinship and tribal groups and Islam, also provide a sense of identity in a region still struggling with transitions resulting from the end of Soviet rule. As in most countries, wide variations exist between the lives of urban inhabitants and rural populations, some of whom remain nomadic. Languages spoken in the region include Turkmen, Uzbek, Tajik, Kazakh, and Kyrgyz. Russian continues to be used widely, particularly in business and government, and is an official language in Kyrgyzstan and Kazakhstan.

History

During the 1st through 15th centuries, the caravan stops of Central Asia were the backbone of trade and cultural exchange between East and West along the Silk Road, which was actually a network of many roads and trails. Silk was only one of many items traded along these routes. Gold, precious metals, ivory, precious stones, and glass were sent east, while ceramics, gun powder, jade, bronze objects, and iron went west. Trade enriched the region and led to the growth of great trading centers such as Samarqand and Boukhara. Literary, artistic, and scientific life flourished, especially from the 8th to the 10th century. Music permeated the culture, and colorful and intricate handicrafts—weaving, embroidery, leatherwork, metalwork—thrived. The mosques and mausoleums were among the architectural and scientific marvels of the world, and writers, scholars, and scientists graced the universities in Samarqand and Boukhara. This abundance gradually faded after the 15th century, however, due to the closing of the border with China for several centuries. Much of the region was taken over by the Russians during the 19th century and became Soviet states in the early decades of the 20th century.

Today, with the reopening of borders and gradual transition to more open societies, the region is once again becoming a crossroads for movement of people and goods from all directions.

Religion

The region's main religion, Islam, was introduced in the 7th century. During the Soviet regime, religion was largely repressed and secularization was widespread. Since the breakdown of the Soviet Union, religion has begun to revive throughout the area as a natural and stabilizing force. The overwhelming majority of Muslims in the region are traditional, tolerant, and moderate and are opposed to the more radical forms of Islam, such as the Taliban in Afghanistan, which they perceive as alien and inherently violent. Political leaders have officially chosen secular regimes as a way to keep more radical factions under control. Due to the Russian presence in the region, the Russian Orthodox faith is also well-represented.

Family

Family life in Central Asia reflects the region's nomadic and Islamic roots, but as in many cultures, family culture varies between urban and rural areas. In traditional culture an authoritarian system with an established, patriarchal hierarchy is typical. Deference is given to elders in the family, and the elder man is the head of the family, while women are viewed as subordinate.

The Soviet regime established a variety of social systems in the region, providing health care, education, and improved housing, transportation, water, and electricity at highly subsidized rates. These subsidies disappeared after independence, and the social infrastructure has deteriorated as a result. In the absence of sufficient economic resources, malnutrition has become more common, diseases have begun to spread more easily, unemployment has become a fact of life, hospitals often lack supplies, and some schools have closed. Children in particular have suffered from the economic conditions during the transition period.

Although the ruling secular governments include women in social and political life, women's role is not equal to men's. Discrimination and sexual harassment continue for employed women, and divorce and property laws often put women at a disadvantage. In traditional households women are expected to stay home and raise children. Girls are taught to obey family rules and accept life as it is. Because of economic difficulties, particularly in rural areas, families may not be able to support their daughters or send them to school. In such cases, they commonly marry their daughters at early ages, leading to a high infant mortality rate, female depression, and failed marriages. Despite their lack of economic resources, most of the people in the region are very hospitable and welcoming to outsiders.

Political and Economic Environment for HRD

After gaining independence in 1991, each of the five countries established democratic and market-oriented political structures, including constitutions with separation of powers, legislatures, and judicial systems. In more than a decade of transition, however, these structures have not led to democratic functioning. All five countries are in some way authoritarian, with leaders who emerged from the Soviet power establishment and have perpetuated a Soviet style of centralized power. Turkmenistan and Uzbekistan are repressive dictatorships, while Kazakhstan, Kyrgyzstan, and Tajikistan can be described as more open but still authoritarian. All five countries suffer from corruption and have high levels of foreign debt.

Much of the region suffers from extreme poverty. Border disputes—resulting from the artificially drawn boundaries that often separate ethnic communities and that were imposed on a previously borderless region—exacerbate insecurity in the area. The five countries possess different economic potential and resources, the more developed being Kazakhstan and Uzbekistan, with Turkmenistan having chances for improving its economic situation thanks to its gas and oil and a relatively small population. Kyrgyzstan is a comparatively poor republic, and Tajikistan, devastated by civil war, ranks last.

The postcommunist era of free markets and globalization has generally been difficult for the region. All but Kazakhstan have experienced severe declines in gross domestic product. The GDPs of both Tajikistan and Kyrgyzstan are now only about a third of the 1990 figures. Tajikistan remains one of the world's poorest countries, with an average per capita income of $330 per year. The relative stability of GDP in Uzbekistan and Turkmenistan has resulted from a refusal to reform their economies, which will undoubtedly lead to future declines as equipment left from the Soviet period wears out and old markets are lost and not replaced.

Central Asia has also suffered tremendous environmental damage as a result of irrigation and soil, air, and water pollution. The Aral Sea, on the border of Kazakhstan and Uzbekistan, dramatically illustrates environmental destruction. Once the world's fourth largest lake, it is now the eighth largest due to irrigation for intensive rice and cotton farming during the past thirty-five years. The loss of water has led to salt buildup along the shores, which is spread by the wind over many miles of agricultural land, degrading thousands of acres. Aging irrigation ditches also allow much water to evaporate, causing further reduction in precious water supplies for a dry region. The fishing industry has collapsed, and respiratory diseases have spread due to the salt and dust in the air. Similarly, some scientists consider the Apsheron Peninsula and the Caspian Sea to be the most ecologically devastated area in the world because of severe air, soil, and water pollution, particularly from oil spills, and the use of DDT and toxic defoliants in the production of cotton.

HRD Programs Now and in the Future

Although many of the people of Central Asia are literate and skilled, the area needs qualified managers and governmental employees who understand market economies. With the transition from a centralized Soviet system to a more democratic, open-market structure, training and retraining are essential to the success of nation building. Nongovernmental agencies (Eurasia Foundation, IREX, ACDI-VOCA, IESC, Winrock, and many others) and international companies operating in the area, in partnership with local institutions, provide much of the support for this effort. Following are some examples of HRD initiatives in the region.

European and Central Asia
Virtual University Association (ECAVU)

The European and Central Asia Virtual University Association was founded in 2001 with the cooperation of over forty universities in Russia and Central Asia. Its mission is to improve quality of learning through partnerships and use new technologies in higher education and research environments (Skidén, 2003).

Most of ECAVU's work is accomplished by instructors from the founding universities who have been trained by the World Bank Institute's courses in distance learning. Technical specialists are in charge of developing and improving platforms for the delivery of distance learning programs. When the association was founded, the World Bank Institute donated virtual learning environment (VLE) programs to be used at no cost by association members for creating and teaching distance learning courses. These programs continue to be updated and installed as freeware for universities. In addition, the ECAVU Consulting Center is helping universities train course developers to create new distance learning programs. An upcoming task for ECAVU is to develop distance courses to support and develop technical and humanities faculty and to improve teacher training systems throughout Central Asia.

University of Central Asia

The training and development provided by the University of Central Asia is an example of the development of HRD in the region. The University of Central Asia was established by a treaty between the aga khan (hereditary imam of the Shi'ite Muslims) and the governments of Tajikistan, Kyrgyzstan, and Kazakhstan and with assistance from experts from around the world. Its mission is to promote socioeconomic development of Central Asia's mountain areas through education and research.

In addition to conferring formal education degrees at the bachelor's and master's levels, the Division of Continuing Education and Training plays a critical role in achieving the university's mission. Although the university's campus sites are still under development, the division operates in all three countries, where about 1,000 people have completed courses. The division uses a network of local learning centers, as well as distance education technologies and ongoing analyses of local communities to meet learners' needs. The division hopes to develop civil servants and leaders, as well as retrain teachers and other professionals, so as to build the intellectual capacity of the regions served. Technical education in trade, agriculture, artisan work, business, economics, computing, the English language, entrepreneurship, and natural resource management will provide a wider range of educational possibilities for those living in rural areas and small towns.

The Caucasus Region

The Caucasus region includes Armenia, Azerbaijan, Georgia, and part of southern Russia. The region is generally inhospitable, with forty-three mountain peaks higher than 14,000 feet, steep valleys, and gorges, although the river valleys offer some good farmland. The total area of the three main countries is 71,853.6 square miles—about the size of Washington state. Climates range from highland continental in Armenia, to semiarid steppe in Azerbaijan, to warm, pleasant weather in Georgia, particularly along the

Black Sea. Azerbaijan's main export is oil and most important resource is petroleum, while Georgia's economy is supported mainly by the cultivation of fruits, tea, nuts, and grapes; some mining; and a small industrial output.

The many ethnic groups, religions, and languages has led researcher Karl Meyer (2003) to describe the region as "a bedlam of identity." Its ethnic and linguistic complexity is due in part to the effects of the many invaders of the region, including Persians, Khazars, Arabs, Huns, Turks, Mongols, and Russians. Over forty languages are spoken in the region today, and Ossetians, Kabards, Circassians, Dagestani, Armenians, Georgians, and Azeris are the primary ethnic groups. Unlike much of the rest of Central Asia, however, Armenia's and Georgia's populations are primarily Christian, while Azerbaijan is mostly Muslim.

All three countries gained independence from the Soviet Union in 1991 and continue to face formidable challenges in transitioning from a Soviet to a market economy and in combating widespread corruption. Unemployment rates are generally 16 to 20 percent. Ongoing conflicts either within or outside their borders further deplete the countries' resources. Azerbaijan and Armenia continue to dispute control of the Nagorno-Karabakh territory, and Georgia is plagued with internal ethnic and territorial disputes.

As in much of Central Asia, HRD activity in the Caucasus stems largely from local partnerships with international public and nongovernmental organizations (NGOs). Training programs in the region run the gamut from teacher training to information technology, from environmental quality to democratic processes. As an example, InterNews, an international nonprofit organization, has been active in Armenia in training television and radio professionals, including station managers, journalists, sales agents, and accountants in media organizations. The Center for Training and Consultancy in Georgia provides training for NGO project managers in organizational management, human resource management, financial management, accounting, nonprofit marketing, effective communications, and other relevant topics. In Azerbaijan the Internet Access and Training Program (IATP) provides software and hardware courses to improve local computer and Internet capabilities.

Afghanistan

Afghanistan is a landlocked country a little smaller than Texas, bordered on the west by Iran, on the east and south by Pakistan, and on the north by Turkmenistan, Uzbekistan, and Tajikistan. The country's climate is arid to semiarid, and much of its terrain is mountainous, with peaks reaching 24,557 feet. Ethnic groups represented in Afghanistan include the majority Pashtun, Tajik, Hazara, Uzbek, and others. As in most of the region, the population is almost entirely Muslim and has a strong Sunni majority. Dari (Afghan Persian) and Pashto are official languages, while Tajik, Uzbek, and Turkmen are spoken widely in the north. More than seventy other languages and numerous dialects are also spoken by smaller groups throughout the country. Average life expectancy is forty-six years, and infant mortality is high. The total population is estimated at over 28 million, with some 4.5 million Afghan refugees living outside the country.

An extremely poor country, Afghanistan is highly dependent on foreign aid, farming, raising livestock, and trade with its neighbors. Its main exports are opium, fruits and nuts, carpets, wool, cotton, hides, and precious and semiprecious gems. The majority of the population suffers from lack of food, clothing, housing, medical care, and jobs.

An ancient civilization, Afghanistan has been called the Crossroads of Central Asia. Its turbulent history includes periods of rule by the Persians, Greeks, Arabs, Mongols (under Genghis Khan), and Moghuls, and its people have battled the British and the Russians. The Soviet Union invaded in 1979 but withdrew ten years later. Subsequently, factions led by warlords fought for control, which led to the rise of the Taliban. Military action in 2001 by the United States and some of its allies reduced Taliban power, allowing the establishment of an interim government.

As a result of war and civil unrest, much of the infrastructure of Afghanistan is in ruins. However, HRD projects, mostly by governmental, public, and nonprofit organizations, have begun to help the country recover. The Afghan government is implementing training for postal workers and has established a training and advocacy center within the Ministry of Women's Affairs. The British Broadcasting Corporation and others are partnering to provide training and equipment to Afghan broadcasters and journalists. Two NGOs, Builders without Borders and Shelter for Life, are using an online forum to work with Afghan builders in an effort to improve housing suited to the region. A public-private partnership providing computer network training at the University Kabul's Cisco Network Academy plans to train over two hundred people in 2003 and is setting up other academies in other areas. Health care training, police and security training, and teacher training are just a few of the many other HRD initiatives in Afghanistan.

Iran

Situated between Iraq and Pakistan, Iran is slightly larger than Alaska at 1.65 million square miles. Its position on the Shatt al-Arab waterway and at the head of the Persian Gulf, as well as its coastline on the Strait of Hormuz and Gulf of Oman, make it strategically important. Iran's climate is mostly semiarid and arid, and its terrain includes a high central basin and mountainous areas.

The country's most important exports are petroleum and natural gas, while handmade carpets are its most famous cultural export, dating back to the 5th century B.C. Agricultural products are also an important part of the economy, although few are exported. Today, Iran's economy is a mixture of central planning, state ownership of oil and other large enterprises, village agriculture, and small-scale private trading and service ventures.

The ancient nation of Persia was an empire in its own right but was overrun numerous times throughout history by Arabs, Seljuk Turks, Mongols, and others. Each time, however, the nation reasserted its unique political and cultural identity. Known as Persia until 1935, Iran became an Islamic republic in 1979 after the ruling shah was forced into exile. Since that time, it has suffered from eight years of war with Iraq, economic turmoil, and internal political unrest. Although Iran was traditionally an agricultural society, by the 1970s, it had attained a considerable level of industrialization and economic modernization. This pace of growth slowed dramatically by 1978, just before the Islamic revolution; since the revolution, the government's increased participation in and control of the economy has slowed growth even more. The development of coherent economic policies has often been hindered by mismanagement and ideological disputes.

The dominant ethnic groups, Persians and Azeris, make up three-quarters of the population, and the main languages are Persian (Farsi) and Turkic dialects. Islam is the religion of 99 percent of the population, primarily of the Shi'ite branch. Conservative Islam pervades all aspects of life, including the government and social norms. Clerics, called mullahs, dominate politics and nearly all aspects of Iranian life, both urban and rural.

Since much of the economy is controlled by the government, HRD initiatives often are headed by governmental departments. For example, the National Iranian Productivity Organization (NIPO) was established in 1992 within the Ministry of Heavy Industries. The Training Department within NIPO is responsible for implementing training programs to provide managers and workers with productivity concepts and tools, as well as developing its own staff with internal and external training. Specific information on HRD activities in the country area is not easily accessible. However, HRD seems to be led primarily by Iranian government ministers, international aid organizations, and international corporations working in the region.

Iraq

Situated between Iran and Kuwait, Iraq is landlocked except for a small portion of coastline on the Persian Gulf, including the ports of Basra and Umm Qasar. Iraq has about twice the land area of Idaho. Its climate is mostly arid, and its terrain consists of broad plains, marshes, and mountains. Despite the arid climate, the Tigris and Euphrates rivers provide water for irrigation. Its main resources are petroleum, natural gas, phosphates, and sulfur.

Arabs make up about 75 percent of the population, while another 20 percent is of Kurdish origin, and the main languages are Arabic and Kurdish. As in much of the region, Islam is the religion practiced by almost all Iraqis. Shi'ite Muslims comprise about two-thirds of the Muslim population, while Sunnis make up the rest. Islamic beliefs govern the values and practices of most Iraqis, although there has been some influx of Western thought and politics over the last century.

Iraq traces its beginnings back 8,000 years ago to Mesopotamia, often called the "cradle of civilization." By 3000 B.C., the Mesopotamians had already invented the wheel, developed writing, and created cities. Sumerians, Babylonians, Assyrians, Persians, Greeks, and other civilizations occupied the region over the centuries, until the Arab conquest in 637. Other groups followed, including the Mongols, Turkmen, and the Ottoman Turks. Iraq was occupied by Britain before becoming an independent kingdom in 1932. A republic was established in 1958, but a series of military leaders have ruled since that time, the most recent being Saddam Hussein.

Many Iraqis work in agriculture, but massive oil fields have provided a much more substantial source of income since they were discovered in the early part of the twentieth century. Iraq's economy has traditionally provided about 95 percent of foreign exchange earnings. However, the wars with Iran, Kuwait, and the United States, plus international economic sanctions, have seriously damaged the infrastructure and economy.

As a result of the 2003 war with the United States, much of the HRD activity in Iraq is focused on developing skills needed to rebuild and improve the economy and quality of life. For example, the Foundation for Enterprise Development (FED) recently announced the signing of a strategic alliance with the Iraqi-American Chamber of Commerce and Industry (IACCI) to create and manage a business training facility in Iraq. In another initiative, the University of Colorado is providing telecommunications training in basic telecommunications, traffic engineering, and local area network management, while Canada and other nations are providing training to Iraqi police officers. USAID projects include training for telephone and postal operators and engineers, train-the-trainer programs for medical professionals, teacher training, and training in many other skill areas.

Turkey

Located in both Southeast Europe and Southwest Asia, Turkey could just as easily be discussed in the chapter on Europe or on the Middle East. Turkey's location makes it a strategic bridge between Europe and Asia where many cultures and civilizations meet. Inhabited since at least the 8th millennium B.C., the country was shaped historically from both east and west. The Egyptians and Greeks fought for the area for centuries, followed by the Persians and then Alexander the Great. Roman rulers followed until the growth of the Byzantine Empire, which was succeeded by control of the Seljuk Turks, European Crusaders, and Ottoman Turks.

The populations of Turks, Kurds, Arabs, Georgians, Circassians, Armenians, and other groups in Turkey reflect its history. A member of NATO (the North Atlantic Treaty Organization), Turkey is an applicant to join the European Union as well, reflecting its European identity. Although the population is overwhelmingly Muslim, its government is secular yet constantly trying to maintain a balance between secular and Muslim interests.

Business customs in Turkey stem from its own cultural traditions as well as Islamic beliefs and are similar to those found in many other Muslim countries. Appointments must be made well in advance, and a personal introduction helps one gain acceptance much more easily. Punctuality is expected. English is widely used, although the use of at least a few Turkish phrases is appreciated. Both secular and Islamic holidays are celebrated, and appointments may be difficult to obtain from June through August, the period in which Turkish businesspeople take extended vacations. Business dress should be conservative—dark suits for men and suits and heels for women. Women should avoid low necklines, sleeveless outfits, and short skirts.

The pace of business, particularly negotiations, is slow in Turkey, and politeness is essential. Most meetings start with introductory small talk and cups of coffee or tea before moving on to the business at hand. One should have plenty of business cards to offer. Elders are treated with deference, and social hierarchies exist based on social class, ethnic group, and religion. Education is one of the keys to moving up within the social hierarchy. While most Turkish workers have a strong work ethic, their attitude toward time is quite relaxed. In keeping with Eastern influences, truth is viewed as coming not entirely from empirical evidence and facts but mainly from immediate feelings, beliefs, and values.

Recommended topics of conversation in Turkey are personal hobbies and interests, families, and professions. One should avoid taking sides in any Turkish political issue or discussing the Turkish-Greek dispute over Cyprus. If invited to a Turkish home, one is wise to bring a gift. Appropriate music or books in English, pastries, flowers, candy, glassware (such as a vase, goblet, or decanter) are usually welcome, as well as small toys or chocolate for children. Since orthodox Islam prohibits alcohol and depictions of humans (drawings, photographs, etc.), one should find out the hosts' beliefs before giving gifts of this nature. Tea is the most popular drink and is served in small glasses with sugar but never with milk. Turkish coffee is very strong and is served with sugar. Visitors should be careful not to drain the cup, since fine coffee grounds remain at the bottom. Milk is served only with instant or American-style coffees. Smoking is common everywhere.

Isbank

Founded in 1924, Isbank is the leading private bank of Turkey. Its system includes 2,278 ATMs, 832 branches, seven overseas branches, and Isbank GmbH in Germany, which manages sixteen branches across Europe, all connected by real-time computer networks. Isbank has over 16,000 employees, all of whom are company shareholders as well. Isbank is the only bank in Turkey whose employees own weighted shares of capital and are represented on the Board of Directors. Through training and communications Isbank makes sure that all of its employees have a wide understanding of the banking industry, so they can easily adapt to changes. The company also works to ensure that employee objectives are aligned with the bank's overall vision, strategies, and policies.

Isbank offers training and internship opportunities for its employees at training centers, universities, and bank facilities within and outside Turkey, as well as offering ongoing internal training. Since the bank's policy is to fill open management positions from lower levels of employees, training is a normal part of work life.

Summary

The boundaries of the region of Central Asia are not carved in stone. The authors chose to discuss key cultural and economic aspects of, as well as the most prevalent types of HRD in, five former Soviet countries—Kazakhstan, Kyrgyzstan, Tajikistan, Turkmenistan, and Uzbekistan—and the countries of the Caucasus (Armenia, Azerbaijan, Georgia), Afghanistan, Iran, Iraq, and Turkey.

Australia and the South Pacific

I was asked to look into the future of our country and the options before us. Frankly, I am equally concerned with where we have come from, what we are becoming and what's going on in our minds at the moment. But ahead of us, I see an unending process of discovering and responding. . . . A healthy society is one which handles this process properly. The journey is as important as the destination."

Sir Paul Reeves, governor general
of New Zealand, July 4, 1989

Introduction

HRD in the South Pacific is rich in innovation and economic impact. The national training and development societies of Australia and New Zealand have been among the most dynamic in the world, and their members have implemented highly successful HRD programs in the surrounding island nations of Papua New Guinea, Fiji, Tuvalu, and Tonga. This chapter explores the interesting array of cultures in which HRD operates in the South Pacific, the economic environment in which it operates, and the history and practice of HRD in the region.

Cultural Factors Impacting HRD

Geography and Demographics

The South Pacific region includes Australia, Papua New Guinea, the large islands of New Zealand, and Oceania. The last consists of some 25,000 islands
scattered across the South Pacific and is usually divided into three major
groups: Melanesia, Micronesia, and Polynesia. Except for New Zealand and
the southern part of Australia, the entire region lies well within the tropics
and enjoys continuously warm temperatures.

The region is home to an estimated 31 million people, more than 91 percent
of whom live in Australia, New Zealand, and Papua New Guinea. The vast majority in Australia and New Zealand are Caucasian, most of Anglo-Celtic descent. Formerly restrictive immigration policies have been liberalized in
Australia over the past twenty years. As a result, Australia has growing populations of immigrants from many European and Asian countries, as well as some
from Latin America. Since 1986, ethnic groups with the fastest growth rates
have been South and East Asians, with Chinese, Vietnamese, and Indians more
than doubling in number by 2001. The original inhabitants make up 1 percent
of the current population of Australia and 9 percent of New Zealand's.

Papua New Guinea has two major population groups, Papuans (84 percent)
and Melanesians (15 percent). Approximately 70 percent of Oceania's 1.2 million people are Melanesian, Micronesian, and Polynesian peoples native to the
islands; 20 percent are of Asian origin; and 7 percent have European ancestry.
In some cases, such as that of Fiji, there is a large population descended from
Asian Indians brought as laborers during the British colonial period.

Language

With more than seven hundred distinct languages, Papua New Guinea is one
of the most complicated linguistic areas in the world. Pidgin English and
Motu are the most widely spoken languages and are used for trade throughout the country. The number of native Australian languages is thought to be
more than five hundred, with more than fifty of them broadcast regularly on
the radio. There are an estimated five hundred Eastern Manayo-Polynesian
languages spoken in Oceania. Hindi is widely spoken in Fiji as a result of earlier migration from India. English is the official language of Australia and
(with Maori) in New Zealand and is used as a lingua franca throughout the
region. In Australia Chinese is the second most widely spoken language after
English; in Sydney Arabic is the second most commonly spoken language.

Religion

Christianity is professed by the vast majority of the people, with Catholicism and Protestantism both well represented in Australia, New Guinea, New Zealand, Fiji, and many smaller island groups. An estimated 50 percent of those living in Oceania practice indigenous religions. Newer immigrants, especially in Australia, include substantial numbers of Buddhists, Hindus, and Moslems.

History

Little is known of the early history of the South Pacific region. Zhivotovsky, Rosenberg, and Feldman (2003) show that modern DNA research suggests that migration from Africa to Eurasia, Oceania, East Asia, and the Americas began more than 65,000 years ago. Early migrations from the Asian continent are reflected in some of the region's languages, but many other languages are of unknown origin. The islands we now call Fiji were apparently settled more than 3,500 years ago by people now known as the Lapita and thought to be of Asian origin. Maori migrations from Polynesian islands to New Zealand probably began around 900 A.D. and increased until the historical "great migration" of the 13th and 14th centuries. Except for Antarctica, Australia was probably the last continent to be inhabited by humans and the last to be explored and settled by Europeans. An estimated 300,000 aborigines distributed among some five hundred tribes lived in Australia when the Europeans arrived.

The Dutch thoroughly explored the South Pacific region in the early 17th century but never returned to colonize the lands they found. In 1769 and 1770, Captain James Cook visited New Zealand and then took formal possession of the eastern coast of Australia for Britain. The British established penal colonies in 1788 in areas that have become Sydney, Hobart, and Brisbane. Free settlements were established in Melbourne, Adelaide, and Perth, and with the discovery of gold in 1851, the number of free immigrants to Australia increased considerably. In 1840, the Maoris ceded sovereignty to the British in return for legal protection and rights to perpetual ownership of Maori lands. The six colonies of Australia became a member of the British Commonwealth in 1901, with New Zealand following in 1907.

Papua New Guinea was governed under various British, Australian, and UN territorial and trust arrangements until its independence in 1975. The king of Fiji voluntarily ceded the islands to Britain in 1874; Fiji gained its independence in 1970. A military coup in 1987 resulted in Fiji's withdrawing from the Commonwealth.

Cultural Characteristics

The people of the South Pacific region are friendly, outgoing, and hospitable. The pace of life, even in those urban areas that are not tropical, is slower than that of most of the industrialized world. Leisure activities and family events play an important part not only in life but also in everyday conversation.

Family and Leisure

Families continue to play a central role in the non-European communities, where extended families are common, women are usually at home, and the family unit is likely to be male dominated. In these communities three or four generations may live together in one house, and extended family connections are important in both work and leisure activities.

Australians and New Zealanders are avid sports enthusiasts and enjoy rugby, field hockey, cricket, sailing, and football. Weekends spent on the beach or excursions to the outback are common.

Economic Environment for HRD

The South Pacific region has a high GDP per capita, bolstered by the economies of Australia and New Zealand, where gross domestic products are about ten times those of Papua New Guinea and Oceania. The region hosts vast mineral resources and diverse topographical terrains. Six Australian companies were among the largest one hundred global firms in 2000.

Australia is the fourth largest economy in the Asia-Pacific region, behind Japan, Korea, and China. It was also the fifteenth largest market for U.S. exports in 2001. Australia's markets reflect those of the United States: The country's growing economy is diversified, with strong mining, agricultural, manufacturing, transport, financial, and service sectors.

History of HRD in the South Pacific

The role of HRD has changed drastically during the past thirty years as the South Pacific region has entered the global marketplace as part of the Pacific Rim. According to Frank (1998a), the status of HRD professionals in Australia prior to 1970 was not high. Trainers lacked any professional association, and employers "saw their incumbency as a short interlude" while they looked for a better position. It was even considered "fatal" to remain too long in the HRD role (p. 50).

It was the National Conference on Training, convened by the government in Canberra in 1971, that focused widespread attention within Australia on the country's poor performance relative to other industrialized countries in the provision of HRD programs for the workforce. The three hundred leaders from corporate and government organizations recognized the "critical links between training and productivity performance" (Frank, 1998a, p. 51). The Australian National Training Council was formed with the purpose of improving the quality of training in Australia. (Similar training councils were later established in New Zealand, Papua New Guinea, and Fiji.)

Today Australia and New Zealand are home to two of the most active HRD associations—the Australian Institute for Training and Development and the New Zealand Society for Training and Development. Australian and New Zealand HRD professionals are highly respected in their own countries and have served in major leadership roles in the International Federation of Training and Development Organizations. Australia has hosted two of the federation's global conferences (1976 and 1984). The importance of HRD in promoting self-reliance and improved living standards in developing nations is fully recognized by the Australian International Development Assistance Bureau, which recently stated:

> The lack of suitable qualified human resources is recognized as a significant obstacle to economic and social progress in most developing countries. Training and education is the main way in which aid donors can contribute to enhance human resources in these countries, and such aid is therefore seen as a priority form of assistance. (Quoted in Frank, 1998a, p. 52)

HRD Programs in the South Pacific

University of the South Pacific, Institute of Management and Development

The University of the South Pacific (USP), with campuses in Fiji, Samoa, and Vanuatu, serves the Cook Islands, Fiji, Kiribati, the Marshall Islands, Nauru, Niue, Samoa, the Solomon Islands, Tokelau, Tonga, Tuvalu, and Vanuatu. In addition to the three campuses, USP has smaller centers in each member country and supports distance education students enrolled through university extension. Nearly half of USP students use the university's sophisticated satellite communications network, USPNet, to study via distance education from their own homes.

Established in 1999, the Pacific Institute of Management and Development (PIMD) has as its mission to be the premier provider of postgraduate management and business education, training, applied research, and consulting in the South Pacific. PIMD provides management education to meet the needs of senior managers and public policy makers in the region. It is linked to the School of Social and Economic Development, and SSED's academic staff contribute to the delivery of PIMD courses and activities.

PIMD's mission is to contribute to the development of the Pacific island countries and their people, in innovative and culturally appropriate ways, by providing quality postgraduate education in business administration; by providing continuing professional upgrading and training for senior executives and managers; by providing advisory services; and by undertaking consultancies and applied research on issues in development.

PIMD focuses on the areas of professional business education, public sector reform and privatization, information management systems, entrepreneurship, and small-business development. PIMD's corporate plan specifies the following goals:

1. To play an influential role across the region in the professional development of senior civil servants, ministers, and leaders in both the public and private sectors
2. To enhance the reputation of the master of business administration course across the region as a high-quality program specifically designed to meet the needs of both public and private sector senior managers
3. To be recognized as a center of excellence in management and development education by providing innovative, high-quality courses using appropriate communication technology and flexible teaching methods
4. To establish a reputation as an institute that provides regional governments with sound policy advice in areas related to public sector reform, strategic management, economic development strategies, and public policy analysis
5. To assist organizations throughout the region in improving their management practices by undertaking and disseminating applied research on Pacific business issues and by producing management case studies on Pacific business enterprises
6. To widen PIMD's sphere of influence by establishing and maintaining a program of collaborative activities with the regional and international organizations such as the Forum Secretariat and Asian Development Bank

7. To play an active role in international organizations such as the Association for Development, Research, and Training Activities in the Asia Pacific (ADIPA)

8. To keep well informed of the leading issues in management research and in MBA teaching practice at international business schools by attracting to PIMD visiting professors to teach MBA courses and international research scholars to bring their research experience to the clients of PIMD in the region

9. To establish strong links with the private sector in the Pacific island economies

10. To assist the institutional strengthening of national organizations responsible for the delivery of advanced management and policy analysis training to senior public servants

11. To promote among governments and organizations in the region the use of management information systems and information technology for better management

PIMD's main functions consist of the following:

1. Conducting graduate business administration courses, including the master of business administration (MBA), the postgraduate diploma in business administration, and postgraduate certificates in human resource management, financial administration, entrepreneurship, and marketing.

2. Offering professional short courses, seminars, and conferences focused on the senior management level. PIMD also conducts regional workshops in collaboration with organizations such as the Pacific Forum, South Pacific Community, and Commonwealth Secretariat and has developed a regional network and database directed at promoting improved management of organizations in the region.

3. Conducting applied research and consulting.

The Institute conducts a research program and undertakes consulting assignments on management and development issues. Such projects include:

- Undertaking a review of the Fiji Islands Trade and Investment Bureau and conducting a strategic change conference for all the staff;
- Assisting the Yaqara Pastoral Company prepare a five-year corporate plan and statement of corporate intent;
- Undertaking a job evaluation study for the Suva City Council; and

• Conducting a strategic planning workshop for the Fiji Ministry of Health and assisting the ministry in preparing a corporate plan.

New Zealand Institute of Management

The New Zealand Institute of Management (NZIM) was founded in 1946 as a nonprofit professional organization with a mission of enhancing managerial and organizational effectiveness in New Zealand. NZIM caters to the professional and organizational needs of its members, currently numbering over 6,500 nationally, and expanding. NZIM provides both its corporate and individual members with networking opportunities, workshops and seminars, training and career development, professional qualifications, management information, mentoring, scholarships, and awards.

NZIM's national office develops and administers a range of certificate and diploma qualifications delivered by secondary and tertiary providers throughout New Zealand. Programs range from short courses for supervisory staff to concentrated residential courses for senior management. NZIM sets the standards for much of the management education and training in New Zealand and, through its role in management education, serves nearly 20,000 individual managers and 1,500 New Zealand businesses.

The institute functions as a decentralized divisional organization with a central secretariat and support. This structure provides a high degree of responsiveness to local needs while preserving the efficiencies of centralized resources and leadership.

Members of NZIM are members of their local divisions, among which those in Auckland, Wellington, Canterbury, and Otago are strongly established. Each division has its own council and management executive responsive to its members and maintains services and support to meet local needs. The national office in Wellington manages and administers the formal NZIM management qualifications. It also provides central support and coordination for the divisions working together on national projects or issues. The national office manages and coordinates the courses of study, provided by polytechnic institutes, that lead to the awarding of the institute's formal national qualifications.

Industry Training Federation of New Zealand

The Industry Training Federation (ITF) is a membership-based organization that represents industry training organizations (ITOs) to government and works with agencies and sector groups to improve policies for and delivery of industry training. ITF's national office in Wellington has four main functions: research, policy, advocacy and lobbying, and promotion of best practices. In 2002, ITF had forty-two members, representing around 95 percent of all training funded by government.

The Industry Training Federation's key objectives are to:

- Promote and support the continuous improvement of ITO performance within a quality-oriented culture;
- Lead the development of policy advice, research, and evaluation in all key vocational education and training policies, including industry training; and
- Influence government, government agencies, and key public sector groups to improve policies for and delivery of industry training.

Industry Training Organizations. Industry training organizations (ITOs) were created by the Industry Training Act of 1992. ITOs have three main roles:

- Develop and maintain national industry education and training standards
- Implement industry-based training programs and qualifications that meet the current and emerging needs of industry
- Provide leadership within their industry on matters relating to skill and training needs

ITOs do not deliver industry-based training. Rather, they manage the quality assurance of industry-based training by setting training standards, registering employees as workplace assessors who monitor training and assessment, and managing learning and reporting systems. Industry-based training is delivered by individual enterprises, often in conjunction with tertiary education providers. These arrangements mix training in the workplace with training delivered in institutions. The Local Government Industry Training Organization and the New Zealand Journalism Training Organization are two such ITOs.

Local Government Industry Training Organization

The Local Government Industry Training Organization (LGITO) is a self-funded business unit of Local Government New Zealand with its own board, which is accountable to Local Government New Zealand. LGITO facilitates training for Local Government staff to enable them to achieve qualifications specific to the Local Government industry. LGITO offers diplomas and certificates in skills ranging from building and plumbing inspection, to plant pest control, to civil defense management.

The New Zealand Journalists Training Organization

The New Zealand Journalists Training Organization (NZJTO) is a voluntary organization funded by newspaper, magazine, radio, and television companies. All major media employers belong to it. Its purpose is to guide and foster training and to raise standards generally by setting qualifications and training standards for journalism schools. NZJTO helps accredit schools, writes training standards, and monitors approved schools. In 2001, about 80 percent of the graduates of approved schools obtained jobs in the news media. NZJTO publishes textbooks and a quarterly journal for journalists called *NOTED*. It also provides an online grammar and writing course for students who want to improve their skills and runs seminars for working journalists. Finally, it provides a point of contact for discussion of professional issues and for jobs, work permits, and so forth.

Westpac Group (Australia)

The Westpac Group is a financial services group headquartered in Sydney with nearly 50,000 employees. Spending on training is approximately 8 percent of the payroll. Westpac's renewed emphasis on training began in 1987, when a comprehensive review was made of the effectiveness of its training efforts. The review found a wide disparity of quality in design and delivery, as well as inefficiencies where training was done for training's sake and areas where very little training was done at all. Although there was an efficient staff of professional trainers, the mangers tended to abrogate their responsibility to identify training needs and acquire training solutions by simply regarding these matters as trainers' functions.

Based on these discoveries, Westpac created a separate business entity called Westpac Training Pty, Limited, to manage the provision of training services to the Westpac Group. Westpac Training quickly developed a system for identifying training needs and determining training strategies for all the business units of the Westpac Group. It linked training strategies to overall human resource strategies, which in turn were linked to corporate business objectives. Each business unit now sets the training budget it believes necessary to support its staff development.

By serving in a facilitative role in determining training needs and strategies, Westpac Training gets involved at the early stages as each unit examines training solutions. This enables coordination throughout Westpac and brings efficiencies such as the elimination of duplication of development or acquisition of similar training products by different units. Westpac has also established the Westpac Manager Training Institute, which provides structured training in various management skills at key stages of employees' careers. Customer service and technology training have become central training programs of the institutes.

Westpac looks far into the future to determine its staff's training needs. It has taken a lead role both in anticipating the impact of the retirement of baby boomers and in more fully integrating women into the corporate structure. Westpac is reshaping its workforce to prepare for the impact of aging baby boomers on the labor market and the graying of its customers. "We have looked out to 2020 across all our labour markets, all the states in Australia and in New Zealand. Within a decade everybody will be competing for a very diminished pool of young labour," says Ann Sherry, Westpac's group executive for people and performance (quoted in Porter, 2002, p. 1).

At the top end of the group, Westpac has created part-time figurehead roles in some states and hired retired executives who can engage with the business community and provide coaching and leadership for staff. For its frontline jobs, Westpac's subsidiary Bank of Melbourne has deliberately gone after women returning to work after having children.

Westpac is the only Australian bank supporting a business unit with specialists in every state dedicated to women's financial needs. Westpac's innovative groupwide program Bank on Women in Business includes a training initiative educating bank employees on how most effectively to serve women business owners. Sponsorship of business education seminars, trade expos, and networking events across Australia assist women in areas such as cash management, wealth creation, and e-business.

Qantas

Queensland and Northern Territory Aerial Services Limited (Qantas), the oldest airline in the English-speaking world, was formally established in 1920. In 1947, the Australian government became the sole owner of Qantas and remained so until 1993, when it began privatization by selling a 25 percent share of the airline to British Airways.

By 1999, Qantas was servicing 120 Australian destinations and carrying passengers to thirty-five other countries, using 102 Boeing aircraft in its main fleet and 38 other aircraft operated by regional subsidiaries. In 1997, Qantas was named, for the eighth year running, the Australian company with the best corporate image, and in February 1996 it was named Airline of the Year by *Air Transport World*.

Qantas employs 30,000 people in ninety-five cities in over thirty countries and operates in more than 50 languages. Qantas's diverse workforce includes some 6,000 engineers, 6,000 cabin crew, 2,000 pilots and technical crew, and 1,500 sales staff. Seventy percent of employees are shift workers.

Qantas College.   Qantas College was established in 1994 with three main aims:

- To enhance business performance through corporate learning
- To provide access to the college for all staff regardless of where and when they work
- To provide line managers with flexible resources to support their learning and development strategies and programs

Qantas College is responsible for company-wide corporate learning and development. It offers a range of learning programs for Qantas staff, including people management, language and literacy, communication, frontline supervisor training, and compliance training in such areas as equal employment opportunity (EEO) and occupational health and safety. Most of these courses are accredited and lead to a nationally recognized qualification.

From the very first days of Qantas College, the training and development department made a point of consulting broadly with stakeholders to make sure its operations were aligned with business needs and directions. Qantas has introduced an interactive Internet education system that provides access to online training courses for the airline's staff worldwide.

Qantas College Online (QCO).   Qantas College Online, launched in 1996, is one of Australia's first Internet-based learning systems. Three learning principles underpin the learning model developed by QCO: relevance, online tutor facilitation, and accredited training. These inform virtually all the programs and services operating through QCO and are considered to be its core educational strengths.

By 2001, Qantas College was offering online a suite of some sixty company-wide tutor-facilitated programs to enhance individual and organizational development. There were more than 5,000 registered users, representing 20 percent of Qantas staff. Increasingly, Qantas business units are seeing the potential for online learning and are using QCO for their technical and compliance training. The system provides self-paced learning for staff through Qantas College Online, which offers corporate and operations training courses via the Internet. Courses are available to staff in the workplace, in crew hotels, or at private residences that have Internet access. Qantas Group General Manager of Human Resources George Elsey says that QCO "is a way for our people to undertake quality and consistent training at a time and place that suits their workplace and their individual circumstances. It also suits staff who work on a roster system because the training is self-instructional and self-paced" (Qantas introduces online training for staff worldwide, 1998, p. 17).

According to Schofield (2002), the establishment of Qantas College and QCO has had three critical impacts on Qantas's corporate training and development function.

1. Corporate learning and development have been strategically repositioned within the company, making it more directly relevant to business needs and integrating it with other elements of human resource management and organizational development.
2. The Web-enabled support for training administration, learning, and development has freed HRM staff to act as internal consultants and project managers rather than old-style training officers.
3. The relationships between learning and development and line management have changed and continue to change. Senior management looks to the college to improve training consistency, quality, and cost across the company, making the training attractive to all individual business units.

Qantas College Online has come a long way since its launch in 1996 and is widely acknowledged to be at the leading edge of online training delivery. Qantas traditionally separated learning and development training from both organizational development (OD) and broad HR functions. Qantas College people recognize that there is still a long way to go before learning and development is fully integrated with other HR and OD functions. It is an issue they struggle with, but overall they feel that learning and development has never been so well integrated.

Summary

The South Pacific consists of over 25,000 islands, ranging from the world's largest—Australia—to many that are only a few hundred yards in circumference. The cultural milieu includes European, Asian, and indigenous elements. HRD has rapidly become a significant factor in the economic development of the region. The region's successful HRD programs include the Pacific Institute of Management and Development (Oceania), the New Zealand Institute of Management, the Industry Training Federation of New Zealand, the Westpac Group (Australia), and Qantas (Australia).

Canada

Canadians are not Americans and do not want to be Americans. . . . The worst insult you can give a Canadian is to say we are the same as Americans.

David Peterson, former premier of Ontario

Introduction

Despite its long (5,525 miles) border with the United States, "guarded only by neighborly respect and honorable obligations," the most important thing to understand about Canada is that it is *not* the United States. However, Canada's proximity to the United States and the similarities in the two countries' history, language, and culture uniquely affect Canada.

Even though the United States and Canada share a long history of cooperation and friendship, the two countries are distinct in a number of important ways. Canada's vast borders contain important differences in culture, beliefs, attitudes, and practices that the HRD practitioner must understand in order to succeed. This chapter considers the HRD environment in Canada and the many faces of this diverse nation.

Cultural Factors Impacting HRD

Geography, Demographics, and Language

Extending over an area of 3.85 million square miles, Canada is the second largest country in the world, exceeded in size only by Russia. Its topography ranges from snowy mountains to open plains, with hundreds of miles of ocean shoreline. Approximately 27.5 percent of the Canadian area is arctic tundra and ice fields, while another 43 percent is forested. In addition, some 2 million lakes cover about 7.6 percent of the total landmass.

Canada's 31.6 million people are spread across ten provinces and three territories, but almost 40 percent live in Ontario, and 85 percent of the population is concentrated within two hundred miles of the U.S.–Canadian border. Much of the land is sparsely populated because of the harsh conditions in the northern subarctic and arctic climate zones and the difficulties encountered when developing in permafrost zones. If Canada's population density were applied to Manhattan, there would be 283 residents sharing the island.

More than 28 percent of the Canadian population is of British Isles descent, with another 23 percent of French origin and 15 percent of other European origins, particularly German, Italian, and Ukrainian. Aboriginal groups scattered throughout Canada make up about 3.5 percent of the population.

In answering the 2001 census question on ethnic ancestry, Canadians listed more than two hundred ethnic groups, reflecting a rich cultural mosaic. The People's Republic of China was the leading country of birth among individuals who immigrated to Canada in the 1990s, followed by India, the Philippines, Hong Kong, Sri Lanka, Pakistan, and Taiwan. These seven Asian countries alone accounted for over 40 percent of all immigrants who came to Canada in the past decade. As might be expected, Asian populations are particularly numerous in British Columbia due to its location on the Pacific. During the same period, 11 percent of new immigrants came from the Caribbean or Central or South America, and 8 percent from Africa.

Language

Although Canada has a great deal of cultural diversity, the two dominant cultures are the British and French. English and French, spoken by about 83 percent of the population, are the two official languages of Canada, and legislation supports their equal status throughout the country in matters of business, education, government, and culture. Chinese is the third most commonly spoken language, followed by a wide variety of other Asian and European languages. Aboriginal culture continues to play an important role in areas with higher concentrations of these groups, such as in the Nunavut territory, but has relatively little impact on the cultural identity of the majority of Canadians. Although many aboriginal languages were once spoken in

Canada, the number of Canadians speaking one of these languages at home continues to drop, and many languages have become extinct.

Religion

Christianity is the predominant religion in Canada, with about 43 percent of the population practicing Roman Catholicism and 30 percent Protestantism. As might be expected, the majority of the residents of Quebec are Roman Catholic, while Protestantism dominates the English-speaking provinces. The majority of the remaining inhabitants report no religious preference, with the rest being Eastern Orthodox Christians, Apostolic and Evangelical Christians, Muslims, Jews, and a variety of other religions. Some of the fastest-growing religious groups have been Muslim, Buddhist, Hindu, and Sikh, as immigration from countries in which these religions is prevalent has increased.

A Dual Identity: French and English

From its earliest days Canada has been influenced by its two strongest cultural identities, French and British, and the conflicts that can emerge from major differences in cultural beliefs, attitudes, and behaviors. Disputes arose in the 17th and 18th centuries between the British and French over land, the fur trade, and fishing rights. Clashes continue between Quebec, with its overwhelmingly French-speaking population and French heritage, and the rest of Canada, which is predominantly British in origin. Several referenda have been held to decide whether Quebec should secede from Canada; each has been defeated. Much of Quebec retains a distinctly French identity, particularly as a result of laws that require French as the predominant language on signs. However, in Montreal 50 percent of the inhabitants are not of English or French origin, and 30 percent are trilingual. It is a city of ninety different cultural communities and 110 languages. Similarly, on the west coast of Canada, the influx of Asians creates a multiculturalism in which the English/French dichotomy seems somewhat lost in a sea of other cultures and languages. In Vancouver, where at least ninety different languages are spoken, nearly half the city's people do not speak English as a first language.

Such demographic changes, as well as the need to address the challenges of competing in a global environment, may tend to erode the traditional rivalry between English and French. In fact, recent studies show that although Canadians have traditionally identified strongly with their respective provinces, more are describing themselves as "Canadian First," particularly those under the age of thirty-five. Canada remains a very decentralized federation, however, and interregional tensions continue between Quebec and other provinces. Friction also results from a perception that Ontario benefits most from the Canadian federation, to the detriment of other provinces. Most Canadians are sensitive to policies, attitudes, or remarks that seem to favor one province or one culture over another.

Common Values

Mendelsohn (2001) shows that while Canadians have become more fiscally and economically conservative, their top priorities remain social issues: education, health care, unemployment, and child poverty. Overall, most Canadians believe that strong social programs lead to a more productive, competitive country. A majority of Canadians also support bilingualism, multiculturalism, immigration, and internationalism. They are increasingly open to trade liberalization and support an expansion of international institutions.

While most Canadians support a continued strong relationship with the United States, they want to retain their own distinct identity and remain independent so as to protect their own interests and make their own decisions. More than one expert has pointed out that while the United States was founded out of a revolution, Canada was built on compromise. This fundamental distinction has led to differing views on defense, support for the United Nations and other international agencies, and relationships with nations around the globe.

Leisure

Modern Canada was carved from a vast wilderness by explorers, trappers, miners, and settlers who faced enormous obstacles and challenges. This sense of adventure and challenge continues today; in Canada nature is never very far away. Thousands of Canadians participate in outdoor sports, particularly golf, baseball, swimming, soccer, skiing, ice hockey, and curling, to name a few. Hundreds of outdoor events attract crowds throughout the year, including the Calgary Stampede rodeo, Ottawa Tulip Festival, Winter Carnival of Québec, Bard on the Beach Shakespeare Festival in Vancouver, and many others. Indoor events and attractions include a wide variety of museums and galleries, as well as world-class film, music, and theater festivals. The Stratford Theater Festival and Shaw Festival are world renowned for their theatrical presentations of plays by both classical and contemporary authors.

Economic Environment for HRD

Canada's population and economy are roughly one-tenth the size of the United States'. However, because of the close economic links between Canada and the United States, the two countries' economic cycles have been similar. Significant growth of Canadian manufacturing in the 1950s transformed the nation from a rural agricultural society into a more industrial and urban society.

According to the Organization for Economic Cooperation and Development (OECD), Canada ranks seventh in the world in gross domestic product (GDP). Service industries employ about 74 percent of the labor force, followed by manufacturing (15 percent), construction (5 percent), and agriculture (3 percent). Canada is the world leader in the export of forest products, which contributed $20.8 billion to Canada's GDP in 2000. In addition to being one of the world's largest producers of minerals, Canada also produces agricultural and fishery products, energy products, industrial goods and materials, machinery and equipment, and automotive products.

A number of changes have contributed to the opening of Canada to the world market, including free trade agreements such as the Canada–U.S. Free Trade Agreement (FTA), the North American Free Trade Agreement (NAFTA), the World Trade Organization Agreement on Government Procurement (WTO-AGP), and the Canada–Korea Telecommunications Equipment Agreement (CKTEA); privatization; and tax reform. The United States is Canada's largest trading partner, accounting for 85 percent of its export market and 74 percent of its import market.

One of the most influential of Canada's trade agreements has been NAFTA, a trilateral agreement between the United States, Mexico, and Canada that went into effect in 1994. The agreement eliminates barriers to trade and to cross-border movement of goods, increases investment opportunities, and promotes fair competition among the three nations.

HRD in Canada

Canadians have always valued education very highly. By 1995, 48 percent of Canada's working-age population had a postsecondary degree, more than double the average for all industrialized countries. Approximately 26 percent of Canadians are university graduates. But, as in most countries, challenges remain. Canada is a leader in the amount of money spent on education, but the question remains, whether it is spent in the right places. Many high school graduates lack the basic skills required in a knowledge economy, while well-paid jobs for people with little education are disappearing.

As in many countries, illiteracy remains a challenge, with significant negative impact on business objectives, management, and operational processes. Twenty-two percent of adult Canadians have serious problems dealing with any printed materials. An additional 24 percent of Canadians can read only simple texts.

Comparing statistics across countries concerning participation in training is difficult because of differences in government control of education, the regulatory environment, the degree of formal versus informal learning, and other variables. In Canada training for employment is a shared responsibility between the provinces and the federal government, although in practice the bulk of public expenditures on training comes from the federal level. Larger Canadian companies are heavily committed to investment in employee training and development, with an average of 4.2 percent of payroll spent on training, but in the small-business sector, formal training is less common. When taken together, Canadian companies spend an average of 1.6 percent of annual payroll on training.

A recent study by the Conference Board of Canada found that Canadian organizations continue to lag behind other nations in training and development investment (Canadian Society for Training and Development, 2003). Formal training expenditures by Canadian organizations in 2001 amounted to $768 per employee, as compared to $1,137 per employee in the United States. This underinvestment could have a negative effect on productivity and competitiveness in an increasingly global economy. The same study found that only 23 percent of respondents to the Conference Board survey consider themselves "learning organizations."

In an increasingly global environment, Canadian organizations are recognizing that retaining the talent they have and attracting top talent from across the globe are critical to building competitive advantage. Since 2000, the number of managers and professionals moving to the United States has accelerated, while those moving from the United States to Canada has declined. Overall, Canada is suffering a net loss of workers in occupations critical to a knowledge-based economy. More than half of Canadian graduates who moved to the United States in 1995, for example, were concentrated in health, engineering, mathematics, and the sciences. Changes in the tax structure have been suggested as a key strategy to stop this brain drain.

In response to the needs of both HRD professionals and employees throughout Canada for continuing learning, the Canadian Society for Training and Development (CSTD) was established in 2003. CSTD represents 1,700 training and development professionals, suppliers, and service providers in every sector of the economy, including government, health care, finance, manufacturing, transportation, and IT. Created as a nationalization of the Ontario Society for

Training and Development, CSTD has as its mission setting the standards for and promoting excellence in the training and development profession and providing its members with the opportunity to enhance their professional abilities and share best practices within their fields.

HRD Programs in Canada

RBC Financial Services

Toronto-based Royal Bank of Canada (RBC) Financial Services is one of North America's leading diversified financial services companies. Its five major lines of business include personal and commercial banking (RBC Banking), wealth management (RBC Investments), insurance (RBC Insurance), corporate and investment banking (RBC Capital Markets), and securities custody and transaction processing (RBC Global Services). Canada's largest company as measured by assets and market capitalization, RBC serves more than 12 million personal, business, and public sector clients worldwide from offices in more than thirty countries with a total of 57,000 employees. In 2002, it was recognized as Canada's most respected corporation overall and in a number of specific categories including human resource management.

RBC has been recognized several times by the American Society for Training and Development for excellent practice in the field. For example, its Personal Learning Network (PLN) was cited as an excellent use of electronic learning technology. The program is a competency-based learning management system that provides employees and managers with PC-based multimedia learning activities, planning tools, and information that are directly aligned with the corporation's business strategies and goals. The company's Developing People Management Competencies Program received similar recognition for providing a significant financial return to the organization and improved leadership competencies. The company was also awarded an Excellence in Practice Citation for its Royal Coaching Journey, a series of courses, resources, and tools designed to improve interpersonal communication, with particular emphasis on employee development and performance improvement. The program is available in English and French and expected to reach all of RBC's almost 60,000 employees through leader-led workshops and a five-hour interactive multimedia CD-ROM.

New Brunswick Province

Located along the Gulf of Saint Lawrence, New Brunswick province relied for generations on lumber mills, mines, and fishing as its primary sources of income. In the 1990s, however, the government's economic planners realized that the economic bases would need to change or the province would face a bleak economic future. At the time, the unemployment level was 15 percent, and projections showed that during the 1990s, the province would lose another 5 percent of the its workforce. The province's premier, Frank McKenna, decided that New Brunswick had to reposition itself; he focused on information technology and multimedia—businesses in which location was less important than initiative.

One of the biggest challenges to the success of this transformation was finding a strategy for training thousands of people throughout the mostly rural province. Building on the existing first-class telecommunications infrastructure, the government set up "TeleEducation" centers throughout the province. The province has continued to increase the number of centers and today offers thousands of courses in several languages. As part of this effort, New Brunswick Community College set up the Multimedia Learning Technology Center of Excellence, a program dedicated to educational technology, including instruction in virtual reality, game design, computer animation, online course design, and other technical skills. Internet access was expanded to schools, recreation centers, and other local gathering places. The province also established an incubator for technology start-ups.

Today the success of this HRD strategy is obvious. Unemployment in New Brunswick has dropped 5 percent, and over 20,000 people are now employed in high-tech areas. In fact, with IT employment growing rapidly, people are moving into the province to find jobs. The province has become a global leader in software production and content for distance learning and online training, with as many as 100,000 companies worldwide using its information products. In 2002, the province won the *Workforce* Magazine Optimas Award for Innovation.

Dofasco Steel

"Our product is steel. Our strength is people."

Dofasco, Inc., is one of North America's most progressive and profitable steelmakers and a market leader in the specialty steel industry. Headquartered in Ontario, its operations also include joint ventures and subsidiaries in Mexico and the United States. Dofasco, which shipped over 4.8 million tons of steel in 2002, has a strong commitment to sustainable development, including limiting the environmental impact of its production processes.

Ranked among Canada's best companies to work for, Dofasco credits its workforce as its greatest competitive advantage. The first Canadian company to introduce profit sharing for its employees, it spends more than $15 million each year to develop and enhance its workers' skills. Attrition is less than 1 percent, and productivity has increased 50 percent since 1990. Since Dofasco is a team-based organization, each of its 7,400 employees is part of a proactive team, entrusted to suggest better ways of working, maximize the performance of new technologies, discover ways to improve quality, enhance customer service, and find ways to save money for both customers and shareholders. Employees are empowered to take responsibility for their own learning, and each has an individual learning and development plan.

HRD initiatives support both structured training and more informal peer-to-peer learning. Technical training, for example, occurs at the company's training center and on the job through informal trainers in each plant. Dofasco's HRD efforts do not stop at training, however. The company has a strong commitment to becoming a learning organization through a variety of approaches including a formal mentoring program to help new employees adjust more quickly to the organization, education reimbursement programs, and personal improvement programs. In addition, its "Essential Skills" program, designed to improve literacy, numeracy, and basic computer skills, is a benchmark for other organizations. Learning alliances with its clients are also important. In one case, employees were able to work with a client automobile manufacturer to produce a car using one hundred fewer welds, which greatly reduced the client's production costs.

Summary

Canada's mosaic of cultures, particularly French, British, and Asian, provides a rich environment for HRD. The country boasts a number of highly successful corporate and governmental entities with award-winning HRD programs, although spending on HRD still lags in some other developed countries. The retention of workers in Canada also poses problems, since many highly educated professionals leave the country, partly because of high Canadian taxes.

The examples of successful public and private HRD programs described in this chapter, from RBC Financial Services to New Brunswick Province and Dofasco Steel, illustrate the key role that training and development can play in organizational success.

Latin America and the Caribbean

We . . . must set our face sternly against corruption and extravagance. We cannot have a Cadillac-style living with donkey-cart economies. Our leaders must set the example of democratic, accountable, clean, lean and efficient governance.

Cheddi Jagan, president of
Guyana, 1992–1997

Introduction

Like other regions of the world, Latin America and the Caribbean struggle to understand and interpret their past in hope of creating a brighter future. That past is diverse, violent, glorious, cruel, and full of hope. The HRD profession in Latin America and the Caribbean has had the complicated task of serving a diverse people who must deal not only with their own deep cultural currents but also with those that flow from the north. This chapter surveys the HRD environment in Latin America and the Caribbean, including cultural and economic influences, and describes some of the region's successful HRD programs.

Cultural Factors Impacting HRD

Geography and Demographics

Stretching from the Caribbean to Cape Horn, Latin America comprises an enormous land area of nearly forty countries with a population of 513 million people in 2000. These one-half billion people live in a rich diversity of cultures with various indigenous, European, African, and Asian roots. As is true with many regions of the globe, the population of the Latin American and Caribbean region is aging. As the population growth rate drops (the estimated rate for 2000–2015 is 32 percent less than that for 1975–2000) and the population under age fifteen decreases, the population over age sixty-five is increasing. The life expectancy in the region between 1995 and 2000 was 69.4 years, a 14 percent increase over the period 1970–1975 (Fukuda-Parr, 2000). Urbanization continues apace in the region. Seventy-five percent of the population lived in urban centers in 2000; by 2015 urban residents are expected to exceed 80 percent.

History and People

When the European explorers began to arrive in Latin America in the early 16th century, the region was home to an estimated 30 million native people. Ranging from the powerful Mayan and Incan empires to the relatively isolated cultures of the Amazon basin and Patagonia, these peoples had a wide variety of lifestyles, languages, beliefs, rituals, and behaviors. While their numbers were decimated by diseases brought from Europe (Diamond, 1999) and their empires were eclipsed, the modern descendants of these native peoples remain an important determinant in the social, political, economic, and cultural life of their various countries. Along the Caribbean coast and in Northeast Brazil, there are numerous African influences and traditions brought to the area by slaves of earlier times.

The region's people fall into five general ethnic groups: Indian, Mestizo, Mulatto, Black, and White. Despite this diversity the mainstream of Latin American culture, politics, economics, and business has evolved principally from the invading cultures of Europe, particularly those of the Spanish and Portuguese colonizers.

Religion

Roman Catholicism is the predominant and, in many cases, official religion of the region's countries. European Protestantism also is practiced, along with beliefs and rituals evolved from traditional African and indigenous animistic religions.

Family Roles and Responsibilities

The family, and by extension the group, plays an important role in both the Spanish/Portuguese and native Latin American cultures. Throughout the region, political and economic power has in many cases remained for generations in the hands of a few powerful families. As a consequence, Latin Americans are accustomed to deferring decisions and actions to the people in charge. The strong, decisive ruler is a much feared and envied figure in both politics and business. Within Native American communities, however, this imported feature is modified by a strong tradition of family and community consensus building, much like that seen in Asia. As a result, these families and communities look outward in one tradition and inward in another.

The authority assumed by the strong leader, of course, has concomitant responsibility and honor. Latin American men, in those contexts where they are taken to be the leader, are much concerned not only with their ability to provide and protect but also with their honor. For many Latin American men, honor, or *machismo,* is what matters most. Sometimes they value it over human life; honor routinely affects day-to-day life at home, in the community, and in business.

The role of women is largely circumscribed and defined by this cultural tradition. While in reality Latin American women carry enormous burdens in the family, the community, and the economy, they are often viewed as maidens and mothers, fragile creatures needing protection from the harsh realities of life by their natural protectors—fathers, brothers, and husbands.

Time: Relative and Imprecise

Carlos Fuentes (1968), the Mexican author and educator, observes that North Americans and Latin Americans have trouble understanding each other because they don't have a common place in time. Latin America looks first to its past, while North America lives almost completely in the future. As for the present, it is the scene of constant misunderstanding, disappointment, and irritation between the two cultures. From the North American point of view, Latinos are always late. For Latin Americans, their northern neighbors never take enough time to develop relationships or understand situations. The one culture is driven by time; the other sees it as a resource to be enjoyed and experienced. North Americans "spend, gain, lose, waste, and invest" time; they are only in time when they are "on time." Latin Americans "have" time today, and if that's not enough, there's always tomorrow. There is always time for family and friends, for romance and politics, for a cup of coffee or a long lunch.

Social Behavior and Communication Styles

Latin American culture puts a premium on relationships. Whenever possible, one does business with friends. When dealing with enemies, one is firm but polite. Formality is often more important than content. For example, great attention is given to rank and title, often simply as a matter of respect, not necessarily as a reflection of accomplishment. It is common in Latin America to refer to a prominent leader as *doctor* even though he might not have finished primary school. *Don, jefe,* and *licenciado* are all titles of respect used with people who might not be patriarchs, chiefs, or licensed practitioners. What's important is the appropriate show of respect to others and the gracious acceptance of it when granted by others.

Latin Americans are typically both warm and effusive. There is much touching, and the distance between speakers is small. Formality is again very important, and content is context specific. Business commitments and promises made in a social context need to be revisited in a work environment. Latin Americans, more than people in almost any other culture, take great pleasure in social interaction for its own sake.

Economic Environment for HRD

The investments that Latin American and Caribbean countries have made in human resources are paying off. By 2000, the literacy rate in the region was 88.3 percent for the whole population, 94 percent for youth aged fifteen to twenty-five. The gross domestic product (GDP) per capita was $7,234 in the region in 2000, and the GDP growth rate between 1990 and 2000 averaged 1.7 percent. A more skilled workforce is increasing the region's manufacturing capacity and has bolstered exports, including high-tech products. Between 1990 and 2000, manufactured goods increased 41 percent (to 48 percent of total exports) and high-tech products increased 166 percent to 16 percent of total exports.

Serious regionwide problems remain. Selbin (1998) reported that nearly half the region's 460 million people were poor in 1998—reflecting an increase of 60 million in one decade. Meanwhile, the number of Latin American billionaires rose from six in 1987 to forty-two in 1994, a figure widely reported and resented in Latin America.

Foreign debt for the region was nearly $800 billion by 2000, with some countries in arrears in debt payments. Unemployment remains unacceptably high, productive capacity is going unused, and the dramatic skew in income distribution persists. Latin American nations, however, are forming regional trading blocs. Brazil, Argentina, Uruguay, and Paraguay created a common market, called Mercosur, in 1995. Mexico has joined the North American bloc with Canada and the United States.

According to Venner (2003), Latin America suffered the worst economic downturn in two decades in 2001–2002. Overall GDP for the region is estimated to have fallen by 0.5 percent, in contrast to the 0.4 percent increase achieved in 2000–2001. A number of factors influenced this downturn, including an adverse international environment, slow growth in the developed countries, and deterioration in the terms of trade for the region. In addition, there were a number of country-specific problems. The economic crisis in Argentina had spillover effects in Paraguay and Uruguay. A political crisis in Venezuela disrupted oil production and put upward pressure on oil prices, while Brazil was affected by a weakening in free market sentiment. The economies of Mexico and Chile suffered least from the adverse external financing conditions as these countries are highly integrated with the world economy and their economic performance was underpinned by sound policies.

Throughout all of these changes and challenges, HRD has served as an important lever for economic development. Nadler (1990) points out that most of the region's countries have some kind of government-sponsored or -directed national HRD activity. Public management, particularly in developing countries in Latin America and the Caribbean, depends on the development of administrative systems in general, which in less-developed countries tends to progress in accordance with models valued by international lenders as indicators of effective government and economic development. As these countries continue to develop, they will transition to a range of alternative HR systems.

Improvements in literacy and the decline in the population growth rate have helped to stabilize economies in the region, as the workforce becomes better prepared for the technical and managerial jobs required in the global competitive marketplace.

Events Affecting HRD in the Twentieth Century

McGinn (1990) suggests a number of major events that are likely to occur as we enter the 21st century, each of which would have a profound impact on HRD in Latin America and the Caribbean:

1. Increasing mobility of labor across national boundaries. Although the overall flow of less educated people to the United States is likely to decrease as a result of increased capital investment in Latin America and the Caribbean, labor flows among countries in Latin America are

likely to increase. Industrial development will be concentrated in a few countries where there has been less investment. The more educated people will flock to technological centers in Argentina, Brazil, and Mexico, as well as to the United States and Canada.

2. Pressures to improve the quality and relevance of education and training. This will mean less emphasis on teaching of classics and more on mathematics, science, and applied language. The quality of public education programs will likewise be under pressure to improve.

3. Rapid growth in private education and nonformal training programs aimed at both children and adults. McGinn cites three reasons:

   A. The changed attitude toward state-controlled education and the spread of the ideology of privatization have led many people to seek private schools and institutes.

   B. Global firms have found that trainees at private institutions are more "international" in attitudes and values.

   C. Graduates of private schools have better opportunities to gain admission to higher-level educational programs in other countries.

4. Increased autonomy for school managers. The sum of the forces described above will increase pressure on public education and training "to produce graduates who can be certified to possess certain knowledge, skills and attitudes" (McGinn, 1990, p. 65). To achieve these results, managers will be encouraged to use considerable initiative in the finance, organization, and operation of their schools.

HRD Programs in Latin America

Organization of American States

The Organization of American States (OAS), with thirty-five member countries, is the world's oldest regional organization, dating back to 1890. One of its purposes is to promote by cooperative action the economic, social, and cultural development of the Latin American–Caribbean region. OAS sponsors a large number of assistance and training programs to fulfill this purpose. OAS works to improve traditional programs of education and training by promoting innovation and technology.

With direct project assistance, regional partnerships, and innovative programs, OAS is transforming populations in the region, giving them technical and political skills to negotiate the complexities of the 21st century.

Project Assistance

St. Kitts and Nevis Small Business Development Project. This project provides training in business marketing for young entrepreneurs and small-business owners; gives opportunities to young adults to develop entrepreneurial skills; provides additional job opportunities for the unemployed, particularly young adults; reduces unemployment and poverty through the creation of new business; and offers year-round training courses and business assistance. Project participants have represented a wide range of businesses. The majority were already owners of small businesses; others were in the process of starting a business or intended to start one in the near future.

Caribbean Hazard Mitigation Capacity Building Program. The OAS and the Caribbean Disaster Emergency Response Agency (CDERA) are implementing a three-year program to assist countries in the Caribbean region in developing comprehensive national hazard vulnerability reduction policies and associated implementation programs, as well as help with the development and implementation of training and certificate programs to ensure the construction of safer buildings.

Hurricane-Resistant Home Improvement Program. In Saint Lucia, the National Research and Development Foundation (NRDF) offers a hurricane-resistant home improvement program (HRHIP) for low-income earners. This program trains local builders in safer construction, offers small loans to families wishing to upgrade their homes, and provides the services of a trained building inspector to ensure quality control.

Regional Partnerships

Institute of Advanced Studies for the Americas (INEAM). The Institute of Advanced Studies for the Americas aims to strengthen the development of human resources in the Americas, including the updating of professional skills and continuing education. Begun in 2002, this new center supports efforts that deepen and consolidate training in social development and generation of productive employment, education, economic diversification and integration, commercial opening and access to markets, scientific development and the exchange and transfer of technology, the strengthening of democratic institutions, sustainable development of tourism, environmentally sustainable development, and culture. This initiative is a product of a strategic alliance between the Inter-American Agency for Cooperation and Development (IACD) of the OAS and Western universities of the Hemisphere.

INEAM's mission is to support quality, innovative professional training in an inter-American context, by using not only traditional means but also new information technologies and telecommunications. The educational experiences achieved through this training will help address the specific problems and realities faced by the different countries and subregions and will contribute to their development and social transformation. INEAM will have at its disposal numerous applications of the Educational Portal of the Americas (http://www.educoas .org) and the OAS Fellowships and Training Program, which has provided a variety of educational financial assistance since 1945 (see http://www.oas.org).

IACD Fellowships. The Inter-American Agency for Cooperation and Development (IACD) of the OAS administers one of the hemisphere's largest multinational fellowship and training programs. Every year, the agency provides several hundred fellowships for graduate studies and research, fellowships for undergraduate studies at universities through the region, and awards for specialized short-term training at educational institutions and training centers in OAS member and observer states.

As one of its strategic objectives, IACD has implemented a multifocused plan to increase fellowships and training opportunities and to expand access to knowledge through greater use of information technology. To this end, it is establishing a broad-based consortium of universities to cofinance fellowships.

Innovative Programs

FEMCIDI. FEMCIDI is a special multilateral fund established to finance cooperation projects presented by OAS member states. The fund is composed of voluntary contributions from member states and is structured according to priority areas identified in the current Strategic Plan for Partnership for Development. In recent years the voluntary contributions have totaled between US$8 million and US$9 million.

Educational Portal. IACD has established an Educational Portal for e-learning in order to promote new educational methods such as distance learning; to disseminate training opportunities of high academic quality; to advocate continuing education for students of all ages; and to urge teachers to adopt more flexible teaching methods and strategies.

The Educational Portal facilitates training and education in remote communities, as well as for traditionally underserved populations such as women and children, indigenous communities, and those with disabilities. As a component of this portal, the Division of Human Development has launched and currently manages a program of electronic fellowships (e-fellowships) as a more cost-effective mechanism for expanding fellowship and learning opportunities.

Regional National Training Centers

Many countries in Latin America and the Caribbean have vocational training programs that focus primarily on assisting small- and medium-sized enterprises (SMEs). Two of the best-known and most successful are SEBRAE in Brazil and SERCOTEC in Chile.

SEBRAE has been a Brazilian leader in developing culturally appropriate training materials, including visual aids and case studies. SERCOTEC (Servicio de Cooperacion Tecnica) has traditionally been the Chilean government organization in charge of the educating SME entrepreneurs. According to Roofthooft (1996), SERCOTEC has discovered the concept of "multiplication": Instead of running courses itself, the service realized it would be far more practical and effective to build a corps of consultants for SMEs in Chile. SERCOTEC collaborated with the International Labor Organization to devise a program for the training of sixteen development executives who would in turn train the SME consultants. The development executives received their training in Turin and Flanders, where there is a fund of rich experience in HRD support for SMEs. In Turin the executives learned fundamental SME business concepts and the didactical skills needed to transmit these concepts. The sixteen development executives then trained 308 consultants. This training program shows every sign of becoming a permanent tool for the professional development of SMEs in Chile.

Other highly acclaimed vocational training centers include SENA in Columbia; SENATI in Peru, which trained 128,000 participants in 1997; INA in Costa Rica; and INFOTEP in the Dominican Republic. Funding for these training programs has been raised through a training tax on all industries in the respective countries, which enables these institutions to offer the programs free of charge.

Eastern Caribbean Central Bank

The Eastern Caribbean Central Bank (ECCB) was formed in 1983 by the governments of Antigua and Barbuda, the Commonwealth of Dominica, Grenada, Montserrat, Saint Kitts and Nevis, Saint Lucia, and Saint Vincent and the Grenadines. The government of Anguilla became a member in 1987. ECCB is headquartered in Bird Rock, Saint Kitts. The bank's mission is to maintain the stability of the Eastern Caribbean (EC) dollar and the integrity of the banking system in order to facilitate the balanced growth and development of member states. The bank's purposes are:

- To regulate the availability of money and credit,
- To promote and maintain monetary stability,
- To promote credit and exchange conditions and a sound financial structure conducive to the balanced growth and development of the economies of the territories of the participating governments, and
- To actively promote through means consistent with its other objectives the economic development of the territories of the participating governments.

ECCB's envisions building and supporting a continuous learning culture in the bank where staff may utilize their skills in a more fluid manner. ECCB developed a new training policy in 1993 that acknowledges staff's critical role and affirms the bank's ongoing commitment to sustaining a vibrant learning institution and providing systematic performance improvement strategies at all levels.

The bank recognizes that ongoing performance improvement and development of its staff is critical to the attainment of the bank's mission. ECCB is committed to ensuring that staff participate in relevant professional and personal developmental activities. It plans to build a learning organizational culture driven by up-to-date knowledge workers and professionals. Strategies to reach this goal include gap analyses, on-the-job training, coaching, and overseas training.

Principles on which staff development at ECCB are based include the following:

1. Learning is ongoing, and the bank will provide opportunities for staff to continue to grow professionally and personally.
2. The individual, the head of department/head of unit, and the bank, through the Performance Development Unit, will collaborate to ensure that such learning is shared within the organization.
3. At ECCB all positions are important, and excellence is desired from each employee.

Following are ECCB's broad performance and training objectives:

- To facilitate optimum returns on the bank's investment in the training function,

- To develop and establish an in-house management development program,
- To coordinate relevant and effective short-term overseas technical programs to staff on the basis of current and anticipated need, and
- To strengthen partnerships with international organizations in order to deliver high-quality regional and international training programs at the bank's headquarters.

The bank's Performance Development Unit in the Human Resource Department is charged with managing the performance and training functions. The core values underpinning the unit's work are teamwork, cost effectiveness, relevant and timely human interventions, and customer focus. The bank offers training in critical thinking, problem solving, and time management; information technology; professional and personal development; management development, team building, and organizational development; and risk-focused supervision seminar for regulators.

Following are some of the initiatives that the bank has been undertaking:

1. The learning contract is an instrument that documents the commitment of staff, the supervisor, and the human resource department so as to provide a measure of return on the bank's training investment.
2. Mobilization of in-house subject matter experts and resource persons who design and facilitate internal training programs.
3. Use of structured analyses to determine performance gaps throughout the bank.
4. The Learning Resource Center is an HR department repository of professional and personal performance-related material available to staff.
5. The bank formed a Performance Development and Training Committee, a cross-departmental group that develops policies and guidelines regarding performance development, including training matters, and sets priorities for bankwide training and performance issues.
6. The ECCB sets aside a Fun at Work Day every year to give staff the opportunity to dress in business casual attire and take part in various fun activities throughout the day. The idea is that a happy workforce usually tends to be a productive workforce.

As part of its commitment to the development of the Organization of Eastern Caribbean States (OESC) region, the bank hosts an internship program for students from the University of the West Indies (UWI) to develop their skills in a dynamic work environment. The objectives of the internship program are:

- To provide opportunities for ECCB economists to exchange ideas with graduate students who have been exposed to the more recent academic training in economics,
- To do basic research in areas of interest to the bank,
- To provide interns with experience in a central bank environment, and
- To strengthen research links with UWI and other institutions.

ECCB recognizes that human performance is dynamic and directly impacts the success of the institution. In light of this and the imperatives of today's business environment, the bank continues proactively to pursue excellence in performance. Through appropriate business processes and human and other performance interventions and strategies, the bank aims to ensure that staff are adequately equipped with the appropriate technologies, knowledge, skills, and aptitudes.

Summary

Latin America and the Caribbean represent a number of rich cultures with European, African, Asian, and indigenous roots. The economic climate for HRD has improved noticeably in the past decade, though structural problems remain. Major events that are likely to affect HRD in the near future include increasing mobility of labor across national boundaries, increased pressure for improved quality and relevance in training institutes, rapid growth in private education and training programs, and an increased autonomy for school managers.

A variety of HRD programs are being provided in the region, including the diverse technical assistance projects of the Organization of American States in the Caribbean; INEAM, the regional Institute of Advanced Studies; FEM-CIDI, the innovative multilateral fund for development; and the Educational Portal that extends educational opportunities to traditionally underserved populations. There are also national training centers such as SERCOTEC, the highly successful vocational training program in Chile, and other national programs that support vocational training in Brazil, Colombia, Peru, Costa Rica, and the Dominican Republic. The Eastern Caribbean Central Bank is transforming itself into a learning organization.

United States

The future ain't what it used to be.

Yogi Berra

Introduction

During the last half of the 20th century, the United States was seen as the epicenter for HRD ideas and programs. Historically, it is the country in which HRD first emerged, and it continued for many years to host the top HRD programs and foster the best HRD theories. But globalization is changing this situation, and U.S. leaders and HRD professionals must struggle to stay abreast of the rapid improvements in HRD around the world. According to the *2003 ASTD State of the Industry Report*, as well as the activity reported throughout this book, great HRD programs now exist worldwide, and some of the best new HRD ideas now come as often from elsewhere as they do from the United States. This chapter examines the cultural factors that help to create and expand HRD over the past sixty years, describes the rapidly shifting roles and activities of HRD, and presents five of the top corporate and public HRD programs in the United States that continue to help make the country a benchmark for the world's best in HRD.

Cultural Factors Impacting HRD

Geography and Demographics

The fourth largest country in the world, the United States is the third most populous (soon to top 300 million) following China (1.3 billion) and India (1.1 billion). The United States is an increasingly diverse society, expected to become less than 50 percent white European in the next twenty-five years. Hispanic Americans are now the largest minority, with 14 percent of the population; African Americans constitute slightly more than 12 percent. Asians and Pacific Islanders, the fastest-growing minority groups, currently make up 4 percent of the population; Native Americans, less than 1 percent. The aging U.S. workforce means more retirees and potential gaps in the availability of experienced workers. By 2015, nearly one in five U.S. workers will be age fifty-five or older.

History

Although North America's history prior to the arrival of Europeans is not fully known, it is clear that the earlier inhabitants had large empires and advanced civilizations. Isolated European explorers probably reached North American shores as early as the 11th century, but exploration began in earnest in the late 15th century. At that time an estimated 1.5 million Native Americans lived within the borders of what became the United States. England, France, and Spain were the principal nations to establish colonies, though the Netherlands, Sweden, and in the west, Russia also took part. Many of the early inhabitants had fled religious persecution in England and France; others came as a part of ventures funded by European commercial companies. The American Revolution of 1776 led to a loose confederation of states that was formalized with the Constitution of 1787.

Throughout the 19th century, explorers, trappers, hunters, and settlers spread westward, and the U.S. government acquired territory from France, Mexico, and Spain until the country stretched from the Atlantic Ocean to the Pacific. A long and brutal civil war broke out in 1861 between the industrial states of the North and the more agrarian states of the South that had seceded over the issue of slavery and the rights of states. The war ended in 1865 with the victory of the northern forces, and the country was reunited politically.

During the 20th century, the United States was a major world power, playing significant roles in the outcomes of World Wars I and II and in other geopolitical events around the world. In the early stages of the 21st century, the country remains a global military and economic power.

Language

English is the official language of the United States and is spoken by most citizens. However, in large urban and suburban areas, such as Washington, D.C., containing numerous recent European, African, and Asian immigrants, as many as two hundred languages are spoken at home. With over 30 million U.S. speakers, Spanish has rapidly become the second most common language, particularly in parts of Florida and much of the southwestern United States. Chinese has become the third most spoken language in homes, with over 2 million speakers.

Religion

Fifty-two percent of all Americans give their religious affiliation as Protestant, with another 24 percent identifying themselves as Catholic and 1 percent as Jewish. There are small, but growing numbers of citizens representing other major world religions, including Eastern Orthodox, Islam, Buddhism, Hinduism, and Baha'i.

Patriotism

Although there is a great deal of diversity and lately no small amount of acrimony among cultures and ethnic communities in the United States, Americans, especially when facing outward, continue to be first and foremost Americans. They are extremely patriotic, and although they may be critical of the U.S. government or its policies, they will almost always argue that, even with its faults, the United States continues to be a good place, if not the best place in the world, to live.

Freedom, Democracy, and Equality

Americans see themselves first as individuals and only secondarily as members of families, communities, religions, or organizations. It is this pervasive sense of the individual self that accounts for much of what puzzles people from cultures in which the individual exists primarily as a unit of the family or other group. Perhaps more than anything else, Americans value what they call "individual freedom." As soon as they are able, most leave their family home and community to strike out on their own.

Along with their impassioned commitment to the individual, Americans have an equally strong belief in democracy, which they commonly equate with freedom, believing that one is not possible in the absence of the other.

Although they will quickly cite examples of where it has not worked, Americans basically believe in equality. Most continue to think theirs is a land of opportunity where any individual may rise to a position of wealth, power, and influence. Even in the face of their own failure to realize the "American Dream," many Americans continue to blame themselves and avoid questioning the validity of their notions. With a fervor that often surprises people from other cultures, most Americans believe not only that all people are created equal but that there is equal social, political, and economic opportunity for all.

Globalization of the U.S. Work Environment

U.S. corporations have invested $1 trillion abroad and employ over 100 million overseas workers; over 100,000 U.S. firms are engaged in global ventures valued at over $2 trillion. For instance, McDonald's operates more than 30,000 restaurants in 120 countries and is adding over 1,200 new restaurants per year. McDonald's restaurants served 16.5 billion customers in the year 2003. Coca-Cola earns more money in Japan than in the United States. The United States' $30 billion music industry earns more than 70 percent of its profits outside the country, and global viewers are largely responsible for the most successful Hollywood movies. Over one-third of U.S. economic growth has been due to exports, providing jobs for more than 11 million Americans.

At the same time, 10 percent of U.S. manufacturing is foreign-owned and employs 4 million Americans. Mitsubishi USA is America's fourth largest exporter, and Toyota has displaced Chrysler as the third largest in U.S. auto sales. Foreign investment in the United States has now surpassed the $3 trillion mark. Over half of the Ph.D.'s in engineering, mathematics, and economics awarded by American universities in 2002 went to non-U.S. citizens.

Shifts in Workplace Learning in the United States

The HRD profession in the United States has encountered the following major shifts since the start of the 21st century.

Shift of Emphasis

In addition to a growing increase in time and expenditure devoted to training and education programs, corporations are shifting from nice-to-know, fill-the-classroom courses to those that clearly connect to business. Instead of a patchwork of unconnected training courses, companies are developing training programs tied clearly and closely to their strategic goals.

Training programs emphasize the building of practical, usable, and quickly applicable skills. Preoccupied with concern about higher productivity in the competitive global marketplace, organizations are focusing increasingly on achieving corporate goals rather than training goals. Improving performance rather than providing enjoyable learning experiences is the new emphasis.

Shift of Status

The responsibility for workplace learning within organizations is gradually moving upward as top executives increase their support for and recognition of such learning's contribution to corporate success. Accordingly, HRD managers must increasingly demonstrate training programs' effectiveness. Managers throughout the organization are now more likely to be involved in planning and assessing training programs provided to their staff. Trainers are enjoying greater organizational status, as well as more decisionmaking authority, budget responsibility, and respect. Compensation studies show a sharp jump in HRD managers' median salaries.

Shift of Provider

More and more of the training and education being conducted for companies is being contracted to outside instructors and consultants. This outsourcing is chosen either because of the fixed-cost effectiveness or because of the greater and wider range of expertise needed but not available within the organization. In addition, corporations are seeking more help from universities and other training institutions. A recent phenomenon is the growing number of degree-granting corporate training institutes and colleges.

Another shift in the provision of training is the greater reliance on managers themselves and other staff outside the HRD department for planning and delivering training. Companies increasingly recognize that a manager's primary role and responsibility is the development and learning of his or her staff.

Shift of Content

Just as the external business environment continues to change rapidly—technology, the information-based economy, global competition, trade, finance, and terrorism—so have corporate strategies and priorities and hence the content of training and development programs. In corporate settings where improved productivity is a critical need, HRD programs are focusing more on aspects of team productivity and quality training. If the corporate goal is to gain competitive advantage, the major training content areas are marketing and sales, as well as customer training and service. If the goal is gaining technological superiority, training programs emphasize skills and knowledge needed by technical workers. Communication skill training is growing in all companies as they attempt to develop and transmit corporate culture and increase employee motivation. And finally, leadership and management development programs, especially action learning programs, continue to expand as companies change strategic direction or strive to manage more with fewer managers.

Shift of Recipients

As technological competence and skills updates become more critical in the global marketplace, training for nonmanagerial staff is also increasing. Customer service training has become essential for larger numbers of people within organizations. At the other end of the scale, top executives also realize that they must become continuous learners and become knowledgeable in areas such as global economics, competitive benchmarking, culture, marketing, and international finance.

Shift of Methods

Methods for the delivery of training programs have moved from classroom-only training to technology-based (especially Web-based) learning and blended (classroom and technology) learning. Because training is becoming more tailored and individualized, more electronic performance support systems (EPSS) training is occurring. Computer-assisted learning continues to expand as it allows for individual employees to learn immediately and asynchronously rather than waiting until a larger group has been identified and is available to be trained. Computer-embedded instruction is also becoming more common. A growing number of companies, including Ford Motor, are making extensive use of company-wide satellite networking to provide training in new products for sales, update employees on corporate policies and activities, and educate engineers and other technical professionals.

HRD Programs in the United States

Federal Express

Federal Express is the world's largest express transportation company, delivering more than 2 million items to recipients in 186 countries each working day. Headquartered in Memphis, Tennessee, all the numbers at FedEx are large and growing: With over 120,000 employees, FedEx flies into more than 325 airports and maintains 1,400 staffed facilities and more than 30,000 drop-off locations. Fiscal year 2001 sales approached $20 billion. The company prides itself on setting "the standards in the shipping industry for reliability, innovative technology, logistics management, and customer satisfaction." FedEx has received numerous awards, including the Malcolm Baldridge National Quality Award.

Under the guidance of CEO Fred Smith, Federal Express has made a conscious and deliberate effort to build a learning organization. Since 1991, many company staff have worked with Peter Senge at the MIT Center for Organizational Learning. FedEx leaders are quick to point out that in becoming a learning organization, the company has boosted its intellectual capacity, agility, and resourcefulness.

Technology application is one learning organization subsystem in which Federal Express has placed considerable resources and attained significant success. Since its founding, the company has developed and implemented several new technologies to set all aspects of its business apart from its competitors. In addition, Federal Express has made a huge investment in interactive training resources—more than $40 million in 1,200 systems in eight hundred field locations. Each is stocked with thirty interactive videodisc programs, which have been used to train many of FedEx's 30,000 couriers and 3,000 customer service employees.

In recent years Federal Express has replaced some of its classroom training programs with a computer-based training system that uses interactive video on workstation screens. This training system can capture and interpret input from learners in order to determine whether a task is being performed correctly. If a learner makes a mistake, the system recognizes the error, points it out, and shows the proper method. The interactive video instruction system presents training programs that combine television quality, full-motion video; analog or digital audio; text; and graphics using both laser disc and CD-ROM. Learners can interact with the system using a touch screen or keyboard.

The interactive video training closely correlates with job testing. Using the system, employees can study about their job and company policies and procedures and brush up on customer service issues by reviewing various courses. All interactive video workstations in the seven hundred U.S. field locations are linked to the Federal Express mainframe in Memphis. Each location has twenty-one videodiscs that make up the customer-contact curriculum. There is virtually no subject or job-related topic that the customer-contact workers cannot find on the interactive video instruction platform.

Once the CD-ROM courseware is written, FedEx knows it must keep the material up-to-date, for the workforce relies on systems to provide accurate and current information. For them, out-of-date information is worse than no information at all. For this reason, a new CD-ROM is sent to each location every six weeks, updating the curriculum through text, PC graphics, and digital audio. Over 1,000 updates are made on an annual basis.

FedEx recently created a mandatory performance improvement program for all of the company's employees who deal with customers either face-to-face or over the phone. The primary goals of this program are (a) to completely centralize the development of training content while decentralizing delivery and (b) to audit employees' ability to retain what they learn.

The pay-for-performance program consists of job knowledge tests that are linked to an interactive video instruction (IVI) training curriculum accessed on workstations in more than seven hundred locations nationwide. More than 32,000 Federal Express customer-contact employees around the country are required to take the job knowledge tests annually via computer terminals at their work locations. The tests, which measure employees' knowledge in their specific jobs, correspond with employees' annual evaluations. In fact, the results of the tests make up approximately one-tenth of the employees' performance ratings. By testing customer-contact employees on product knowledge services, policies, and various aspects of their jobs, FedEx obtains two major benefits, according to William Wilson, manager of training and testing technology:

- All employees operate from the same book, ensuring that all customers receive accurate and consistent information during each transaction. This helps the company maintain its high service levels and commitment to quality.
- Managers have an objective way to measure job knowledge for all customer-contact employees.

Federal Express provides many incentives for workers to quickly increase their learning. For example, employees are paid for two hours of test preparation prior to each test, two hours of test time, and two hours of post-test study time. The current average amount of time that all workers total use the IVI program is approximately 132,000 hours per year. Compared to traditional training, this equates to approximately eight hundred one-day classes for twenty employees per class. Yet no trainer or travel costs are incurred.

Federal Express also developed a test program called QUEST (Quality Using Electronic Systems Training) to ensure that all of the learning tests are valid, relevant, and fair and meet appropriate learning standards. This was done by creating focus groups composed of trainers, managers, and job incumbents. The focus groups designed each of the tests, which consisted of multiple-choice questions pertaining to all important aspects of employees' jobs. To keep the tests timely, FedEx had the original focus groups meet quarterly to discuss existing test questions to ensure that they were still valid and also to write new questions. Over a period of time, FedEx has built up a bank of several hundred questions for each test. If questions are eliminated, they are pulled from the bank and equally weighted questions are inserted for the same topics.

Federal Express has found that the QUEST automated program saves hours in clerical and administrative activities because the computer does all of the scoring, record keeping, item analysis, and score reporting. Additional features of the program are real-time registration, real-time test score reporting, and item analysis.

Federal Express has invested large amounts of money in technology-based learning but is quick to highlight the many benefits and even greater savings for the company. Internal studies have shown that the company's system for just-in-time training works. Instruction time on some modules has been reduced by 50 percent, with no loss in retention or quality of training. Since the implementation of interactive video training, job knowledge test scores have increased an average of twenty points. Locations that have higher usage of interactive video training have higher job knowledge test scores. When correlating test scores and performance evaluation ratings, Federal Express learned that, in general, the employees who have the highest scores on the test are in fact the company's better performers.

Federal Express firmly believes that its philosophy "Train to the job, perform to standards, and test for competency" provides customers with a value-added program that translates into outstanding service and a competitive edge. Well-trained, knowledgeable, and empowered employees support this philosophy and the company's goal of 100 percent customer satisfaction.

Hewlett-Packard

Headquartered in Palo Alto, California, Hewlett-Packard (HP) exceeds $50 billion in annual sales, employs over 130,000 people worldwide, and operates in over 120 countries. *Fortune* magazine (Stewart, 1998) recognized it as America's Most Admired Computers/Office Equipment Company. Lew Platt, HP's former chairman, president, and CEO, recently said that "successful companies of the 21st century will be those who do the best jobs of capturing, storing and leveraging what their employees know." In keeping with this philosophy, the firm's consulting unit—which offers IT service management, enterprise desktop management, customer relationship management, and enterprise resource planning services—has undertaken a Knowledge Management Initiative to transform the decentralized knowledge of its consultants from a "latent asset into a resource available to everything within the organization."

At one time the sharing of knowledge at HP Consulting was informal and serendipitously based on personal networks or accidental encounters at meetings. But HP Consulting recognized that success would be "highly dependent on the ability to manage and leverage organizational knowledge—and that this knowledge, appropriately leveraged, was as valuable as financial assets" (Martiny, 1998).

To accomplish greater dissemination and diffusion of knowledge, HP Consulting had to create an environment where everyone was "enthusiastic about sharing knowledge and institute processes that ensured this occurred." As Martiny observes, "The human side of knowledge management is the hard part—it involves creating a strong foundation where an organization moves from individual knowledge to organizational knowledge, where it energizes itself to create knowledge sharing and reuse behaviors to tap its collective wisdom. HP Consulting had come to believe that sharing, leverage, and reuse of knowledge had to become part of its culture" (pp. 75–76).

In 1996, a knowledge management initiative was launched with four key objectives:

1. To deliver more value to customers without increasing hours worked
2. To bring more intellectual capital to solutions
3. To create an environment where everyone is enthusiastic about sharing knowledge and leveraging the knowledge of others
4. To leverage and reuse knowledge, an initiative that required organizational change—especially on the part of leadership

Jim Sherriff, HP Consulting's general manager, recognized a significant opportunity to improve both the value delivered to customers and the profitability of the organization by tapping into the knowledge of the more experienced consultants—or in his words, "to make the knowledge of the few the knowledge of the many." He strongly believed that all consultants in the organization needed to feel and act as if they had the knowledge of the entire organization at their fingertips when consulting with customers.

HP Consulting launched the Knowledge Management Initiative using pilot programs that focused on several behavioral elements:

- Taking time to reflect and learn from successes and mistakes.
- Creating an environment that encouraged sharing of knowledge and experiences between consultants.

- Encouraging the sharing of best practices and reusable tools and solutions that could be leveraged by other consultants.

Leadership also identified four values for sustaining knowledge sharing, leverage, and reuse in HP Consulting:

- Leveraging other people's knowledge, experience, and deliverables is a desired behavior.
- Innovation is highly valued when both successes and failures are shared.
- Time spent increasing both one's own and others' knowledge and confidence is a highly valued activity.
- Consultants who actively share their knowledge and draw on the knowledge of others dramatically increase their worth.

The results have been dramatic and extremely profitable for HP. Along the way, knowledge management has progressed from an initiative to becoming a transformation leverage for HP Consulting's knowledge-based business.

Motorola

For over seventy years, Motorola has been recognized as a world-class leader in a wide range of communications and electronics markets. Its reputation for quality, innovation, and customer service has resulted in numerous awards; it was one of the first companies to receive the Malcolm Baldridge National Quality Award and to be named as a Top Training Company by the American Society for Training and Development (ASTD).

Since the early 1980s, companies from all over the world have made pilgrimages to Motorola's headquarters in Schaumburg, Illinois, to explore and examine the high-performance work practices at Motorola. What they have discovered is that Motorola's success is built on a foundation of corporate-wide learning that is leveraged to (1) create new products and services, (2) delight new and old customers, (3) quickly respond and adapt to the rapidly changing global environment, and (4) develop high-impact teams. The cornerstone for this corporate learning is Motorola University, an institution that has served as the impetus for Motorola's becoming one of the top global companies as we enter the 21st century.

Motorola's commitment to continuous innovation in new products and services continues to the present day. The company's successes over the years in a wide range of communications and electronics markets cannot be ascribed purely, or even primarily, to a goal of beating the competition, even though that has very often been the outcome. The most important motivation is the more technical objective of always trying to do better than before. Mobilizing the entire company around apparently impossible goals has long been a central part of Motorola's corporate strategy.

Since quality is a way of life at Motorola, everything from the antenna on a two-way radio to accelerometer sensors on automobiles is touched by this commitment to attaining perfection. Targets, such as the famous "Six Sigma" quality goal of reducing the error rate in every one of the company's processes to fewer than 3.4 mistakes per million operations, have helped create a common vocabulary and sense of purpose for Motorola. Even more important, motivating people to think continuously of ways to improve has kept the organization moving and searching for new opportunities.

This commitment to quality has resulted in numerous awards over the years. Motorola was recently named as leading supplier in the worldwide embedded systems industry by *Electronic Engineering Times* for launching its Digital DNA brand around the world. This award was won as a result of being best in its class for each of sixteen supplier attributes including documentation, pricing competitiveness, application support, customer orientation, and technology leadership—a phenomenal achievement.

Some of the best training in the world takes place at Motorola. The tradition of training began in the 1920s and has continued to grow in importance ever since. Until the early 1980s, Motorola Corporation had its own array of traditional employee development activities, in which training was a key component. The firm's decision in 1980 to build its own university outside the human resource department of the corporation was a radical one. The university would not displace the role of training within the company; rather, training would continue as a department within the human resource area.

By the end of the 1980s, the university had expanded its operations both in the United States and around the world. Motorola University also began offering new and more comprehensive services such as online learning systems, translation and cultural training, and an expanded portfolio of executive education programs. Nearly all of Motorola's training organizations are integrated and serve the business. Nowadays, Motorola University has ninety-nine sites in twenty-three countries on five continents that deliver over 100,000 days per year of training to employees, suppliers, and customers.

At Motorola U, factory workers study various business-related topics, from the fundamentals of computer-aided design to robotics and from communication skills to customized manufacturing. They learn not only by reading manuals or attending lectures but by inventing and building their own products, as well. The university employs few professors. Instead, it relies on a cadre of outside consultants—including engineers, scientists, and former managers—to teach most of its courses. Their role is to guide people into thinking as well as remembering. In a class on reducing manufacturing-cycle time, for example, senior managers break quickly into teams to devise new ways to get a product to market faster.

Thousands of workers have learned skills at Motorola University that have helped create new businesses as well as improve existing businesses. As a result, hot-selling products pour off Motorola's assembly lines. The company became the first American electronics firm to defeat Japanese competitors, even in their home market. Motorola later organized a course that dramatically reduced product development cycle time.

Motorola's training program is considered a model in corporate circles because of its strong link to the company's business strategy. "Motorola's whole system is driven from the shop floor," explains Anthony Carnevale (1992), a labor economist with the Committee for Economic Development in Washington, D.C. "The company trains to solve performance problems. It doesn't just put a little red schoolhouse in the workplace."

Experts also point out that Motorola extends its training programs to every one of its workers around the world. In contrast, most companies provide training only for certain employees such as general managers or technicians. Motorola is further recognized for the way it monitors its training programs. In order to move training efforts closer to operations, for example, the company now offers an increasing number of on-the-job apprenticeships.

Motorola calculates that every $1 it spends on training delivers $30 in productivity gains within three years. Since 1987, the company has cut costs by $10 billion—not by the normal expedient of firing workers but by training them to simplify processes and reduce waste. Motorola executives believe that the company's sizable training commitment has contributed to strong financial results. In 1999, Motorola will spend over $300 million to deliver a minimum of eighty hours of training to each of its 132,000 employees. Altogether, the company lays out more than 4 percent of its payroll for training, far above the average of 1 percent invested by American industry. Over the past five years, Motorola has seen annual sales increase by an average of 18 percent, while annual earnings growth has soared at a 26 percent clip. Productivity measured by sales per employee has climbed 139 percent during the same period.

Throughout most of the 1980s, Motorola University built credibility within the organization by developing educational experiences that addressed a number of imminent business needs. The tie between education and business strategy was seen as a key objective, whether it came to reducing costs in operations, improving product quality, or accelerating new product development.

In today's uncertain and turbulent business environment, Motorola University is focused on raising questions where the answers do not yet exist. The university's role, which parallels the changing competency requirements of individuals within the organization, is to raise the level of inquiry within the company through a diversely structured dialogue with customers, experts, and industry representatives (suppliers, regulators, policymakers, and special interests groups).

Motorola University's initiatives in recent years look more like new business development activities than classic educational programs. The purpose and outcome of a months-long project may be to understand how to create and manage a software business. Or the learning may include dialogues extended to customers, experts from both within and outside an existing network for the company, and industry representatives who are new to the company.

Thus new business development in an era of discontinuous change is not a new business development as it has been understood in the past. And while at first blush it appears that Motorola University merely serves as an incubation center for the more entrepreneurial activities of the company (it is not by accident that the new business development offices for the company are right next door to the university), the university has a more deeply rooted focus of change: knowledge creation. In raising questions where the answers do not yet exist for the company, Motorola University is creating the forum within the company to explore beyond the known boundaries of its business and its industry. The objective of the university is to develop the company's critical competencies so as to generate for itself new models or maps for making sense of the market when the environment becomes uncertain or ambiguous.

Business Council for International Understanding

Since 1958, the Business Council for International Understanding (BCIU) Institute has trained over 40,000 U.S. and non-U.S. managers and technicians to live and work in over 170 countries around the world. Programs are custom designed for each company and are directed toward corporate staff, negotiating teams, departing expatriates and their families, and reentering staff and their families, as well as international corporate executives coming to the United States. Training programs are conducted at BCIU headquarters in Washington, D.C., New York, and London, as well as on-site.

BCIU delivers special instruction in commercial affairs to U.S. foreign service officers in an effort to help further their promotion of U.S. commerce overseas. The special commercial training courses provided by BCIU are designed to familiarize U.S. embassy personnel with fluctuating issues such as international property rights, sanctions policy, and market access.

BCIU's programs cover the following topics:

- Knowledge of how people in other cultures think and make decisions
- Insights into various cultural perspectives
- Skills for coping with unfamiliar and frustrating personal and business situations
- Knowledge about the social, political, and economic institutions and customs of the people of a particular country or countries
- Understanding of how to do business in other countries
- Awareness of pertinent international events that affect corporate operations overseas
- Special programs for spouses, children, and multicareer families

BCIU's tailored intercultural communications, area and country studies, and language programs of three, four, five, and ten days are conducted for relocating families on an ongoing basis and provide a cost-effective alternative for successful adjustment and performance overseas.

The BCIU Institute supports the complete training cycle through extensive research and intensive follow-up in the foreign country. Graduates are visited regularly in country by the BCIU Institute staff and resource persons, allowing them insight into the progress of their graduates and their projects worldwide. Knowledge gained on these follow-up trips is then incorporated into future training and development programs for business personnel and their families headed overseas to join these or similar projects.

Meridian International Center

In contrast to BCIU's training of Americans preparing to live and work abroad, the Meridian International Center (MIC) trains foreigners who come to the United States to live, work, and/or study. Over the past fifty-five years, Meridian has trained people from every country in the world. Programs are conducted in English, Spanish, French, Arabic, and Japanese at sites in Washington, D.C., Seattle, and Miami. Over sixty current and former heads of state have been trained at MIC.

Each year, Meridian designs and implements exchange, technical assistance, and training programs for more than 2,000 international professionals. Much of this activity is carried out for the U.S. Department of State's International Visitor Program. The objective of its professional exchange programs is to provide participants with the knowledge, skills, and resources they need to work more effectively in their areas of expertise.

Study programs implemented in the United States provide foreign participants and their American counterparts with opportunities to exchange information and ideas and to develop enduring professional relationships. These programs also give visitors insights into American society, culture, and institutions. Meridian's exchange programs promote person-to-person contact and help to build international understanding.

Meridian conducts programs for a wide variety of audiences:

- Cultural training for managers and students consists of one-week cultural orientation courses for senior managers from developing countries of Eastern Europe, Asia, Africa, and Latin America. The program introduces participants to American cultures and values and prepares them for their work or study experience in the United States.
- U.S study programs for senior international leaders. Each year, MIC coordinates tailored professional study programs for some 2,000 people, including political leaders, journalists, business executives, agronomists, and manufacturers. Group and individual projects are conducted on topics such as the U.S. political process, economics, education, and the environment and take place in cities throughout the United States. Examples might include a Pakistani learning about commercial and investment banking, Brazilians learning about American trade policies, and Thais meeting with Americans to develop refugee polices.
- World affairs seminars. Every year ambassadors and high-level diplomatic officials from some 150 countries attend Meridian seminars to discuss topics on a variety of international political and economic issues. MIC also provides language training and recreational activities for diplomatic families.

Growing Importance of HRD in the United States

According to the ASTD's *2003 State of the Industry Report,* expenditures for HRD continue to expand, the use of learning technologies continues to grow, and assessment of the long-range impact of training receives ever greater scrutiny. Just as they are in other regions described in this book, HRD professionals in the United States are challenged, more than ever, to ensure that workplace learning leads to workplace success.

Part 5

Future of Global HRD

Megatrends in Global HRD

*Our task is not to make societies safe for globalization,
but to make the global system safe for decent societies.*
John J. Sweeney, U.S. labor leader

The empires of the future are the empires of the mind.
Winston Churchill

Introduction

The accelerating pace of change that has ushered more than 6 billion people in earth's 182 countries into the 21st century shows no signs of slowing. We are all buffeted by the compression of time and space that characterizes this acceleration. How should HRD professionals prepare themselves for a world that may be significantly different in twenty years? What major forces will have an impact on global human resource development? What global issues will significantly affect the work of HRD professionals all over the world? What are the emerging opportunities and the potential pitfalls for those aspiring to HRD careers?

The authors' personal experiences in more than 150 countries, as well as their research relative to HRD programs and literature throughout the world,

1. Globalization
2. Global technology
3. Changing global workforce
4. Creativity
5. Ascendancy of knowledge
6. Learning organizations
7. Ethics in the workplace
8. Global quality and service
9. Spiritual values and religion
10. Emerging roles of women
11. Work and family life
12. Sustainable development
13. Safety and security
14. Environment

FIGURE 24.1　Global Megatrends

have led them to identify fourteen global megatrends (see Figure 24.1) that we believe will have increasing impact on HRD and the workplace as we enter the 21st century. This chapter will examine each of the global HRD megatrends and identify the ways in which leading global "cutting edge" organizations have already begun to incorporate these trends.

Globalization

Many scholars think of globalization as an *environment* to which we must adapt. As an environment globalization is a compression of time and space that makes everything seem equally far and near. As Scheuerman (2002) notes, globalization increases possibilities for action between and among people where latitudinal and longitudinal location seems immaterial to the social activity at hand. Deterritorialization becomes a facet of globalization as does the growth of social interconnectedness across existing geographical and political boundaries.

Globalization will continue to be characterized by value clashes, as cultural norms and popular beliefs are shared around the world. Within the past fifty years many products have become globalized. McDonald's restaurants and Toyota autos are recognized in nearly every country in the world. The globalization of ideas and attitudes has also occurred and will assume an even more important role than the globalization of products.

One factor accelerating globalization is the rapid proliferation of the English language. There are more than 1 billion English speakers in the world. In nearly one hundred countries English is the primary or secondary language. English is the language of global media, of computers, and of business. Government and business leaders recognize the importance of English language capability for survival in the global marketplace. In January 2003, the president of Madagascar, Marc Ravalomanana, urged citizens of that francophone island to learn English, saying, "The children of Madagascar must keep in step with globalization." Nevertheless, HRD professionals in English-speaking countries must understand that English as a communications skill is different from English as a key to cultural identity. HRD professionals should be on the leading edge of learning other languages and appreciating other cultures.

More and more companies will seek globalization training, realizing that such training is the single most critical element for global success. Corporations will realize that HRD is the primary tool for mediating local cultural differences. Chapter 7 provides a wide range of roles that can and should be played by HRD professionals in making globalization a more positive force for the development of all peoples.

Global Technology

Toffler (1990) writes that the advanced global economy cannot run for thirty seconds without the technology of computers and other new and rapidly improving complexities of production. As information processing capability continues to expand, employment will tilt even more toward knowledge work—scientific and technological research, sophisticated software, advanced telecommunications, and electronic finance, all requiring a better-trained workforce.

In the new millennium, every industrial country will have advanced technology: microelectronics, biotechnology, new materials (ceramics, plastics, and composites), telecommunications, robotics and machine tools, and computers and software. The results of this spread of technology will be mixed. On one hand, the possibilities for collaborating to combat disease, malnourishment, and poverty will be enhanced in proportion to the increase in international collaboration. On the other hand, the inappropriate use of leading-edge technologies can create a fear that paralyzes, driving nations into isolationist tendencies or into fragmented and hostile alliances. For example, the events since the bombing of the World Trade Center Towers and the Pentagon in 2001 have increased suspicion, fear, and concerns about safety and security.

Driven by profit motives, many high-tech global corporations will seek inexpensive labor around the globe, just as their counterparts in the textile and apparel industries did in the 20th century. Already, computer technical support is increasingly deterritorialized; many U.S. citizens who call toll-free numbers for help with personal computers have their calls routed to experts in India or other countries. Equipped with manuals and with training about how to deal with American attitudes and communication styles, these experts are extensions of the technical support services provided by computer manufacturers. The provision of technical support across cultures will increase dramatically and will provide additional opportunities for HRD professionals to train technical service providers.

Changing Global Workforce

Continuing immigration and the need for specialized skills, particularly in more economically advanced countries, will deepen the already diverse nature of the global workforce. Corporations increasingly will reach across borders to bring jobs to workers or workers to jobs. Movements of workers will be driven by the growing gap between the world's supply of labor and the demands for it. While many of the world's skilled and unskilled workers live in the less developed countries, most of the well-paid jobs are generated in the cities of the industrialized world.

Johnston (1991), in an extensive study of global work patterns, foresaw four major implications of this mismatch for HRD practitioners:

1. There will be a massive relocation of people, including legal and illegal immigrants, temporary workers, retirees, and visitors. The greatest relocation will involve young, well-educated workers flocking to the cities of the developed world.
2. Some industrialized nations will reconsider their protectionist immigration policies as they come to rely on, and compete for, foreign-born workers.
3. Labor-short, immigrant-poor countries like Japan and Sweden will be compelled to improve labor productivity dramatically to avoid slow economic growth. Increased training and outsourcing of jobs will become necessary.
4. There will be a gradual standardization of labor practices around the world in areas of vacation time, workplace safety, training, and employee rights.

Citizens of highly developed countries are keenly aware of the impact of immigrants from less developed countries on their economies. They may be less aware that jobs have been moving from high-producing economies to countries whose educational systems produce prospective workers faster than their economies can absorb them. According to Deloitte Consulting, in the next five years 2 million jobs in the financial services business will move from the United States and Europe to cheaper locations. The exodus of service jobs across all industries could be as high as 4 million. Three-quarters of leading financial institutions and investment banks will allocate tasks to Third World countries in the next five years. Global financial institutions, for example, will invest US$350 billion in India for outsourcing projects.

Immigration flows of highly skilled workers will decrease as companies find ways to bring work to the labor market. Just as Nike has traveled the globe to set up factories where pockets of cheap labor can be found, computer makers have begun providing technical support by routing help-desk calls and e-mails to India and other countries that produce workers skilled in IT. Establishing overseas technical support services has become so successful that some policy-makers fear a serious loss of IT jobs in the United States. According to Jyoti Malhotra (2004), in India, where a 30 percent increase in outsourcing was predicted for 2004, government officials are concerned that state and local governments in the United States will prevent service jobs from going overseas.

The combination of a globalized workforce and global corporations means that managers and employees must be able to work effectively with more and more people with differing cultures, customs, values, beliefs, and practices. Cross-cultural training will become ever more important. Training firms that specialize in managing cultural diversity will continue to enjoy high demand for their services. HR staff with experience in other cultures and languages will be increasingly valuable assets to organizations.

Creativity

Einstein once wrote that "imagination is more important than information." As the technological revolution continues to reduce the number of rote workers, more creativity will be required of all. Ohmae (1990) laments that people in business have forgotten how to invent. Corporations need to relearn the art of invention, especially for industries or businesses that are global, where one must achieve world-scale economies and yet tailor products to key markets. Global business leaders need to create sustaining values for the customer in a world that has come to view corporate advertising as cynical manipulation of the marketplace.

White (1992) talks about the importance of world-class leaders who need to be "creative, to see possibilities globally, be open to learning, and possess an innovative spirit. . . . They need to prefer vision to numbers" (p. 51). Creativity training has been around for a long time, but the need for it will grow rapidly all over the world as companies realize its importance in developing sustaining relationships of value with customers.

Toffler (1990), in his book *Powershift*, states that an "innovation imperative" will be essential since no existing market share will be safe, no product life will be indefinite. The corporate need for creativity will encourage worker autonomy, implying a totally different power relationship between employer and employee, one that tolerates error and encourages "a multitude of bad ideas to harvest a single good one" (p. 213).

Many corporations do make efforts to encourage creativity among their employees. One celebrated approach was taken by 3M (Minnesota Mining and Manufacturing), which has taken specific actions to encourage creativity in the workplace:

1. Managers are rewarded for encouraging new, creative projects among their staff.
2. Research and development people are allowed to spend up to 15 percent of their time working on their own ideas.
3. Division managers have discretionary power to finance new, creative ventures.

HRD professionals will need to keep abreast of industry trends in promoting creativity and inventiveness and share best practices among organizations.

Quoting Bernard Lonergan, Grudin (1990) reminds us that "strokes of genius are but the outcomes of a continuous habit of inquiry that grasps clearly and distinctly, all that is involved in the simple things that anyone can understand" (p. 10). Development of the imagination can be a daunting task in societies like the United States where a cultural and spiritual dualism tends to see values, outcomes, and choices in binary terms. Yet exposure to music and art from other cultures has helped Americans to become more open to values that others place on time, space, and their importance to the decisionmaking process. HRD professionals in particular must be open to creative approaches to training employees for the changing world of the 21st century, as people around the globe become more respectful of one another's values and more willing to integrate plurality into the workplace.

Ascendancy of Knowledge

The power of knowledge has been celebrated from the beginning of human history. But its intimate relationship with appointed, elected, and self-proclaimed authority is rapidly coming to an end. For most of human history the most knowledgeable were at or close to the seats of power, and their authority endowed their pronouncements with credibility. The words of elders, professors, physicians, prelates, parents, police, and princes were accepted as true because of the authority vested in their positions. All of this is coming undone.

Knowledge, delinked from authority, has become ascendant because electronic media have put the equivalent of thousands of encyclopedias in hovels and huts as well as in halls of ivy; now even the least among us can create knowledge by weaving information available everywhere into the cultural framework of one's village, town, city, or metropolis.

The ascendancy of knowledge creates wonderful opportunities and terrible pitfalls for government, corporate, and nongovernmental organizations. Organizations that learn how to manage knowledge, become flexible learning organizations, and encourage lifelong learning among workers are likely to succeed; those that seek to constrain or contain knowledge or to limit workers' access to knowledge are likely to fail. As knowledge is created in myriad cultural contexts, organizations can adapt to changing environments through knowledge management and can empower their managers and workers through action learning.

Knowledge Management

The concept of knowledge management takes into account the fact that workers, exposed to information from innumerable sources, are capable of creating knowledge useful to an organization by applying information to their organizational context, culture, problems, and initiatives. Yogesh Malhotra's (2000, 2001) notion is that knowledge, because it is contextual and related to environment and experience, has potential for action and is thus linked to performance. It is the creative and innovative capacity of human beings that transforms information into knowledge.

Knowledge management really involves the management of people whose capacity for creating knowledge does not relate in any significant way to an organization's hierarchical structure. Thus managers, in the age of knowledge ascendancy, leave behind tendencies to micromanage workers and processes and instead become coaches, mentors, and facilitators, guiding workers toward accomplishing organization mission and goals, but not necessarily determining the successful paths they will take. In environments that are subject to rapid and frequent change, knowledge management assists organizations in adapting, surviving, and retaining competency.

Action Learning

Organizations that embrace knowledge management should also embrace action learning, which can heighten the creation of knowledge within a learning organization. Action learning is a creative cycle of inquiry, action, and reflection that can enhance problem solving within organizations and simultaneously create successful leaders, teams, and individuals.

The power of action learning is that it strengthens teams and creates insightful and confident employees while it focuses on solving organizational problems. According to Marquardt (2004), action learning has such potential because it flows from the best practices of many fields: management science, psychology, education, political science, economics, sociology, and systems engineering.

Action learning includes and requires six basic components:

- An important and urgent problem
- A diverse group of four to eight people
- A reflective inquiry process
- Implemented action
- A commitment to learning
- An action learning coach

Action learning also requires normative behavior among team members. All must adopt an attitude of inquiry that creates an atmosphere of open questioning among team members; and all must commit to continuous learning, before, during, and after taking action. This helps teams to continue the cycle of inquiry, action, and reflection.

Learning Organizations

There is an increasing concern among global corporations that individual learning will not be an adequate response to the learning needs of the 21st century, especially for corporations that must collect, analyze, and utilize information from hundreds of sources worldwide. Collaboration in the processing of information and knowledge must gradually supplant the traditional withholding of information that characterizes the competitive organization. Competition in the future will come to designate man's common efforts to compete with the natural and manmade forces that block human development. Competition will gradually give way to collaboration, as joint activities, considered valuable enough to pursue, will capture the imagination of citizens around the world. People competing against people and companies against companies to claim greater wealth, comfort, and power must become widely recognized as destructive to the human race.

As people from around the world become more acquainted with one another and respectful of their diverse value holdings, competition will come to mean the struggle against the forces that would overwhelm the human race: depletion of natural resources, environmental destruction, global wars, poverty and disease, loss of meaning and hope, selfishness, and greed.

Senge (1990) states that work must become a continual process for learning how to create our future rather than reach to our past. Successful learning organizations must possess the five disciplines of systems thinking, personal mastery, mental models, shared vision, and team learning. Learning organizations allow people to "continually expand their capacity to create the results they truly desire, where new and expansive patterns of thinking are nurtured, where collective aspiration is set free, and where people are continually learning how to learn together" (p. 3).

The future global organization will find itself as both guest and host in a sea of diverse cultures. A collective learning environment that promotes sharing of experience on a worldwide scale and fosters an easy dialogue between different countries and cultures will be a key to both the survival and success of 21st century organizations.

Although the focus of HRD professionals has traditionally been on individual learning (and that still is important), organizations must accelerate the development of a macro view of learning and a deeper understanding about how the organization as a system learns. The economic future, according to Barham and Devine (1991), is "not just about international competition or international collaboration. It is also about international learning. Managing across borders means learning across borders" (p. 37).

Ethics in the Workplace

As business becomes more global, so do the ethical dilemmas and complexities facing global organizations. Is it acceptable for American businesspeople to bribe Nigerian customs officials, a practice some say is as accepted there as contributing money to politicians' campaigns is in the United States? Do emerging markets present a social responsibility as well as a business opportunity? Does one give Muslim workers time off during the Islamic holy month of Ramadan?

In addition to these and other ethical choices that face international organizations, the delinking of global organizations from local culturally based ethical systems can leave these organizations without a moral compass. A "greed is good" attitude, well known in the United States since the era of the "robber barons," dominated the latter part of the 20th century and has served up the gross scandals of BCI, Pentagon waste, Japanese investment houses, Solomon Brothers Trading, the Union Carbide disaster in Bhopal, India, and the Enron, Anderson, and WorldCom scandals. A regular feature of one of the major network news broadcasts in the United States (*NBC Nightly News*) at the turn of the 21st century was "The Fleecing of America," a weekly expose of fraud and mismanagement that wastes the tax contributions of the working public and attacks the spirit of trust in public authorities. These examples are supplemented by daily reports of corruption at state, local, and national government levels both in the United States and abroad.

William H. Donaldson, appointed chairman of the Securities and Exchange Commission, expressed surprise in February 2002 at the lack of ethical behavior he witnessed in the securities industry. "I am surprised at the day-in and day-out, steady level of malfeasance that comes in under the radar," he said in the *Washington Post* (May 7, 2003).

According to Blake and Carroll (1989), corporations have focused efforts on ethics training for corporate workers. The Center for Business Ethics at Bentley College in Massachusetts found that 45 percent of the largest U.S. companies have ethics programs or workshops. More than 350 universities teach courses in business ethics. All courses at Georgetown's highly regarded MBA program must include both a global and an ethical component.

Most of these courses focus on individual behavior, as do many of the areas of ethical challenge developed by the American Society for Training and Development. Among ASTD's ethical prescriptions for HRD professionals are maintaining appropriate confidentiality, saying "no" to inappropriate requests, and using power appropriately.

Yet understanding of the obligations of human beings and the corporations they create must become better integrated with other business concepts and know-how. As Korten (1999) points out, global technology, especially communications technology, allows us to function with a "global species intelligence" (p. 14), one that allows us to anticipate the future consequences of our collective actions and make a conscious collective choice to act. Corporations must reconnect with the absolute value of human life and establish productive relations with the communities where they exist. What would not be tolerated in the CEO's backyard must not be tolerated on the commons.

Global Quality and Service

The ability to attract and retain customers with quality products and quality service will be a key survival issue for global businesses in the 21st century.

Global corporations realize that a focus on quality turned Japan into an economic powerhouse. Even the public sector will be expected to be service- and quality-oriented or face privatization or loss of funding.

Developing a quality product is only the beginning. How it is delivered is equally important in the global marketplace. Poor service sends more customers to global competitors than price or quality. In a global study by Forum Corporation, customers were asked to rate service quality. Lack of reliability and lack of cultural empathy were the top complaints. The Forum study also found a direct correlation between employee turnover and service quality: Companies with the lowest service quality ratings also had the highest employee turnover rates. In other words, quality can lessen the need to continually hire and train new workers.

Perhaps in reaction to the intensity of the quest for personal and corporate profits, leaders of many business schools in the United States are finding ways to stress the importance of service to corporate success. Autry (1991) talks openly of the importance of the servant's role to corporate behavior. HRD professionals will be on the forefront of initiatives to orient employees to service prototypes within organizations and to create opportunities for corporations to strengthen human communities. Increasingly, HRD practitioners will assist workers to understand how the social obligations of companies impact workers' roles in society.

Spiritual Values and Religion

Naisbitt and Aburdene (1990) observed in *Megatrends 2000* that people around the world are turning toward religion and spiritual values in overwhelming numbers. They are realizing that "science and technology do not tell us what life means. We learn that through literature, arts, and spirituality" (p. 293). By reaffirming the spiritual, people experience a "more balanced quest" to better their lives.

In reaction to the intensity of the quest for personal and corporate profits, leaders of many business schools in the United States are finding ways to stress the importance of spiritual values to corporate success. Unfortunately, this instruction does not always seem to translate into application.

James Autry's (1991) best-seller among HRD professionals, *Love and Profit: The Art of Caring Leadership,* begins with the author's three basic beliefs:

1. Work can provide the opportunity for spiritual as well as financial growth;
2. The workplace is rapidly becoming the new neighborhood;
3. Good management is largely a matter of love. (p. 13)

In the workplace, Autry believes, everyone should be treated with dignity and respect, honesty and trust, and with love. Such a workplace would be like "heaven" (p. 156).

Michael Ray (1991), a professor at Stanford University, sees the emergence of spiritual values as part of the new paradigm in business. Spirituality in this new paradigm refers not to religion but rather "to the power of inner wisdom and authority and the connection and wholeness in humanity" (37). It is a move to the spirit, to inner qualities such as intuition, will, strength, joy, and compassion.

William Miller (2001) describes how the director of Hewlett-Packard Laboratory, Frank Carrubba, concluded that the most successful teams are built on the quality of spirit and truth within themselves. According to Miller, an appreciation of deep cultural values and a conscious development of those values are essential to corporate growth and the quality of life.

Insofar as spiritual values assume greater importance in corporate behavior, HRD professionals will function increasingly as mediators among global collaborators who interpret the same reality in different ways or will replace litigation as the primary tool for settling differences, as lawsuits give way to win-win situations. Corporations will need HRD specialists who understand how to mediate value statements and achieve compromises regarding work conditions, benefits, and other conditions of service.

Emerging Roles of Women

The changing roles of women and the impact of these changes on family and the organization will gain significance in the global arena during the 21st century. The flow of women into the industrial work force is a worldwide phenomenon. In Japan 58 percent of females between ages fifteen and sixty-four are in the workforce. In Canada one-third and in France one-fifth of all businesses are owned by women. In Great Britain women are establishing new businesses three times faster than men; in the United States, twice as fast. In the United States, women represent nearly 60 percent of college graduation classes and are taking two-thirds of the new jobs being created, most of them in the information/service industry (the primary industry of the 21st century).

Even in less developed countries, where women have traditionally shouldered the bulk of agricultural work and nonformal sector work, more and more have joined the formal sector as educational opportunities have increased. The percentage of females in the workforce is now at nearly 50. As cooking and cleaning technologies ease the burden at home, as agricultural jobs disappear, and as service jobs (which generally require less education) begin to proliferate, an even higher number of Third World women will enter the labor force. Even now China and Thailand have a higher percentage of female workers (75 percent) than any industrialized nation except Sweden (79 percent). In countries where female labor force participation remains low (e.g., Pakistan, at 12 percent), the reasons are often religious and cultural.

Women have faced serious difficulties, however, as they have entered the labor market: the glass ceiling that prevents many from emerging into senior management positions, sexual harassment, limited elder care and child care facilities, and being placed in the "mommy track."

As difficult as the corporate world has made it for women to attain power in organizations, it is precisely the female style of leadership that may be most needed in the global corporation of the 21st century, according to Naisbitt and Aburdene (1990), who see the "new corporate archetype" as being more feminine than masculine. They see the dominant principle within future global organization shifting from management in order to control an enterprise to leadership in order to bring out the best in people and to respond quickly to change. As wasteful competition gives way to collaboration, the leader in the 21st century global corporation will be more of a teacher, facilitator, and coach who will encourage the new, better-educated worker to be more entrepreneurial, self-managing, and oriented toward lifelong learning.

Work and Family Life

Coping with conflicts between work and family will be one of the greatest employment challenges in the early 21st century. Over the past two decades, the number of working women in the workforce has nearly doubled on a worldwide basis. Single working mothers are becoming more common, stay-at-home dads are increasing in the United States, and two-career families are becoming the norm in many countries. Recessions, mergers and acquisitions, relocations, corporate downsizing, longer commutes to find affordable housing, and the soaring costs of heath care—all have increased pressures on traditional families.

Many companies have adopted family-friendly policies to help employees deal with their family and work obligations. These policies include:

- Flexible work arrangement—alternative work schedules and telecommuting
- Leaves—maternal and paternal leave, leave donations to sick and disabled employees
- Financial assistance—flexible benefits, long-term-care insurance, child care discounts

- Corporate giving/community service—funding for community or national work-family initiatives
- Dependent-care services—child and elder care referral, on-site centers, sick-child programs
- Management change—work-family training for managers, work-family coordinators
- work-family stress management—wellness programs, relocation services, work-family seminars

One corporate leader, Johnson & Johnson, provides flextime, maternity leave, working at home after childbirth, part-time work, on-site day care, on-site aerobics, health care for part-timers, payment to employees who adopt, and most important, a firm commitment by top management to change the corporate culture to be family-friendly.

The recognition by corporations that employees are not simply factors of production, but rather creative beings with the potential to fashion new products and new relationships that will benefit society and the company will reinforce efforts to make the work experience family-friendly. HR professionals will be key players in managing increasingly diverse arrangements to meet needs of workers and companies in high-tech societies.

Sustainable Development

At the beginning of the third millennium, a broad consensus is developing about the meaning and urgency of "sustainable development." Introduced by the Bruntdland Report on our common future in 1987, the term has come to mean a meeting of the world's present needs without denying or compromising the ability of future generations to meet their own needs. The aim of sustainable development is to achieve balance in global economic, environmental, and social needs for the present and future generations. Sustainable development requires a long-term integrated approach to developing a healthy global environment by jointly addressing economic, environmental, and social issues while avoiding overconsumption of key natural resources.

The key factors to achieving sustainable development are economic development, social equity and justice, and environmental protection. Sustainable development requires that these three factors subsist in a harmonious relationship, but in fact they were in conflict in the latter half of the 20th century, as rich nations wrestled with their role in supporting sustainable development and with the paradigm shift that delinks unbridled economic growth and sustainable development.

For development to become sustainable, excesses at both ends of the global economic system must be curbed. Excessive consumption, pollution, and individual acquisition must be restrained among the wealthy countries, while excessive poverty, ignorance, and population growth must be reduced among the poor countries. The gap between the wealthy and the poor must be diminished both within nations and among the populations of the globe. Such gaps within and between nations contribute to resentments among people, anger at government authorities, divisions among populations, insecure institutions, and a growing willingness by desperate people to resort to extreme measures while seeking simple justice.

How should sustainable development be measured? Henderson (1995) and others have pointed out that measures, such as per capita income and gross domestic product, are inadequate because they give no indication of the disparities among people. These critics have come up with a number of indicators intending to bring the three factors of economic development, social equity and justice, and environmental protection into harmony. These indicators include the following.

Economic Indicators

- Numbers of hours of paid employment at the average wage required to support basic needs
- Diversity and vitality of the local job base
- Number and variability in size of companies
- Number and variability of industry types
- Variability of skill levels required for jobs
- Wages paid in the local economy that are spent in the local economy
- Dollars spent in the local economy that pay for local labor and local natural resources
- Percent of local economy based in renewable local resources

Environmental Indicators

- Use and generation of toxic materials
- Vehicle miles traveled
- Percent of products produced that are durable, repairable, or readily recyclable
- Total energy used from all sources
- Ratio of renewable energy used at renewable rate compared to nonrenewable energy

Social Indicators

- Number of students trained for jobs that are available in the local economy
- Number of students who go to college and come back to the community
- Number of voters who vote in elections
- Number of voters who attend town meetings

HRD, especially through its workforce and community development functions, should take a lead role in promoting the social, environmental, and economic factors that affect sustainable development. Already HRD is addressing issues of appropriate resource deployment and allocation in the various environments in which global corporations operate. Issues, such as centralization of operations and outsourcing of services, must be balanced with the importance and impact of a company to the community where it operates. HRD can use powerful tools, such as action learning, to address and assess issues of corporate citizenship as well as productivity and efficiency.

Safety and Security

Humankind has developed three approaches to the search for safe and secure environments in which to raise children and to live peacefully with neighbors: defense, deterrence, and acceptance. Defense assumes walls can be built thickly enough to protect from even the most powerful weapons. Castles, forts, firewalls, steel doors, bunkers, barbed wire, armored cars, and space shields are a part of the inventory of defense machinery. Despite the collapse of the walls of Jericho, the storming of the Bastille, the breaching of the Alamo, and the clever attacks of computer hackers, defense strategists continue to have faith that a more perfect defense can be devised to protect us from enemies.

Deterrence assumes that a potential enemy will be disinclined to attack once he realizes how powerful will be the counterattack. High-tech surveillance, smart bombs, the best-trained troops, and sophisticated intelligence networks should deter all but the foolhardy from attacking. The Cold War of the 20th century—when the United States and the Soviet Union built up nuclear arsenals, client states, and vast spy networks—offers a classic case of mutual deterrence.

Yet deterrence, too, has its limitations. In September 2001, the United States, which has the most costly and most sophisticated deterrence capability in the history of mankind, was attacked by a group with a mission and objectives but with neither homeland nor impressive systems of defense or deterrence. Al-Qaeda inflicted unimagined damage on both the commercial and military pulses of the United States, the World Trade Center, and the Pentagon. Even so, U.S. officials' faith in the value of deterrence was unshaken. More resources were devoted to deterrence, and a Department of Homeland Security was created to coordinate the efforts of states and cities to prepare for, prevent, or mitigate future attacks.

Acceptance requires a different type of engagement. In the Old Testament of the Bible, when Jacob's son Joseph went to Egypt, he learned the language and customs of his hosts. He accepted the value of the culture in which he was exiled, even though it was different from his own. The Egyptians, in turn, protected him, valued his gifts, and made him powerful in their land. Joseph was able to extend this protection to his whole family.

In the 20th century, countries in every part of the globe invested in acceptance as an approach to security when they created opportunities for volunteers to live and work in other countries. The largest of these organized efforts was the peace corps in the United States. By the turn of this century, more than 150,000 Americans had served as peace corps volunteers overseas in more than one hundred countries. Typically, volunteers lived among the poor, either with host families or in dwellings characteristic of the communities where they lived. They became sons and daughters of local families.

Volunteers who managed to learn the local language and to adapt to the local culture reported feeling safe and secure. Incidents of violent behavior toward these volunteers in their local communities were few. Because they learned local languages and respected local customs, they were protected by the communities where they lived and worked. The protection afforded by mutual acceptance is based on openness to diversity and a respect for other belief and value systems. On a global scale the United Nations also represents an investment, by the whole family of nations, in acceptance as an approach to a safe and secure world.

These approaches to safety and security have always coexisted uneasily because they evoke our contradictory views of human nature. We see others potentially as both enemies and friends, recognizing our human capacity for great good and great evil. Two of these approaches, defense and deterrence, anticipate others as potential enemies and seek, as Galtung (1996) notes, a negative peace, the absence of war. The acceptance approach views others as potential friends and fosters a positive peace, one that promotes conditions favoring political equality and social and economic justice.

The 21st century will see increasing tension between these conflicting approaches to safety and security. Wealthy nations, influenced by those who create the newest technology and concerned for the safety of their citizens, will continue to employ ever more sophisticated mechanisms to detect, assess, and deter hostile currents around the globe and will add even smarter weapons of mass destruction to their arsenals. Concurrently, from the grass roots will come voices, louder each generation, to proclaim that sustainable security will come only from attending to the physical and spiritual needs of mankind: food, clothing, shelter, education, means of sustenance, freedom to choose.

Human resource professionals must be aware of these conflicting currents and be able to identify those that influence the behavior of their organizations and the societies in which they practice. Their responsibility should be to build a bridge connecting these seemingly irreconcilable orientations in order to broaden and humanize the relentless process of globalization.

Environment

Our world is at a crisis point with respect to stress on the environment. The earth's air, water, forests, fish, and wildlife are at risk due to a combination of rapid human population increase, economic development, a lack of regulation of the commons, idealization of high consumption societies, and poor understanding of how the global environment works, among other factors. Some believe that in time, humanity's creative intellect will find technical solutions to the depletion of our renewable resources. Others caution that we must act now to prevent irreversible damage to the global ecosystem. Virtually all nations now admit that global warming presents a serious problem. Yet there is little consensus on what we should do about this problem, which may threaten the very existence of those just three generations away from ourselves.

The World Bank reported in April 2003 that rich countries, with 15 percent of the world's population, account for half of all energy consumption and carbon dioxide emissions. The Organization for Economic Cooperation and Development says that because of economic growth in thirty advanced capitalist nations, their municipal waste output increased 40 percent—almost twice as fast as population growth—from 1980 to 2000.

At the beginning of the 21st century, the United States and other wealthy countries offer numerous examples of the combination of profit motive as an end and individualism as a cultural institution. Thousands of corporate executives wrap themselves in riches, draining corporate earnings while basic benefit programs for corporate employees are placed at risk. As if Leo Tolstoy (2001) had never instructed us on how much land a man needs, top executives of large corporations commonly amass property on several continents; travel about in expensive cars, boats, and planes; and insulate themselves effectively from the risks and realities of life on the street.

Many of the rest of us follow behind, settling on the second, third, or even fourth tier of the "good life," buying a second home, fancy car, or modest boat. We in the West, particularly the United States, are a people of rights. We raise our personal rights to the level of moral goods, and our religious leaders bless these rights as God given.

As the 21st century opens, many believe that this may be our last chance to avert environmental damage so severe that future generations will be unable to meet basic requirements for food and energy. Business leaders are increasingly aware that the earth operates as a single unified ecosystem and that what occurs in one place will have repercussions in another. Companies in the West that are moving, albeit slowly, toward ecoresponsibility are doing so without consistent government support.

The forms and impact of future technologies will become more energy efficient, produce less waste, and contribute to human betterment with minimal consumption of natural resources. Shifts in these directions are already occurring in information technology, biotechnology, and advanced materials. Renewable energy sources—solar, wind, hydro, biomass, and photovoltaic— will become more competitive with conventional energy sources.

Human resource development professionals will need to provide leadership in helping corporations develop environmental strategies that can become competitive, profitable, and secure and can lead to successful and ethical growth. HRD practitioners should pose hard questions to a world in crisis, assist those ready for dialogue to find the words that illuminate our common humanity, and reinforce the best tendencies of the human spirit—those that seek justice and peace.

Summary

The authors' personal experiences in over 150 countries as well as their research relative to HRD programs and literature throughout the world have led them to identify fourteen global megatrends that will significantly impact HRD and the workplace in the 21st century (see Figure 24.1). HRD practitioners in many global organizations have already begun considering these trends in their planning and practices. They are helping their colleagues to understand the impact of these trends on the world of work and on economic success and global well-being.

Helpful Web Sites

Abu Dhabi National Oil Company (ADNOC). http://www.adnoc.com

America-Mideast Educational and Training Services (AMIDEAST). http://www.amideast.org

Arab Air Carriers Organization. http://www.aaco.org

Canada. http://www.canadainfolink.ca/teach.htm

Caribbean Disaster Emergency Response Agency (CDERA). http://www.oas.org/cdera/champ/

Central Intelligence Agency (CIA) World Factbook. http://www.cia.gov/publications/factbook

Dofasco, Inc. http://www.dofasco.ca

Encyclopedia of Sustainable Development. http://www.doc.mmu.ac.uk/aric/esd/

Hurricane-Resistant Home Improvement Program. http://www.oas.org/cdmp/hrhip/

International Council for Educational Media (ICEM). http://www.icem-cime.com

International Council for Open and Distance Education (ICDE). http://www.icde.org

International Federation of Red Cross and Red Crescent Societies. http://www.ifrc.org

International Federation of Training and Development Organizations (IFTDO). http://www.iftdo.org

International Labor Organization (ILO). http://www.ilo.org

International Project on Technical and Vocational Education of the United Nations Educational, Social, and Cultural Organization (UNESCO-UNEVOC). http://www.unevoc.unesco.org

Knowledge Management Network. http://www.brint.com/km/

Kuwait Institute for Scientific Research (KISR). http://www.kisr.edu.kw

Organization of American States (OAS). http://www.oas.org

ProLiteracy Worldwide. http://www.proliteracy.org

Qatar Info. http://www.qatar-info.com

RBC (Royal Bank of Canada) Financial Group. http://www.rbc.com

Society for Intercultural Education, Training, and Research (SIETAR). http://www.sietar.org

The International Council for Educational Media (ICEM). http://www.icem-cime.com

United Nations. http://www.un.org

United Nations Development Program (UNDP). http://www.undp.org
United Nations Industrial Development Organization (UNIDO). http://www.unido.org
Wall Street Executive Library. http://www.executivelibrary.com
World Bank Institute (WBI). http://www.web.worldbank.org
World Education. http://www.worlded.org
World Rehabilitation Fund (WRF). http://www.worldrehabfund.org

References and
Suggested Readings

Adler, N. J. (2002). *International dimensions of organizational behavior* (4th ed.). Cincinnati, OH: South-Western.

Al-Faleh, M. (1987). Cultural influences on Arab management development: A case study of Jordan [Electronic version]. *Journal of Management Development, 6*(3), 19–34.

Ali, A. J. (1995, Fall). Cultural discontinuity and Arab management thought [Electronic version]. *International Studies of Management & Organization, 25*(3).

_____. (1995). Teaching management in the Arab world: Confronting illusions [Electronic version]. *International Journal of Educational Management, 9*(2), 10–18.

Allen, D., & Alvarez, S. (1998). Empowering expatriates and organizations to improve repatriation effectiveness [Electronic version]. *Human Resource Planning, 21*(4), 29–39.

Allen, T. (1997). *Managing the flow of technology.* Cambridge, MA: MIT Press.

American Society for Training and Development. (1988). *Models for HRD practice.* Alexandria: ASTD (American Society of Training and Development) Press.

Arnold, M., & Day, R. (1998). *The next bottom line: Making sustainable development tangible.* Washington, DC: World Resources Institute.

Autry, J. (1991). *Love and profit: The art of caring leadership.* New York: William Morrow.

Axtell, R. (1998). *The do's and taboos of body language around the world.* New York: John Wiley.

Aziz, Z. (1993). *Introduction to Islam.* Lahore, Pakistan: American Association of Individual Investors (AAII) Press.

Barham, K., & Devine, M. (1991). *The quest for the international manager: A survey of global human resource strategies.* London: Business International Press.

Bartlett, C., & Ghoshal, S. (1998). *Managing across borders.* Boston: Harvard Business School Press.

Bas, D. (1989). On-the-job training in Africa. *International Labor Review, 128*(4), 485–496.

Bates, R. (2003). Human resource development objectives. In *Encyclopedia of life support systems.* Oxford, UK: Eolss, under the auspices of UNESCO.

Berger, N. O. (1999). Human resource issues in Russia: A case study. *Advances in Developing Human Resources, 4,* 38–54.

Berger, N. O. (2003a). Elements of planning strategies for HRD. *Encyclopedia of Life Support Systems.* Oxford, UK: Eolss, under the auspices of the UNESCO.

_____. (2003b). Needs assessment in HRD. *Encyclopedia of Life Support Systems.* Oxford, UK: Eolss, under the auspices of UNESCO.

Bhagwati, J. (2002). *Free trade today.* Princeton: Princeton University Press.

Bierstadt, R. (1963). *The social order: An introduction to sociology.* New York: McGraw-Hill.

Bissell, T. (2003). *Chasing the sea: Lost among the ghosts of empire in Central Asia.* New York: Pantheon.

Black, J., Gregersen, H., Mendenhall, M., and Stroh, L. (1999). *Globalizing people through international assignments.* Boston: Addison-Wesley.

Blake, R. B., & Carroll, D. A. (1989, June). Ethical reasoning in business. *Training and Development Journal, 43*(6), 99–104.

Blua, A. (2003, May 22). Charter university to bring education to remote mountain regions. *Radio Free Europe Report.* Retrieved December 29, 2003, from http://www.rferl.org/nca/features/2003/05/22052003161630.asp

Boyce, B. (n.d.). Say the magic word. *Shambala Sun On-line.* Retrieved April 4, 2004, from http://www.shambalasun.com/Archives/

Brake, T., Walker, D. M., & Walker, T. (1995). *Doing business internationally: The guide to cross-cultural success.* Burr Ridge, IL: Irwin Professional.

Budhwar, P. S., Al-Yahmadi, S., & Debrah, Y. (2002, September). Human resource development in the Sultanate of Oman [Electronic version]. *International Journal of Training and Development, 6*(3), 198–215.

Burleigh, A. (1988, April). New Zealand updates apprenticeship. *Vocational Education Journal, 63*(4), 36–38.

Calori, R., & Dufour, B. (1995). Management European style. *Academy of Management Executive 9*(3), 61–74.

Canadian Society for Training and Development. (2003, July 4). Conference Board T&D survey. *CSTD e-Newsletter.* Retrieved July 4, 2003, from http://www.cstd.ca.

Carmel, E. (1999). *Global software teams.* Upper Saddle River, NJ: Prentice-Hall.

Carnevale, A. (1992, February). Learning: The critical technology. *Training and Development Journal, 46*(2), S1–S14.

Casse, P. (1982). *Training for the multicultural manager.* Yarmouth, ME: Intercultural Press.

Chalofsky, N. (1992). A unifying definition for the human resource development profession. *Human Resource Development Quarterly, 3*(2), 175–182.

Chapnick, S. (2000, December). Thinking outside the states. *Learning Circuits* (ASTD online newsletter). Retrieved December 15, 2003, from http://www.learningcircuits.org/dec2000/chapnick.html

Chesanow, N. (1985). *The world class executive.* New York: Rawson Associates.

Clayton, A., & Radcliffe, N. (1997). *Sustainability: A systems approach.* London: Earthscan.

Copeland, L., & Griggs, L. (1985). *Going international.* New York: Random House.

Cornell, S. E., & Spector, R. A. (2002, Winter). Central Asia: More than Islamic extremists [Electronic version]. *Washington Quarterly, 25*(1), 193–206. Retrieved December 29, 2003, from http://www.twq.com/02winter/spector.pdf

Cox, T. (1994). *Cultural diversity in organizations.* San Francisco: Berrett-Koehler.

Dahlman, C. (2002, September 9–12). *Challenges to Middle East and North African countries from the knowledge revolution.* Paper presented at Knowledge for Development: A Forum for Middle East and North Africa, Marseilles.

Dalton, M., Ernst, C., Deal, J., & Leslie, J. (2002). Success for the new global manager. San Francisco: Jossey-Bass.

Davenport, T., & Prusa, K. (1998). *Working knowledge.* Boston: Harvard Business School Press.

Davison, S., & Ward, K. (1999). *Leading international teams.* London: McGraw-Hill.

Day, K., & Johnson, C. (2003, May 7). New strength at the SEC's helm surprises consumer advocates. *Washington Post,* E1.

Deal, T., & Kennedy. (1982). *Corporate culture: The rites and rituals of corporate life.* Reading, MA: Addison-Wesley.

DeMente, B. (1990). *How to do business in Japan.* Lincolnwood, IL: NTC.

Devereaux, M., & Johansen, R. (1994). *Globalwork: Bridging distance, culture and time.* San Francisco: Jossey-Bass.

Diamond, J. (1999). *Guns, germs, and steel: The fates of human societies.* New York: W. W. Norton.

Doke, D. (1993, February 25). Pulling power—People management is the key. *Personnel Today.* Retrieved February 6, 2004, from http://www.personneltoday.com/Article 17662.htm

Drucker, P. (2001). *The essential Drucker.* New York: HarperBooks.

Edgar, A. L. (2001, October 26). Identities, communities, and nations in Central Asia: A historical perspective. Panel presentation sponsored by the Institute of International Studies at UC Berkeley. Retrieved December 23, 2003, from http://ist-socrates.berkeley.edu/~bsp/caucasus/articles/edgar_2001–1029.pdf

Elliot, J. (1999). *An unexpected light: Travels in Afghanistan.* New York: Picador.

Encyclopedia of sustainable development. (n.d.). Manchester Metropolitan University, Department of Environmental and Geographical Sciences. Accessed February 7, 2004, at http://www.doc.mmu.ac.uk/aric/esd/

Expat study identifies policy trends [Electronic version]. (1997, July). *Workforce, 76*(7), 9.

Fielding workforce interests in global assignments. (1999, June). *Institute for International Human Resources Update, 3,* 6–7.

Frank, E. (1998a, May). HRD in Australia. *Journal of European Industrial Training, 12*(5), 49–56.

_____. (1998b, May). HRD in India. *Journal of European Industrial Training, 12*(5), 32–38.

_____. (1998c, May). HRD in Japan. *Journal of European Industrial Training, 12*(5), 42–49.

Friedman, T. (1999). *The Lexus and the olive tree.* New York: Random House.

_____. (2001). Speech at Elliott School of International Affairs, George Washington University, Washington, DC.

Fucini, J. J., & Fucini, S. (1990). *Working for the Japanese.* New York: Free Press.

Fuentes, C. (1968). *A change of skin.* New York: Noonday Press.

Fukuda-Parr, S. (2000). *Human development report 2000.* New York: Oxford University Press.

Galagan, P. (1991a, October). Creativity and work. *Training and Development Journal,* *45*(10), 23–32.

____. (1991b, October). The learning organization made easy. *Training and Development Journal, 45*(10), 37–44.

Galagan, P. (2003, December). The future of the profession formerly known as training. *T+D, 57*(12), 26–38.

Galtung, J. (1996). *Peace by peaceful means.* London: Sage.

Gannon, M. (2001). *Understanding global cultures: Metaphorical journeys through 23 nations.* Thousand Oaks, CA: Sage.

Gannon, M. J., & Associates. (1994). *Understanding global cultures.* Thousand Oaks, CA: Sage Publications.

Geary, S. (2002, Fall). What does it take to implement the learning organization? *Canadian Learning Journal, 6*(2), 27–30.

Gibson, M. K. (1998, November). Avoiding intervention pitfalls in international consulting [Electronic version]. *Journal of Management Consulting, 10*(2), 59–66.

Global Banking Alliance for Women convenes first summit to promote women entrepreneurship: Four international banks converge in Boston to share best practices. (2001, June 20). *Business Wire.* Retrieved February 6, 2004, from http://www.find articles.com/cf_0/m0EIN/2001_June_20/75663595/p1/article.jhtml

Green, S. (2003, May 27). Japanese banks hemorrhage. *Sydney Morning Herald.* Retrieved February 6, 2004, from http://www.smh.com.au/articles/2003/05/26/1053801342977.html

Gregerson, H., Hite, J., & Black, S. (1996). Expatriate performance appraisal in U.S. multinational firms. *Journal of International Business Studies, 27*(4), 711–738.

Grudin, R. (1990). *The grace of great things: Creativity and innovation.* New York: Ticknor & Fields.

Gundling, E. (2003). *Working globesmart: 12 people skills for doing business across borders.* Palo Alto, CA: Davies-Black.

Hachey, J.-M. (2003, January). Why do people go overseas? Important characteristics for overseas workers. *Access Learning.* Retrieved January 23, 2004, from http://www.accesslearning.com/careerstv/pdfs/working_overseas.pdf

Hall, E. (1976). *Beyond culture.* Garden City, NY: Doubleday.

Hamel, G., & Prahalad, C. K. (1994). *Competing for the future.* Boston: Harvard Business School Press.

Hamilton, E., & Asiedu, K. (1987, Summer). Vocational-technical education in tropical Africa. *Journal of Negro Education, 56*(3), 338–355.

Hampden-Turner, C., & Trompenaars, F. (2000). *Building cross-cultural competence.* New Haven, CT: Yale University Press.

Handy, C. (1995). *The age of paradox.* Cambridge, MA: Harvard Business School Press.

Harris, P. R., & Moran, R. T. (1996). *Managing cultural differences* (4th ed.). Houston: Gulf.

Hassett, K. A., & Shapiro, R. (2003, July 1). How Europe sows misery in Africa. *AEI Online.* Retrieved February 11, 2004, from http://www.aei.org/research/filter.economic,subjectID.8/projectpub_list.asp

Hayashi, S. (1988). *Culture and management in Japan.* Tokyo: University of Tokyo Press.

Head, T., Haug, R., Krabbenhoft, A., & Ma, Chunhui. (2000, Summer). Issues and trends in international business law: Implications for O.D. consultants [Electronic version]. *Organization Development Journal, 18*(2), 62–78.

Hedley, A. E. (2002). *Running out of control: Dilemmas of globalization.* West Hartford, CT: Kumarian Press.

Henderson, H. (1995). *Paradigms in progress: Life beyond economics.* San Francisco: Berrett-Koehler.

Herman, S. (2000). Counterpoint: Notes on O.D. for the 21st century—Part 1 [Electronic version]. *Organization Development Journal, 18*(2), 108–111.

Hofstede, G. (1980). *Culture's consequences.* Thousand Oaks, CA: Sage.

____. (1991). *Cultures and organizations.* London: McGraw-Hill.

____. (2001). *Culture's consequences: Comparing values, behaviors, institutions, and organizations across nations.* San Francisco: Sage.

Huey, R. J. (1989, March). Financial services training—The Westpac experience. *Journal of Management Development, 8*(3), 50–54.

Irving, J. (1999, June). Making development gender sensitive. *Africa Recovery Online, 13*(1). Retrieved February 7, 2004, from http://www.un.org/ecosocdev/geninfo/afrec/subjindx/131wm.htm

Isbister, J. (2001). *Capitalism and justice.* West Hartford, CT: Kumarian Press.

Ishida, H. (1986, Spring). Transferability of Japanese human resource management abroad. *Human Resource Management, 25*(1), 102–120.

Johnston, W. (1991, March–April). Global workforce 2000: The globalization of labor. *Harvard Business Review, 69*(2), 115–127.

Jones, A. (Ed.) (1966). *The Jerusalem bible.* Garden City, NJ: Doubleday.

Jones, M. L. (1991). Management development: An African focus. In M. Mendenhall (Ed.), *International Human Resource Management* (pp. 234–247). Boston: PWS-Kent.

Kanter, R. (1995). *World class: Thriving locally in a global economy.* New York: Simon & Schuster.

Kaplan, R. (2001). *The coming anarchy: Shattering the dreams of the post cold war.* New York: Vintage Books.

Katzenbach, J. R., & Smith, D. K. (2003). *The wisdom of teams.* New York: Harper.

Keeley, S. (2003, December 5). Employees in China just can't get enough training. *China Business Infocenter Newsletter.* Retrieved January 21, 2004, from http//www.cbiz.cn/News/showarticle.asp.

Kelleher, A., & Klein, L. (1999). *Global perspectives: A handbook for understanding global issues.* Upper Saddle River, NJ: Prentice-Hall.

Kelly, M. J. (1995). Electronic manufacturing and packaging in Japan. *Japanese Technology Evaluation Center Panel Report.* Retrieved February 4, 2004, from Loyola College, Baltimore, Web site at http://www.wtec.org/loyola/ep/toc.htm

Kemper, C. L. (1998, February). Global training's critical success factors. *Training & Development, 52*(2), 35–37.

Kiechel, W. (1990, March 12). The organization that learns. *Fortune, 12*(5), 133–136.

Kiger, P. J. (2002, July). Training transforms a region's economy. *Workforce, 81,* 46–50.

Kohls, L. R. (1981). *Developing intercultural awareness.* Washington, DC: Society for Intercultural Education, Training, and Research (SIETAR).

Korten, D. C. (1999). *The post-corporate world: Life after capitalism.* West Hartford, CT: Kumarian Press.

_____. (2001). *When corporations rule the world* (2nd ed.). West Hartford, CT: Kumarian Press.

Laurant, A. (1983, Spring–Summer). The cultural diversity of western conceptions of management [Electronic version]. *International Studies of Management and Organization,* 75–96.

Lindberg, K. (1991, Summer). The intricacies of training and development in Japan. *Human Resource Development Quarterly, 2*(2), 101–114.

Linsky, M., & Heifetz, R. (2002). *Leadership on the line.* Boston: Harvard Business School Press.

Lippitt, G., & Lippitt, R. (1986). *The consulting process in action* (2nd ed.). San Diego: Pfeiffer.

Long, D. (2003, March 10). The role of the extended family in Saudi Arabia. *Saudi-American Forum,* Essay Series #09. Retrieved July, 7, 2003, from http://www.arabialink.com/SAF/Newsletters/SAF_Essay_09.htm

MacFarland, J. R. (1997, August). Increasing expatriate success while decreasing corporate costs. *Performance Improvement, 36*(7), 22–30.

Malhotra, J. (2004, February 3). Outsourcing: US "advice" rankles Sinha. *Indian Express.* Retrieved February 5, 2004, from http://www.indianexpress.com/full_story.php?content_id=40342

Malhotra, Y. (Ed.) (2001). *Knowledge management and business model innovation.* Hershey, PA: Idea Group.

_____. (Ed.) (2002). *Knowledge management and virtual organizations.* Hershey, PA: Idea Group.

Marquardt, M. J. (1999a). The global advantage: How world class companies improve performance through globalization. Houston: Gulf.

_____. (1999b). *Successful global training.* Infoline #259913. Alexandria, VA: American Society of Training and Development (ASTD) Press.

_____. (Ed.). (2003). Human resources and their development. Volume 10 of *Encyclopedia of life support systems.* Oxford, UK: Eolss, under auspices of UNESCO.

_____. (2004). *Optimizing the power of action learning.* Palo Alto, CA: Davies-Black.

Marquardt, M. J., & Berger, N. O. (2000). *Global leaders for the 21st century.* Albany, NY: State University of New York Press.

_____. (2003). The future: Globalization and new roles of HRD. *Advances in HRD, 5*(3), 283–295.

Marquardt, M. J., & Engel, D. W. (1993). *Global human resource development.* Englewood Cliffs, NJ: Prentice-Hall.

Marquardt, M. J., & Kearsley, G. (1998). *Technology-based learning: Maximizing human performance and corporate success.* Boca Raton, FL: CRC (Chemical Rubber Company) Press.

Marquardt, M. J., King, S., & Erskine, W. (2002). *International comparison report 2002: An annual accounting of worldwide patterns in employer-provided training.* Alexandria: American Society for Training and Development (ASTD) Press.

Marquardt, M. J., King, S., & Koon, E. (2001). *International comparison report 2001: An annual accounting of worldwide patterns in employer-provided training.* Alexandria: American Society for Training and Development (ASTD) Press.

Marquardt, M., Nissley, N., Ozag, R., & Taylor, T. (2000). Training and development in the United States. *International Journal of Training and Development, 4*(2), 138–149.

Marquardt, M. J., & Reynolds, A. (1994). *The global learning organization.* Chicago: Irwin Professional.

Marquardt, M. J., & Snyder, N. (1997). How companies go global: The role of global integrators and the global mindset. *International Journal of Training and Development, 1*(2), 103–116.

Marquardt, M. J., & Soffo, F. (1999). Preparing human resources for the global economy. *Advances in Developing Human Resources, 4*, 3–21.

Martin, C. (1987, January). Centers of excellence: New Zealand Programme for the training of trainers. *Journal of European Industrial Training, 11*(1), 23–25.

Martiny, M. (1998). Knowledge management at HP Consulting. *Organizational Dynamics, 27*(2), 71–77.

Masey, J. (2003, April–June). Elearning withstands economic slowdown in Europe. *The Learning Citizen, 5.* Retrieved April 4, 2004, from http://www.hope-project.org/documents/

Mathai, S. (2001, September 11). Out of work in the Gulf. *AME Info On-Line Newsletter.* Retrieved January 2, 2003, from http://www.ameinfo.com/news/Detailed/16655.html

Maynes, C. W. (2003, March–April). America discovers Central Asia [Electronic version]. *Foreign Affairs, 82*(2), 120–132.

McCarthy, P. (1990, November). The art of training abroad. *Training & Development Journal, 44*(11), 13–19.

McGhee, P. (1999, April). They who laugh, last. Retrieved January 11, 2004, from http://www.laughterremedy.com/humor.dir/humor4_99.html

McGinn, N. (1990). Economic integration within the Americas: Implications for education. *La Educacion, 106*, 55–69.

McGrath-Champ, S., & Yang, X. (2002). Cross-cultural training, expatriate quality of life and venture performance [Electronic version]. *Management Research News, 25*(8–10), 135–140.

McLean, G. (2001). Human resource development as a factor in the inevitable move to globalization. In O. Aliagra (Ed.), *Academy of Human Resource Development 2001 Conference Proceedings* (pp. 731–738). Tulsa, OK: Academy of Human Resource Development.

Mendelsohn, M. (2001). Canada's social contract: Evidence from public opinion. Canadian Policy Research Network. Retrieved December 21, 2003 from http://www.cprn.org.

Meyer, K.E. (2003). *The dust of empire: The race for mastery in the Asian heartland.* New York: PublicAffairs.

Micklethwait, J., & Wooldridge, A. (2000). *A future perfect: The challenge and hidden promise of globalization.* New York: Times Books.

Miller, W. (2001). *The spiritual revolution in leadership.* Lexington, MA: Linkage.

Morrison, T., Conaway, W., & Borden, G. (1994). *Kiss, bow, or shake hands.* Avon, MA: Adams Media.

Mujumdar, N. A. (2003, March 13). Rediscovering the priorities. *Hindu Business Line, Internet Edition.* Retrieved February 4, 2004, from http://www.blonnet.com/2003/03/13/stories/2003031300060800.htm

Nadler, Z. (1990). Latin America. In L. Nadler (Ed.), *Handbook of Human Resource Development* (2nd ed., pp. 24.1–24.11). New York: John Wiley.

Naisbitt, J., & Aburdene, P. (1990). *Megatrends 2000.* New York: Avon.

Noor, Queen. (2003). *Leap of faith: Memoirs of an unexpected life.* New York: Miramax.

Ohmae, K. (1990). *The borderless world.* New York: Harper.

Peters, T. (1992). *Liberation management.* New York: Knopf.

Peterson, D. (2001). How do Canadian provinces and U.S. states view the importance of their relationship with their cross-border counterparts? [Electronic version]. *Canadian/US Law Journal, 27,* 147–153. Retrieved June 26, 2003, from http://lawwww.cwru.edu/academic/canadaus/new/volume27/147Peterson.pdf

Pledge, T. A. (1998). *Saudi Aramco and its people: A history of training.* Dhahran, Saudi Arabia: Saudi Arabian Oil Company.

Population and the environment. (1999). Retrieved February 7, 2004, from http://www.populationconnection.org/Reports_Publications/Reports/report29.html

Porter, J. (2002, January 23). Work older, work smarter. *Sydney Morning Herald,* 1.

Prince, D., & Hoppe, M. (2000). *Communicating across cultures.* Greensboro, NC: Center for Creative Leadership.

Prusher, I. R. (2000, August 8). Kuwaiti women seek the vote. *Christian Science Monitor Online.* Retrieved April 3, 2004, from http://www.csmonitor.com/atcsmonitor/specials/women/rights/rights080800.html

Pucik, V. (1997). Human resources in the future: An obstacle or a champion of globalization? In D. Ulrich, M. R. Losey, & G. Lake (Eds.), *Tomorrow's HR management: 48 thought leaders call for change.* New York: John Wiley.

Qantas introduces online training for staff worldwide. (1998, April). *Training and Development in Australia, 25*(2), 17.

Ramchandran, V. (1984). Training for work in an alien culture. In T. Japp (Ed.), *Global strategies for human resource development.* Alexandria, VA: American Society for Training and Development (ASTD) Press.

_____. (1990). HRD in Asia. In L. Nadler (Ed.), *The Handbook for Human Resource Development* (2nd ed., pp. 26.1–26.23) New York: John Wiley.

Ray, M. (1991). The emerging new paradigms in business. In J. Renesch (Ed.), *New traditions in business* (pp. 33–45). San Francisco: New Leaders Press.

Rhinesmith, S. H. (1996). *A manager's guide to globalization.* New York: McGraw-Hill.

Rice, J. C., Coleman, M. D., Shrader, V. E., Hall, J. P., Gibb, S. A., & McBride, R. H. (2001). Developing Web-based training for a global corporate community. In B. H. Khan (Ed.), *Web-based training* (pp. 191–202). Englewood Cliffs, NJ: Educational Technology.

Richmond, Y., & Gestrin, P. (1998). *Into Africa: Intercultural insights.* Yarmouth, ME: Intercultural Press.

Ricks, D. A. (1999). *Blunders in international business* (3rd ed.). Malden, MA: Blackwell.

Roberts, L. (1990). HRD in Africa. In L. Nadler (Ed.), *The handbook for human resource development* (2nd ed., pp. 25.1–25.25). New York: John Wiley.

Robinson, T. (1998, November 23). Toyota tunes up training program. Internet Week.com. Retrieved February 9, 2004, from http://www.internetweek.com/case/study112398–1.htm

Roofthooft, W. (1996). Five ways to REALLY support the SME. Center of International Business and Education Research, Mexico City Universidad Anáhuac del Sur. Retrieved February 8, 2004 from http://www.uas.mx/Posgrado/pos/cieni/Articulos/jouward2.doc

Rosen, R. (2000). *Global literacies*. New York: Simon & Schuster.

SABMiller (2003). *Corporate accountability report, 2003*. Johannesburg, South Africa. Retrieved February 5, 2004 from http://www.sabmiller.com.

Saphiere, D. H. (2000, October). Online cross-cultural collaboration. *Training & Development, 54*(10), 71–72.

Schein, E. (1997). *Organizational culture and leadership*. San Francisco: Jossey-Bass.

Scherer, C. W. (2000). *The internationalists: Business strategies for globalization.* Wilsonville, OR: BookPartners.

Scheuerman, W. (2002, Fall). Globalization. In E. N. Zalta (Ed.), *The Stanford encyclopedia of philosophy* [Electronic version.] Retrieved February 9, 2004, from http://plato.stanford.edu/archives/fall2002/entries/globalization

Schofield, K. (2002). The first five years: A case study of Qantas 1996–2001. Online learning: Case studies of the corporate experience. Australian Center for Organizational, Vocational and Adult Learning. Retrieved February 8, 2004, from http://www.oval.uts.edu.au/papersdl/02–01_ks_rp115.pdf

Schrage, C. R., & Jedlicka, A. (1999, June). Training in transition economies. *Training & Development, 53*(6), 38–41.

Schwandt, D., & Marquardt, M. J. (2000). *Organizational learning: From world-class theories to global best practices.* Boca Raton, FL: St. Lucie Press.

Selbin, E. (1998). *Social justice in Latin America: Dilemmas of democracy and revolution.* Paper presented at the 1998 meeting of the Latin American Studies Association, Chicago, Illinois. Retrieved February 8, 2004, from http://216.239.41.104/search?q=cache:ZbbEtzSyg-sJ:168.96.200.17/ar/libros/lasa98/Selbin.pdf+selbin+social+justice+in+latin+america&hl=en&ie=UTF–8

Senge, P. M. (1990). *The fifth discipline.* New York: Doubleday.

Skidén, U. (2003, September 14). European and Central Asia Virtual University Association improves distance learning programs. Retrieved December 28, 2003, from http://www.centerdigitaled.com/converge/?pg=magstory&id=68038.

Smith, A. (1999, December). International briefing 4: Training and development in Australia. *International Journal of Training and Development, 3*(4), 301–313.

Smith, L. (1987, March). Divisive forces in an inbred nation. *Fortune, 119*(4), 24–28.

Snell, S., Snow, C., Davison, S., & Hambrick, D. (1998). Designing and supporting transnational teams. *Human Resource Management, 37*(2), 247–148.

Snow, C., Snell, S., Davison, S., & Hambrick, D. (1996). Use transnational teams to globalize your company. *Organization Dynamics, 24*(4), 50–68.

Solomon, C. M. (1995, January). Repatriation: Up, down or out? *Personnel Journal, 74*(1), 28–37.

Stewart, T. (1997). *Intellectual capital.* New York: Doubleday.

____. (1998, March 2). America's most admired companies. *Fortune, 137*(4), 70–75.

Storti, C. (1989). *The art of crossing cultures.* Yarmouth, ME: Intercultural Press.

____. (1994). *Cross-cultural dialogues.* Yarmouth, ME: Intercultural Press.

____. , & Bennhold-Samann, L. (1997). *Culture matters: The Peace Corps cross-cultural workbook.* Washington, DC: Peace Corps.

Sveiby, K. (1997). *The new organizational wealth.* San Francisco: Jossey-Bass.

Swaminathan, S. (2002, September 20). The overstretched dichotomy. *The Hindu.* Retrieved February 4, 2004, from http://www.hinduonnet.com/2002/09/20/stories/2002092002211600.htm

Swanson, R., & Holton, E. (2001). *Foundations of human resource development.* San Francisco: Berrett-Koehler.

Tanaka, T. (1989). Developing managers in the Hitachi Institute of Management Development. *Journal of Management Development, 8*(4), 12–21.

Taylor, A. (1990, November 19). Why Toyota keeps getting better and better and better. *Fortune, 122*(13), 66–77.

Thompson, A. R. (1981). *Education and development in Africa.* Harare, Zimbabwe: College Press.

Tjepkema, S., Horst, H., Mulder, M., & Scheeren, J. (2000). Future challenges for HRD professionals in Europe. Retrieved April 4, 2004, from http://www2.trainingvillage.gr/download/ero/woukaol.rtf

Toffler, A. (1971). *Future shock.* New York: Bantam.

____. (1990). *Powershift.* New York: Bantam Books.

Tolstoy, L. (2001). *How much land does a man need?* Northampton, MA: Crocodile Books.

Tomlinson, J. (1999). *Globalization and culture.* Chicago: University of Chicago Press.

Trompenaars, F. (1994). *Riding the waves of culture.* New York: McGraw-Hill.

Ulrich, D., Losey, M. R., & Lake, G. (Eds.). (1997). *Tomorrow's HR management: 48 thought leaders call for change.* New York: John Wiley.

UNESCO in Central Asia. (1999). Brochure retrieved December 29, 2003 from http://www.unesco.org/webworld/centralasia/intro.html

Varner, I. I., & Varner, C. H. (1994, Winter). A culture-based framework for successful business training in Russia [Electronic version]. *Human Resource Development Quarterly, 5*(4), 361–369.

Venner, K. D., et al. (2003). Report and statement of accounts for the financial year ended 31 March 2003. Eastern Caribbean Central Bank, St. Kitts. Retrieved February 8, 2004 from http://www.eccb-centralbank.org/About/vac-perfomance.asp

Wallace, C. P. (2003, August 4). A difficult labor. *Time Europe Online, 162*(5). Retrieved January 7, 2004, from http://www.time.com/time

Wederspahn, G. (2002). Expat training: Don't leave home without it. *Training & Development, 56*(2), 67–70.

Weiss, A. (1998, July). Global doesn't mean "foreign" anymore. *Training, 35*(7), 50–55.

White, B. (1992). *World class training.* Dallas: Odenwald.

World Bank report on knowledge and development. (1999). Washington, DC: Oxford University Press.

Yip, G. (1992). *Total global strategy.* Englewood Cliffs, NJ: Prentice-Hall.

Zhang, X. (2003, July). Enhanced vocational training needed to increase human resources. *People's Daily.* Retrieved February 5, 2004, from http://english.peopledaily.com.cn/200207/29/eng20020729–100497.shtml

Zhivotovsky, L. A., Rosenberg, N. A., & Feldman, M. W. (2003, May). Features of evolution and expansion of modern humans, inferred from genomewide microsatellite markers. *American Journal of Human Genetics, 72,* 1171–1186. Retrieved February 6, 2004, from http://www-hto.usc.edu/~noahr/features.pdf.

Index

ABANTU for Development, 212–213
Abu Dhabi National Oil Company (ADNOC), 197–198
Aburdene, P., 345, 347
Acculturization, 44, 58, 59. *See also* Culture(s); Training, acculturization of training programs
Acronyms/abbreviations, 56
Adler, Nancy, 3
Administrative issues, 5–6, 11, 32, 34, 37, 39, 80–91, 154, 309
  administrative tasks, 82–83
ADNOC Technical Institute (ATI), 197–198
Advertising, 153, 339
Advocates, 71–72
Afghanistan, 273, 277–278
Africa, 9, 21, 24, 67, 76, 90, 126, 128, 129, 131, 177, 202–217, 306
  North Africa, 34–37, 189–201, 203, 204
African Virtual University (AVU), 213–214
Age, 66, 190, 237, 247, 249, 262, 306, 308, 318
AG Learning Systems Polska, 187
Agnelli, Giovanni, 186
Agriculture, 176, 205, 206, 209, 249, 272, 275, 279, 346

Ainu people, 232
Al-Faleh, Mahmoud, 195
Algeria, 190, 211
Ali, A. J., 196
Allen, D., 107
Allen, T., 12
Alternatives, 72–73
Alvarez, S., 107
America-Mideast Educational and Training Services (AMIDEAST), 198
American Society for Training and Development (ASTD), 183, 317, 327, 332, 344
Annan, Kofi, 123, 135
Apprenticeship system, 211
Arab Air Carriers Organization (AACO), 200
Arab cultures, 9, 21, 27, 31, 34–37, 50, 52, 55, 57, 189–201, 280
Aral Sea, 275
Aramco, 199–200
Argentina, 129, 309, 310
Armenia, 276–277
Arnold, M., 167
Asia, 4, 9, 21, 31, 50, 63, 74, 88, 90, 128, 307
  Asian Productivity Organizations (APOs), 255–256
  Central Asia, 271–282
  East Asia, 32–34, 162

South Central Asia, 246–259
Southeast Asia, 235, 260–270
Asiedu, K., 211
Assumptions, 17, 28, 55, 77
ASTD International Comparisons report
   (2002), 183
*ASTD State of the Industry Report
   (2003)*, 317, 332
Australia, 5, 283, 284, 286, 292–295
   Australian Institute for Training and
      Development, 287
   National Conference on Training
      (1971), 287
   Westpac Group, 292–293
Autry, James, 345–346
Azerbaijan, 276–277

Bahrain, 194
Bangladesh, 22, 125, 247, 248, 249
   National Productivity Organization,
      254–256
Bank of Melbourne, 293
Banks, 143, 224, 235, 282, 293, 302,
   313–316
   electronic banking, 270
Barham, K., 343
Bartlett, C., 3, 112
Bates, R.. 158
Becton Dickinson, 145
Belgium, 176, 204
Bentley College, Center for Business
   Ethics, 344
Bierstadt, R., 17
Birth rates, 190
Black, S., 85
Blake, R. B., 344
Body language, 102
Bolivia, 38
Borneo, 261
Boyce, B., 55
BP. *See* British Petroleum
Brake, T., 48
Brazil, 306, 309, 310
   SABRAE training program in,
      313

British Broadcasting Corporation, 278
British Petroleum (BP), 121–122, 157
Brown and Root design/engineering
   firm, 122
Browne, Sir John, 121
Buddhism, 22, 32, 88, 177, 210, 232, 247,
   262, 285, 298, 319
Bureaucracy, 76
Burma, 261
Burundi, 204
Business Council for International
   Understanding (BCIU), 330–331
Business schools, 345

Calori, R., 181
Cambodia, 126, 129. 130, 131,
   261, 262
Cameroon, 28–29
Canada, 30–32, 184, 296–304, 310, 346
   Canadian Society for Training and
      Development (CSTD), 301–302
   Center for Intercultural Learning,
      Canadian Foreign Service, 97
   dual identity in, 298–299
   New Brunswick province, 302–303
   training expenditures of Canadian
      organizations, 301
*Canadian Guide to Working and Living
   Abroad, The* (Hachey), 96
Capital, 143
Career paths, 151, 222, 244
Caribbean area, 305–316
Caribbean Hazard Mitigation Capacity
   Building Program, 311
Carnevale, Anthony, 329
Carroll, D. A., 344
Carrubba, Frank, 346
Caterpillar, 228
Caucasus region, 276–277
Central Asia, University of, 276
Ceremonies, 88
Chalofsky, N., 4
Chapnick, S., 185
Chen Zhili, 225
Chiang Kai-shek, 219

Children, 17, 63, 104, 125, 132, 162, 167, 192, 249, 274, 293, 299, 348, 350
Chile, 161, 309
    SERCOTEC training program in, 313
China, 21, 32, 33, 60, 65, 76, 81, 131, 144, 161, 162, 218–230, 261, 273, 297, 318, 347
    importance of HRD in, 229–230
    national development strategy, 221
    state-owned enterprises, 223–224
    top 500 firms, 222–224
Christianity, 177, 178, 204, 219, 262, 277, 285, 298, 306–307, 319
Churchill, Winston, 175, 335
Class structure, 21, 31, 33, 36, 38, 39, 74, 87, 205, 233
Climate, 176, 278, 279
Clothes, 64, 65, 182, 281
Coca-Cola, 320
Cold War, 350
Colgate Palmolive, 113
Collaboration, 342. See also Competition/cooperation
Colombia, 5, 313
Colorado, University of, 280
Colors, 57, 65
Communication(s), 10, 53, 81, 89–90, 91, 96, 98, 121, 125, 151, 163, 213, 322
    communication styles in Latin America/Caribbean, 308
    and cultural differences, 24–27, 51, 138
    and geographic distances, 12–13
    global system for global communication, 270
    Japanese communication styles, 234–235
    mobile, 187
Competition/cooperation, 27, 99, 136, 342–343, 347
Competitive advantage, 143, 144, 164, 166, 301, 303, 321

Computers, 56–59, 78, 87, 198, 235, 282, 322
    technical support for, 337–338, 339
    See also Learning, e-learning; Web sites
Conferences. See Global conferences
Conflict avoidance/resolution, 51, 75, 234, 263
Confucianism, 32, 219, 220, 232, 260, 262
Consensus, 234, 236, 240, 244, 307
Consultant News, 70
Consulting, 70–79, 89, 118, 186, 243, 289, 313, 321, 326–327
    challenges concerning, 75–76
    phases of global, 73–74
    roles of global consultants, 71–73
Contextual issues, 12, 13, 24–25, 32, 89
Contracts, 89
Cook, James, 285
Corporations, 90, 135–157, 235, 250, 320, 338, 339, 344, 347, 352
    corporate culture, 28, 51, 102, 140, 147, 263, 348
    corporate universities, 119, 185, 186–187, 242, 243, 327, 328–329
    phases of, 136–140
Corruption, 76, 160, 180, 344
Costa Rica, 313
Costs, 107, 109, 112, 113, 116, 122, 140–142, 166, 180, 184, 304
Cranfield University, 125
Creativity, 339–340, 341
Credentials, 47, 89
Crime, 6
Criticism, 75
Cultural Orientation Inventory, 98–99
Culture(s), 7, 15, 16–39, 61, 66, 81, 89, 176–179, 189–201, 207–208, 218–220, 231–238, 246–249, 260–263, 284–286, 296–299, 306–308, 318–320, 332, 351
    adjusting to host culture, 103
    and communication practices, 24–27

cultural differences, 8–9, 10, 11, 12,
13, 14, 24–27, 44, 46, 53, 63, 70, 74,
75, 77, 84, 99, 109, 115, 138,
145–146
cultural sensitivity, 137, 139
cultural synergies, 145–146
culture shock, 83, 96
culture-specific guidelines,
64–66
defined, 5, 16–17
and HRD practice, 29–39
vs. human nature/personality, 17
in-control vs. controlled, 22
influences on cultural environment,
19–22. *See also individual factors*
knowledge of, 101, 331
levels/types of, 28–29
and phases of global consulting,
73–74
variables of, 22–28
See also Corporations, corporate
culture; Training, acculturization of
training programs
Curricula, 47–49, 72, 156, 254,
269, 324
Customer base, 144–145
Customer loyalty, 142
Customer service, 322, 323, 324, 327,
344–345

Databases, 54
Davison, S., 111, 113, 115
Day, R., 167
Deal, T., 28
Decisionmaking, 9–10, 27, 49, 72, 79, 88,
91, 118, 122, 138, 164, 170, 171,
178, 180, 234, 236, 244, 264, 307,
340
and Arab management, 195–196
Deloitte Consulting, 339
Democracy, 160, 180, 206, 249, 319
Democratic Republic of the Congo
(DRC), 203, 204
Demographics, 176–177, 190, 247, 260,
272, 284, 297, 298, 306, 318

Deterrence, 350–351
Deterritorialization, 336, 338
Developing countries, 82, 85, 86, 87, 108,
124, 161, 338, 346
Devereaux, M., 109–110
Devine, M., 343
Distribution systems, 153–154
Diversity, 79, 121, 139, 176, 181, 204. *See
also* Culture(s), cultural differences
Divorce, 179, 192, 274
Documents, 87, 127
Dofasco, Inc., 303–304
Doing vs. being, 24
Dominican Republic, 313
Donaldson, William H., 344
Downsizing, 76, 166
Drucker, Peter, 80
Dryland Development Knowledge and
Learning Network, 125
Dufour, B., 181

Eastern Caribbean Central Bank
(ECCB), 313–316
Eastern cultures, 24
Economic issues, 6–7, 20, 30, 31, 32, 35,
38, 56, 71, 81, 144, 180, 193–194,
205–207, 219, 235–236, 238,
249–251, 273–274, 286, 300,
308–309
global economic growth, 161
knowledge economies, 118, 300
and sustainable development, 349
transition economies, 64–65
Economies of scale/scope, 140–141
Education, 20, 30, 31, 32, 34, 35, 38, 90,
123, 125, 128, 130, 131, 162, 176,
178, 194, 213, 220, 249, 251, 263,
279, 281, 299, 300
distance education, 132, 185–186,
275, 287, 303. *See also* Training,
distance training
environmental, 241–242
generalist orientation in, 237
nonformal programs in Africa,
211–212

private/public schools, 310
vocational. *See* Training, vocational
See also Learning
Educational Media International (EMI),
133
E-Forum, 128
Egalitarianism, 27, 50, 60, 61, 81, 181,
236
Egypt, 35, 129, 204
E-learning. *See under* Learning
Electronic Engineering Times, 328
Elsey, George, 294–295
Emotion, 25–26, 54, 65, 96
Employment, 76, 160, 185, 186, 192, 194,
206, 303, 320, 338, 339
in China, 225–226
in Japan, 233, 237, 238
job rotation, 240–241, 245
job testing, 323, 324–325
new employees, 240
in South Africa, 215
Environment, 22, 98, 125, 157, 164, 165,
167–168, 169, 170, 171, 197,
241–242, 275, 348
in crisis, 352–353
and sustainable development, 349
Equality, 319, 320
Ernst & Young consulting firm, 118
Erskine, W., 184
Ethics, 166, 167, 268, 343–344
Ethiopia, 126, 131, 209
Ethnicity, 28–29, 66, 176–177, 179, 225,
233, 272, 284, 297, 306
Ethnocentricity, 99, 137, 138
Europe, 26, 48, 50, 90, 143, 175–188,
212–213, 251, 306, 339
business guidelines for,
181–182
cultural factors, 176–179
European Council, 185
European Union (EU), 90, 175, 176,
178, 180, 185, 281
European Values Survey,
178–179
meaning of term *Europe,* 176

European and Central Asia Virtual
University Association (ECAVU),
275–276
Expatriates, 104
vs. global professionals, 103
predeparture preparation for,
105–106
See also Repatriation; Working abroad
Expectations, 60, 62, 63, 67, 73, 79, 81,
84, 108

Families, 21, 30, 32–33, 35–36, 38, 39, 89,
176, 179, 191, 219–220, 233, 238,
249, 262, 273–274, 307, 319
of expatriates, 103, 104, 106, 107,
151
extended, 192, 249, 286
family-friendly policies, 347–348
Fatalism, 193, 205, 248
Federal Express (FedEx), 322–325
Feedback, 52, 54, 66, 69, 73, 74
Feldman, M. W., 285
FEMCIDI fund, 312
Festivals (film, music, theater), 299
Fiat, 186–197
Fiji, 283, 284, 285
Financial issues, 85–86, 143, 152–153,
207, 314, 337, 339
Financial Mail, 215
Finland, 176
"Fleecing of America, The" (*NBC
Nightly News*), 344
Food issues, 162, 204, 206. *See also*
Agriculture; Meals
Ford Motor, 322
Foreign debt, 308
Foreign investments, 228, 251, 320
Formality/informality, 26–27, 36, 54, 60,
62, 65–66, 102, 196, 308
Fortune 500, 222, 228
Forum Corporation, 345
France, 27, 48, 65, 68, 81, 177, 181, 184,
190, 247, 318, 346
Frank, E., 252, 286
Freedom, 136, 160, 319

Friedman, T., 135, 160, 170
Fuentes, Carlos, 307

Galtung, J., 351
Games, 50
Gandhi, Mohandas, 248
Gender, 66, 179, 194. *See also* Women
General Electric, 143
General Motors, 142
General Motors University, 119
Geography, 21–22, 31, 176, 189–190,
    202–205, 218, 231, 246–247,
    260–261, 271–272, 276, 284,
    296–297, 306, 318, 336
  geographic distances, 10–11, 12–13,
    81–82, 109
Georgia (in Caucasus region), 276–277
Germany, 26, 89, 179, 181, 184, 185
Ghana, 161
Gibson, Melissa, 70
Global conferences, 120, 128, 132, 133
Global Development Learning Network,
    126
Global intergovernmental organizations,
    124–128
Globalization, 3, 102–103, 114, 115, 116,
    119, 123, 135, 146, 161, 184, 317,
    336–337
  global culture, 29
  with a human face, 158
  opponents of global companies,
    135–136
  as positive/negative, 170, 250–251,
    274
  of U.S work environment, 320
Global megatrends. *See under* Human
    resource development
Global mindset, 148, 165, 168
GlobalSuccess Model, 147–156
Global teams, 109–122, 163
  Total Productivity Maintenance
    (TPM) global team, 113
Global Training Model, 43, 44, 45, 58.
    See also Training, acculturization of
    training programs

Global workforce, 338–339
Goshal, S., 3, 112
Government relations, 90
Great Britain, 65–66, 177, 179, 182, 190,
    247, 248, 285, 318
Greece, 179
Green, S., 235
Gregersen, H., 85
Gross domestic product (GDP), 160,
    178, 180, 205, 249, 250, 274, 300,
    308, 309, 349
Groups, 66–67, 78, 236–237, 307
Grudin, R., 340
Guanxi, 220. *See also* Relationships
Guatemala, 38
Guinea-Bissau, 129
Gulf States, 190
Gulf War, 195, 197
Guyana, 125

Hachey, Jean-Marc, 96
Hambrick, D., 113, 115
Hamel, G., 118
Hamilton, E., 211
Handy, C., 10
Harris, P. R., 66
Hassett, K. A., 205
Health issues, 161, 162, 167, 169, 170,
    275, 299, 337, 348. *See also*
    HIV/AIDS
Heifetz, R., 114
Heilongjiang Engineering University
    (China), 228
Henderson, H., 349
Hewlett-Packard, 325–327
Hierarchies, 9, 26, 27, 65, 76, 85, 89, 195,
    208, 238, 273, 281, 341
Hinduism, 32, 88, 177, 247, 248, 249,
    262, 285, 298, 319
Hispanic Americans, 318
History, 21, 31, 33, 34, 36, 38, 74, 317
  African, 204–205
  Arabian, 190–191
  Central Asian, 272–273
  Chinese, 219

European, 177–178
Japanese, 232–233
of Latin America/Caribbean, 306
of South Central/Southeast Asia,
    247–248, 261–262
of South Pacific region, 285
Turkish, 281
of United States, 318
Hitachi, 235, 241–243
Hite, J., 85
HIV/AIDS, 125, 126, 131, 162, 205–206
Hofstede, G., 16, 17
Holton, E., 4
Hong Kong, 218, 219, 224–225, 297
Honor, 307. *See also Machismo*
Horst, H., 182
Housing, 85, 161, 162. *See also*
    Overnight accommodations
Human Development Report 2000, 205
Human resource development (HRD),
    317
    capabilities/roles of professionals,
        14–15
    centralized/decentralized approach to,
        156–157
    challenges of global, 8–14, 109
    commitment to, 100
    competencies of professionals, 76–79,
        99–103
    culture's impact on, 29–39
    defined, 4, 182
    evaluating, 53–54, 69, 74
    evaluating staff, 84–85, 97
    expatriate failures, 103, 104
    expenditures for, 332
    and the future, 170–171
    global HRD associations, 131–133
    global megatrends, 15, 335–353
    global vs. traditional domestic, 5–8
    guidelines for delivering programs,
        62–66
    vs. human resource management
        (HRM), 4–5, 55, 82, 182
    implementation, 31–32, 36–37, 39,
        59–69, 74, 168–169
    and in-country partners, 8, 61
    for individuals, 95–108, 169
    instructional
        methodologies/materials, 49–52,
        54–55, 56, 63, 86–87
    marketing, 81, 88–89
    positive impact on globalization of,
        159–168
    resources for, 6, 76, 82, 86
    staff, 82–86, 97, 104, 339
    and sustainable development, 350
    team members, 11
    See also Training
Human resource management (HRM),
    131, 221. *See also under* Human
    resource development
Hurricane-resistant homes, 311

IBM, 116, 157, 266
Icons (computer), 57
Idealism, 193
Incomes, 193–194, 321, 349
India, 21, 27, 55, 60, 143, 144, 247, 248,
    249, 297, 318, 338, 339
    economic development in, 250–251
    government of Punjab's Directorate
        of Technical Education and
        Industrial Training, 253–254
    Indian Academy of Human Resources
        Development (AHRD), 256–257
Individualism/collectivism, 27, 99, 181,
    233, 237, 352
Individuals, 89, 192, 319. *See also under*
    Human resource development
Indonesia, 68, 74, 262, 268–270
Industry, 176, 206, 221, 235–236, 279
    Industry training organizations
        (ITOs), 291
    See also Manufacturing
Industry Training Federation (ITF) of
    New Zealand, 290–291
Informal sector, 207, 208
Information, 144. *See also* Knowledge
Innovation, 121, 144, 145, 184, 196, 223,
    228, 229, 327, 340, 341

Institute of Advanced Studies for the
Americas (INEAM), 311–312
Instructors, 60, 62, 66
Insurance, 187, 225
Intellectual capital, 3
Inter-American Agency for Cooperation
and Development (IACD),
312–313
Interdependence (within/between
teams), 11–12
International Council for Educational
Media (ICEM), 133
International Council for Open and
Distance Education (ICDE),
132–133
International Federation of Red Cross
and Red Crescent Societies,
129
International Federation of Training and
Development Organizations
(IFTDO), 131–132, 243, 287
International Labor Office, 56
International Labor Organization (ILO),
126–127, 132, 221, 313
International Living and Working
Inventory, 97–98
International Project on Technical and
Vocational Education (UNEVOC),
128
International Society for Intercultural
Education, Training, and Research
(SIETAR), 132
International Training Center (ITC),
126–127
Internet, 229, 270. *See also* Learning,
e-learning; Web sites
InterNews, 277
Invention, art of, 339. *See also*
Innovation
Iran, 278–279. *See also* Iran/Iraq War
Iran/Iraq War, 6, 195
Iraq, 279–280. *See also* Gulf War;
Iran/Iraq War
Irrigation, 275
Irving, J., 212

Isbank, 282
Islam, 9, 21, 34–37, 47, 58, 88, 177, 190,
191, 192, 193, 203–204, 247,
248–249, 262, 272, 273, 277, 278,
279, 280, 281, 319
Isvor Fiat, 186–187
Italy, 179, 181, 186
Ivory Coast, 211

Japan, 27, 33, 54, 55, 181, 231–245, 261,
320, 338, 345, 347
automotive industry in, 235–236
culture and HRD in, 236–238
Japanese Society for Training and
Development (JSTD), 243
and United States, 236
Jedlicka, A., 64
Jews, 58, 177, 298, 319
Johansen, R., 109–110
Johnson & Johnson, 348
Johnston, W., 338
Jones, M. L, 207, 210
Jordan, 192, 195

Kanter, Rosabeth, 146
Karma, 248
Kazakhstan, 271–276
Keeley, S., 222
Kemper, Cynthia, 59
Kenya, 205, 209, 213
Kenya Village Polytechnics, 208
King, S. 184
Knowledge, 118, 120–121, 143, 154, 155,
330, 331, 337
ascendancy of, 340–342
knowledge and power, 267
knowledge workers, 228
See also Learning;
Managers/management, knowledge
management; *under* Technology
"Knowledge for Development" (World
Bank report), 167
Korea, 32, 33, 161, 261–262, 263–264,
300
Korten, D. C., 344

Kuwait, 190, 194, 195
Kuwait Institute for Scientific
Research (KISR), 197
Kyrgyzstan, 271–276

Labor unions, 90–91, 181
Lake, G., 91
Land mines, 125, 130
Language(s), 7–8, 19–20, 30, 31, 32, 34,
35, 37, 52, 53, 57, 65, 84, 102, 105,
109, 138, 139, 157, 187, 278, 280,
319, 351
African, 203
Arabic, 190, 284
in Canada, 297–298
Central Asian, 272
Chinese, 218
European, 177
guidelines for, 62–63
Japanese, 232
proliferation of English, 336–337
in South Central/Southeast Asia, 247,
261
in South Pacific, 284, 285
translations, 49, 51, 55–56, 64,
67, 90
Latin America, 21, 24, 26, 29, 37–39, 67,
74, 90, 128, 305–316
labor flows in, 309–310
Laurant, A., 16
Leading Edge, The (newsletter), 120
Leadership development, 165–166. *See
also* Managers/management
League of Nations, 124
Learning, 3, 4, 17, 31, 33–34, 36–37, 68,
91, 114, 120, 139, 163, 170, 237,
265, 295, 314, 327
action learning, 342
and corporate success, 321
e-learning, 184–185, 185–186, 214,
322
from expatriates, 103
learning centers, 186–187, 214,
303
learning contracts, 315

learning organizations, 120–121, 122,
146, 155–156, 257, 258–259, 301,
323, 342–343
learning plans, 47–48
learning programs, 31, 33–34, 36, 39,
77, 119
learning styles, 6, 20, 48, 53, 61–62
workplace learning in the United
States, 320–322
See also Education; Training
"Learning for Life, Work and the Future:
Stimulating Reform in Southern
Africa through Sub-regional
Cooperation" (conference), 128
Lebanon, 130, 190, 192
Leisure, 286, 299
Lesotho Council of Non-governmental
Organizations (LCN), 209
Liberia, 22
Libya, 190, 194
Life expectancy, 162, 278, 306
Lindberg, K., 236
Linsky, M., 114
Lippitt, Ronald and Gordon, 71
Literacy, 131, 160, 162, 170, 176, 194,
247, 301, 309
Local Government Industry Training
Organization (LGITO) of New
Zealand, 291
Lonergan, Bernard, 340
Losey, M. R., 91
Loss of face, 51, 64, 69, 75
*Love and Profit: The Art of Caring
Leadership* (Autry), 345–346
Lufthansa School of Business, 185

Maastricht, Treaty of, 178
McDonald's. 320, 336
McGhee, Paul, 100–101
McGinn, N., 309–310
McGraw-Hill, 156
Machismo, 38, 39, 307
McKenna, Frank, 303
McLean, G., 158, 164
Mada, Gadjah, 268

Madagascar, 337
Malaysia, 32, 89, 262
Malcolm Baldridge award for quality, 327
Malhotra, Jogesh, 341
Malhotra, Jyoti, 339
Managers/management, 9, 11, 12, 64, 75–76, 80, 84, 88, 90, 119, 120, 125, 139, 183, 199, 217, 265, 268, 288, 290, 295, 301, 321, 322, 340
  African management, 208
  Arab management, 195–196
  global dimensions of HRD management, 81–82
  global materials/inventory management, 153
  Japanese management, 233, 236, 237, 240, 241
  knowledge management, 163, 164, 224, 325–327, 341
  and love, 345, 346
  management training, 187
  managers in sites away from headquarters, 117–118, 137, 138
  participatory management, 236
  school managers, 310
  Western European model of management, 180–181
  See also Administrative issues; Training, management training
Manufacturing, 140, 141, 144, 145, 152, 186, 206, 221, 228, 241, 300, 308, 320
Maori people, 285
Mao Tse-tung, 218
Marketing, 153, 264, 311, 321. See also under Human resource development
Marquardt, M. J., 184
Marriage, 249, 274
Marriott hotels, 113–114
Martiny, M., 326
Massachusetts Institute of Technology (MIT), 214
Massey, J., 184

Mass Transit Railway Corporation (MTR), Hong Kong, 224–225
Materials. See Human resource development, instructional methodologies/materials
Meals, 68, 85, 88, 182, 193
Mechanical engineering, 228
Media, 292, 337, 344
Meetings, 109, 122, 182, 193
Melanesia, 284
Mendelsohn, M., 299
Mercosur, 309
Meridian International Center (MIC), 331–332
Mesopotamia, 280
Mexico, 68, 81, 300, 309, 318
Meyer, Karl, 277
Micklethwait, J., 136
Micronesia, 284
Microsoft, 143, 228–229
Middle Ages, 204
Middle class, 179, 251
Middle East, 24, 26, 29, 34–37, 67, 74, 128, 189–201
Migration, 177, 194, 250, 261, 284, 285, 297, 298, 338, 339
Miller, William, 346
Minorities, 179, 203, 225, 250
Mitsubishi USA, 320
MMD pharmaceutical company, 116
Moran, R. T., 66
Mortality rates, 160, 161, 274, 278
Motorola/Motorola University, 327–330
Mulder, M., 182
Muslims. See Islam

Nadler, Z., 309
Naisbitt, J., 345, 347
National Iranian Productivity Organization (NIPO), 279
Nationalism, 205
National productivity organizations (NPOs), 254–255, 279
Native Americans, 307, 318

Natural resources, 21–22, 31, 33, 36, 38–39, 136, 195, 197, 204
Needs analysis, 45–46, 56
Nehru, Jawaharlal, 248
Nepal, 6, 247, 248, 249
Nepotism, 196
Nestlé, 185–186
Netherlands, 176, 179, 285, 318
New Partnership for Africa's Development (NEPAD), 106
New Zealand, 283, 284, 285, 286
    New Zealand Institute of Management (NZIM)m 290
    New Zealand Journalists Training Organization (NZJTO), 292
    New Zealand Society for Training and Development, 287
Nigeria, 203
Nongovernmental organizations (NGOs), 131, 132, 133, 207, 209, 210, 212, 213, 254, 275, 277, 278
Norms, 54, 61, 65, 68, 69, 76, 105, 336
North American Free Trade Agreement (NAFTA), 300
North Atlantic Treaty Organization (NATO), 281
Nutrition, 161, 162–163, 169, 273, 337
Nyerere, Julius K., 202

Objectives, 46–47, 169–170, 182–183, 212, 253, 282, 314–315, 329
Oceania, 284, 286
Odaira, Namihei, 231
Ohmae, K., 339
Oil, 35, 36, 115, 122, 197, 272, 274, 275, 277, 280, 309
Oman, 194
Opportunities Industrialization Center (OIC), 211–212
Oracle Workforce Development Program, 229
Organization for Economic Cooperation and Development (OECD), 300, 352

Organization of American States (OAS), 310, 311, 312
Organizations, public and nonprofit, 123–134
Outsourcing, 82, 321, 337–338, 339
Overnight accommodations, 87–88

Pacific Institute of Management and Development (PIMD), 288–290
Pakistan, 247, 248, 251, 297, 347
Palestinians, 190, 195
Pan-African Institute for Development, 209
Panama, 129
Papua New Guinea, 283, 284, 285, 286
Paraguay, 309
Partnerships, 146
Patience, 96, 100, 193
Patriotism, 319
Peace corps volunteers, 351
Performance, 4, 25, 91, 169, 209, 239, 316, 321, 324
Perry, Matthew, 233
Personalismo, 38, 39
Personality traits and work overseas, 95–96
Personal space, 27, 98, 308
Peru, 38, 313
Peters, Tom, 110
Pfizer, 117
Philippines, 143, 261, 262, 297
Platt, Lew, 325
Poland, 187
Political issues, 6–7, 20–21, 30, 31, 32, 34, 35, 38, 74, 81, 206, 248, 274–275
    political development, 159–161
Polkomtel, 187
Polygamy, 192
Polynesia, 284
Populations, 176, 177, 190, 202, 203, 218, 221, 231–232, 247, 261, 272, 274, 297, 300, 306, 309, 318
Portugal, 38, 177, 179, 204, 306, 307
Poverty, 125, 161, 162, 170, 207, 225, 249, 251, 274, 299, 308, 337

Power issues, 9, 25, 51, 76, 88, 89,
     98, 252
  knowledge and power, 267
  power of global teams, 111–112
Powershift (Toffler), 340
Prahalad, C. K., 118
PricewaterhouseCoopers (PWC),
     266–267
Privacy, 233–234
Private sector, 194, 196, 235, 238, 253
Privatization, 71, 310
Problem solving, 10, 22, 72, 75,
     244, 342
  and technical vs. adaptive problems,
     114–115
Productivity, 221, 223, 224, 254–255,
     321, 329, 338
Profits, 223, 320, 337, 352
Project teams, 110–111, 121
ProLiteracy Worldwide, 131
Publications, 118, 127, 144, 196
Public sector, 71, 85, 90, 194, 206, 235,
     345
Pucik, Vladimir, 80, 103
Punctuality, 24, 86, 193, 196, 281
Putin, Vladimir, 180

Qantas airline, 293–294
Qantas College/Qantas College Online,
     294–295
Qatar, 190, 194
Quality issues, 152, 163, 327, 328,
     344–345

Ramadan, 191
Ramchandran, V., 75
Ravalomanana, Marc, 337
Ray, Michael, 346
Reasoning, deductive/inductive,
     28, 99
Reeves, Sir Paul, 283
Regional issues, 29, 30, 308, 311–312
  multiregional companies, 138–139
Regulations, 7, 28, 47, 82, 223, 225, 250
Relationships, 220, 234, 237, 307, 308

Religion, 7, 8, 9, 19, 30, 31, 47, 61, 74,
     179, 232–233, 345. *See also*
     individual religions
Relocations, 338
Repatriation, 83, 107–108, 151
*Report on the Development of Chinese
     Enterprises, A,* 223
Research and development (R&D), 142,
     143, 145, 152, 186, 223, 235, 340
Resources, 6, 72, 76, 86, 111. *See also*
     Natural resources
Rhinesmith, S. H., 165
Rice, J. C., 57
Risk taking, 196
Roberts, L., 208
Robinson, T., 244
Roofthooft, W., 313
Rosenberg, N. A., 285
Royal Bank of Canada (RBC) Financial
     Services, 302
Royal Dutch Shell, 115
Rubbermaid, 152
Russia, 50, 56, 60, 76, 143, 144, 180, 183,
     272, 273, 275, 276, 318
Rwanda, 204

SABMiller, 214–216, 217
Safety and security issues, 350–352
St. Kitts and Nevis Small Business
     Development Project, 311
Saint Lucia, 311
Samsung, 263–264
SANNO Institute of Management,
     243–244
Satellite technology. *See under*
     Technology
Saudi Arabia, 7, 22, 35, 190, 191, 194
Scandinavia, 27, 177, 181
Scheduling, 67–68, 88. *See also* Time
     issues
Scheerens, J., 182
Schein, E., 17, 28
Scheuerman, W., 336
Schofield, K., 295
Schrage, C. R., 64

Science, 191, 197, 221, 235, 250, 337, 345
Selbin, E., 308
Self-development, 239
Senge, Peter, 323, 343
Sense of humor, 96, 100–101
Sexuality, 7, 191
Shapiro, R., 205
Sharia, 191
Sherriff, Jim, 326
Shinto, 232
Siemens, 229
Sierra Leone, 130
Silk Road, 272
Singapore, 6, 32, 161
Singapore Institute of Management (SIM), 264–266
Skills, 101–103, 143, 164, 165, 186, 194, 208, 210, 211–212, 226, 300, 304, 321, 322, 329, 331, 338
skill competitions, 227–228
Smith, Fred, 323
Snell, S., 113, 115, 117
Snow, C., 113, 114
Software, 229, 266, 277, 303, 327
South Africa, 126, 131, 203, 214–216
South African Brewery (SAB), 214
South Pacific region, 283–295
University of the South Pacific, 287
Soviet Union, 272, 273, 277, 278. *See also* Russia
Spain, 38, 39, 68, 177, 179, 181, 306, 307, 318
Specialization, 71, 72
Sports, 286, 299
Sri Lanka, 28, 247, 248, 249, 297
Central Bank of Sri Lanka, 257–259
Standardization of labor practices, 338
Starvation, 162
State-owned enterprises, 223–224, 267
Status, 9, 26, 34, 35, 51, 66, 76, 87, 88, 208, 210, 238, 321
Stereotypes, 60

Stock exchanges, 143, 235
Stress, 100–101, 103
Sullivan, Reverend Leon, 211
Sumatra, 261
Support systems, 68, 83, 84, 86, 104, 106–107, 151, 187
Sustainable development, 348–350
Swahili speakers, 203
Swaminathan, S., 251
Swanson, R., 4
Swaziland, 126
Sweden, 59, 81, 318, 338, 347
Sweeney, John J., 335
Switzerland, 89
Syria, 192, 194

Taiwan, 219, 297
Tajikistan, 271–276
Taliban, 273, 278
Tanaka, T., 241
Tanzania, 203, 209
Tanzania Association of Nongovernmental Organizations (TANGO), 209
Taoism, 262
Taxation, 145, 184, 301, 313
Teachers, 60
Teams, 86, 244. *See also* Global teams; Virtual teams
Technology, 12, 56, 58, 77–78, 87, 110, 111, 113, 121, 122, 125, 136, 163, 221, 250, 263, 264, 303, 312, 323, 345, 353
global, 337–338
and knowledge, 166–167
satellite technology, 268–269, 270, 287, 322
See also Telecommunications
Telecommunications, 144, 154, 184, 187, 213, 221, 228, 269, 280, 300, 303, 312, 337
Teleconferencing. *See* Videoconferencing
Teleworking, 82
Terrorism, 6, 195, 337, 350–351
Thailand, 27, 32, 33, 74, 261, 262, 347

Thompson, A. R., 12
3M (Minnesota Mining and
    Manufacturing), 152, 340
Tibet, 129, 261
Time issues, 22–24, 49, 66, 67–68, 75, 79,
    86, 88, 98, 100, 193, 196, 281
  in Latin America/Caribbean,
    307–308
  time zones, 109, 116
Tjepkema, S., 182
TNT, 4
Toffler, A., 337, 340
Togo, 211
Tolerance for minorities, 179
Tolstoy, Leo, 352
Tomlinson, John, 16
Tonga, 283
Toyota, 5, 142, 244–245, 320, 336
T+D (journal), 4
Trade, 161, 195, 236, 272–273, 300
  trading blocs, 309
Trafalgar House construction company,
    122
Training, 5, 6, 7, 8, 14, 29, 31, 32, 33–34,
    37, 39, 56, 88, 90, 91, 128, 129,
    156–157, 168, 185–186, 195, 198,
    199, 208, 210–211, 216, 236, 238,
    250, 255, 263, 275, 282, 292–293,
    304, 312
  acculturization of training programs,
    43, 44, 46–47, 48–49, 49–54, 57,
    65–66
  of blue-collar and white-collar
    workers, 240
  and Chinese employees, 222
  creativity training, 339–340
  cross-cultural, 83, 104, 105
  distance training, 268–270. *See also*
    Education, distance education
  global, 150–151
  interactive video instruction, 323,
    324, 325
  management training, 187, 209–210,
    221, 244–245
  on-the-job, 239, 263

and productivity, 329
self-instructed, 187
shift in corporate, 320–321
skills-training programs, 211–212
teacher training, 269
training bases, 226–227
training expenditures, 183–184
training venue, 87
vocational, 163–165, 184, 221,
    225–226. 227, 229, 238, 251, 313
of women, 252, 254
Training Managing Company, 98
Transportation, 163, 322
Treaty of Paris (1763), 247
Trust, 10, 25, 74, 89, 193, 220, 267, 346
Tunisia, 190
Turkey, 280—282
Turkmenistan, 271–276
Tuvalu, 83

Ukraine, 126
Ulrich, D., 91
UNDP. *See* United Nations,
    Development Programme
Unemployment, 78, 161, 225, 273, 277,
    299, 303, 308
Unilever, 140–141, 267
United Arab Emirates (UAE), 190, 194,
    197–198
United Kingdom. *See* Great Britain
United Nations (UN), 124, 299, 351
  Agenda 21 Forum, 164
  Development Programme (UNDP),
    124–126, 130, 162, 192
  Educational, Social, and Cultural
    Organization (UNESCO), 128, 133
  Industrial Development Organization
    (UNIDO), 127
United States, 5, 7, 21, 22, 23, 24, 26,
    30–32, 48, 53, 54, 57, 60, 66, 67, 74,
    99, 145, 178, 179, 181, 184, 209,
    221, 233, 237, 250, 251, 278, 286,
    317–332, 339, 346, 352
  business schools in, 345
  and Canada, 296, 299, 300, 301

Department of State's International
    Visitor Program, 331
and Japan, 236
Los Angeles County, 29
United States Agency for
    International Development
    (USAID), 209, 210, 280
workplace learning in, 320–322
World Trade Center Towers/Pentagon
    attacks, 337, 350–351
Universities, 118, 144, 194, 213–214, 228,
    250, 265, 268, 269, 273, 275–276,
    312, 316, 320, 321, 344. *See also*
    Corporations, corporate
    universities
Urbanization, 306
Uruguay, 309
USPNet, 287
Uzbekistan, 271–276

Values, 17, 27, 28, 55, 61, 77, 79, 84, 99,
    108, 114, 139, 152, 315, 327, 336,
    339, 340
    African, 210
    American, 332
    Canadian, 299
    European, 178–179
    global, 148
    spiritual, 345–346
Venezuela, 309
Venner, K. D., 309
Videoconferencing, 78, 187, 269
Videos, 52, 64
Vietnam, 261, 262, 266–268
Virtual teams, 78, 82, 113, 121
Volunteers, 239, 351

Wages, 78, 91, 209
Walker, D. M. and T., 48

Ward, K., 111
Wars, 178, 195
Washington Post, 344
Water, 162, 195, 204, 275, 280
Web sites, 56–58, 78, 102, 125, 128, 187,
    251, 322. *See also* Internet
West Indies, University of, 316
Whirlpool, 119–120
White, B., 339
Whitwam, Dave, 119
Wilson, William, 324
Women, 7, 8, 35, 38, 52, 76, 127, 129,
    162, 179, 212, 238, 249, 252, 281,
    286, 307
    Bank on Women in Business
        (Australia), 293
    emerging roles of, 346–347
    and Islam, 192, 193, 194, 273, 274
Wooldridge, A., 136
Work ethic, 75, 281
Workforce Magazine Optimas Award for
    Innovation, 303
Working abroad, 83, 96–99, 151, 163. *See
    also* Expatriates
World Bank, 167, 187, 209, 210, 213,
    221, 250, 352
    World Bank Institute (WBI), 126, 275
World Education, 128–129
World Rehabilitation Fund (WRF), 130
World Trade Organization (WTO), 219,
    221, 300

Yemen, 35, 190, 192
Yen Trinh, 266–267

Zambia, 6, 203
Zhang Xiaoji, 221
Zhivotovsky, L. A., 285
Zimbabwe, 203